ERODING A WAY OF LIFE

ERODING A WAY OF LIFE

Neoliberalism and the Family Farm

MURRAY KNUTTILA

University of Regina Press

Copyright © 2023 University of Regina Press

All rights reserved. No part of this work covered by the copyrights hereon may be reproduced or used in any form or by any means—graphic, electronic, or mechanical—without the prior written permission of the publisher. Any request for photocopying, recording, taping, or placement in information storage and retrieval systems of any sort shall be directed in writing to Access Copyright.

Printed and bound in Canada at Imprimerie Gauvin. The text of this book is printed on 100% post-consumer recycled paper with earth-friendly vegetable-based inks.

Cover art: "Vanishing Point" by David Thauberger, from the collection of Merrilee Rasmussen
Cover design: Duncan Campbell, University of Regina Press
Interior layout design: John van der Woude, JVDW Designs
Copyeditor: Ryan Perks
Proofreader: Alison Strobel
Indexer: Patricia Furdek

Library and Archives Canada Cataloguing in Publication

Title: Eroding a way of life : neoliberalism and the family farm / Murray Knuttila.
Names: Knuttila, Kenneth Murray, author.
Description: Includes bibliographical references and index.
Identifiers: Canadiana (print) 20230439349 | Canadiana (ebook) 2023043939X | ISBN 9780889779488 (hardcover) | ISBN 9780889779457 (softcover) | ISBN 9780889779464 (PDF) | ISBN 9780889779471 (EPUB)
Subjects: LCSH: Agriculture and state—Canada. | LCSH: Agriculture—Economic aspects—Prairie Provinces. | LCSH: Grain trade—Economic aspects—Prairie Provinces. | LCSH: Family farms—Prairie Provinces. | LCSH: Neoliberalism—Prairie Provinces. | LCSH: Prairie Provinces—Economic conditions. | LCSH: Prairie Provinces—Social conditions.
Classification: LCC HD1787 .K58 2023 | DDC 338.1/8712—dc23

10 9 8 7 6 5 4 3 2 1

University of Regina Press, University of Regina
Regina, Saskatchewan, Canada, S4S 0A2
TEL: (306) 585-4758 FAX: (306) 585-4699
WEB: www.uofrpress.ca

We acknowledge the support of the Canada Council for the Arts for our publishing program. We acknowledge the financial support of the Government of Canada. / Nous reconnaissons l'appui financier du gouvernement du Canada. This publication was made possible with support from Creative Saskatchewan's Book Publishing Production Grant Program.

CONTENTS

List of Maps, Figures, and Tables   ix
Preface   xi

Introduction   xv
Chapter 1   Confederation to Depression: Western Canada Enters the Global Economy, 1867–1930   1
Chapter 2   Phase 1—Activist Government: Promoting the National Policy and Family Farming in the West, 1867–1930   27
Chapter 3   Phase 2—Crisis and Stability: Keynesian Fordism and Maintaining the Family Farm, 1930–1969   71
Chapter 4   Phase 3—Unleashing the Market: Neoliberalism and Family Farming, 1970–2014   125
Chapter 5   A Tenuous Location in the Food Chain   195
Chapter 6   Meanwhile, Back on the Farm   231
Epilogue: Unanswered Questions   253

Acknowledgements   259
Notes   261
Index   319

LIST OF MAPS, FIGURES, AND TABLES

MAPS

Map 1. Provinces of Canada: July 1, 1867, to July 15, 1870   8
Map 2. Northwest Territories, 1898   11
Map 3. Canada in 1898   14

FIGURES

Figure 2.1. Number of Farms, 1901–31   59
Figure 2.2. Acres under Cultivation, 1901–31   59
Figure 3.1. Number of Saskatchewan Farms, 1921–71   119
Figure 5.1. Agricultural Operations in Saskatchewan, 1921–2016   201

TABLES

Table 3.1. Total Farm Income Saskatchewan, 1926–37 (in 1961 Dollars)   79
Table 3.2. National Farm Input Costs, 1935–61   116
Table 3.3. Composite Index of Farm Prices of Agricultural Products, and Realized Gross Farm Income, Saskatchewan, 1945–61   117
Table 5.1. Twenty Years of Change in the Types of Saskatchewan Farms, 2001–21   202

Table 5.2. Estimated Value of Major Productive Assets on
 Saskatchewan Farms, 1981–2021   **203**
Table 5.3. Classification of Saskatchewan Farms Based on
 Total Capitalization   **204**
Table 5.4. Hours of Paid Non-farm Work by Saskatchewan
 Farm Operators, 2016   **205**
Table 5.5. Decline in Primary Elevators in Saskatchewan,
 1962–2019   **219**
Table 5.6. Major Inland Terminal Operators in Saskatchewan   **221**

PREFACE

The family farm on which I was born and raised no longer exists. It has not existed for nearly fifty years. During the 1970s—the decade in which my parents decided to sell—nearly 10,000 other family farms disappeared in Saskatchewan. In the 1960s, nearly 17,000 Saskatchewan farms disappeared; the 1980s saw another 6,500 farms vanish. During all this time I was aware the countryside was changing, if for no other reason than the proliferation of farm auction sales I attended. In casual conversations with high school friends, some of us wondered if there was "enough money in farming." We sometimes blamed ourselves or other individual farmers for the exodus—some had made bad decisions, had old equipment, had bad luck, or simply had not worked hard enough. In the language of the day, some of us "trucked on" since there were still plenty of bonspiels in the small towns and villages in my little corner of the province, although some towns were in obvious decline, and not all the rinks were in prime condition. Of course, many of us were busy living, and so did not really think very systematically about why all these changes were occurring around us and what they meant.

For me, that started to change because my parents discouraged me from thinking about farming as a career, and like many others in the 1960s, I subsequently went to university. I remember the day that Dr. James Napier McCrorie came to my introductory sociology class at the University of Regina and, using the work of Vernon Fowke, explained the importance of the so-called National Policy for understanding the development of farming on the Prairies. He described how Western settlement by a non-Indigenous agrarian population was an integral plank in an industrial development strategy that Canadian governments implemented in the decades after Confederation. I was captivated by the notion that complex developments such as the depletion of family farms did not "just happen," but were instead the result of causal forces and mechanisms that could be isolated, studied, and ultimately understood. It started to dawn on me that my parents had not failed, nor had they forsaken the dreams of their first-generation settler parents—they, too, were part of a historical process. I was fortunate to subsequently develop a long association with a sociology department that Professor McCrorie and others were building, a department that was committed to a critical analysis of the history and trajectory of Saskatchewan and the West. This recognition carries, of course, no implication that Dr. McCrorie or any of my erstwhile colleagues and friends would agree with or bear any responsibility for the analysis of events to be found in the coming pages; however, they did teach me the merits of taking a longer view and of adopting a "big picture perspective."

Fowke argues that in order to understand a region such as Saskatchewan and the West, we must understand its role in the larger national and international political economy. This book attempts to follow in this scholarly tradition, but with one important conceptual addendum: explicit attention to social class. The rationale for this particular approach is linked to a critical-realist orientation to understanding the world. Critical realism tends to assume that phenomena—events, trends, occurrences, and important decisions—tend not to "just happen," but rather are linked to causal, influencing, underlying, or contributing mechanisms. Investigation, understanding, and analysis of events and developments involves uncovering such mechanisms through the use of conceptual frameworks that guide and focus our attention. In what follows, I attempt to use what I call the prism of social class to partly understand the transformation of rural Saskatchewan.

Understanding social class is an inherently difficult task given both the dynamic and the ever-changing nature of class structures and the existence of multiple and contested explanations and understandings of class. As explained in the introduction, this book adopts a particular structural understanding of class and focuses on a specific segment of the class whose members constitute the bedrock of the family farm: agricultural independent commodity producers. This is a class whose very existence and subsequent fate has been aided and abetted by the policies and actions of various federal governments. I will argue that this class played a central role in the development of the National Policy, the industrialization policy in play from just after Confederation to the Great Depression. During this period, federal governments tended to adopt policies and undertake actions that were geared toward facilitating the establishment of family farms on the Plains and in the province of Saskatchewan after it was created in 1905. The economic crisis of the Great Depression and the Second World War marked a shift in Canadian political economy, from that of a national, east–west orientation to a more continental, north–south one. During this period, federal governments tended to adopt policies and undertake actions that were geared to maintaining Western family farms even as the internal dynamics of the market was facilitating a restructuring of agricultural production. The 1970s brought a definitive end of the postwar economic "happy days" as a shift to neoliberal market-oriented government actions, policies, and legislation no longer protected family farmers, but rather "freed" them to harness the winds of change associated with so-called market discipline. The market and its "logic" were increasingly granted the status of a natural force that governed most of the affairs of humans, including the fate of family farming.

The story that unfolds in these pages is one of radical change but not necessarily progress. It involves the acquisition of the lands of the West by federal governments, the displacement of Indigenous Peoples and First Nations, the creation of a new class, the temporary support of that class, and then deliberate actions and decisions that were known to have a radically transformative impact on its members. History, in this case the history of Saskatchewan and the West, teaches us that classes come and go, and with them joy and heartbreak, prosperity and hardship, hope and despair, and all the other elements of the human condition.

INTRODUCTION

My father's first major heart attack happened in 1977, when he was just fifty-nine years old. It happened while he was feeding cattle on my parents' traditional mixed family farm in eastern Saskatchewan. The 1970s were, despite the contemporary popularity of the TV sitcom *Happy Days*, hard times in the country for family farmers in rural Saskatchewan, many of whom relied largely on cereal grain and oilseed income supplemented by a few cattle and/or hogs. In 1970, amid instability in international commodity prices and continually rising input prices associated with corporate concentration, a major Canadian government study had recommended the elimination of many small farms. My parents were having a hard time covering the costs of production no matter how hard they worked. As the family patriarch, and in the finest tradition of liberal individualism, my father blamed himself. Somehow, it was his fault: he must have not worked hard enough, or made bad decisions, or bought the wrong inputs, or done something else wrong. The debts piled up, the stress accumulated, and the worries intensified until his heart literally gave out.

My father survived his heart attack, but he and my mother were forced to quit farming, and they soon ended up in the paid labour force. In what is surely an ironic twist of fate, they ended up working for the Saskatchewan Wheat Pool, my mother as a cook for an elevator construction crew and my father her paid cook's helper. They were certainly not alone in experiencing such a radical change in their positions, having gone from being independent farmers to members of the paid labour force. Indeed, a great many first-generation Canadian farmers whose parents immigrated to Saskatchewan in the late eighteenth and early nineteenth centuries experienced similarly dramatic changes in their life circumstances in the latter decades of the nineteenth century and beyond. The larger economic and political changes that weighed on my parents' dreams is what this book is about.

What Charles Knuttila lacked was not intelligence, ambition, energy, drive, or determination, but rather the ability to systematically link what was happening to him and my mother, Allie, with the larger context of the global food system and the patterns and structures of wealth production and accumulation that were unfolding in the global marketplace. Yes, he knew about the power of banks, and had felt this in his own life. He understood the fact that the prices of everything he needed to buy constantly increased while the prices he and his neighbours received for their products fluctuated radically, often falling below the cost of production. Yes, he occasionally railed against "the system." But he was never quite able to fully link his biography and his personal troubles with their larger historical context. Had he possessed a more robust ability to locate his biography within the context of the unfolding national and global economic structures, my family's personal story might have ended differently. American sociologist C. Wright Mills termed the ability to link our biographies with the historical epoch in which they unfold the "sociological imagination." Such a contextual view, Mills argued, allows us to differentiate personal problems from public issues. My parents needed to understand that falling wheat prices resulted from national and global developments well beyond the farm gate and were subject to structural forces and dynamics beyond their control, and that as hard-working and efficient farmers, they were not to blame.[1]

In his doctoral dissertation, later published as *Canadian Agricultural Policy*, Vernon Fowke demonstrated a keen sociological imagination by locating the object of his studies in this larger social and historical context. Fowke argued that the best way to understand the development and fate of agriculture in an industrial society like Canada was to place it within the larger economic and political context. He wrote:

That agricultural policy can best be explained by an historical consideration of agricultural functions. Essential to an understanding of governmental treatment of the agricultural community...is an historical knowledge of the uses to which agriculture has been put from time to time and from place to place. If we can learn why agricultural development was wanted at a particular time and place there arises the possibility of knowing why agriculture was encouraged or neglected, what groups were interested in its development, and the political pressures under which agricultural assistance was extended. In support of this contention...[I seek] to portray the role or roles of agriculture within territories which now form the Dominion of Canada, and to relate these roles to the formation of the agricultural policies of the respective governments.[2]

The present volume is informed by Fowke's approach. To this end, it links Prairie agriculture, and more specifically cereal grain and mixed family farming in Saskatchewan, to the larger patterns of economic and political change in Canada. The approach adopted here moves beyond Fowke, though, by focusing explicitly on class structures and placing the Canadian economy within the context of the larger evolving global capitalist system.

It could be said that Fowke represents the perspective that Paul Baran describes as characteristic of an intellectual. Baran does not mean the intellectual as a stereotypical "egghead" sitting in an office using incomprehensible language; rather, his intellectual is someone whose "concern is the entire historical process" and who is capable of taking "the longer view" with an eye to understanding the interconnectedness of what might seem on the surface like separate, autonomous, and isolated aspects of complex totalities.[3] It is clear that Fowke was such an intellectual because he understood the settlement of the West not as an isolated development, but rather as part of a much larger national undertaking with international overtones.

Examining and describing complex phenomena such as the changing roles of agriculture in a national economy and the political and economic forces that impact those roles requires the employment of various analytical tools. One such tool that we shall use is historical periodization, an analytical process whereby larger pieces of history are divided into discrete periods or epochs. Periodization can be used to study events ranging from the evolution of humanity to economic or political systems, institutions, or even the work and life cycle of an individual.[4] Periodization will be used here to facilitate an understanding of the dynamic nature of modern capitalism, the economic system within which Canada has developed. Further, we will periodize the development of Canadian federal government agricultural policies that have had a direct impact on the Western family farm. The first such periodization we will use draws on the work of several scholars in suggesting that capitalism is best understood as having evolved through several distinctive stages since it emerged around 1500.[5]

THE CONTEXT: EVOLVING GLOBAL CAPITALISM

Chapters 1 through 4 are each introduced with a brief comment on the evolving stages of the dynamic global capitalist economic order, and how the relevant stage impacted the subject matter of each chapter. To preview this approach, we will begin with the first stage of English capitalism, known as merchant capitalism, or mercantilism, which dates from about 1500 to the Industrial Revolution and the emergence of industrial capitalism around the 1770s.[6] The evolution of industrial capitalism after the 1770s to the end of the American Civil War (1865) marks the second stage, which we might call the era of classical competitive industrial capitalism. Continued technological innovation, the growth of the stock markets, and the expansion of banks and other financial institutions, particularly in the United States after the victory of the industrial North in the Civil War, resulted in the emergence of a new form of economic organization. Increasingly the highly productive joint-stock corporation emerged as the dominant economic actor replacing family-owned enterprises in major sectors of the economy. This is the era of corporate capitalism often referred to as the Gilded Age (1880s–1920s). It marks the emergence of the first societies in human history capable of mass material production and concomitant mass consumption. After a half century, the era of corporate capitalism ended abruptly with the stock market crash of 1929. The Great Depression that followed represented the first international financial crisis to threaten the entire capitalist economic order. It resulted in the emergence of a new school of economic and political thought and action that legitimized the role of activist states providing social stability through massive spending linked to the creation of welfare states and supplemented by economic stability that was at least partly the result of increased regulation. We refer to the period from the 1930s through to the postwar boom (lasting into 1970s) as the era of Keynesian corporate capitalism.

By the 1970s, social, political, and economic forces began to undermine Keynesian corporate capitalism as a neoliberal economic, ideological, and economic revolution began to radically change the role of the state and re-establish an unfettered and deregulated market. The neoliberal nation-state redirected spending away from social programs to corporate support, while promoting privatization, deregulation, and the emergence of a fully-fledged globalized economic order. Although the world changed radically under neoliberalism, after about forty years the era of neoliberal globalized capitalism collapsed as a result of the economic crisis of 2008–09. The stock market imploded, as did several financial corporations and many other businesses along with the housing market, generating a dramatic increase in unemployment. It became clear that deregulated, fully globalized economies, unregulated international financial markets, and liberalized trade were incapable of generating sustained economic stability. After 2008–09, massive government spending and intervention prevented the total collapse of the global economic order, but the result was an age of confusion. Despite massive public spending, the era did not see a return to classical Keynesianism, but rather a continuation of key elements of neoliberalism as politicians and powerful economic interests advocated social restraint while targeting spending and assistance to the most powerful actors in the economy. The term "age of confusion" implies multiple contradictions, including increased national and global inequalities in a much-touted era of freedom, concurrent expanded economic globalization, renewed nationalisms, and calls for greater equality amid various emerging fundamentalisms, leading one observer to designate it as an "age of anger."[7] We will return to this context-setting overview in the introductions to chapters 1, 2, 3, and 4.

CANADA AND THE GLOBAL ECONOMIC ORDER

Canadian history is best understood when placed in alignment with the evolution of global capitalism. Canada emerged as an independent nation in 1867, albeit one with colonial connections, just as corporate capitalism was emerging in the 1860s. As a result, the new Canadian state set out its future economic strategy for nation building in an era in which the large corporation was emerging as the dominant economic actor. The crises of the Great Depression and the Second World War shifted Canadian economic strategy away from previous efforts to build a national economy in favour of greater integration into the powerful North American economy. The modest success of the Canadian version of a Keynesian approach during and after the Depression and the war could not prevent powerful Canadian economic interests and policy-makers from seeking greater North American economic integration. During and after the Second World War, continental economic integration—so-called continentalism—replaced the National Policy as the dominant economic and political world view. In the 1950s and '60s, the Canadian economy, and many Canadian families and individuals, experienced a version of the postwar boom. However, after the early 1970s, Canada followed the United States and Great Britain in adopting neoliberal and neoconservative social, economic, and political policies. Like their other Western counterparts, Canadian governments, under the leadership of both major political parties, undertook the typical neoliberal approach of privatization, deregulation, major reductions in state expenditures, lower taxes, and the application of market rationality to the funding and operation of most social institutions. The collapse of global neoliberalism after the 2008–09 economic crisis led Canadian governments to spend massively to bolster key sectors of the economy through various forms of aid to the corporate sector, even while articulating the ethos of rule by the market and individual responsibility.

Returning to Fowke's approach, we will use another periodization to organize the main arguments in chapters 2 through 4, which examine select agriculture-related federal legislative actions. This schema draws from a significant body of scholarship that suggests that distinctive phases or periods of agricultural policy have impacted family farming on the Prairies.[8] For simplicity's sake, we will designate these as follows: phase 1 (Confederation to 1929–30); phase 2 (Great Depression to the 1970s); and phase 3 (the 1970s–present). Phase 1 was the period from the instigation of post-Confederation industrialization policies that we call the National Policy to the Great Depression. During this period, Western family farming played a central role in the National Policy and the efforts of successive federal governments to facilitate industrial development in Canada. Phase 2 encompasses the period from the Great Depression through the end of the postwar boom. After the crises of the Depression and the Second World War, the National Policy ceased to be the dominant economic development framework, and as a result Western agriculture no longer played a central role in Canadian economic development. During this same period, Western farmers, no longer an important market for Canadian industry, became just one of many export-oriented sectors in a more complex economy. During the heyday of Keynesian state capitalism (1945 to the beginning of the 1970s), some supports for family farming and Western agriculture were maintained, but they were increasingly marginalized amid a range of other spending priorities. The Western farming sector itself was also rapidly changing. Phase 3 begins in the 1970s and covers the period up to the present, during which globalization and neoliberalism came to dominate economic and political policy. By the beginning of this period, the economic role of Prairie agriculture had long since lost the central place it once held and was increasingly irrelevant as a market for industrial goods in a fully globalized marketplace. Deregulation, privatization, and dramatic cuts to a variety of forms of government assistance soon took a toll on the grain and emerging plant-based oil-producing family farms in Saskatchewan and the West.

CHAPTER OUTLINE

Chapter 1 begins by noting how British North America was integrated into the global capitalist order from the time of European colonizers' first contact with Indigenous Peoples. It sets the stage for the transition from British North America to the creation of the independent nation-state of Canada in 1867. The chapter presents Confederation as a framework for solving a variety of political, economic, geographical, and military problems. It also establishes the importance of the West in the post-Confederation economic development strategy premised on a three-pronged industrialization program involving tariffs, Western settlement, and transportation, or what we have already termed the National Policy. It provides the context for understanding why, given its dual roles as a tariff-protected captive market and producer of export commodities in the form of cereal grains in phase 1 of Canadian agricultural development, the Western family farm was a central pillar of the Canadian economic project.

In chapter 2, we track the specific actions and legislative initiatives of a variety of federal governments as they sought to encourage the expansion of agriculture, particularly cereal grain production and mixed farming, in Saskatchewan and on the Prairies between the 1870s and the Great Depression. Having undertaken actions to, in the words of James Daschuk, clear the Plains of much of its Indigenous population, a succession of governments sought to make the land available to settlers and to use immigration policies and activities to attract further numbers of largely white immigrants.[9] Institutions were created to develop crops and farming methods appropriate for the region, and governments undertook to facilitate the establishment of a transportation network and the infrastructure to handle the purchase and export of agricultural commodities for national and international markets. When necessary, governments enacted legislation and regulations to ensure a smooth-functioning grain trade that placed an adequate cash flow into the hands of farmers to purchase industrial inputs. It was a new society predicated on the principles of agrarianism.

The frantic expansion of the Prairies came to a crashing halt in 1929 with the onset of the Great Depression, the drought of the 1930s, and the Second World War. In chapter 3, we explore phase 2 as an era of crisis followed by the relative stability brought about by the postwar boom. Governments in Canada were forced to adopt a Keynesian approach to managing these crises and steering the Canadian economy. The crisis of the Depression and the economic growth spurred by the Allied war effort marked a major turning point for the Canadian economy. As global capitalism continued to develop and US-based multinational corporations emerged as the dominant global economic actors, many Canadian businesses looked south rather than west for market opportunities. The central role that the Prairies enjoyed in the era of the National Policy began to wane as continental economic integration and north–south trade flourished. The rapid mechanization of agricultural production in the postwar era was an important factor in the development of internal differences within the farm community. The number of Prairie farms began to decline after 1945 with the trend toward larger and larger but fewer and fewer farms. By the 1960s, a variety of factors produced increasing poverty and discontent among some farmers, so much so that by the end of that decade, the federal government was moved to re-examine the future of family farming in Canada.

Chapter 4 examines another important milestone in the Canadian economy and federal government policy, with the 1970s marking the beginning of phase 3. Facing uncertainty and potential political problems, the federal government of the day established the Task Force on Agriculture. Its final report recommended a significant restructuring of family farming, including a reduction in the number of farms. The 1970s also mark a significant transition in the dynamics of global capitalism. What we will refer to as a neoliberal assault on the Keynesian state emerged, bringing with it significant changes to many agricultural legislative initiatives. By the end of the first decade of the twenty-first century, legislation informed by neoliberalism had radically transformed the environment of the family farm in Western Canada. Government assistance to agriculture was increasingly crisis-focused—that is, geared to stabilizing incomes when needed. The historic Crow's Nest Pass Agreement was abrogated, the Canadian Wheat Board eliminated amid a wave of deregulation and massive privatization of assets and services. Grain, oilseed, and mixed-crop farmers increasingly spoke with many political voices as the class to which they belonged was transformed, with many relying on income they earned in the labour market to keep their operations viable while others increasingly relied on the employment of wage labour to operate their large agricultural enterprises.

In chapter 5, we investigate the radically changed external environment in which Saskatchewan family farms, and indeed all agricultural producers, operate. By examining the place of Western agricultural producers in the global food chain, including input and output enterprises, processors, and retailers, we can better understand the complexities of the system and appreciate the vulnerabilities of the actual "grounded" producers. We examine Western grain farmers' status as part of a fractured class whose members had different interests and concerns and spoke with different voices. What they had in common, however, were relationships with agricultural input and output sectors characterized by a high degree of capital concentration and centralization.

The final chapter considers a few important social, economic, and political implications of a transformed and restructured class of agrarian independent commodity producers. After examining the implications of an ideological shift from agrarianism to an individualist and entrepreneurial world view, we consider the implications of class restructuring for community viability and producer health and wellness before turning, finally, to the shifting political sands in Saskatchewan. The epilogue asks some difficult questions, including how the narrative presented here might be related to the question of truth and reconciliation vis-à-vis Indigenous Peoples.

A NOTE ON CLASS

We will be utilizing the concepts of class, class structure, and class interests in our extension of Fowke's analysis, and to better understand the dynamics and interests behind the creation of a class of independent agricultural commodity producers in the West, their temporary preservation, and their eventual decline. In the social sciences, the concept of class remains one of the most debated, contested, complex, and difficult. No effort will be undertaken here to summarize the decades of controversy surrounding this issue; however, some clarification is in order.[10]

To cut through some of the complexities attending the concept of class, several scholars have argued that the multiple theories that characterize the field can be understood as falling into one of three types of analysis.[11] The first approach is nominal. Without a systematic theoretical basis for the designation, a nominal approach merely identifies a group, aggregate, or collection of individuals who share some common attribute, and then attaches a name to them. For example, those whose income or worth is over a billion dollars could be called the "super rich," or those whose income is less than two thousand dollars per annum are "the poor." There are no necessary theoretical or empirical relationships between the different classes.

The second approach also understands classes as representing groupings of people sharing some set of characteristics or attributes. This "lifestyle approach" generally links the criteria for class membership to some element in the social structure.[12] This is typically possession of one or more common attributes, such as income level, education, occupation, dwelling size, neighbourhood, authoritative position, and other social factors that produce common lifestyles, interests, attitudes, or patterns of interaction. This type of class analysis does not typically postulate significant relationships among members of a class other than mere coexistence. Even when quantitative characteristics such as income levels are used, the focus is difference, not inequality.

The third approach to class focuses on individuals' societal/structural locations and their positions in major social institutions, with one's place within the dominant economic institutions being primary. Class position or location is not the product of simple aggregation, nor are classes a matter of lifestyle groupings based on some common attribute. By focusing on individuals' positions in market relationships, the relational approach adopted here refers to what individuals bring to the market. In multiple markets that characterize advanced capitalism, individuals buy and sell a variety of different assets, commodities, or items of exchange. Some come to the market with capital and wealth eager to invest with an eye to profit, while others bring commodities and services that they and their families produce, while still others lacking capital or the capacity to produce commodities sell their capacity to work—their labour power—for wages and salaries. When class is understood in the context of one's position in the economic structures of a market-based society, the inevitable social and economic dynamics involve transfers of wealth, structural inequality, class conflict, and economic coercion.

It is important to remember that the emergence of capitalist societies in which markets are the dominant mechanism for organizing and controlling the production, exchange, and distribution of goods and services is a relatively recent development in human history. As capitalism has changed and evolved over the last four hundred years, new and increasingly complex forms of organization have emerged among those who bring capital to the market, as have new forms of control and management. A structural constant is the fact that to "make a living," those without capital are required to offer or sell their capacity to work. Changes in technology and the social organization of production, distribution, and exchange create new occupations, opportunities, and professions requiring new skills, knowledge, credentials, qualities, and qualifications, while others pass into oblivion, thus generating a complex and dynamic class structure with multiple shifting in internal divisions, or class fractions. Additionally, markets constantly see new types of independent commodity and service production and provision. Within this complexity, it remains true that the welfare and fate of most individuals in a capitalist society are ultimately tied to the market, yet debates continue as to what really happens when buyers and sellers meet in various markets.

A scholar who succinctly penetrated a core issue relating to the essential nature of market relationships in a capitalist economic order is the renowned Canadian political philosopher C.B. Macpherson. While classical liberal political and economic thought trumpeted the triumph of markets as beacons of individual rights and freedoms, Macpherson pointed out that the market in capitalist society is not just a mechanism of exchange or trade in goods and services, it is also a mechanism that involves a net transfer of powers. A pre-eminent Macpherson scholar, Phillip Hansen, argues that when it comes to the market relationship between owners and non-owners of productive resources, the key to understanding the relationship is Macpherson's concept of the net transfer of powers within a capitalist economic order driven as it is by a ceaseless drive to accumulate wealth.[13] I want to extend the point.

The concept of a net transfer of powers has both quantitative and qualitative dimensions. The qualitative dimension relates to the notion that an essential element of the human condition is our capacity to produce what we require to survive, but also, very importantly, to find a sense of fulfillment and satisfaction in that activity. This is what Macpherson calls our *developmental power*. As Hansen points out, when individuals are forced to sell their labour, they forfeit control of the use of their human creative capacities to fully realize their full potential, their developmental power, and thus their developmental power is diminished. I would extend the logic of this argument to the inevitable loss of developmental power experienced by independent commodity producers; this would of course include family farmers who, for example, experience inner satisfaction as creative producers of quality foodstuffs, but who know they will not control the quality or destination of its final form.

But that is not all that is happening in the market transaction because there is a quantitative dimension, a net transfer of what Macpherson calls *extractive power*. Hansen writes, "Extractive power points to the ability to use, along with one's own power, the power of others to achieve one's purposes. That is, it is the power over others, the power to extract benefit from them."[14] When the owners and non-owners engage in the marketplace, and the owners purchase the capacity of the non-owners to operate their productive resources (mines, mills, factories, etc.), they do so only when there is an extractable profit for the owners. Again, in Hansen's words, "non-owners enjoy no extractive power and little power overall because of the necessity to transfer control over the exercise of their capacities in order to gain access to the means of life and labour."[15] I would again suggest that the logic of the notion of extractive power in market transactions articulated by Macpherson and Hansen would apply to the multiple market relations entered into by independent commodity producers.

The substantial debates surrounding the details of the net transfer of powers when capital and the various types of labour meet in the marketplace need not concern us here; however, the mechanisms through which the net transfer of power functions when independent commodity producers enter the market is of interest. For the purposes of this study, we are dealing with a class typically called the "petite bourgeoisie," in this case independent agricultural commodity producers. The precise nature of this class and its many fractions will vary across time, locale, and the position of a society in the international economic order.[16] In advanced capitalism, for example, professionals such as lawyers, physicians, or accountants may be understood as independent commodity producers (even if what they sell lacks the physicality of a bushel of wheat) if they operate their own firm and with minimal hired labour offer their services on the market. Alternatively, they may be employed by a large enterprise for a salary, changing what they bring to the labour market, perhaps making them part of a new middle class or an upper fraction of the working class.

Our focus going forward will be a particular type of independent commodity producer—namely, Western Canadian agrarian or agricultural independent commodity producers who were economically dependent largely on the sale of cereal grains and, later, oilseeds. Although it is perhaps not conceptually rigorous, to avoid the monotonous, even annoying, repetition of a single turn of phrase we will use several terms to represent this class. In short, the text will variously use "farmers," "family farmers," "Western farmers," and "Western cereal grain producers" to refer to individuals and families engaged in agricultural production who nominally own productive resources (land, buildings, tools, equipment, and livestock) and who employ their own and unpaid labour from within their household to produce commodities for sale in various markets.

One last point requires attention before we move on. A volume of this sort has many inherent limitations, some linked to the vicissitudes of book publishing, but also to the intellectual limitations of the author and the inherent complexity of the object of investigation. When we study any social phenomena, we must be constantly aware of the complexity of what we are investigating and the impossibility of ever fully grasping it. German sociologist Max Weber identified what he called the infinite complexity of reality and the fact that we possess finite minds, necessitating the selection of specific elements or aspects of that reality on which to focus our attention. In the jargon of the social scientist, we engage in abstraction when we focus on certain aspects of reality while deliberately neglecting others. Abstraction involves acknowledging, but then withholding from detailed consideration, potentially important dimensions of the phenomenon under consideration.[17]

Obviously, limiting the focus of an analysis through abstraction necessarily results in omissions, lacunae, and simplifications. This study focuses on some of the impacts of federal agricultural policy, action, and regulation on cereal grain and oilseed family farming while leaving aside very important issues such as provincial activity. This is clearly a limitation. While the importance of examining matters such as agricultural commodity production through a gendered lens is unquestionable, as is the vital requirement of examining ethnicity, nationalism, and racism, these matters are not addressed here. The analysis assumes the existence of a patriarchal gender order with its concomitant relations of domination, subordination, and inequality.[18] Likewise, we acknowledge the existence of systemic and systematic racism in the colonial projects that led Europeans to North America and legitimized the granting of much of the West to a colonial company and then later the removal of hundreds of thousands of Indigenous people from their traditional lands and their replacement by largely white settlers. While the mere acknowledgement of these lacunae and the attendant weaknesses in this account is insufficient, I nonetheless look forward to further analyses of these events by those more qualified and through prisms and lenses that further expose those dynamics.

Before turning in detail to the policies that characterized each of the phases described above, it is necessary to briefly recount the circumstances that led to the creation of Canada as an independent nation-state in 1867 and the important role the Prairies have played in Canadian economic history.

CHAPTER 1

CONFEDERATION to DEPRESSION

Western Canada Enters the Global Economy, 1867–1930

MERCANTILE CAPITALISM AND BRITISH NORTH AMERICA

As merchant capitalism emerged in the sixteenth and seventeenth centuries in England and western Europe, merchants and state-sponsored agents increasingly exploited new sources of wealth beyond Europe, for example, in the abundant stocks of North Atlantic cod. Contact with Indigenous Peoples in North America introduced another source of wealth in the form of furs, and soon after that Europeans began to tap into the wealth of North American forests.[1] A new form of economic organization was emerging as alliances forged between monarchs and merchants resulted in the formation of international charter companies. Merchants were eager to find new products to buy and sell, while monarchs were eager to enhance their power and dominance through the acquisition of colonies and territories.[2]

As merchant capitalism developed, the Great Plains of North America became integrated into events in England after the restoration of Charles II. To cement alliances with the emerging merchant classes, in 1670 Charles granted his cousin Prince Rupert a charter to form a company under the name of the Governor and Adventurers of England Trading into the Hudson Bay, or what has since come to be known as the Hudson's Bay Company (HBC). The terms of this charter were astonishing, involving a land grant of 1.5 million square miles composed of the watershed of Hudson Bay, an area that soon came to be known Rupert's Land. The land grant included "nearly 40 percent of today's Canadian provinces, including what would become Ontario, Quebec, north of the Laurentian watershed and west of the Labrador boundary, Manitoba, the better part of Saskatchewan, southern Alberta, and much of the Northwest Territories."[3] Not only was the HBC granted ownership of the land and all wealth and resources therein, as well as power over the inhabitants, it was essentially recognized as a sovereign state: "Powers are given to the Company to make laws, impose penalties and punishments, and to judge in all causes civil and criminal according to the laws of England." Further, the company's representatives "may employ an armed force, appoint commanders, and erect forts."[4]

Other developments on the international scene had major implications for North America. The first Treaty of Paris (1763), which ended the Seven Years' War in Europe, radically changed the political structures of North America when France ceded its major North American territories to what was then British North America (BNA). Shortly thereafter, Britain in turn lost much of its North American territory with the 1783 Peace of Paris that ended the American Revolution. After the formation of the Montreal-based North West Company in 1779, the HBC attempted a different tack to solidify its position in the West by promoting settlement in the Red River region.[5] Following the British conquest of New France, the primary immigrants to British North America shifted from French to British. The number of English-speaking immigrants to the northern colonies increased significantly when more than 40,000 United Empire Loyalists moved north to escape the American Revolution.[6] The fifty years that followed the revolution saw a significant increase in the population of Upper Canada (what is today southern Ontario), however, the period from 1800 to 1850 saw even faster growth, particularly in English-speaking Upper Canada, where the population increased from about 158,000 in 1825 to nearly 1.5 million by 1861.[7]

In the West, the quasi-state status of the HBC in Rupert's Land—comprising what Daschuk calls a "de facto government"—was extended when the British government granted Vancouver Island to the HBC in 1849.[8] After the discovery of gold in the 1850s stimulated a dramatic increase in the region's non-Indigenous population, the British created a new mainland colony called British Columbia in 1858. The actions of the British in claiming this territory were partly in response to the American push westward. In 1844, James Polk's presidential platform included the slogan "Fifty-four Forty or Fight!," meaning the Americans should claim all the West Coast—this in spite of the Anglo-American Convention of 1818, which set the border west of the Great Lakes at the 49th parallel. The matter was settled in 1846 when the Oregon Treaty confirmed that everything north of the 49th parallel to the Pacific Ocean (with the addition of the southern tip of Vancouver Island) would remain entirely British.[9]

INDUSTRIAL CAPITALISM AND FLEDGLING INDUSTRIES IN BRITISH NORTH AMERICA

As British industrial capitalism developed, the role of Britain's colonies also changed from being the source of trade goods to that of raw materials and markets for manufactured goods. By the mid-1800s, the British began to advocate free trade; as the leading industrial nation, Britain required enhanced sources of imported raw materials and expanding markets for its rapidly growing industrial output. The British realized that direct control of a vast colonial empire was difficult and costly, and they concluded that some of their colonies could have a greater degree of domestic political control and still provide Britain with the necessary inputs for its industrial machine and as a market for its products.

As the population of BNA continue to increase, so did its exports of timber, lumber, wheat, and other commodities, supplementing the continuing fishery. Along the St. Lawrence River, the timber, lumber, and shipbuilding industries, in addition to a more general growth in the population, provided a local demand for a vast variety of products, resulting in the development of small-scale industries in textiles, leather, brewing and distilling, food processing, milling, iron, and other manufactured goods. The construction of railroads and canals to move various products served to further stimulate local industry and small-scale manufacturing. Kenneth Norrie and Douglas Owram observe that in the first half of the nineteenth century, the economy of Upper Canada was transformed from a simple pioneer economy to a "mature agricultural-commercial" one. The latter was to become the stepping stone for the emergence of an industrialization process, a fundamentally important transformation for the future of the Prairie West.[10]

By the 1860s, two decades of continued economic and population growth along the St. Lawrence generated new problems as well as possibilities in BNA. Among the problems was the fact that population growth in predominantly English-speaking and Protestant Upper Canada (otherwise known as Canada West) was outpacing that of French-speaking and predominantly Catholic Lower Canada (Canada East). Each colony had equal representation in the joint assembly created in 1840 in reaction to the 1837–38 Rebellions. As a result, some in Canada West began to call for increased parliamentary representation to match their larger population, while in Canada East there was fear that local linguistic and religious interests would not be protected by the anglophone majority. The best agricultural land along the upper reaches of the St. Lawrence was already occupied, resulting in diminished opportunities and increased emigration to the United States. Additionally, Canadian industry and manufacturing, fledgling and established alike, lacked a vital element for industry in a capitalist economy—an expanding and dynamic market. To the south, the post–Civil War era was characterized by rapid expansion of American railroads and westward settlement over the Appalachians and into the Mississippi region, exemplified by Minnesota joining the Union in 1858, posing a serious threat to the future of the West and Rupert's Land. While the doctrine of Manifest Destiny may have been coined with reference to the annexation of Texas, it came to represent a larger ideology characterized by the United States' mission of North American expansionism.

Facing political deadlock in the Canadian assembly, declining economic prospects, and real or perceived military and territorial threats, the political elites and emerging dominant economic classes in BNA began to act. In the early 1860s, political and business leaders in the colonies of Nova Scotia, New Brunswick, and Prince Edward Island began discussions about a Maritime Union; however, when news of the discussions reached the Canadas, the assembly requested permission to send a delegation that included George-Étienne Cartier and John A. Macdonald. The delegation from Canada essentially hijacked the Charlottetown Conference. A subsequent meeting was held in Quebec City in the fall of 1865. At Quebec, the delegates, all of them male and without any Indigenous representation, developed seventy-two resolutions outlining the essential constitutional structures of a new nation-state to replace the existing colonial entity of BNA. Britain had matured into the world's most developed and powerful capitalist economy and was moving toward free trade and away from all vestiges of mercantile regulation. The British were interested in gaining access to markets and raw materials worldwide, exemplified by the repeal of the Corn Laws in 1846, and the Canadians were confident they could convince the British Parliament to take action on their request to create a new nation, albeit one that would remain firmly allied to Britain.[11] A further conference was held in London in late 1866 and early 1867, resulting in the British Parliament passing the *British North America Act*. It was enacted on March 29, 1867, creating the federal state of Canada made up of Ontario, Quebec, Nova Scotia, and New Brunswick.

CONFEDERATION: A NEW NATION-STATE

New nation-states do not just happen but rather are typically created by a combination of internal and external social, economic, cultural, and political forces and interests. In the case of Canada, Confederation can be seen as a framework to address the problems noted above. The adoption of a federal system created a strong national government capable of developing and implementing an industrialization strategy and protecting the West from American intrusion. Politically, a federal system with specific provincial jurisdiction over language, culture, education, and civil law provided the francophone population of Quebec with some basic protections. A national government would also be in a stronger position when it came to raising funds necessary for investment in transportation; it also offered a united front on matters relating to international trade. Vernon Fowke argues that Confederation was only the first step in a series of actions that were to be undertaken to facilitate economic development in Canada:

> A few important steps were necessary to the creation of a second national, economic, and political unit in BNA territory. The first of these was the creation of a national constitution. The main outlines as well as a good deal of the detail of such a constitution were provided for in the BNA Act of 1867. Development and integration were the indispensable and inseparable economic requirements. Both rested heavily on the possibility of facilitating trade among the existing colonies or provinces. Confederation removed the tariff barriers which had previously existed between the separate units, and the BNA Act provided for the completion of an intercolonial railroad by the national government. Further development, however, would require the exploitation of some vast new areas of resources, the establishment of a new frontier of investment. Attention was thus directed even before confederation to the prospects in Rupert's Land and the Pacific colonies.[12]

A critical issue in the creation of a federated state such as Canada is the distribution of powers between the component parts—in the case of Canada, between the federal government and the provinces. The BNA Act was clear about which level of government would be most powerful regarding matters related to economic development: these powers were given to the federal government. Gérald A. Beaudoin explains the principle that guided the division of powers: "The Fathers of Confederation took as their guiding principle that jurisdiction over matters of national interest would be given to Parliament and those of particular provincial interest, to the provinces."[13] He notes that federal jurisdiction included "trade and commerce, direct and indirect taxation, currency, the postal service, census taking and statistics, national defense, the federal civil service, navigation, fisheries, banking, copyright, Aboriginals and Indian reserves, naturalization, marriage and divorce, criminal law, penitentiaries and interprovincial works and undertakings." The provinces, on the other hand, had more limited and local or regional controls: "Provincial legislatures have jurisdiction, among other things, over their internal constitutions, as well as direct taxation for provincial purposes, municipalities, school boards, hospitals, property and civil rights (their largest area of responsibility), administration of civil and criminal justice, penalties for infraction of provincial statutes, prisons, celebration of marriage, provincial civil service, local works and corporations with provincial objectives."[14]

The decisions by Prince Edward Island and Newfoundland not to join Confederation in 1867 produced a nation with a small geographical footprint, and it was made even smaller by the fact that Rupert's Land was still under the control of the HBC. Even before Confederation, however, it was clear that the new nation-state would not be limited by these boundaries forever. The second of the Quebec City resolutions reads in part, "Provision being made for the admission into the Union, on equitable terms, of Newfoundland, the North-West Territory, British Columbia and Vancouver." The point is repeated in resolution 10: "The North-West Territory, British Columbia and Vancouver shall be admitted into the Union on such terms and conditions as the Parliament of the Federated Provinces shall deem equitable and shall receive the assent of Her Majesty; and in the case of the Province of British Columbia or Vancouver, as shall be agreed to by the Legislature of such Province."[15]

Map 1. Provinces of Canada: July 1, 1867, to July 15, 1870

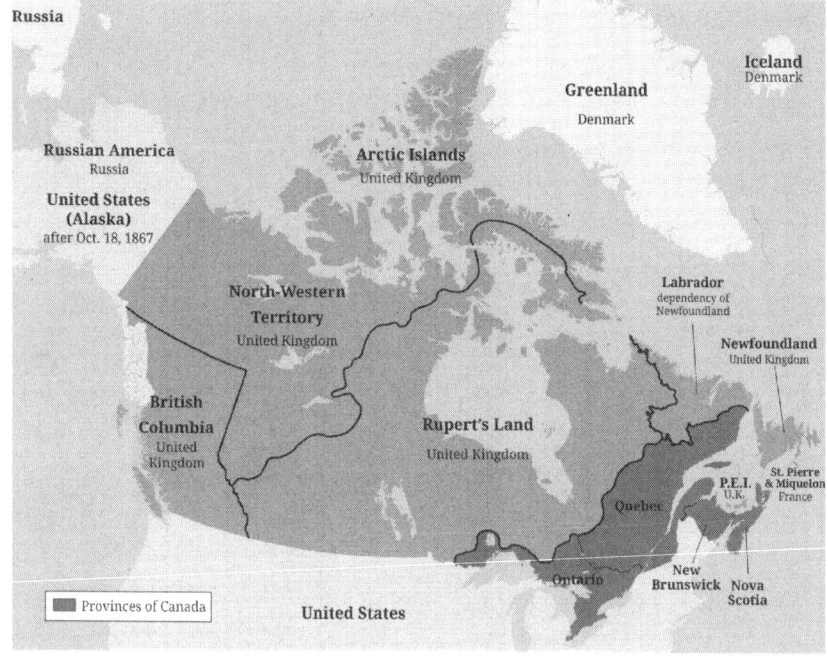

Canada and British North America in 1867. *Source: Coates and Girard, "Reconsidering the Debates over Canadian Confederation."*

That geographical and economic expansion were priorities for Canada from the beginning is made clear by the actions of the very first session of the new Parliament, when the speech from the governor general spoke of the foundation of a new nationality that "will, ere long, extend it bounds from the Atlantic to the Pacific Ocean." The speech also noted that the House of Commons "will also be invited to the important subject of Western Territorial extension."[16] In the debate that followed, the remarks of Charles Tupper typify what was envisioned: "With 11 millions of acres of public soil in the Red River and Saskatchewan Country to invite the immigrant and increase our population, this question of Western extension becomes one of greatest importance."[17] The intentions of the new government with regard to the West was immediately apparent when one Mr.

William McDougall moved notice of a bill incorporating Rupert's Land into the Dominion of Canada.[18]

The extensive debate and commentary by a group of white, male, and relatively wealthy parliamentarians that followed included numerous references to Indigenous people, but not in a manner that indicated any immediate interest in involving them in the process. Mr. Thomas Parker expressed the concern that "If we were to acquire this property it would be necessary to extinguish the claims, not only of the Hudson's Bay company, but of the Indians by whom a great portion of it was inhabited." Mr. Parker went on to indicate that he was prepared to support acquiring the territory "for the purpose of Christianizing its Indian population" or to "raise the Indian to the position of civilized humanity," but he worried that the only intent of such a project was monetary. Mr. Henry Joly and Mr. Charles Connell both indicated concern with the possibility of the United States making a deal with the HBC for the purchase of its land. Mr. Robert Harrison noted the need for Canadian immigration and the valuable contribution immigration was making to the development of the American economy: "In this North-West, we had prairie land equal to any in the western states. Possessing these lands, we could not only give the immigrants land equal in fertility and natural facility for cultivation, but also the protection of British laws. The moral power we would acquire by this acquisition of territory would be something very great."[19] Mr. Alexander Mackenzie, speaking to the American threat to occupy the West, stated that he "was aware of the grasping and avaricious spirit that prevailed in the United States in regard to the acquisition of territory, and he had no doubt many people there were anxious to lay their hands on the rich and fertile regions of the North-West." Later in the same debate, Mr. McDougall suggested that in its pursuit of profit the HBC had mistreated the Indigenous population, but with an unmistakable sense of paternalism he stated, "It had been the practice of our government to recognize some rights as belonging to the aborigines of the country, making treaties with them, and giving them compensation for their lands—dealing with them in a measure as with minors incapable of management of their own affairs, but always acting generously towards them." He suggested that the Canadian approach would produce no fear of disturbances.[20] In discussing the matter, Prime Minister Macdonald invoked a common, racist, debasing trope to justify colonial domination, noting that the government is proposing "the protection of the Indian inhabitants from white aggression and their guardianship as of persons underage, incapable of the management of their own affairs."[21]

Since the acquisition of Rupert's Land required action by the British Parliament, the Canadian Parliament prepared a resolution and dispatched a delegation to present it to Queen Victoria.[22] The resolution prayed that Her Majesty "unite Rupert's Land and the North-West Territory with this Dominion, and to grant to the Parliament of Canada authority to legislate for their future welfare and good government, and assuring Her Majesty of the willingness of the Parliament of Canada to assume the duties and obligations of government and legislation as regards those territories."[23] The HBC formally signed over the land in November 1869 according to terms that one historian describes as follows: "After six months of negotiations, the HBC agreed to transfer Rupert's Land to Canada for the bargain price of 300,000 British pounds in addition to continued HBC title over various trading posts, and five percent of the territory—mostly fertile prairie farmland."[24]

The importance of federal control of the newly acquired lands is illustrated by the speed with which the government introduced and passed the *Act Respecting the Public Lands of the Dominion*.[25] Shortly thereafter, an Order-in-Council established a land survey system, similar to that used in the United States, in which the land was to be divided into square blocks of 640 acres (commonly called "sections"), which were in turn subdivided into quarter sections of 160 acres.[26] Certain lands were set aside, the sale of which would provide revenue to establish schools; other land was reserved for the HBC as part of the Rupert's Land purchase. Still other land was reserved for sale to support railroad construction, with some areas reserved for road allowances. The *Dominion Lands Act* made provision for the granting of 160 acres of land to settlers for a ten-dollar registration fee. The conditions were minimal: the homesteader had to be twenty-one years of age or older, build a permanent residence, and plant 30 acres of land within three years; they also had to maintain residence on the land for at least six months during the first three years. Women were excluded unless they were the sole heads of families.

Along the Red River, the arrival of survey crews and the subdivision of already-occupied farmland generated unrest and, eventually, a militant response from the local Métis and Indigenous population led by Louis Riel. In response to the declaration of a provisional government in 1869, negotiations between Ottawa and Riel and his followers produced an agreement to form a new province, Manitoba. In August 1870, British and Canadian troops arrived to enforce the agreement, thus formally establishing the region as part of Canada.[27] Although the new country's western borders with the United States had been settled, some felt that it was important for Canada to definitively establish its presence from sea to sea. British Columbia joined Confederation in 1871 with a promise from the Government of Canada to join it by rail with the rest of Canada within ten years.

Map 2. Northwest Territories, 1870

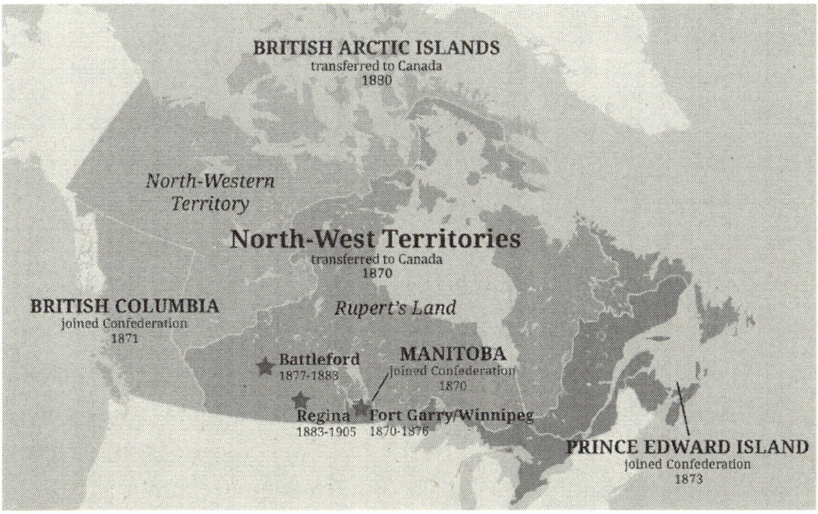

Canada's post-Confederation expansion to the west and north. *Source: Wilcox, "North-West Territories Act."*

The terms under which British Columbia was admitted made it clear that a transcontinental railroad was a matter of national importance, a point made repeatedly in Parliament, where the US practice of using public lands to promote railroad construction was upheld as a model. In 1871, Samuel Tilley argued that a railroad through the West was important for a number of reasons; he noted that "there was a tract of Prairie Land, immense in extent, magnificent in character, and how could immigration be conducted to that country, how could supplies be carried to settlers, how could the produce of that country be brought to a market unless there was a railway[?]"[28] In spring 1872, a bill was introduced to incorporate the Canadian Pacific Railway (CPR). The bill seems to have not been particularly controversial, receiving royal assent in only two months.[29] The Pacific railroad was soon to become a matter of national importance as a scandal erupted following the victory of the Conservative Party in the summer and fall election of 1872.

The Speech from the Throne that opened the Second Parliament was an ominous sign of things to come since the governor general felt obliged to mention a scandal relating to the CPR that seemed to be occupying public attention.[30] The matter quickly became a crisis in the form of a motion of non-confidence claiming that "arrangements were made between the Government and Sir Hugh Allen by which large sums of money were to be paid to the government for the purposes of influencing the recent elections; in return for which Sir Hugh Allan and his friends were free to receive the contract for the construction of the railway, and that was done."[31] As intriguing as the details of the scandal are, we will not consider them here other than to note that Sir John A. Macdonald, Canada's first prime minister, was forced to resign in the midst of the controversy on November 5, 1873.[32]

In the aftermath of these events, the 1874 election resulted in the defeat of the Macdonald Conservatives by Alexander Mackenzie and the Liberal Party. The key deciding factor in the election was not so much the Liberals' platform as the Conservatives' corruption, to which voters reacted harshly. Added to the situation was a significant worldwide recession that began in

1873, which negatively impacted most of the capitalist world and resulted in the loss of jobs and slow growth in virtually every sector of the British, American, and Canadian economies.[33] As the Mackenzie Liberals prepared to govern, they also faced several daunting domestic issues, including the future of the Western territories, relations with Indigenous Peoples, the promised railroad to British Columbia, and the need to stimulate economic development in the new nation in the face of the depression. The cautious nature of the Mackenzie government is illustrated by the lack of action on the Pacific railroad question. The government was "reluctantly conscious that the line would have to be built, in the main, with public funds." Manitoba remained essentially isolated, with transportation along Canadian routes requiring the loading and unloading of cargo from Central Canada up to seventy times over a mixture of trails and waterways. The other option, undesirable to many, was to use American rail and shipping lines.[34]

The governance of the enormous and complex area of the West was also an important issue. After 1870, the territory that now encompasses the northern parts of Quebec, Ontario, and the Prairies west to the Rocky Mountains and north from the 49th parallel to the Arctic Ocean was governed from Ottawa. In 1875, the Mackenzie Liberals passed the *North-West Territories Act*, thereby replacing the lieutenant-governor of Manitoba as the political leader of the Prairie region with a new lieutenant-governor residing in the newly designated territorial capital of Battleford. The territorial lieutenant-governor presided with the aid of a governor's advisory council appointed by Ottawa.[35] In the House of Commons, Mr. Mackenzie noted that the hope was to bring political stability to facilitate settlement on the Prairies by providing the basis for a territorial police force.[36] Later, even as settlement lagged, the North-West Territories was further subdivided into four provisional territories or districts—Assiniboia, Saskatchewan, Alberta, and Athabasca.[37]

The fact that Canada had formally acquired Rupert's Land meant that the Mackenzie Liberals had to address the issue of Indigenous Peoples and their relationship to the land. Beginning virtually with first contact,

Map 3. Canada in 1898

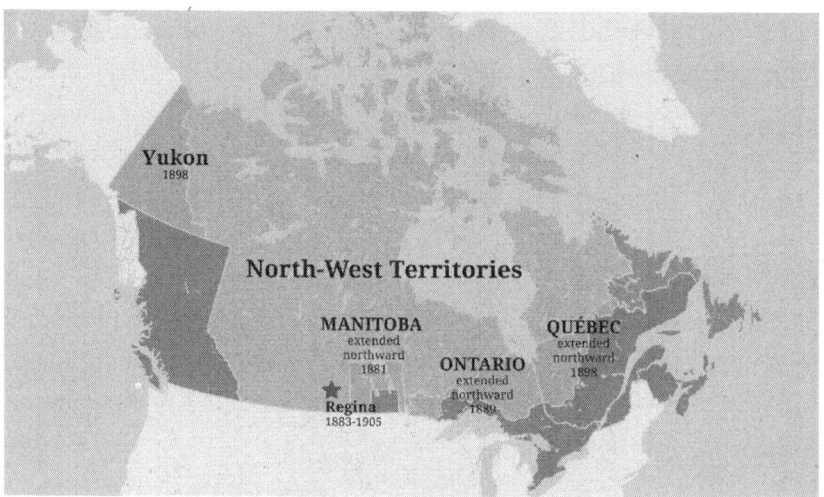

The evolution of political jurisdictions in Canada as of 1898. *Source: Natural Resources Canada, "Atlas of Canada."*

European powers, particularly the French and then the English, had engaged Indigenous populations with both violence and diplomacy. On the diplomacy side, Europeans had engaged—albeit often for commercial and self-serving reasons—in negotiations and established various treaties and agreements that allowed them to extract various forms of wealth from Indigenous communities and provide certain European technologies in return. So numerous were these treaties and agreements that the secretary of state for the provinces indicated in 1870 that there were 107 different treaties.[38] Negotiations began again in August of 1871 with Treaties 1 and 2, giving the Canadian government access to most of the lands of what is now southern Manitoba and a corner of what is now Saskatchewan. As we shall see, most of the remaining agricultural lands of was to become Saskatchewan were addressed in Treaties 4 and 6.[39]

The fate of Indigenous people, particularly in Western Canada, was to some extent tied to the fate of the American Indians as the so-called Indian Wars were drawing to a tragic end in the mid- to late 1800s. The slaughter of the buffalo in the United States impacted the Canadian Plains. A study of buffalo killing in Canada notes that "the animals were gone years before the tracks of the Canadian Pacific arrived."[40] That over thirty million buffalo could be slaughtered in less than a century should shock everyone, yet it was but a preview of what would be visited upon the people who had lived on the Plains since time immemorial.[41] While there was less open warfare north of the border than was typically the case in the United States, the loss of the buffalo was an international ecological catastrophe, and brought starvation and economic ruin for many First Nations in Canada.

As the depression dragged on through the 1870s, the Liberals remained unprepared to undertake any systematic action to connecting Central Canada and the West, thus seeming to frustrate the dreams of some that Confederation would unite the land from sea to sea. The creation of Manitoba and the admission of British Columbia and Prince Edward Island marked geographical consolidation of sorts, but economic growth lagged, particularly in manufacturing and industry. As Norrie and Owram note, "The three decades after Confederation were disappointing to those who wished to see Canada emulate the industrial success of its neighbour to the south."[42] The Liberals were also facing a dire situation in terms of government revenue and growing debt. The main source of government revenues was tariffs, but the Liberals were a free-trade party and could not agree on tariff increases despite the fact that many American manufacturers, protected from competition by import tariffs, were dumping goods into Canada, creating what has been called a "slaughter market" and driving Canadian companies into bankruptcy.[43] During the debate on the Mackenzie Liberals' 1878 budget, Macdonald, having recovered from the Pacific Scandal, actively promoted his vision of a new direction for Canada by advocating the so-called National Policy. In an amendment to the budget, he argued "that the welfare of Canada requires the adoption of a National Policy, which will by judicious readjustment of the Tariff, will benefit and foster the agricultural, the mining, the manufacturing and other interests of the Dominion." He went on to suggest that such a step would result in fewer Canadians having to leave the country to find employment and stop Canada from "being made a sacrifice market."[44]

AN INDUSTRIALIZATION STRATEGY: THE THREE-PRONGED NATIONAL POLICY

Donald Creighton summarizes the situation as the 1870s dragged on as follows: "The Liberals, or Reformers, had gained office, not on their own merits, but simply because of the overwhelming discredit of the Conservatives. A national Liberal Party could scarcely be said to exist; certainly, it was not prepared to rule."[45] Despite having been routed in the 1874 election and driven out of power by the Pacific Scandal, Macdonald sensed that the economic and political malaise was an opportunity, and he began what would be an astonishing comeback. In the aftermath of the Civil War, the Americans were effectively using a variety of tariffs to ensure that the settlers in the United States who were rapidly pushing west would buy American-made goods.[46] Macdonald argued that a similar approach would work in Canada as he began to link tariffs, Western settlement, and a national railroad as the basis of a national policy of industrial development.[47] Despite a personal setback in his home riding, the results of the 1878 election, coming just four years after the Pacific Scandal, were astonishing: the Conservatives gained 60 seats for a total of 124 while the Liberals lost 66 and were reduced to 63.

What was this National Policy that cast the die in Canadian politics for the next thirty years or more, serving as the cornerstone of Canadian economic and political wisdom and eventually adopted by both parties? Donald Smiley notes, "The term 'national policy' has been used in three somewhat different ways in Canada." He explains:

> First, the National Policy—by tradition dignified by capital letters when used in this sense—has referred to the explicitly protectionist direction of Canadian commercial policy taken by the Macdonald Conservatives after they were returned to power by the general election of 1878.

Second, "national policy" has been taken to mean what W.A. Mackintosh designated as the "three basic national decisions" of the new Dominion of Canada to (1) acquire and subsequently settle and develop Rupert's Land and the North-west Territory as a Canadian frontier region, (2) cause the construction of a transcontinental railway wholly on Canadian territory, (3) effect the industrialization of the Canadian heartland through protective tariffs.[48]

K.A. MacKirdy and colleagues strike a similar note: "Various meanings have been given to the phrase. The narrowest definition is the policy of protective tariffs advocated by the Conservative party in opposition prior to the election of 1878. A broader definition links the attempt to stimulate industry through tariff protection with the development of eastwest channels of communication, notably railway expansion and the settlement of the prairie west."[49] We will use the "National Policy" moniker to refer to the general development strategies that were designed to facilitate economic and industrial development in Canada after Confederation, what Fowke described as "that group of policies and instruments which were designed to transform the BNA territories of the midnineteenth century into a political and economic unit."[50]

Once in power, the Macdonald Conservatives moved quickly to put into place and link the trio of policies that we have since come to call by a single name. With the *Dominion Lands Act* in place, the important task became overseeing the removal of the Indigenous Peoples from the land via the treaty-making process in an attempt to formally allow the subdivision of lands through a comprehensive survey project. The establishment of the North-West Mounted Police (NWMP) in 1873 was part of the strategy of orderly settlement. It was perhaps one of the least-debated elements of the entire Western settlement project, having been introduced by Sir John A. Macdonald himself in May 1873 and quickly passed.[51]

Referring to the complexities of the impact of Canadian colonialism on Indigenous Peoples, Andrew Woolford noted that "the combined effects of land appropriation, violated or ignored treaties, legal domination, and forced assimilation were devastating for Aboriginal peoples. However, they did not entirely succumb to these experiences."[52] Daschuk as well as Ray, Miller, and Tough, document how the devastation brought on by the destruction of the buffalo was fundamental in forcing Indigenous Peoples to sign treaties.[53]

The question of Western land in hand, the Conservatives, after returning to power, announced in their first Speech from the Throne the government's intention to implement the second element of the National Policy through a "readjustment of the tariff with a view to increasing revenue, and at the same time, of developing and encouraging the various industries of Canada."[54] The first budget brought in by the new Macdonald government announced a change in policies relating to tariffs, indicating clearly that the tariffs in the budget were geared to protecting Canadian industry. In Mr. Samuel Tilley's words, "Today many of the furnaces are cold, the machinery in many cases is idle, and those establishments that are in operation are only employed half time and are scarcely paying the interest on the money invested."[55] He went on to speak of the importance of the National Policy, the new revenues that the proposed tariffs will generate, and trade difficulties with the Americans. And yet, the purpose of the tariffs was clear—the protection of Canadian industry.

The National Policy's emphasis on protective tariffs was at first attacked by the free-trade Liberals; however, they were not able to mount any significant opposition inside or outside the House, leaving the "Liberal front bench drained of energy" and Liberal leader Mackenzie, in the words of one contemporary, looking "like a washed out rag, limp enough to hang upon a clothes line."[56] Edward Blake replaced Mackenzie as leader in 1880, after which time the Liberals downplayed the anti–National Policy rhetoric. In 1882, the Conservatives won 139 seats compared to 71 for the Liberals, in part because manufacturers supported the Conservatives' tariff policy. The Liberals' error was that they "consistently underestimated the power the manufacturers could exercise."[57] Despite the fact that the Canadian economy remained bogged down by the economic depression of the late nineteenth century, the Conservatives rode the National Policy to another victory in 1887, although their margin of victory was this time somewhat reduced.[58] Mr. Wilfrid Laurier replaced Blake as Liberal leader, but the Conservatives won again in 1891. After that loss, the Liberals changed trade policy, essentially adopting the elements of the National Policy.

Having put in place tariff protection for Canadian industry and having appropriated the land that was to be used for non-Indigenous settlement, Macdonald and his Conservatives quickly moved on the other key element of their policy—the Pacific railroad. Unperturbed by the fiasco and corruption of the Pacific Scandal, Macdonald announced in his 1879 Speech from the Throne, "It is the purpose of my Government to press for the most vigorous prosecution of the Canadian Pacific Railroad."[59] Speaking to the matter in the House, Charles Tupper acknowledged the previous failures and restated the Conservative position on the need to construct a railroad to the Pacific, and that it should be done not by the government, but by private enterprise, aided by grants of land and money.[60] After days and days of debate, the House approved the measure and the CPR was born. This was accomplished with the aid of $25 million in cash, twenty-five million acres of Western land, assurance of a monopoly for twenty years, perpetual tax exemption, and an already completed section of railroad worth $35 million.[61]

Even though the 1880s did not bring the economic prosperity or growth that was envisioned, Macdonald and the Conservatives fought the 1891 election focused on "The Old Flag, The Old Policy, The Old Leader," winning 117 seats compared to the Liberals' 90 under their new leader, Wilfrid Laurier. Following Macdonald's death shortly after the election, the Conservative Party had four leaders in four years. Meanwhile, the Liberal Party was busy reinventing itself under Laurier's leadership. To this end, it moved cautiously but definitively toward an embrace of the National Policy, including a move away from free trade. Creighton described Laurier as a politician who "belonged to the tradition of Macdonald, not the tradition of Mackenzie and Blake."[62] Laurier fully endorsed the objectives of the National Policy as well as the philosophical position of state support of private enterprise in realizing the grand design.

THE WEST'S ROLE IN THE NATIONAL POLICY

If there is any doubt as to the key role Western Canada and the region's settlement was to play in the National Policy, we need only look to the words of three important political leaders after all the measures were in place. First, in the House of Commons, Charles Tupper made the essential role of the West in the National Policy clear:

> No person can look abroad over the Dominion without feeling that the Great NorthWest Territory is the district to which we must look for our strength and development. Just as the older of the United States look to their Great NorthWest, with its rapidly increasing population, adding hundreds of thousands and millions to their strength, not only may we look for strength by reason of an additional Customs Revenue from the increased population of that Territory, but we must look upon that western country as a field for the manufacturing industries of the older and more settled parts of Canada. Every person acquainted with this country knows we have exhausted to some extent its bread growing power, but under the National Policy that Canada has adopted, we must look forward not only to building up thriving centres of industries and enterprise all over this portion of the country, but to obtaining a market for those industries after they have been established; and I say where is there a greater market than that magnificent granary of the NorthWest, which, filled up with a thriving and prosperous population, will make its demands upon Ontario, Quebec, Nova Scotia and New Brunswick for these manufacturing products that we, for many years, will be so well able to supply.[63]

Reflecting their party's shift from free trade to protectionism, a subsequent generation of Liberal politicians would repeat this theme, as the following statement by Clifford Sifton in 1904 indicates:

> I do have to say a word as to what we expect western Canada will do for itself. But it will not be enough that it shall do only for itself. It is a portion of Canada. Canada is a national entity. Canada is an organism, and you cannot develop a single part of an organism satisfactorily. Each and all parts must contribute to the vitality of the whole. What then will western Canada do for the Canadian organism? Sir, it will give a vast and profitable traffic to its railways and steamship lines. It will give remunerative employment to tens of thousands of men, to keep the permanent way in order, to man the trains and ships, and to engage in the multitude of occupations which gather around the great system of transportation. It will do more. It will build up our Canadian seaports. It will create volume of ocean traffic which shall place Canada in short time in its proper position as a maritime nation. It will furnish a steady and remunerative business to the manufacturers of eastern Canada, giving assured prosperity where uncertainty now exists. These are things which the west will do for the east. In a word, I may say it will send a flood of new blood from one end of this great country to the other, through every artery of commerce.[64]

Finally, Sir Wilfrid Laurier, speaking to the Canadian Manufacturers' Association, invoked in similar terms:

> They [the settlers filling up the Prairie West] will require clothes, they will require furniture, they will require implements, they will require shoes—and I hope you can furnish them to them.... They will require everything that man must be supplied with. It is your ambition, it is my ambition also, that this scientific tariff of ours will make possible that every shoe that has to be worn in those prairies shall be a Canadian shoe; that every yard of cloth that can be marketed there shall be a yard of cloth produced in Canada; and

so, on and so on. It does not follow that I do not want to trade with other nations, and I still hope that our scientific tariff will not prevent the trade with other nations. I want to give a preference to Great Britain, but I do not hesitate to say that I have no hard feelings against the Americans.[65]

Owing to historical circumstances that included a global depression and the availability of land in the American West and Midwest, attracting settlers to Canada initially proved difficult. The actual responsibility for attracting settlers to the new lands was a somewhat complex issue because the terms of the BNA *Act* provided concurrent provincial and federal jurisdiction on immigration matters. At the federal level, the Department of the Interior was given broad powers after its creation in 1873:

> The eventual mandate of the department was to explore the western region; remove the natives from the open plains; settle outstanding grievances with the Métis; survey and subdivide the area; establish land reserves for natives, schools, the HBC Company, railways, towns and swamp lands; grant or sell millions of acres of homestead lands; encourage immigration; lease lands for timber, grazing, mining and water rights; create the national park system; protect wildlife; and administer and conduct scientific research on a whole range of natural resources.[66]

The first *Immigration Act* had been introduced in spring 1869 and moved through the House with no record of discussion.[67] It was primarily concerned with adequate health and safety protection for immigrants during their transit to Canada.[68] Despite the efforts of the government through this bill and the presence of the Commons Committee on Immigration and Colonization, the efforts to settle the West with immigrants in the first three decades after Confederation have been described as "an almost unredeemed failure."[69] Nevertheless, during the 1896 budget debate, Prime Minister Laurier stated that there was "no question more important to us" (meaning the government) than immigration, and although he had concerns with some aspects of the previous government's approach, he supported the overall system. He went on to note that fertile lands in the United States were nearly fully occupied, and, therefore, there was an opportunity for Canada to accommodate more settlers. At various points over the course of the debate, speakers spoke to the desirability of certain types of settlers, particularly those from Scandinavia and Iceland.[70] While the Liberals adopted the intent and objectives of the National Policy, on the matter of immigration they changed course after forming government in 1896. The Department of Agriculture controlled immigration until 1892, when responsibility for that portfolio was transferred to the Department of the Interior, where it remained until 1917, when the Department of Immigration and Colonization was created.[71] We will return to this in due course.

Following Fowke, this is the framework in which an analysis of Western Canadian history must be placed. As the nineteenth century ended and the Liberal government replaced the Conservatives, the main features of the National Policy remained intact. The fact that the Liberal budget of 1896 was the first explicit legislative manifestation of the party's shift toward the National Policy tariffs gave great pleasure to the Conservatives as they debated the budget. Mr. George Foster, a Conservative, speaking of Liberal tariff policy in 1897, argued that the Liberals had seen the light and adopted an essentially Conservative protectionist policy; he noted that on tariff policy, "Whatever may be said in palliation, or excuse or extenuation, the fact is one which remains from this time forward on the statute-books of the country, that there is today in this Parliament as between the two sides, practically no difference upon the expediency of the principle of protection as the guiding principle of our fiscal system."[72] He went on to call the Liberals' tariff principles "avowedly, founded absolutely on the principle of protection." Describing this era, J.M.S. Careless notes that "it spelt success at long last for the National Policy, which the Liberals now took over as their own. The National Policy of protection was firmly fixed in Canada until the Great Depression since both major parties accepted it."[73] James

McCrorie, for his part, summarized the role of the West in the national economy at the time in these terms:

> The decision to settle the West was part of an overall plan to develop a national industrial economy. The National Policy treated agricultural development in the West as functional yet subordinate to this goal. The tariff policy was designed to foster industrial growth in the East; the railway policy was designed to integrate the Atlantic with the Pacific and provide transportation of goods and services across Canada. The immigration program was designed to create new markets for Canadian products in the West and to provide a new investment frontier for the East; agriculture was developed to serve an emerging industrial complex.[74]

CAPITALISM TRANSFORMED, 1860–1929

Even as Canada emerged as a nation-state and began undertaking industrialization via the National Policy, the overall nature and character of capitalism as a global economic order was changing. By the middle of the nineteenth century the dynamic nature of capitalism once again became apparent. As competitive industrial capitalism continued to develop sophisticated technologies and new modes of organizing production, two processes that were to fundamentally change the nature of the capitalist economic order were occuring—the concentration and centralization of capital. The concentration of capital occurs when individual enterprises expand production, adopt new technologies, and invest in new machinery, thus increasing (concentrating) the amount of capital per enterprise. Centralization of capital occurs as a result of the normal outcome of market competition in which successful enerprises expand and buy out their less successful competitors or take over their markets as some firms go out of business. The centralization of capital is supported and made possible by the credit system, investment banks, and stock markets that bring multiple smaller amounts of capital into one firm, heralding the emergence of joint-stock companies. The outcome of both processes tends to be fewer but larger enterprises, which in turn come to dominate and characterize production of most key commodities.[75] We will put aside the interesting question of whether this was fortuitous, offering Canadian enterprises an opportunity to develop profitable relationships with emerging large enterprises, or an unfortunate happenstance that subsequently resulted in large non-Canadian enterprises coming to control the country's economy.

Summarizing some points in our argument, we can see that Canada emerged as a nation-state during the period in which the leadership of the global capitalist economic order was beginning to pass from Britain to the United States. This era also was marked by the emergence of large joint-stock and other corporate enterprises as the dominant players in many sectors of the economy. The fact that Canada was a relative latecomer in terms of industrialization pushed the new Canadian state to adopt an activist stance and engage in efforts to create the necessary conditions to facilitate industrial development.

The major post-Confederation initiative in this regard was the three-pronged National Policy, the central plank of which was the creation of a white settler society in the West. We will now turn our attention to an examination of the specific actions and legislative initiatives that various federal governments undertook in the fifty years between the instigation of the National Policy and the onset of the Great Depression, with a focus on efforts to create a new class of agricultural producers in the West.

CHAPTER 2

PHASE 1— ACTIVIST GOVERNMENT

Promoting the National Policy and Family Farming in the West, 1867–1930

POST-CONFEDERATION: AN ACTIVIST STATE

CONFEDERATION OCCURRED AT A HISTORICAL moment when representatives of capital and political leaders in nations with more fully developed industrial economies such as the United States and Britain tended to espouse laissez-faire ideologies; however, nations undergoing later industrialization, like Canada and Germany, had no qualms about using activist states to provide the necessary conditions for economic development. An examination of the frequent disjuncture between the ideology of laissez-faire and actual government actions during the nineteenth century notes that it was often the case that, while "the desirability of non-interference was conceded in principle, expediency demanded and secured policies which breached both the letter and spirit of lasses-faire."[1] Canada represents a classic example of the use of state action and support to facilitate the establishment and operation of a market-based, capitalist society. As Karl Polanyi notes, "Economic history reveals that the emergence of national markets was in no way the result of gradual and spontaneous emancipation of the economic sphere from government control. On the contrary, the market has been the outcome of a conscious and often violent intervention on the part of government which imposed the market organization on society for noneconomic ends."[2]

Seen in this light, the National Policy was a clear example of a state taking actions to facilitate the development of a capitalist industrial economy. We will now examine some specific policies and actions, and their impact on the West, as they were deliberately designed and implemented to bring the National Policy to fruition.

SECURING LAND FOR SETTLERS

We have noted that the process of treaty making between First Nations and the Government of Canada was part of the plan to make the Canadian Plains available for agrarian settlement. An important question is what role did the Canadian government envision for the Indigenous people who already occupied the land? The question of land, both access and ownership, is of fundamental importance when establishing a society of agricultural producers. Based on a wide range of evidence and documentation, Sheldon Krasowski analyzed the question of land ownership in the interactions between Indigenous people and Europeans dating back to the Royal Proclamation of 1763, although he focuses on the context and content of the eleven numbered treaties signed between 1871 and 1921. Krasowski notes that the protocols that informed the negotiation and signing of these treaties were established before the Royal Proclamation. These protocols prevented private individuals from negotiating treaties with Indigenous people, required that advance notice of negotiations be provided to all parties, and that all such negotiations be held at a public meeting or assembly involving members of the relevant Indigenous community.[3]

In *No Surrender: The Land Remains Indigenous*, Krasowski points to what was and still is a fundamental question for Canadian society: By signing treaties, did Indigenous people surrender the land, or were the treaties an agreement based on the assumption that Indigenous people would share land in return for certain benefits offered by the Canadian government? Krasowski offers a clear answer: "Indigenous oral histories state that there was no surrender of the lands through the treaty process. First Nations agreed to share their land in exchange for benefits offered by the Canadian government."[4] While Krasowski notes that "the texts of the numbered treaties clearly state that First Nations surrendered their 'rights titles and privileges to the land,'"[5] there is a major problem in the fact that the precise wording of the treaties was not part of the negotiations, nor is it very likely that clear translations of the texts were provided to the chiefs before they agreed to each document. Moreover, during the negotiations the government tended only to speak of the benefits of the treaty-making process, and not the resulting surrender of the land.[6]

For our purposes, the most important of the numbered treaties is Treaty 4 since it covers much of the area that was to be settled in what is now southern and central Saskatchewan. Daschuk explains that the signing of Treaty 4 at Fort Qu'Appelle in the fall of 1874 followed the prior establishment of relations that saw Indigenous people grow increasingly dependent on the health and viability of the declining fur trade, and that, when coupled with the destruction of the bison, this resulted in the loss of sustainable economic activity and the attendant onset of deprivation, disease, food shortages, and hunger.[7] Treaty 4 contained meagre and totally inadequate provisions to support any potential development of meaningful agriculture among the Indigenous population. In the words of the treaty,

> It is further agreed between Her Majesty and the said Indians that the following articles shall be supplied to any band thereof who are now actually cultivating the soil, or who shall hereafter settle on their reserves and commence to break up the land, that is to say: two hoes, one spade, one

scythe and one axe for every family so actually cultivating, and enough seed wheat, barley, oats and potatoes to plant such land as they have broken up; also one plough and two harrows for every ten families so cultivating as aforesaid, and also to each Chief for the use of his band as aforesaid, one yoke of oxen, one bull, four cows, a chest of ordinary carpenter's tools, five hand saws, five augers, one cross-cut saw, one pit-saw, the necessary files and one grindstone, all the aforesaid articles to be given, once for all, for the encouragement of the practice of agriculture among the Indians.[8]

It is obviously ludicrous to suggest that a family, of whatever size, would be able to secure a living on the unbroken plains and parkland using two hoes, a spade, a scythe, an axe, and some seeds to plant on "such land as they have broken up" when none had the opportunity to break land! The breaking of land would surely be made nigh on impossible by the fact that there was one plough and two harrows for every ten families and one yoke of oxen, one bull, four cows, and some tools to be dispensed for the entire group by the chief.

Indigenous people who attempted commercial farming in the 1880s confronted the very same harsh conditions that were then preventing non-Indigenous settlers from homesteading, including drought, early frost, fires, and marketing difficulties. Indigenous people were faced with additional restrictions such as the prohibition against seeking homesteads after the *Indian Act* was passed and the "pass system" subsequently imposed, which severely constricted the off-reserve movement of Indigenous people. Additionally, after complaints from non-Indigenous farmers, "in 1889 the federal government imposed a 'peasant' farming policy. Indigenous farmers were to reduce their acreages dramatically to no more than 40 acres and to grow root crops, not wheat."[9] A further obstacle to Indigenous agriculture was the rather blatant appropriation and theft of a significant amount of Indigenous treaty land as white settlement proceeded. Peggy Martin-McGuire studied the loss of Indigenous lands in the West around the turn of the century. She concluded that "over 100 surrenders of treaty reserve land were obtained by the Crown in this region between the late 1890s and the 1930s. In the study period alone—1896 to 1911—21 percent of the lands reserved to prairie First Nations were surrendered to the Crown to make way for western expansion and an influx of immigrants."[10]

There was one instance of an experiment without any ethical or moral oversight relating to Indigenous farming during this period. In the late 1880s, a residential school was opened on the Little Black Bear Reserve, north of Balcarres, Saskatchewan. Much of the curriculum at the school centred on farming and agriculture, with many of the boys actively involved in producing various vegetables while girls were taught traditional domestic skills. The boys were being groomed to be farmers and the girls as farm wives. The vision of the school administrators and Indian Affairs inspector William Morris Graham was to establish a Christian Indigenous farming colony made up of a hand-picked group of former students from the residential school. The story is one of colonialism, exploitation, and community division. Indeed, Drew Bednasek notes that the tensions that emerged within the Indigenous community are still apparent: "There is a friction and resentment between colonists and original members about the construction of the colony and who should be compensated in land claims." He further notes that, "ultimately, everyone has been victimized, and this victimization has reached across many generations and still persists today."[11] In August 2022, federal minister of Crown-Indigenous relations Marc Miller travelled to Peepeekisis Cree Nation to issue a government apology. Chief Francis Dieter noted that, "in creating and implementing the colony scheme, Canada breached its fiduciary duty to the Nation by failing to protect the Nation's interest in (the allocated farmland) and not providing any compensation to the Nation," while expressing his hope that the community can move to close this unfortunate chapter in its history.[12]

In sum, the dispossession of Indigenous people and their replacement by white colonial settlers was one matter to which both major political parties were committed, meaning that the Indigenous population, "with its hunting, fur-trading and freighting economy, should be thrust aside, [and that] the North-West should be settled as quickly as possible and stamped with the social, cultural, and political institutions of Canada."[13]

HOMESTEAD ACTS

The other actions necessary to transform the West were undertaken with relative dispatch. As we have seen, Rupert's Land was acquired, the *Dominion Lands Act* put into place, and a land survey system established (through an Order-in-Council) creating blocks of land to be distributed to incoming settlers. Subsequent amendments were made to the *Dominion Lands Act* to make Western Canada more attractive to settlers. In 1884, the age requirement was lowered (to eighteen years), as was the amount of land that a settler must prepare and plant to secure title. The importance of what was called in Parliament the North-West, and the settlers the government hoped to attract to the region, was recognized by the Opposition in a proposed amendment that read in part, "The settler is the foundation rock upon which the superstructure of a great country must be built in the North-West."[14] Still further amendments to the act were introduced by making the residence conditions slightly less restrictive to allow prospective homesteaders an opportunity to earn off-homestead income for two years before building a habitable home. It also made men who had served in the Canadian military during both the Red River Resistance and the Riel Rebellion eligible to receive 320 acres.[15]

Other opportunities to acquire farmland were available to incoming settlers, including the purchase of land retained by the HBC at the time of the sale of Rupert's Land (amounting to 5 percent of the total area).[16] Many farmers bought land from the CPR, which had been granted 25 million acres (about 10 million hectares) of land in close proximity to the railway.[17] Additionally, some farmers bought "school land," the two sections (640 acres apiece) in each township set aside in the *Dominion Lands Act* to be sold to provide funding for schools.

SETTLING THE WEST: IMMIGRATION LEGISLATION

When the Liberals took office in 1896, Laurier announced that attracting immigrants was one of the main priorities of his government. Clifford Sifton's election that year and subsequent appointment as minister of the interior in 1897 was a turning point in the history of Canadian immigration. By this point, several external circumstances had changed, including the declining availability of agricultural land in the United States. The depression that began in the early 1870s was ending, resulting in increased prices for many agricultural products. Coupled with the lower freight charges for shipping Western Canadian grain, these changes meant that farming on the Canadian Plains was more becoming economically viable. Sifton immediately reorganized the department, pressured the CPR and the HBC to sell off their vast tracts of land, and engaged in a massive promotional campaign across northern Europe.[18] He used budget increases to develop pamphlets, newspaper advertisements, and displays to be used at regional exhibitions, and added significant numbers of immigration agents in Europe. In 1896, the department produced sixty-five thousand promotional items, but under Sifton's leadership that number exploded to over one million in the first six months of 1900.[19] The promotional information included non-photographic pictures of depicting the idealized possibilities of white patriarchal families in the west. Such images typically included strong men holding bundles of wheat and a child against the background of cattle and farm animals, men with outstretched arms looking over a vista of farms and a village, or well-dressed women waving to men working in fields, sometimes holding a baby in their arms.[20]

The message was clear: come to Canada, come to the Prairies, and you will prosper. And come they did. As we have seen, the agricultural emphasis was not a result of happenchance. In 1922, after he was no longer in charge of immigration but Canada was still attempting to attract immigrants, Sir Clifford Sifton penned an article in *Maclean's* magazine entitled "The Immigrants Canada Wants." Using a hypothetical example,

Sifton described the cohort of people the federal government was then hoping to attract: "If one should examine twenty people who turn up at Hamburg to emigrate, he would find one escaped murderer, three or four wasters and ne'er do wells, some very poor shopkeepers, artisans or labourers and there might be one or two stout hardy peasants in sheep-skin coats. Obviously, the peasants are the men we wanted here." He went on to note that the booking agents "winnowed out this flood of people, picked out the agriculturalists and peasants and sent them to Canada, sending nobody else." In his conclusion, he notes that the search for settlers was confined to northern and eastern Europe, where there are "hundreds of thousands of hardy peasants, men of the type described above, farmers for ten or fifteen generations who are anxious to leave Europe and start life under better conditions in a new country." Further, "they have been bred for generations to work from daylight until dark. They have never done anything else and never expect to do anything else."[21]

The creation of the new provinces of Alberta and Saskatchewan in 1905 was necessitated by the success of the federal government's immigration campaign. Given that most of the Prairies was still largely governed from Ottawa, a political restructuring was required. The premier of Manitoba was eager to extend his province by moving its western boundary to the border with British Columbia.[22] On February 21, 1905, Prime Minister Laurier introduced two bills that he said were intimately connected, one each to create the provinces of Saskatchewan and Alberta. Laurier spoke to the measures using another version of his much-quoted observation: "It has been observed on the floor of this House, as well as outside of this house, that the nineteenth century had been the century of the United States, so the twentieth century would be the century of Canada." He went on to note that this claim was accepted internationally "as a statement of truth, beyond controversy."[23] It is important to note that the new provinces were being admitted to Confederation with an important jurisdictional difference. The other provinces had ownership and control over their lands, "but when the two new provinces come into the Dominion, it cannot be said that they can retain the ownership of their lands, as they never had ownership." The Dominion government was to hold ownership of these lands because the immigration to and the settlement of the region was considered to be of national importance.[24]

The population growth that followed was phenom. In the three decades between 1901 and 1931, Saskatchewan increased from 91,279 inhabitants to 921,785, Manitoba from 255,211 to 700,139, and Alberta from 73,022 to 731,605.[25] The vast majority of those coming to the Prairies were farmers. In 1901 there were about 13,500 farms in what was to become Saskatchewan. By 1911, the number grew to over 95,000, then to 104,006 in 1916, despite the global disruption of the First World War. Postwar growth saw that increase to about 119,500 in 1921, reaching 136,472 at the beginning of the Great Depression in 1931.[26]

BUILDING A TRANSPORTATION SYSTEM

After Confederation, governments of all stripes used public money, land grants, and regulation to ensure that private interests built, owned, and operated the railroads. The construction and operation of the CPR was a case in point; however, there were many other publicly supported private railroads. The first railroad in the West was opened in 1878 with a line from St. Boniface, Manitoba, to St. Paul, Minnesota. While the completion of the CPR in 1885 was an essential element of the National Policy, the company's southern main line opened only a miniscule part of the Great Plains for settlement. Even the completion of a few branch lines, north to Saskatoon and to the Yorkton region via Manitoba, left most of Saskatchewan without viable transportation to move settlers and manufacturing goods west and their cash crops east. Clearly, more railroads were required.

Provincial governments also played an active role in railroad construction. The Manitoba government used land grants and other forms of support to guarantee company bonds toward the construction of railroads. The Canadian Northern Railway expanded both east and west from Manitoba, first building a line to Port Arthur (now Thunder Bay, Ontario) in 1902 and then west to the Pacific by 1915.[27] The Grand Trunk Railway had been part of the history of BNA since the mid-1850s, so it is not surprising that it played a role in the expansion of the West. With state support, a deal was struck that involved the government building a National Transcontinental Railway and the Grand Trunk constructing a companion railroad, the Grand Trunk Pacific. The economic disruptions associated with the First World War, high construction costs, a measure of mismanagement, and a tragic accident took a toll on the project. As the war ground on, the Grand Trunk and the Canadian Northern were both facing serious financial problems. The high degree of government involvement in the whole scheme meant that further federal action was required.

In July 1916, the government appointed a Royal Commission to investigate "the general problem of transportation in Canada" with specific reference to the issue of the future of the Grand Trunk, Grand Trunk Pacific, and the Canadian Northern Railway. The commission's report, tabled in 1917, documented the enormous amount of public money in various forms that had been granted to the different railroads over the years, including $298,253,263 to the Canadian Northern, $228,500,925 to the CPR, and $114,470,884 to the Grand Trunk Pacific. The total public investment in these and other railroads was estimated to be close to a billion dollars (in 1917; that figure would of course be even higher today). In addition, each of the three Prairie provinces provided railroads within their boundaries with various forms of grants and subsidies to facilitate settlement.[28] W.A. Mackintosh estimates that Manitoba had allocated over $33 million in bond guarantees and line rentals to the Northern Pacific by 1920, while Saskatchewan's bond guarantees were over $28 million by 1919–20, and Alberta assumed liabilities of over $39 million.[29]

Considering the enormous public expenditures that went to private enterprise, an argument might have been made that these railroads had essentially been paid for by the public, and should therefore be a public asset; however, the commission immediately ruled out government ownership and transferred the railroads to a new, private commercial enterprise. The commission recommended that an independent board of trustees, the Board of Railway Commissioners, oversee the operation of a new company to be created by an act of Parliament.

In August 1917, Sir Thomas White, minister of finance, introduced the commission's recommendations to the House of Commons, thereby setting in motion a process that would eventually involve the government in the ownership of railroad assets.[30] The subsequent debates were described as "long and at times bitter," and "ran throughout the whole of August, and it was only by vigorous use of closure that the government was able to bring it to an end."[31] The Canadian Northern was not the only railroad in difficulty during this period, and in short order the federal government was forced to assume the assets of the Grand Trunk and the Grand Trunk Pacific as well. An Order-in-Council in December 1917 authorized the Board of Railroad Commissioners to use the name Canadian National Railroad.[32] By 1923, various government actions eventually resulted in the emergence of a new, fully integrated public railroad company under that name. By the beginning of the Great Depression, there were few areas in the Grain Belt not covered by railroads, one of them publicly owned. The miles of railroad track in the three Prairie provinces increased from 5,966 miles in 1906 to 18,192 in 1930, an increase of over 300 percent.[33]

SUPPORTING SETTLEMENT: EXPERIMENTAL FARMS

The physical environment and climate are among the important factors impacting agricultural production because they determine what crops are suitable and commercially viable in different regions. As the settlement of the Plains proceeded, a significant question emerged regarding the suitability, or lack thereof as the case may be, of existing Central Canadian- and European-based crops and agricultural practices on the Prairies. There was a pressing need for both cereal grain crops and farming practices that were suitable for agriculture on the Great Plains, with their variable and sometimes harsh weather and relatively short growing seasons. The issue became a matter of political debate in 1884 when the House of Commons moved to establish a select committee to "enquire into the best means of encouraging and developing the agricultural industries of Canada."[34] The motion noted that the Americans were studying ways and means of expanding and promoting their agricultural industries through research and the study of crops and production practices appropriate to the region. A ten-person committee was appointed, and soon offered a recommendation: "That the Government take into earnest and favourable consideration the advisability to establishing a Bureau of Agriculture, and an Experimental Farm in connection therewith."[35]

Prime Minister Macdonald himself indicated action was forthcoming, and with the support of both parties a bill entitled *Respecting Experimental Farm Stations* was quickly passed.[36] Initially, five experimental farms were established, including Indian Head, in the North-West Territories; however, other research stations were subsequently established at Saskatoon, Swift Current, Regina, and Melfort. The research focus of the Western experimental farms, including in such areas as animal and field husbandry, crop rotation, cultivation, fertilizer use, and appropriate farm machinery, was very much geared toward facilitating agricultural expansion on the Prairies. The horticultural and cereal divisions were active in plant breeding and the development of new varieties of grains suited for the Plains. The development of new wheat varieties was an important activity: "A major achievement of the Research Branch was the release of Marquis Wheat in 1909....Marquis was a spring wheat that was the first early maturing variety that also had high quality for baking and milling. By 1920, Marquis wheat was grown on more than 6 million acres on the Canadian prairies, about 90% of the total wheat acreage."[37] The federal government also supported agricultural education in other ways, as illustrated by the 1912 *Aid for the Advancement of Agricultural Instruction in the Provinces Act*, which provided federal funding to facilitate the expansion of agriculture through various kinds of horticultural instruction.[38]

THE CROW'S NEST PASS AGREEMENT

Despite having assembled the core elements of the National Policy by the mid-1880s, as the decade progressed there "was mounting apparently irrefutable evidence which seemed clearly to imply that the National Policy was a failure or, at best, a very qualified success."[39] Among the issues raised in the House of Commons that were deemed to be a hindrance to Western settlement was the high cost of moving goods west and east, as the CPR's monopoly allowed the company to set freight rates that were much higher than anything that prevailed in the United States.[40] In the fall of 1896, negotiations began over a deal that would have the CPR lower freight rates in return for a subsidy to build a new railroad through the Crow's Nest Pass. The result was *An Act to Authorize a Subsidy for a Railway through the Crow's Nest Pass*, passed in late June 1897.[41] An assessment of the essential feature of the Crow's Nest Pass Agreement indicates that it was clearly designed to increase the economic viability of Prairie farming:

> The CPR was given a cash subsidy of $3.3 million and title to pass into BC in exchange for reducing, in perpetuity, eastbound rates on grain and flour and westbound ones on a specified list of "settlers' effects" (total rate reduction about 15%). The CPR obtained access to the valuable mining and smelting activities in the BC interior, and the government was able to allay western concerns over national transportation policies. The rate reduction coincided almost exactly with the beginning of the settlement boom, and quickly became enshrined in the public mind as a key part of the economic strategy of the day.[42]

The benefits of the agreement were many, both in terms of the costs of shipping goods west and, more importantly, of lowering the costs of shipping agricultural goods entering the competitive world export market. The Crow Rate, as it came to be called, was suspended in 1918 under the *War Measures Act* owing to the economic disruptions related to the

First World War, but then reinstated in 1925.[43] The decision to reinstate the Crow Rate was a controversial one involving decisions by the Board of Railway Commissioners, activity in Parliament by the new Progressive Party, and a Supreme Court decision.[44] The final outcome was beneficial to farmers because the Crow Rate was not only re-established but made to apply to all railroads in the West.[45] The Crow Rate would become a contentious matter when governments adopted radically different philosophical positions fifty years later.

REGULATING PRIVATE ENTERPRISE: ENSURING GRAIN TRADE FAIRNESS

Robert Burns's much-quoted lines from "To a Mouse" are typically rendered in contemporary English as something like, "The best-laid plans of mice and men often go awry." Canada's post-Confederation National Policy was surely a case of a best-laid industrialization and economic development plan based on legislation, policies, and regulation. As we have seen, the plan was quite simple: promote industrial development by acquiring the lands of the Prairie West, and remove the region's Indigenous Peoples and attract white immigrant settlers. The agrarian population would engage in commercial agriculture, employing tariff-protected Canadian manufactured goods and the services of commercial and transportation interests to market their cash crops nationally and internationally.

What could possibly go wrong? In truth, it did not take long for matters to begin to go awry. The first sources of tension and conflict between the grain farmers and the private grain merchants emerged almost immediately. While the immigrant settlers produced a significant amount of their daily foodstuffs from gardens and barnyard livestock, their ultimate survival depended on the production of cash crops for sale on national and international markets. Farmers required market engagement with grain merchants to realize their income. To facilitate this, the Winnipeg Grain Exchange was established in 1887 in anticipation of a booming grain export sector. In 1904, it expanded its activities to include grain futures trading.[46]

The establishment of the Winnipeg exchange and a futures market in wheat and other commodities was an indication of the rapid development of grain marketing infrastructure across the West. A closely related development was the rapid expansion of the grain trade at the local level involving a multitude of private grain companies operating grain delivery points and elevators eager to buy the farmers' wheat. Dozens of private grain traders and merchants established grain warehouses and later elevators as the rail network spread. A range of American entrepreneurs and merchants such as Peavy entered the field, as did Canadian entrepreneurs like the families of William Parrish, Norman Heimbecker, William Ogilvie of Montreal, and the Richardson family, originally from Kingston.[47] Brett Fairbairn notes that "there were over 100 grain companies that built elevators during the early years of settlement; however, most of these companies were small. Many of the main line companies were initially owned by American interests (e.g., National, Federal, McCabe, Searle); the large Canadian companies were N.M. Paterson and Sons, Pioneer (Richardson and Sons), and Parrish and Heimbecker."[48]

The expansion of the railroad network and the grain trade occurred virtually simultaneously. In 1906 there were just under six thousand miles of railroad lines across the Prairies, but by 1915 that number had more than doubled to over fifteen thousand miles.[49] As the railroads spread and branch lines proliferated, so did the number of grain handling elevators across the Prairies, growing from 421 in 1900 to nearly 3,000 in 1915 and 3,785 by 1920.[50] For reasons of efficiency and profitability, the CPR encouraged a shift from shipping grain in sacks loaded by hand to elevators in which grain was stored in vertical bins and quickly loaded by gravity into railcars. A pattern of settlement emerged with regularly spaced delivery points providing the unique pattern of town and village locations that once characterized the Plains: "The spacing of grain delivery points along the rail lines was to allow a farmer located furthest from the rail line to be able to deliver a load of grain by horse and wagon and return home in one day."[51] It turns out this was about six to eight miles, resulting in a map with towns that were spaced with an amazing degree of regularity.

The naming of many grain delivery points and towns is an interesting story that relates in part to the Grand Trunk's policy of following alphabetical order when naming settlements west of Portage la Prairie, Manitoba. Starting at Portage la Prairie, then, the first station on the original line travelling west was Arona, followed by Bloom, then Caye, Deer, Exira, and so on to the Saskatchewan border. Although some towns, stations, and villages were added and some disappeared, the first original station on the Saskatchewan side of the provincial boundary was Welby, while the last station on the Manitoba side was Victor. At the time, the next town in Saskatchewan after Welby was Yarbo, followed by Zeneta, after which we go back to the beginning of the alphabet with Atwater, Bangor, Cana and on to Xena, Young, and Zelma, then again to Allan, Bradwell, and so on.[52]

The local grain traders made money from the purchase and resale of grain and in some cases by providing agricultural inputs (seed, fertilizer, chemicals, etc.) to farmers. The amount the grain merchants paid a farmer for grain was based on the domestic and international prices and the grain merchant's determination of the quality of the product (grade), the amount of non-grain material such as chaff, weed seeds, etc. (dockage), and the quantity of grain (based on weight). Herein was the rub.[53] The farmers' livelihood depended on their ability to receive the maximum return on the products they produced, so they had an obvious interest in the price, but also in receiving the highest grade possible with a minimal amount of dockage and an accurate determination of the quantity determined by weight. Grain merchants, on the other hand, had a vested interest in buying at the lowest price possible while not overestimating the grade or underestimating the amount of dockage. The quantity the farmer brought for sale was determined by weight on a scale operated by the grain merchant.

While farmers came to the marketplace as individual, independent commodity producers, the members of the grain trade had been co-operating among themselves since the formation of the Northwest Elevator Association in 1899. The Elevator Association subsequently became the North West Grain Dealers Association, with an explicit objective "to reduce unnecessary competition at country points." Farmers soon became suspicious and the association "brought charges from western farmers that they were the victims of a monopoly."[54] Farmers complained that there was collusion to set prices and they questioned the integrity of some grain buyers claiming there was systematic dishonesty in grading, dockage, and weighing.[55]

Added to the potential conflict between farmers and merchants were the actions of the CPR, which, armed with its twenty-year monopoly clause, was co-operating with the grain trade to ensure that farmers were not allocated railcars to allow them to ship directly without the services of the grain trade. Farmers saw the interconnections among and between grain merchants and the transportation network as a problem. For example, the "Lake of the Woods Milling Company, was established in 1887 by CPR entrepreneurs Sir George Stephen and William Cornelius Van Horne."[56]

The conflict between farmers, the grain trade, and the CPR reached the House of Commons as early as 1898, when Mr. James Douglas, the member for East Assiniboia, introduced a bill to force the CPR to allocate railcars to farmers. The bill was referred for study to the Committee on Railways and Canals, but it did not produce any results. Douglas persevered, introducing another bill the following year to regulate the grain trade.[57] That bill, too, was subsequently referred to a select committee, and although there are no records of those deliberations, the continued agitation among farmers was sufficient to prod the Laurier Liberals to action. Eager to ensure a harmonious and effective settlement process, the federal government established a Royal Commission on the Shipment and Transportation of Grain in 1899. It is interesting to note that the commission members were three farmers and a judge.

The commission's report was officially tabled in the House of Commons in April 1900.[58] It documented many of the grievances of the farm community, and in just over a month resulted in the introduction of the

Manitoba Grain Act. Harold Patton notes the importance of this legislation, which simply contained many of the recommendations of the Royal Commission translated into legislative language; Patton further notes that "the *Manitoba Grain Act* was hailed by western grain growers as a veritable agrarian Magna Carta."[59] Although the act addressed many issues, shipping and grain-handling problems persisted, prompting a series of actions and protests that generated a new agrarian organization, the Territorial Grain Growers Association, to counter the actions of the CPR and the grain trade.[60] The *Manitoba Grain Act* was subsequently amended in 1902, with further amendments in 1903 introduced by the minister of the interior himself, Clifford Sifton, after his consultation with Western farmers.[61]

Despite the importance of the *Manitoba Grain Act*, agrarian agitation continued and soon another in a series of Royal Commissions was appointed to investigate grain shipment and transportation.[62] The membership of the 1906 Royal Commission on the Grain Trade of Canada was composed entirely of farmers, including a well-known organizer of the Territorial Grain Growers Association as chair. After the commission issued its report, a major conference on the topic was held in Ottawa. The Royal Commission found the system operated by the North West Grain Dealers Association "is no doubt a trade restriction," but due to legal action under way at the time, it could not say if the restriction was undue.[63]

The collective grievances of Western Canadian farmers were manifesting themselves in what is typically referred to as the Western Canadian agrarian movement.[64] While the details of the political, economic, and social actions and consequences of the agrarian movement are beyond the scope of this volume, the ability of organized farmers to secure federal action on some of their demands is illustrative of an important point—namely, that activist federal governments were willing to address the concerns of Western farmers as long as such concerns were not seen as a threat to the imperatives of the National Policy. At this moment in history, Western farmers represented a growing political constituency, and keeping cash flowing into their hands so they could continue to purchase Canadian-manufactured goods served many interests. The voice of the farm community is seen in further amendments to the *Manitoba Grain Act* that followed. When he introduced the amendments on July 10, 1908, Minister Oliver went so far as to say, "it is in accordance largely with the views that have been expressed directly by grain growing interests that the amendments which have been placed before the House in sheet form have been prepared."[65]

The first decade of the twentieth century saw the rapid development of various Western farm organizations such as the Saskatchewan Grain Growers Association, the Manitoba Grain Growers Association, and the United Farmers of Alberta. With a measure of grain-handling regulation in hand, farmers and their organizations increased their demands, both in the House of Commons and through the farmer-controlled *Grain Growers' Guide*, for actual government ownership of terminal elevators.[66] In 1909, a delegations of farmers visited Ottawa to push their demands.[67] When Prime Minster Laurier toured the West in 1910, he was met by thousands of farmers demanding government terminals. Speaking in Regina, Laurier noted that after "ample conference with the grain growers of the west he was quite prepared for government ownership."[68] Motions advocating government ownership were once again brought to the House in January and February of 1911; however, action on a bill to provide for government ownership was pre-empted by the 1911 general election. In the meantime, various provincial governments, farmer associations, and adjacent organizations were dealing with the question of local elevator ownership at the provincial level.[69]

As important as the grain trade was, the 1911 election was fundamentally about another component of the National Policy: the protective tariff. At virtually every stop of Laurier's tour of the West, he was met by large numbers of farmers and representatives of farm organizations united in their demands for tariff reductions. In 1911, as discussions to this end got under way, a large delegation of farmers converged on Ottawa. The event became known as the Siege of Ottawa and provided an opportunity to present what was called the "Farmers' Platform." The entire 1911 debate over a modest

Liberal proposal to enter discussions with the Americans over some reciprocal tariff reductions came to nothing in terms of actual tariff reform as the Liberals lost the election after all their major industrial and business supporters abandoned them in favour of the pro-tariff Conservatives. The Liberals, thereafter, studiously avoided any significant tariff reductions until the Depression struck.[70]

The victory of the Borden Conservatives in 1911 did not significantly diminish the federal government's willingness to undertake significant measures to ensure the grain trade treated farmers with a reasonable degree of fairness. In the first session of the Twelfth Parliament, the Conservatives introduced a resolution to consolidate and revise the *Manitoba Grain Act*.[71] Following the traditions of the Liberals, the Conservative minister of trade and commerce noted, "This is not my Bill particularly, not the Bill of any party it is, as nearly as possible, a non-partisan Bill."[72] What he was referring to was the continuing support of both major parties for one overall objective of the National Policy—a farm community with sufficient resources to continue to serve as a tariff-protected market and an exporter of cash crops, even if this meant the tighter regulation of the grain-handling system. Some agrarian concerns with that system were alleviated by the producers themselves through their own farmer-owned co-operative elevators and grain-handling companies.

An interesting side note to the 1911 election was the significant disenchantment felt by many Western Canadian agrarian producers with both the Liberals and the Conservatives. The discontent focused on the protective tariff, a policy accepted by both main parties after the Liberals' 1911 wavering. Although the nationalism and pro-empire war hysteria that surrounded the First World War temporarily dampened political agitation, demand for tariff reform emerged again as the conflict came to an end. Several leaders of farm organizations were elected under the Unionist Government banner in 1917; however, after the war they were instrumental in the development of what was called the New National Policy, this one based on free trade. When the Conservative-led Unionist Government refused to move on the protective tariff, steps were taken to form a new Western-based farmers' party, the National Progressive Party. Members of the Progressive Party contested many seats in the 1921 election, winning all but one in Saskatchewan and sixty-five nationally. The Progressives soon fell into disarray, however, in part because many members did not agree that party politics was the best way to further the interests of farmers.[73]

WHEAT MARKETING IN CRISIS: THE FIRST WORLD WAR AND THE FIRST CANADIAN WHEAT BOARD

The success of farmer-owned and -controlled co-operatives buying grain at local delivery points and selling through private agents and their own exporting operations, despite determined opposition from the Winnipeg Grain Exchange, was widely if not universally supported by grain producers. The success of provincial co-operative elevator companies across the Prairies was accompanied by the emergence of retail and wholesale co-operatives, credit unions, co-op creameries, and, eventually, wheat pools, all important elements of both the romantic mythology and actual history of the West. Before the First World War, many farmers had switched their marketing alliances to farmer-owned co-operatives like the Grain Growers' Grain Company. As Brett Fairbairn notes, this company was very successful: "from 1907 to 1912 the number of shareholders went from 1,800 to over 27,000, while grain volume grew from 2.3 million to nearly 28 million bushels."[74]

Like many aspects of life in much of the Western world, the outbreak of the First World War brought radical disruptions to the national and international grain trades. The actions of the British government to fix prices and control markets as well as the activities of the newly created Allied Purchasing Agency eventually pushed the Canadian government to act. To this end, it established the Board of Grain Supervisors with the power to set prices and ensure supplies to Britain. Ultimately, the turmoil led to the suspension of trading activities on the Winnipeg Grain Exchange, followed by the creation, through the powers of the *War Measures Act*, of what was envisioned as a temporary marketing organization, the Canadian Wheat Board (CWB).[75] The CWB operated by paying farmers an initial price on delivery and then a final payment when it sold the wheat. After the war, normal trading resumed, but this was suspended when prices for grain rose sharply. Although the suspension came at a moment when prices were rising, it soon became evident to many farmers that the practice of receiving an assured initial delivery price followed later by a final payment removed some of the uncertainty that accompanied the yearly fluctuations in prices, and especially the drop in prices in the fall when grain was plentiful. The Canadian Council of Agriculture supported the move. On the other hand, future prime minister Arthur Meighen expressed concern on behalf of the railroads and banks.[76]

While the Wheat Board proved beneficial to farmers, when asked whether it would remain on a permanent basis, the minister in charge, Mr. Foster, responded, "My answer is an emphatic no."[77] And indeed, in mid-summer 1920, the government announced that it was going to terminate the operations of the CWB and restore the operation of the Winnipeg Grain Exchange. Significant agrarian protest followed the announcement; however, this was to no avail. The question of federal unresponsiveness without doubt played a role in the Progressive Party's virtual sweep of Saskatchewan in the 1921 election noted above.[78] But while the issue of the Wheat Board never fully disappeared, the attention of many farmers turned to an alternate way of addressing what they saw as the power imbalances in the grain marketing system—producer pools. Among the dynamic stories of the so-called Roaring Twenties was the success of the various wheat pools, supported in any number of ways by the governments of the Prairie provinces.[79]

The success of the pooling enterprises on the Prairies did not mean all issues relating to the marketing of grain disappeared or that federal governments ignored the wishes and concerns of farmers. In June 1922, the Liberal minister of trade and commerce announced the government's intention to bring forth a measure to create a new CWB. The measure envisioned a board with lesser powers; however, it would have the power to buy and sell wheat with the stipulation that two or more provinces enact legislation to facilitate the board's operation.[80] The bill was extensively debated but never proclaimed. Various other issues related to grain handling and transportation resulted in the appointment of a special committee and then yet another full-scale Royal Commission, the Turgeon Commission.[81] Many of the recommendations contained in the commission's report were incorporated into the 1925 *Canada Grain Act*, including provisions to facilitate and ensure the operation of the pools and other co-operatives.[82] The report's introduction contains this interesting observation: "Between the year 1897 and the outbreak of the Great War in 1914, thirteen investigations into various departments of the grain trade were held by Royal Commissions, in some cases appointed by federal and in other cases by provincial authority."[83] It can be said that in general, federal governments demonstrated legislative enthusiasm to encourage the grain trade, as in the 1928 amendments to facilitate the grading of new varieties of cereal grains.[84] Vernon Fowke studied the impact of Royal Commissions on Canadian agricultural policy and concluded that the role of such commissions changed in tandem with the function of agriculture in the national economy. However, he shows that the constant element was the necessity of adherence to the economic and political principles of market capitalism, or as he put it, "the theoretical superiority of the price system."[85] Fowke quotes W.R. Motherwell's cynical comment in the House of Commons regarding commissions in general: "One Commissioner, one master counsel and Presto! You can get any kind of report you like."[86]

The period from the turn of the century to the end of the 1920s was mostly one of expansion and growth on the Prairies. Hundreds of thousands of farms were established, in turn stimulating the growth of cities, towns, and villages across the region. Federal governments aided and supported the establishment of a particular class—independent agrarian commodity producers. It is now time to look more closely at the internal dynamics of that class.

WORKING THE FARM

Labour is a necessary input for human material production; in the case of family farmers, a defining characteristic of the class is reliance on unpaid, household, and family-based labour to produce commodities for the market. Early Prairie settler families were typically large owing to a generally optimistic, future-oriented outlook among those from the "old country" who were now landowners looking forward to a better tomorrow.[87] Prairie settlement also occurred at the end of the Victorian era, a period in which a patriarchal ideology of familialism informed sex and gender relations, meaning there was widespread acceptance of the patriarchal family as part of the "natural order," with men deemed the "heads" of families and thus responsible for their provisioning. After 1900, a variety of factors influenced fertility rates among the early settlers, resulting in large families and a very young population on the Prairies for several decades. In Saskatchewan, a full 34 percent of the population was under 14 years of age in 1906, representing the largest age cohort reported in the census of that year, while 82 percent were under 39. Ten years later, there was an upward shift in age, but those under 19 still accounted for 45 percent while 87 percent were under 44. The prevalence of large families continued in 1926, when the under-19 cohort reached 48 percent; despite a shift in census categories that year, the fact that 76 percent were under 39 sill indicated a young population.[88]

Although the employment of wage labour is not a traditional defining characteristic of independent commodity production, not all labour was provided by farmers and their families, particularly during planting and harvest. One estimate suggests that farmers and their sons made up over 80 percent of the agricultural workforce on the Prairies in 1911, increasing slightly by 1931, meaning that when farmers hired labour they mostly hired neighbours, friends, and relatives.[89] As important as hiring seasonal wage labour was for some farmers during the pre-Depression period, Cecilia Danysk notes an important difference between those working the agricultural sector and other sectors of the economy: "While the industry itself operated according to capitalist economic imperatives, the men involved, whether employer or employees, were motivated by non-economic considerations as well. They wanted to farm."[90] It was common for farm labourers to be the sons or daughters of other farmers working for a while in order to save sufficient money to establish their own farming operations. Estimates place the costs of setting up farms on the Prairies between 1882 and the start of the First World War as low as $300 to $500; however, those more fortunate might have had access to four or five times that amount, and they were able to establish much more substantial operations.[91]

The multiple and necessary roles that women played in the establishment of a new society on the Plains have been recently documented and publicly recognized. The statue in Weyburn, Saskatchewan, for example, depicts a farm woman holding a child alongside a daughter and son, chickens, and a container that was used to sell cream (known as a cream can) to local creameries (dairy plants). The accompanying plaque notes that farm women "left a legacy of hope rooted in the prairie soil." Another statue in Saskatoon, *Egg Money*, depicts a girl and a boy and five chickens beside a granite block containing the names of twenty-five Saskatchewan pioneer women from Britain, France, Germany, Hungary, Norway, Russia, Scotland, Ukraine, and the United States. In 1923, *Maclean's* covered the work of farm women involved in settling the Prairies in a feature whose title drew attention to a key element of their lives: "Women Pioneers in the Canadian West Have Made Good in Many Varied Lines of Endeavor, Involving Even 'Hard Labour.'"[92] Nevertheless, the Prairies were settled in a way that accorded with the power dynamics and structures of a patriarchal society, a situation that meant women's work largely went unnoticed and unrecognized, a fact that feminist historian Ann Leger-Anderson has noted:

> In the late 19th or early 20th century, newcomer females were seen, when noticed at all, as wives, mothers, and homemakers, their triform role central to the agricultural economy that Ottawa deemed the prairie destiny. Women were helpmates, essential to the agrarian enterprise: such

was suggested by promotional literature, travel accounts, eulogies, editorials, even women themselves. Only marriage could end the plight of the bachelor homesteader: the woman could then share the burden of work, give birth to the children who would soon become contributing, productive family members, and make the house a home. Wife, mother, homemaker, then, gave the male a stake in making his enterprise successful. Men themselves sometimes sought wives in newspaper letters or ads. "Getting a mate" was a theme in appeals directed towards women: Come west, fill a badly needed job like teacher or domestic servant, then find a marriage partner, thereby making an even greater contribution to development. Finding mates (or jobs, or both) was also a leitmotif of British women who sought a solution to the surplus female population at home. By the eve of World War I, however, Saskatchewan's gender imbalance had ceased to be a major problem.[93]

In a sweeping history of rural life in Canada, and particularly the lives of rural women, R.W. Sandwell quotes the account of a farm wife described the sometimes difficult reality of agricultural life on the Prairies as follows: "To homestead is to be drenched with rain, caked with mud, choked with dust, chilled with cold, warmed by the sun, to rise early and go to bed late, to wonder whether roads and railway will ever come one's way, whether one has come to the right place or not, what the future holds in store for oneself and one's children, to be tired, to work, to laugh, to help the other fellow and always to hope."[94]

MACHINERY

The type of market-oriented agriculture that was envisioned and that gradually developed on the Prairies involved the use of the most recently available machinery and technology. Two of the most important transitions during the first three decades of the twentieth century were the replacement of animal and steam power with internal-combustion-engine tractors and the replacement of stationary harvesting thrashers with mobile combine harvesters. Bruce Shepard documents the increase in the annual sale of tractors in Saskatchewan from 1,655 in 1921 to 8,703 in 1928, while in all three Prairie provinces annual sales topped out at over 17,000 in 1928 alone.[95] The end result of the application of machinery to production "strengthened the trend towards larger farm size."[96]

Of course, not all farmers could afford the newest innovations and machinery, and the consequences could be dire: "Canadian Plains farmers who did not keep pace with mechanization paid a harsh price...[and were] forced to give up farming."[97] Speaking in the House of Commons in 1930, Mr. Thomas Donnelly commented on the importance of larger machinery in efforts to reduce the costs of production: "To sum up in regard to mass production, the farmer to-day is handling 640 acres of land just as easily as twenty-five years ago he handled 160 acres. This means we have fewer farmers and greater production."[98] David Monod explains how, early on, mechanization "dragged farmers forever, into the orbit of the dominant industrial culture."[99] The costs of not being able to keep up with the trend toward more technologically advanced farming practices were profound: "Those who rejected mechanization came to suffer for their failure to adapt. Farmers who lacked the capital, or who did not have the acreage to profit from industrialization, or whose land was too uneven for the early tractors, binders, and combines to negotiate, found themselves in an increasingly tenuous position."[100] An obvious impediment to mechanization was access to the funds necessary to buy new technology. While the obvious source of such capital was the banking system, the federal government sought to facilitate farm credit. In 1927, the minister of finance introduced a measure to establish the Canadian Farm Loan Board with the power to issue farm loan bonds and provide long-term loans and mortgage credit to farmers.[101]

The development of the farm machinery industry presents an excellent example of the dynamics of capital concentration and centralization. International Harvester (IH), an important company in the post–Second World War farm machinery sector, was founded in the 1840s. By the 1940s, it has absorbed 10 different companies. IH's main postwar competitor also dates back to the 1840s, when Daniel Massey established a shop to repair and make small implements. A decade later, in 1857, Alanson Harris started his farm machinery company, and the two merged in 1891. By 1940, Massey-Harris had absorbed 12 other companies. Indeed, mergers and takeovers seem to be the norm in this sector. At the end of the Depression, the J.I. Case company added 6 other companies to its holdings, while John Deere had absorbed 9, Oliver Farm Equipment acquired 6, Allis Chalmers 7, and Minneapolis Moline 9.[102] Through the absorption and innovation of short-line enterprises (producers of a limited and usually specialized line of equipment), the development of these companies into full-line firms (companies producing and selling a wide range of different types of farm equipment) provides a quintessential illustration of the dynamics of the marketplace.

Some may argue that the growth of these corporations, with their ability to operate across national borders, in the process employing economies of scale and developing better and more efficient machines through research and development, are a net benefit for Prairie farmers. But equipment and machinery costs were always an issue. A persistent theme in the political grievances voiced by Western farmers is the perceived additional costs they were forced to bear because of National Policy tariffs. The issue was raised in the House of Commons in 1925 when Mr. John Evans asked rhetorically, "I should like to know whether the sky-scrapers of Toronto are of more importance to this country than the whole agricultural industry of the Dominion."[103]

In 1937, a select special committee of the House of Commons was established with a mandate to investigate the high prices of farm implements. After more than forty days of extensive work, the committee concluded "that over the period 1891–1936 retail prices of farm implements have been maintained at too high a level as shown by the financial returns to the companies engaged in the industry, during that period."[104] The reasons for the high prices were determined to be related to the tariff, which prevented access to lower-priced US machinery, distribution costs related to the fact that factories were mostly located in Ontario, and industry concentration. The concerns of Western farmers and the conclusions of the select special committee were supported by a 1938 US Federal Trade Commission finding that is relevant to the Canadian scene. The commission found that a small number of companies could "determine the conditions under which all manufacturers and dealers must operate," and that the "similarity of policies respecting prices, terms and competitive practices, to some extent result whether the policies are determined by the companies individually and competitively or by understandings and agreements."[105]

Judging from the issues raised in the House of Commons by members sympathetic to the farm community, it seems that Robert Heilbroner and others were correct in suggesting that price competition declines as competitive capitalism metamorphosizes into corporate capitalism, a system in which fewer and fewer larger companies dominate the market. During the 1923 budget debate, for instance, speaker after speaker bemoaned the difficulties of Western farmers faced with increasing costs and unstable and even declining incomes. Mr. James Steedsman again noted the lower input costs for American farmers and the fact that Canadian and American farmers both sell their products in the same competitive world market. Mr. Tolmie spoke to the difficulties farmers faced with rising costs and falling prices, while John Morrison noted that prices for key commodities had dropped by two-thirds compared to previous levels at the same time that Massey-Harris reported increased profits.[106] Cost and tariff concerns notwithstanding, Western farmers continued to use more and larger machinery, even if the Depression and the Second World War had a temporary dampening effect.

FERTILIZER

While historical data on the use of chemical fertilizers on the Prairies is difficult to come by, the issue of fertilizer costs was important, and was a subject of debate in the House of Commons on several occasions.[107] As early as 1909, a bill was introduced in the House to regulate quality and require the listing of ingredients.[108] In 1921, an *Amendment to Fertilizer Act, 1909* was introduced to ensure manufacturers list components, but the matter appeared to go nowhere. The issue reappeared in 1922, when the minister of agriculture in the new Liberal government called for more regulation of the industry, including better packaging and information on any contents that might poison soil, and the creation of an advisory board.[109] While earlier cost and regional-use data do not appear to be available, between 1926 and 1930 Canadian farmers increased their expenditures on fertilizer from $6.2 million to $12.0 million. After a dip during the Depression, the total rose steadily from 1937, reaching $21 million by the end of the war.[110] The use of fertilizer became more important in the postwar period.

BUILDING COMMUNITIES

At the risk of oversimplifying, it is possible to think of Western family farmers as a relatively homogenous class prior to the First World War. Despite their diverse national, ethnic, and religious backgrounds, pioneer immigrant families often shared the experience of leaving a homeland, and on arrival in the West, they faced the arduous tasks associated with establishing viable family farms on the Prairies. The decades between 1890 and the First World War saw homesteaders and settlers by the hundreds of thousands take up land and farming across the region. Their stories of breaking the land, constructing houses and barns, and working together to build roads and establish schools, churches, community halls, and hospitals are the stuff of myth and legend. Typically, the immigrants arriving from Europe were largely oblivious to the fact that they were acquiring, under the aegis of the Canadian government, land from which native wildlife was fast disappearing, sometimes to the point of extinction, and an Indigenous population was removed through disease, neglect, and sufficient violence to ensure their lands could be appropriated by the state.[111]

Alan Anderson's *Settling Saskatchewan* documents the processes by which many arriving immigrants often gravitated to block settlements characterized by a degree of national, ethnic, or religious homogeneity. The emergence of religious, national, and ethnic communities across the Prairies was the result of several different dynamics, including ethnic and ethno-religious group planning; the efforts of government as well as transportation and settlement company recruiters; chain migration, in which friends and relatives followed those already established; and newcomers settling near others with common cultural and linguistic traditions.[112] The result was a patchwork quilt, not just in the sense of a land physically divided into square blocks, but also of ethnic and national communities with their own cultural traditions, festivals, foods, flags, social patterns, and ways of living.

The process of emigration and immigration is often characterized by both push and pull. That was certainly the case for a relatively small cohort of immigrants who typically do not get much attention in analysis of Prairie agriculture. Beginning in about 1905, approximately fifteen hundred African Americans migrated from Oklahoma, Kansas, and Texas to Saskatchewan and Alberta, largely in response to racist laws in their home states. Even still, it was not uncommon for incoming ethnic and national groups to feel a measure of hostility or ostracization when they arrived in Canada, and the plight of these African American newcomers was exacerbated by the explicit anti-Black racism they encountered upon arrival, both from government officials and from those already living on the land. Despite the desire of the federal government to attract immigrants, in 1911 Sir Wilfrid Laurier's cabinet approved an order banning Blacks from entering Canada under the guise of their unsuitability for the Canadian climate.[113] A number of African Americans did immigrate to Canada, settling in a number of communities, including Maidstone, Saskatchewan, while others took up farming in various locations including near towns of McGee and Fiske. The total number remained small, just 0.1 percent in 1916.[114] Those settling near Maidstone became known as the Shiloh People, based on the name of the church they established, and which is now included on the Saskatchewan Register of Heritage Property.

Among the first institutions that the arriving settlers established were schools. The *Dominion Lands Act* had anticipated this need, and as early as 1884, the territorial government made provision for the establishment of schools, passing *An Ordinance Providing for the Organization of Schools in the North-West Territories*. The ordinance established a Territorial Board of Education to oversee school districts of thirty-six square miles; a school could be established in a district as soon as there were ten school-aged children resident in the area. The growth of the school system after 1905 was nothing short of phenomenal, as data from Statistics Canada shows: "From 1906 to 1911 the number of school districts in Saskatchewan grew from 1,190 to 2,546, and to 3,873 by 1916."[115] Attendance was made compulsory up to grade 8 or fourteen years of age in 1917.

A NEW SOCIETY UNFOLDS

As we think about the period from Confederation to 1930, the success of the National Policy in terms of the settlement of the West is clear. By 1931, the population of Saskatchewan reached 922,000, equal to 8.9 percent of all Canadians. Most of these new arrivals were involved in farming, as illustrated by the rural-urban split. In 1901, the province's rural population was just over 77,000 compared to 14,266 in urban centres. By 1916, both had increased dramatically, but the rural population still outnumbered the urban by 471,673 to 176,162. Between 1901 and 1931, the number of farms in Saskatchewan jumped from about 13,500 to 136,500. During the same period, the total acreage under cultivation rose from about 3.8 million acres to nearly 56 million.[116]

Perhaps the industrial sector, and industrial capital in particular, were the major beneficiaries of the National Policy before the Depression. In 1905, there were about 14,600 manufacturing establishments with five or more employees in Canada, with total production valued at just over

Figure 2.1. (left) Number of Farms, 1901–31
Figure 2.2. (right) Acres under Cultivation, 1901–31

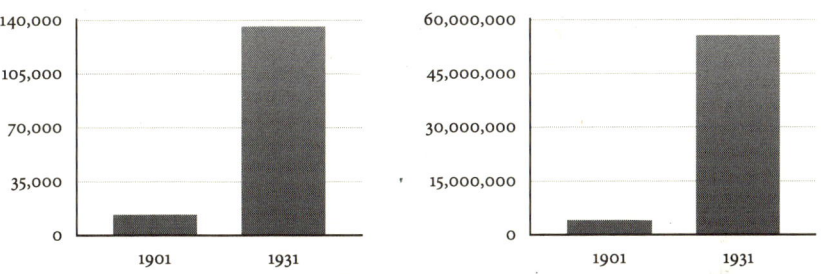

The number of farms and the area under cultivation in Saskatchewan between 1901 and 1931. Source: Statistics Canada, Historical Statistics of Canada, General Statistics (Series M1-248), "Table M1-11: Farm Population, Census Data, Canada and by Province, 1931 to 1971," and "Table M23-33: Area of Land in Farm Holdings, Census Data, Canada and by Province, 1871 to 1971," https://www150.statcan.gc.ca/n1/pub/11-516-x/sectionm/4057754-eng.htm.

$481,000,000. By 1910, the number of such establishments grew to over 19,000, with total production worth 1,165,974,000. By 1922, there were over 22,000 of these firms and their total production value $2,439,846,000. In 1930, as the Depression was beginning and the era of the National Policy was winding down, 22,6000 manufacturing establishments had a total production value of just under $3.5 billion (all dollar values in 1961 dollars).[117] The prevailing optimism was exemplified by Prime Minister Laurier, who in 1904 in Toronto expounded once again on his claim that the twentieth century is Canada's: "The 19th century has been the century of United States' development....Let me tell you, my fellow countrymen, that all the signs point this way, that the 20th century shall be the century of Canada and of Canadian development. For the next 70 years, nay for the next 100 years, Canada shall be the star towards which all men who love progress and freedom shall come."[118]

The transformation or rural Saskatchewan by settlers was accompanied by the emergence of hundreds of villages and towns. The 1911 census—the first full census after Saskatchewan was created—listed 10 urban centres with populations over 4,000, plus 50 towns and 195 incorporated villages.[119] The 1916 census saw a change to the reporting format, but the trend toward growth was nonetheless clear as there were now 3 cities over 10,000, 22 more towns (for a total 72), and 109 more incorporated villages (for a total of 304).[120] In 1921, there were 7 cities, 78 towns, and 344 villages.[121] As the agricultural population continued to increase, the number of cities remained at 7 in 1926; however, there were now 80 towns and 360 villages. In 1926, the average population for a town in Saskatchewan was 797, while the average for a village was 195.[122] In 1931, there were 8 cities with a population of more than 5,000, and 88 towns, defined as having a population of more than 500. There were 384 villages with a population of more than 100.[123] As would be expected, as the availability of land decreased and the dual crises of the Depression and the Second World War took their toll, growth slowed, such that between 1931 and 1941 no new cities emerged, while only 2 new towns (bring the total to 90) and 6 new villages (for a total of 394) were incorporated.[124]

While statistical data is important, they tell very little if anything about the impact of events and processes on those whose lives comprise the raw material of such data. The birth of a settlement that eventually becomes a town or village is the beginning of multiple individual stories, of dreams laden with joy, pain, sacrifice, ecstasy, success, failure, and all the other dimensions of lives that are lived. Everyone who came to the embryonic villages and towns in the West had dreams and high hopes for the future. As farmers flooded the region, they fueled an expanding demand for the goods and services provided by their urban neighbours, with whom they often worked to build a variety of necessary social institutions. This was true of the merchants, bank tellers, teachers, preachers, railway workers, grain buyers, blacksmiths, hoteliers, printers, midwives, carpenters, implement dealers, mechanics, doctors, cooks, postal clerks, hairdressers, barbers, billiard-room proprietors, partners, and spouses. But as one study of the growth of towns put it, "The process of development in these small prairie towns has been dominated by a set of corporate lumber yards, the grain companies, and implement dealers."[125] The expansion of the banking industry is a striking case in point. In 1916, the Royal Bank had 56 branches; a mere ten years later, there were 298. The other major banks expanded as well during the same time frame, with the Canadian Bank of Commerce increasing its branches from 133 to 187, the Bank of Montreal from 26 to 164, and the Bank of Toronto from 31 to 58.[126]

Following the notion of class articulated in the introduction, the class structure of these small urban centres was quite complex. Many of the merchants and some providing professional services (lawyers and accountants) made up either a fraction of the petite bourgeoisie (self-operators) or were small employers, while those working for a wage or salary offered a variety of skills and credentials, with their concomitant income differences. The establishment of an agrarian society in the West was also predicated on mutual assistance and co-operation among new arrivals, co-operation that extended from the building of a variety of different styles of houses and the raising of barns to the erecting of churches and schoolhouses.

A co-operative spirit was also present in how the early settlers addressed the economic and political situation in which the National Policy had placed them. As we have seen, among the issues that federal governments had to address to keep the National Policy rolling out were the persistent protests emerging form the agrarian community over the actions of the private grain trade and the railroads, not to mention a sense that the region lacked adequate political clout. Prior to the First World War, such political action seemed to flow rather seamlessly from a generally homogenous community; however, by the 1920s that community cohesion had begun to fray. For several decades there prevailed a widely shared world view that might be described as not just agriculturally based but *agrarian*.

AN AGE OF AGRARIANISM

Agrarianism has been described as "the celebration of agriculture and rural life for the positive impact thereof on the individual and society," though it is perhaps important to make a distinction between romantic and rational agrarianism.[127] Rational agrarianism, in the tradition of Thomas Jefferson, stresses "the tangible contributions agriculture and rural people make to a nation's economic and political well-being." Romantic agrarianism, on the other hand, in the tradition of Henry David Thoreau, emphasizes "the moral, emotional, and spiritual benefits agriculture and rural life convey to the individual."[128] Others have identified specific elements of the agrarian world view in the form of five themes of Great Plains agrarianism; while these are derived from the American context, they are applicable to Western Canada. These are "agrarian fundamentalism, agricultural naturalism, economic independence, hard work and the family farm as the bulwark of democracy."[129]

The notion that agriculture was important, morally as well as economically, was apparent in the National Policy itself. The content of the immigration campaign initiated under Sifton's leadership in the early 1900s makes this crystal clear. Many of the settlers who flocked to the Prairies well understood their efforts contributed tangibly to the "nation's economic and political well-being," and that their activities had a definite moral, emotional, and spiritual dimension.[130] In the early days of Western settlement, an agrarianist organization, the Patrons of Industry, spread from the United States into Western Canada. One of their publications expressed the essential elements of an agrarian ideology, albeit in patriarchal language: "Every man should be secured in his labor and in his homestead; he should work for himself and not for others, no one should share in the profits who does not share in the production. Labor must have the exclusive right to the produce if we are ever to achieve permanency and stability in agriculture.…Laws must be passed to secure the exclusive right of the occupier of the ground to the fruits of his labor."[131]

In 1908, the *Grain Growers' Guide* published a lengthy article by Henry Thoreau entitled "What Life Means to Me."[132] A later edition published E.A. Partridge's speech to the Annual Meeting of the Grain Growers' Grain Company, in which he decried farmers' exploitation at the hands of the grain trade, the banks, and other commercial interests. Partridge ended his speech with these words:

> We have to create material wealth, but we must also create mental, moral and spiritual wealth.
>
> We must purify, expand and enrich the individual life, the community life and the national life.
>
> Let us fight and win our rights that we may become more efficient champions of the rights of all; looking forward to an ideal commonwealth where strife of competition will be replaced by the peace of co-operation and the lust for private gain by zeal for the common good.[133]

The theme of agriculture as the basic industry upon which all others depend was a prominent aspect of the agrarian discourse during this period. The Farmers' Platform presented to Parliament in 1910 began with the following preamble:

> We come asking no favors at your hands. We bear with us no feeling of antipathy towards any other line of industrial life. We welcome within the limits of Canada's broad domain every legitimate form of industrial enterprise, but in view of the fact that further progress and development of the agricultural industry is of such vital importance to the general welfare of the state, that all other Canadian industries are so dependent upon its success that its condition forms the great barometer of trade, we consider its operation should no longer be hampered by tariff restrictions.[134]

Partridge's call was typically more left-of-centre than many of his peers, but it was founded on a common agrarian trope that intellectual historian Richard Hofstadter used in the title of an essay on the topic, "The Myth of the Happy Yeoman."[135] Hofstadter described the trope as follows: "The yeoman, who owned a small farm and worked it with the aid of his family, was the incarnation of the simple, honest, independent, healthy, happy human being." However, he points out that the United States "was born in the country and moved to the city," and that the notion of America as a community of yeomen tilling the soil was therefore an anachronism promulgated by what he called "the articulate people" who "were drawn irresistibly to the non-commercial, non-pecuniary, self-sufficient aspect of American farm life."

Myths aside, it turned out that many agrarian producers did have a strong sense of fairness and justice, particularly when it came to how they were treated by those they interacted with in the marketplace. We have noted the struggles many farmers had with the organized, private grain trade, and their efforts to establish their own co-operative grain-handling system. A persistent theme in the *Grain Growers' Guide* was the corruption of the political system by what the paper called special interests. Editorial pictures often identified politicians by name. A 1908 entry has Prime Minster Laurier leaning over and lecturing a farmer called "The West," and offering to rent him a horse. The farmer says he does not like the offer and will try to get a better deal from Conservative leader Borden, a supposed alternative, but who is clearly only interested in a poster offering a lot of money to any lawyer who will run the Opposition. We noted how the mistrust of the existing parties was a key factor in the emergence after the First World War of the Progressive Party and, later, during the Depression, the Co-operative Commonwealth Federation. Even before the Depression, Saskatchewan had a history of political candidates and parties representing values and programs that were different than those found among traditional Liberals and Tories.[136] In 1921, for example, eleven different groups and parties from across the political spectrum contested the provincial election, and while many ran only one candidate, their presence illustrates the vibrant nature of Saskatchewan's political scene.[137]

An important element of the agrarian movement, particularly throughout its early iterations, was the Social Gospel. Richard Allen, the pre-eminent scholar of the Social Gospel, offers this definition: "The Social Gospel is an attempt to apply Christianity to the collective ills of an industrializing society, and was a major force in Canadian religious, social and political life from the 1890s through the 1930s."[138] Allen describes the essential elements of this largely Protestant application of religious belief to the effort to realign secular society with the principles of the Gospels as follows: "Its central belief was that God was at work in social change, creating moral order and social justice. It held an optimistic view of human nature and entertained high prospects for social reform. Leaders reworked such traditional Christian doctrines as sin, atonement, salvation, and the Kingdom of God to emphasize a social content relevant to an increasingly collective society." These tenets may vary according to one's specific religious denomination, but the common elements were an emphasis on social justice, the Christian version of the golden rule, and care for others, particularly those in need or difficulty.

Given the diversity of adherents, from reformers and activists in many occupations and professions, ranging from trade unionists to farmers and educators, the Social Gospel was never a unified set of beliefs or practices. The notion that the Gospels could assist in bringing God's Kingdom to earth found traction in many communities among members of local churches, agrarian-based co-operatives, and supporters of new political organizations, from the Progressive Party to the Social Credit Party to the Co-operative Commonwealth Federation.

And yet care must be taken not to overstate the homogeneity of the farming community on the Plains. Indeed, a good deal of ideological fragmentation was evident among farmers through the late 1800s to the 1920s. Looking at Manitoba, Jeffery Taylor has documented fissures resulting from such factors as gender relations in simple commodity-producer households, the differential impact of the integration of the Prairie agricultural economy into global capitalist markets, the ideological role of educational institutions such as the Manitoba College of Agriculture and the farm media. Taylor notes the importance of learning and knowledge for this vulnerable class of new farmers in a new land, making them both susceptible and often receptive to ideological manipulation.[139] Indeed, although some, including E.A. Partridge, espoused a left-wing analysis of the position of family farmers, according to Taylor the dominant tendency in the formal educational system and the press in the rural West was conservative, forging what he calls a pro-business, bourgeois identity. Despite its original left-wing stances, for example, the *Grain Growers' Guide* later promoted an image of the successful farmer as someone capable of producing with industrial efficiency, competitive (winning plow matches and competitive cattle shows), and successful in the market.[140]

THE NATIONAL POLICY REVISITED

As we have noted, the National Policy—with one notable if brief exception in 1911—was embraced by both the Liberals and the Conservatives between the 1890s and the Great Depression. The Liberal Party governed from 1896 to 1911 under the leadership of Sir Wilfrid Laurier; however, the party's dalliance with lower tariffs in 1911 cost it dearly. The Conservatives took office promising to retain all elements of the National Policy under leaders Robert Borden (prime minister from 1911 to 1920, and part of that time head of a Unionist Government) and Arthur Meighen (prime minister from 1920 to 1921). The Liberals under Mackenzie King took power in 1921, relinquished it for eighty-eight days in 1926 before winning that year's election, and then again lost to the Bennett Conservatives on the eve of the Great Depression.[141]

To the extent that a defining characteristic of a capitalist economy is the continual development of new technologies, capital equipment, machinery, and organizational structures, agriculture is no exception. Agricultural expert and analyst Darrin Qualman suggests that the post-1918 period represents a watershed in the development of family farming in North America, marking the beginning of what he calls "high-input agriculture." In a summary that anticipates the next era in our periodization schema, Qualman writes, "It was in 1918 that farmers in Canada and the US began to purchase large numbers of farm tractors. These tractors required petroleum fuels.

Those fuels became the first major farm inputs. In the early decades of the 20th century, farmers became increasingly dependent on fossil fuels, in the middle decades most also became dependent on fertilizers, and in the latter decades they also became dependent on agricultural chemicals and high-tech, patented seeds."[142]

As the Roaring Twenties drew to a close, the National Policy seemed to have worked. Most of the best agricultural lands on the Prairies were occupied by family farms producing an increasingly diverse range of agricultural products, although cereal grains were still dominant. Various federal governments had ensured that agricultural producers were able to market their commodities in peace and war by regulating the private grain trade and even facilitating its replacement by co-operatives and pools. An essential element of the National Policy, the tariffs established in 1878–79, remained virtually untouched despite persistent agrarian protest. The expanding population of family farmers had proven to be a reliable market, readily adopting new products and technologies for over three decades. An extensive transportation system of rail branch lines served hundreds of communities.

The development of closer Canada-US ties was already under way before the Depression. The year 1923 was the first time Canada "exported more to the United States than to Great Britain," and by the end of the decade, the United States "was by far Canada's most important trading partner."[143] The 1920s were important for Western farming for a number of other reasons too, not the least of which was the declining importance of agriculture and rural life as Canada was being transformed from a rural agricultural nation to an urban-industrial society. By 1927, manufacturing had overtaken agriculture in terms of its share of total Canadian production as the agrarian-driven boom of the late nineteenth and early twentieth centuries faded in importance.[144]

By the 1920s, other sectors of the Canadian economy were emerging with the exploitation of new Canadian resources, such as pulp and paper, minerals, and hydroelectric power. Kenneth Norrie and Douglas Owram describe the success of the National Policy in the area of industrial development by noting that "manufacturing—whether primary or secondary—was now an important part of the Canadian economy, accounting for a greater percentage of total Canadian production than did agriculture by 1927."[145] A significant proportion of new investment was undertaken by emerging US-based multinationals, but this was of little concern to business and political leaders because investment from any source yielded growth, development, jobs, and profits; and capitalism, of course, is about growth and development, with little regard for which sectors drive this ultimately derives from. However, as Norrie and Owram make clear, "Just how dependent Canada was on the United States quickly became apparent with the economic collapse in 1929."[146]

Although it was not yet obvious, the global capitalist system was changing. Before the turn of the century, the post–Civil War American economy was transformed during the Gilded Age as mergers, consolidations, and trusts generated fewer and fewer but even larger corporations, which were in turn coming to dominate major sectors of the economy. Many of these enterprises found it profitable to invest in Canada, both in industry and manufacturing and in the exploitation of raw materials. The United States emerged as the dominant economic power after the First World War, and it was Canada's fate to be the reliable neighbour. Throughout the 1920s, the Canadian and US economies were booming, populations were growing, agricultural and industrial expansion seemed never-ending, stock markets reached record highs. But there were of course negative harbingers of the trouble ahead. Broadus Mitchell notes that by the end of the 1920s, there were over twenty-six million cars registered in the United States, "enough to permit every person in America to go riding at once."[147] The decades of excess accurately described in Mark Twain's *The Gilded Age* and F. Scott Fitzgerald's *The Great Gatsby* came to an unhappy end in 1929. The Great Depression that ensued threatened the entire capitalist world order, resulting in yet another series of revolutionary changes in economic thought and the role of the state. Robert Heilbroner notes that during the 1920s, industrial production was growing but employment was not, stock market speculation was rampant, the era of farm expansion was ending, and there was what he calls a "maldistribution of income."[148] The 1920s may have roared, but the next decade would change everything.

CHAPTER 3

PHASE 2 — CRISIS and STABILITY

*Keynesian Fordism and
Maintaining the Family Farm, 1930–1969*

THE KEYNESIAN STATE AND CORPORATE CAPITALISM, 1930s–1970s

ON OCTOBER 29, 1929 (SO-CALLED BLACK TUESDAY), the New York Stock Exchange began a precipitous and catastrophic collapse that would ultimately see over eighty-five thousand US businesses fail, including over five thousand banks.[1] In Canada, overall spending on all goods and services (including by governments and corporations) fell by 42 percent while unemployment rose to over 30 percent.[2] As that latter figure grew, farmers lost their land, businesses failed, and banks closed, leaving depositors empty-handed; this in turn resulted in further social discontent and unrest. Membership in socialist and communist parties increased across the Western world as governments fretted and worried about the potential for social revolution. In the absence of a substantial welfare or social assistance system, the Canadian government initially reacted by pushing the problem on the provinces and increasing repression to address the social protests and discontent.[3]

An important outcome of the Depression was a revolution in economic theory based on the ideas of British economist John Maynard Keynes. Keynes argued that if the total social or aggregate demand for goods and services in an economy declined, resulting in business failures and unemployment, the state should spend money to increase that demand. State spending on education, health care, and welfare, for example, or on infrastructure such as roads and bridges, could kick-start the economy, creating demand for goods and services and thus stimulating investment and employment in the private sector. Once the economy was functioning again, the state would withdraw its activities and use tax revenues to pay off any costs accrued through its stimulus expenditures. As we will see below, the Conservative prime minister R.B. Bennett was forced to make some modest increases in government spending during the crisis, actions that have been likened somewhat to the New Deal policies and actions of US president Franklin D. Roosevelt. The Mackenzie King Liberals, by contrast, were more deliberately Keynesian.[4] Despite these tentative moves in the direction of increased spending, however, it was the massive state spending in the preparation and subsequent conduct of the Second World War that ultimately stimulated economic growth, particularly in those combatant nations, such as Canada and the United States, that were not themselves on the front lines. It might seem that, given the active role the Canadian state played in promoting economic activity and industrialization after Confederation, it had always been something akin to a Keynesian state, but the types of actions that were forthcoming in the aftermath of the Second World War were of a different ilk.[5]

After the war, the acceptance of a more activist state was part of an overarching political and class compromise in many Western industrial nations. The compromise involved a set of social and political arrangements through which business, labour, and the state acted in concert to facilitate a period of economic stability. According to this postwar "social contract," unions focused on improving pay and working conditions. The state provided a social safety net through social programs such as health insurance, medicare, and various forms of social assistance as well as direct investment (especially economic development aid for selected regions and industries) for the benefit of both capitalists and the working class. Corporate and smaller-scale business was free to make most major economic decisions within these broad constraints. In key industrial sectors (e.g., autos, rubber, steel, farm machinery, and chemicals), owners and managers were given a free hand to introduce technological changes and other labour-saving innovations, thereby allowing workers, through their unions, to secure wage increases in line with productivity gains. Beyond the immediate demand created by the war effort, in the postwar era there were numerous investment opportunities providing basic consumer durables to meet the pent-up demand. Under American leadership, the reconstruction of war-ravaged societies stimulated new industries and fostered innovations in such areas as electronics, where wartime military technologies were given a wider application as the Cold War heated up.[6] This overall system has come to be called the Fordist accumulation regime, an era one might call "happy days."[7]

The notion of a Fordist accumulation regime draws its name, in part, from the revolution in mass production and mass consumption associated with Henry Ford's revolutionary use of mass production combined with F.W. Taylor's scientific management techniques. Fordism has been described "as an accumulation regime, a labour process and as a norm of consumption," one based on high levels of mass production and consumption organized and overseen by nation-states operating under broadly Keynesian imperatives.[8] In the words of David Harvey, "Postwar Fordism has to be seen, therefore, less as a system of mass production and more as a total way of life."[9]

As a result of the activities of the welfare state and the surge in economic activity, the post–Second World War era in Canada was characterized by a higher degree of social equality compared to previous decades. It is important to note that the social programs and benefits of this Keynesian and Fordist era were financed through a variety of taxes—including a significant level of corporate taxes and a progressive personal income tax regime—and state borrowing. It was a time when it seemed that the social contract included a conception of the "common good" as something to be paid for by a relatively well-off population. Reflecting on the era, Armine Yalnizyan noted that, "Back then, there were broad-based gains in wages for every type of job, and prosperity was not just a pocketbook issue; it was also a public affair, with more access to health care and education, and creation of a public infrastructure that included community centres, parks, libraries, rinks and pools, theatres and cultural spaces."[10]

While much of the prosperity associated with the postwar boom was felt among society at large, specific sectors such as agriculture were also able to benefit from the widely shared notion that the role of government was to regulate the market and where necessary support various pieces of the economy. After weathering the dual crisis of the Depression and the war with the help of several support programs, family grain farmers benefited from CWB crop insurance and grain advance programs. But before considering some of the legislative initiatives that characterized Keynesian-style attempts to ensure stability, including in the family farming sector, we must first consider changes in the jurisdictional status of Saskatchewan and Alberta.

A MEASURE OF PROVINCIAL AND NATIONAL INDEPENDENCE

The original *Saskatchewan Act* through which the province was created in 1905 contained a clause that gave the federal government control over Saskatchewan's land and natural resources. The relevant portion reads, "All Crown lands, mines and minerals and royalties incident thereto," including water, "shall continue to be vested in the Crown and administered by the Government of Canada for the purposes of Canada, subject to the provisions of any Act of the Parliament of Canada." This changed in 1930 with the *Constitution Act*, passed by the British Parliament after approval from the Canadian Parliament (since it involved a pre-1931 constitutional change). The act stated that "the Province [in this case, Saskatchewan] is entitled to be and should be placed in a position of equality with the other Provinces of Confederation with respect to its natural resources."[11] In March 1930, the minister of the interior, Charles Steward, introduced a motion to confirm an agreement between and federal government and Saskatchewan to transfer natural resources to the province.[12]

Why the change of heart? One could argue that it was because the National Policy had come to fruition—the land was occupied, an agrarian population was in place; plus, Saskatchewan now needed revenues from its natural resources to provide services for its population as the Depression loomed. One aspect of the National Policy had worked, and thus the federal government had no need to micromanage the geography of the region, including by exerting control over Crown land and natural resources. There was another important political change in 1931 that impacted Canada and several other Commonwealth nations, and that was the *Statute of Westminster*, which granted Commonwealth Dominions equal status with Britain and thus more autonomy in both international relations and domestic policy. It has been seen as "Canada's all-but-final achievement of independence from Britain" since it granted Canada, as a member of the Commonwealth, legislative equality with the former metropole.[13]

DROUGHT AND DEPRESSION

The period from the turn of the century to the Great Depression saw some of the most rapid economic development in Canadian history; to that extent, the National Policy had worked to a tee. We know that capitalism is a dynamic economic order, and that change is a constant. This is also true in agriculture. On the agricultural front, we saw that mechanization and expanding farm size in the 1920s resulted in some farmers facing the prospect of losing their farms, but this was merely a harbinger of things to come during the Great Depression. As Gregory Marchildon explains, the early 1930s were particularly difficult in Saskatchewan: "As the wheat province, Saskatchewan was at the epicentre of this economic earthquake. In Ontario and Quebec, provincial per capita incomes fell by 44% between 1929 and 1932. Over the same period in Manitoba, it fell by 49%. In Alberta, the second-most agricultural province in the country, per capita income fell by 61%, while in Saskatchewan, it fell by an astounding 72%."[14] Describing the overlapping natural, economic, social, and political calamities that the Depression brought to Saskatchewan, Marchildon explains how a

> 1931 drought covered the southern half of the province, and, for the first time, net farm income was minus $31 million with numerous farm families no longer able to live off their capital and past resources. In 1932, the south-central portion of the province was again the hardest hit. In 1933, it was the Southwest's turn, although over half of the south-central part of the province was also affected by drought. Much the same area was affected by the drought in 1934. In 1935, the rains finally came, but rust devastated yields through most of the province. In 1936 drought returned to the western and far southern regions. 1937 was the worst drought year of all with two-thirds of the province's farmers losing their crops. In that lowest of years, the average provincial yield was 2.6 bushels per acre, a little more than one-tenth the average yield of 1928. Once again, farm net income was pushed below zero, hitting a record minus $36 million.[15]

CONSERVATIVE INTERLUDE AND CRISIS MISMANAGEMENT

The Progressive Conservative Party under R.B. Bennett had the misfortune of winning a clear majority in the federal election of 1930. A conservative in every sense, Bennett set out to run the government as a one-man show, treating his cabinet as a board of directors without any doubt as to who was the chair.[16] As the Depression worsened, he was forced to act, including by raising tariffs in response to a similar action by the Americans and others. Bennett had famously campaigned on a promise to use tariffs to "blast" Canada "into the markets of the world," but drastic government action was difficult for Bennett to endorse.[17] In 1933, he wrote to former prime minister Robert Borden, making his cautious approach clear: "Any action at this time except to maintain the ship of state on an even keel and trim our sails to benefit but every passing breeze involves possible consequences about which I am hesitate even to think."[18] The economic system was, however, in free fall, and during the debate on the 1931 Speech from the Throne, the Progressive Conservatives were repeatedly pressed about what they were going to do for farmers. A Saskatchewan member, grilling the minister of agriculture, noted that eight months had passed and that "conditions have gone from bad to worse, yet we hear no voice from the government.... What is your program with regard to the grain growers, and what are you going to do to help the farmers of western Canada?"[19]

Eventually, the economic crisis, coupled with Prime Minister Bennett's fear of political radicalism, forced his hand, and in 1931 he introduced a resolution to provide the Governor-in-Council with the power to address unemployment and the need for farm relief. The result was a temporary, one-year bill that Bennett himself described as palliative and not a change in course or philosophy (as was illustrated by the budget cuts introduced later that year).[20] The measures were ultimately ineffective since much of the responsibility for relief fell on the provinces and local governments.[21]

Bennett placed considerable hope in re-establishing Commonwealth economic ties and thereby securing markets for Canadian products, and in so doing he pursued a course of action that had been anathema to Conservatives since 1878: lowering tariffs, albeit only on British goods. The result was ineffective and only served to annoy the Americans.[22] But while the impact of these alterations to Canadian tariffs may have been minor, this change in policy was a precursor of the more significant changes to come. For the first time since the Macdonald Conservatives established tariffs, a Canadian government undertook to significantly lower them, a move that would eventually assume the scope of an alternate economic development strategy. It was, in essence, the beginning of the end for the historic National Policy.[23] Conditions also dictated other measures. In spring 1934, Robert Weir, minister of agriculture, introduced a resolution to allow the development of Dominion marketing boards to improve the "methods and practices of marketing natural products in Canada."[24] The *Marketing Act* eventually passed in July of that year.[25] Ultimately, it was an exercise in futility because in January 1937 the Privy Council declared the measure *ultra vires*—that is, a matter of provincial jurisdiction and therefore outside the constitutional power of the federal government.[26]

As the farm crisis worsened, in May 1932 Prime Minister Bennett gave notice of a bill to "facilitate compromises and arrangements between farmers and their creditors" through appointment of receivers and provincial review boards. He also gave notice of amendments to the *Canadian Farm Loan Act* to "increase the extension of credit to farmers."[27] Bennett finally seemed to understand the grave situation facing Western farmers: "The object, of course, is to keep the farmer on the farm: if possible to keep him cultivating the land upon which he has lived." However, he also noted that the measure would assist those who have loaned the farmer money.[28] The Opposition leader, Mackenzie King, agreed with the purpose of the measure. Immediately following the first reading, Bennett introduced what he called a complementary bill amending the *Canadian Farm Loan Act* and increasing the credit extended to farmers.[29] The measures in the *Farmers' Creditors Arrangement Act* allowed farmers to seek time extensions and alternate payment options with their creditors and, failing agreement, ensured that the matter would be referred to a review board whose decision would be binding.[30]

What we see in measures such as these is the willingness of a Conservative government to act to keep farmers financially viable and on the land. The dire circumstances faced by Saskatchewan farmers during this era is illustrated in table 3.1.

The importance of the *Farmers' Creditors Arrangement Act*, which was given assent on July 3, 1934, is indicated by the fact that by 1939, over thirty-seven thousand farmers outside Quebec had taken advantage of its provisions.[31] In this sense, the act represented a continuation of the legacy of the National Policy, as its preamble made clear: "Whereas in view of the

Table 3.1. Total Farm Income Saskatchewan, 1926–37 (in 1961 Dollars)

Year	Total Farm Income	Year	Total Farm Income
1926	$168,648,000	1932	$–1,473,000
1927	$176,191,000	1933	$–14,483,000
1928	$184,665,000	1934	$–1,821,000
1929	$51,321,000	1935	$27,708,000
1930	$38,202,000	1936	$18,402,000
1931	$–31,117,000	1937	$–36,336,000

Table shows variations in total Saskatchewan farm income from the pre-Depression years to 1937. Source: Statistics Canada, *Historical Statistics of Canada, General Statistics* (Series M89-98), "Table M119-128: Total Farm Net Income, Canada and by Province, 1926 to 1974," https://www150.statcan.gc.ca/n1/pub/11-516-x/sectionm/4057754-eng.htm#1.

depressed state of agriculture, the present indebtedness of many farmers is beyond their capacity to pay; and whereas it is essential in the interest of the Dominion to retain the farmers on the land as efficient producers and for such purpose it is necessary to provide means whereby compromises or rearrangements may be effected [*sic*] of debts of farmers who are unable to pay..."[32]

The ongoing economic and social crisis forced other government actions. Given the virtual collapse of the financial system, in February 1934, Minister of Finance E.N. Rhodes introduced a bill to establish a central bank in Canada, noting that the decision follows on the heels of a thirty-seven-hundred-page, seven-volume *Report of the Royal Commission on Banking and Currency*. Unlike other models for a central bank, the proposed Bank of Canada was to be privately owned but operated as a public trust with a board of directors appointed by Ottawa and with a limit on the profits to shareholders of 6 percent.[33] As might be expected, in the long debate that accompanied the bill's slow progress through the House and committee, Mackenzie King and J.S. Woodsworth criticized the notion of a private central bank.[34] Bennett was also forced to address concerns about

American domination of Canadian culture, particularly the ever-growing popularity of American radio, by establishing a public broadcasting corporation, although it was described merely as a "paper corporation."³⁵

In the spring of 1935, the minister of agriculture introduced a further resolution to bring a measure to assist the rehabilitation of drought areas in Manitoba, Saskatchewan, and Alberta.³⁶ The *Rehabilitation of Drought Areas Bill* was generally well-received, passing the House of Commons with relatively little debate. It allowed action on soil reclamation projects on abandoned lands as well as measures to prevent soil drifting.³⁷ When the new Mackenzie King government assumed office in 1935, the bill took on a new name, *Prairie Farm Rehabilitation Act*. The minister of agriculture noted that the projects undertaken under the act included demonstration farms, strip farming, various types of suitable grass seeds, small dams, dugouts, and irrigation.³⁸ The initiative faced political difficulties in its subsequent implementation as provinces attempted to ward off federal activities in their areas of responsibility; nevertheless, the agency created by the act, the Prairie Farm Rehabilitation Administration (PFRA), which was headquartered in Regina, became an important agency of rehabilitation and stability for beleaguered farmers.³⁹ The *Farmers' Creditors Arrangement Act* was further amended in 1935 and 1938, and again in 1939. The 1939 amendment was made necessary when some provinces opted out of the act, including Manitoba. But based on a request from the Manitoba legislature, the federal Ministry of Finance introduced an amendment to ensure the act was applicable to Manitoba, Saskatchewan, and Alberta.⁴⁰

WHEAT MARKETING IN CRISIS

On assuming office in 1930, the Bennett Conservatives faced several unprecedented crises, including the collapse of the international grain market. The success of the Prairie wheat pools and other co-operative grain enterprises resulted in high payments for wheat deliveries for the 1929 and 1930 crops. However, the collapse of international prices left the pools and other grain companies with millions of bushels of grain that was now worth less on the international market than the companies had paid farmers for the grain. The pools and most grain companies relied on bank loans to pay the initial delivery price to farmers, repaying the banks when the grain was sold to exporters and millers. In the case of the wheat pools, sales were handled by what was called the Central Selling Agency. After the collapse in wheat prices, the pools sought relief from the Prairie provinces because these were governments over which farmers had significant control. There was a problem, however, because the Canadian constitution prevented provincial activity in international trade, which was the federal government's jurisdiction. As a result, not only were the farmers, farms, and the grain companies in jeopardy; so, too, was the Canadian banking system.[41]

Immediately on assuming office, the Bennett government was forced to address the situation. Bennett's initial reaction was to dismiss calls for the reinstatement of a wheat board such as had been employed after the First World War, a solution advocated by many farmers who remembered the income stability that resulted from an orderly marketing system. The Prairie pools were in crisis and the government was forced to provide guarantees for the banks. It also placed its own appointee, a former private grain trader, in charge of the Prairie pools' Central Selling Agency to control its activities and dispose of the massive stockpile of wheat. Uncertain as what to do, the Bennett government appointed another inquiry, the Royal Commission to Inquire into Trading in Grain Futures, headed by Josiah Stamp. The Stamp Commission refused to listen to the recommendations of producers that futures trading should be replaced with a government-controlled wheat board that would buy from producers and sell Canadian grains on national and international markets.[42] Additionally, a series of international conferences addressed the issue as Bennett travelled to London to discuss the crisis with other world leaders in May 1933, and although nothing concrete came of the meeting, it was followed by further international negotiations aimed at increasing the global price of wheat. Simplifying a complex story, the result of numerous meetings was the 1933 International Wheat Agreement, in which the major exporting countries agreed to quotas on export sales.[43]

Despite the efforts of governments to stabilize international prices, in 1932 wheat prices fell again, and the crisis continued unabated. In 1935, the International Wheat Agreement fell apart and pressure mounted on the Canadian government to act. On May 21, 1935, Bennett was asked when action would be forthcoming about a wheat or grain board. While Bennett's reply did not evince any sense of urgency, on June 10 he nonetheless introduced a resolution proposing the creation of a Canadian grain board to purchase, receive, and take delivery of wheat. The measure, he said, was brought about by the exigencies of the war and the fact that the matter of wheat prices was one of the most serious facing Canada.[44] Mackenzie King agreed that this was a serious issue that must not be dealt with in a partisan manner. During the second reading of the bill, Bennett was passionate in his defence of the proposed measure, accusing those who would oppose it of courting "destruction of the entire economic structure we have built up during the last fifty years," even encouraging them to send their "sneering comments" to Western farmers.[45]

When the bill returned to the full House in July following extensive discussion and debate on a variety of amendments in committee, King actively goaded Bennett on the many changes Liberal members had forced on the bill, going so far as to insist it was a different but improved bill creating a wheat board. King noted that the eventual unanimous support of the special committee that worked on the bill deserved credit for the fact that it was about to pass.[46] The *Canadian Grain Bill* was passed in 1935, leading to the creation of the Canadian Wheat Board that same year, although as Alvin Finkle notes, the "reaction of the grain trade and the business community as a whole was unanimously negative." Finkle further shows how the Liberals actually worked hard to dilute the bill, including by removing the monopoly clause and making it a voluntary board that only offered farmers a guaranteed initial minimum price.[47] Apparent Liberal support did not mean the party viewed this as anything more than a temporary crisis-management measure to stabilize prices and deal with the surplus of grain, a theme that was often repeated in the House.[48] For Bennett, the point was moot because the Liberals swept to victory in the fall 1935 election. Circumstances would thereafter force the Liberals to act on several fronts.

In the end, Bennett's mild Keynesian epiphany, and his eventual understanding of the real and radical need for some state action, came too late.[49] In actuality, an important part of Bennett's legacy includes work camps and political repression, as in the case of the Regina Riot, when he ordered the police to stop hundreds of unemployed men from travelling to Ottawa for a political protest. Lorne Brown describes Bennett's general obduracy on the provision of any substantive relief to the unemployed and dispossessed, noting how he "utterly refused to undertake any type of massive government spending."[50]

THE *PRAIRIE FARM REHABILITATION ACT*

As drought continued to devastate the landscape of the Prairies in the mid-1930s, the Liberal minister of agriculture introduced a resolution to amend the *Prairie Farm Rehabilitation Act* so as to facilitate the establishment of an advisory committee, provide additional funding, extend the time period of the act to 1939–40, and expand the work of the agency. In committee, James G. Gardiner indicated his interest in doing "anything else that [might] be found in the interests of the farmers of that area or that might rehabilitate them as farmers," particularly by expanding the activities of the PFRA in the areas of "water conservation, community pastures, regressing, reclamation and reforestation and matters of the kind."[51] In May 1941, a minor amendment was introduced to allow ministerial approval of small projects recommended by the advisory committee, with wartime conditions among the factors necessitating continuing assistance for Prairie farmers.[52]

From its establishment during the Depression to the 1960s, the PFRA was a major actor in the development of water-related resources on the Prairies. Among the activities under its purview were dams along the Frenchman

River and the Rolling Hills irrigation project in Alberta, which helped many farm families resettle near reliable water supplies. In the 1940s, water control structures were completed on several lakes in the Qu'Appelle River system as well as on several rivers in Alberta. In the 1950s, many dikes were constructed in Manitoba to deal with flooding. Approximately five thousand families were resettled near irrigation systems and/or reliable water sources by 1962. Also in the 1950s, a project allowed the pumping of water from the South Saskatchewan River into Buffalo Pound Lake to provide additional water to Regina and Moose Jaw and serve a new potash mine in the area. In 1959, work began on what would become the Gardiner Dam and Lake Diefenbaker. During its existence, the PFRA helped many farmers with its involvement in more than 148,000 dugout projects and assisting with 111,552 wells, nearly 15,000 livestock watering dams, 11,000 irrigation projects, and over 700 water pipelines.[53] Many such measures sought to stabilize the Western rural economy and allow family farmers to survive.

The community pasture initiative was among the important activities of the PFRA. Saskatchewan and Manitoba transferred land to the PFRA under the condition that it be rehabilitated and/or used for community pastures. The overall benefits of the program extended beyond pasture use to include flood prevention, environmental protection, and even income distribution in local areas.[54] Dave Phillips describes the essential features of the community pasture program as follows:

> Arrangements were made in 1939 to establish community pastures to be operated by PFRA to rehabilitate and conserve fragile and marginal lands that had been subject to drought and erosion. The provinces of Manitoba and Saskatchewan identified and assembled blocks of degraded and sometimes abandoned lands to be incorporated into the Community Pasture Program (CPP). While the primary objective of the program was to rehabilitate and conserve lands subjected to erosion, an equally important purpose in establishing the pastures was to help advance economic stability and diversification in the Prairie Provinces.[55]

Phillips reports that by 2006, 85 PFRA pastures covering over 900,000 hectares of mostly marginal land had allowed 3,400 users to graze 220,000 cattle.

One of the bitter ironies, or perhaps tragedies, of the settlement of the Prairies was the extent to which one group's gains were often connected to losses suffered by others. The prime example of this was, of course, the granting of land title to white settlers and the corresponding loss of land by Indigenous people. One particularly tragic story, related to the PFRA, played out in western Manitoba, very near the Saskatchewan border. Situated between the Qu'Appelle and Assiniboine Rivers the community of Ste. Madeleine was established by members of the Métis Nation in the aftermath of the First Riel Rebellion. In 1937, the population of Ste. Madeleine was approximately 250, although it may have been as high as 400 in the past. Because the land was part of an area composed of sandy soil, it had not been desirable for many settlers, although Métis farmers were able to make a living on the land. With the passage of the *Prairie Farm Rehabilitation Act*, the area was designated as one of the areas that would become a community pasture, and as a result the community was told that it must be relocated. Most Canadians would find the actions related to that "relocation" abhorrent. Ste. Madeleine was literally burned to the ground by government officials, some of its dogs shot, and its residents removed. Trevor Herriot offers a harrowing description of these events:

> The land—more than three thousand acres where Métis families lived—was being reclaimed by the federal government to make a community pasture. Those with title and paid-up taxes would receive equivalent parcels nearby. People who did not have title, or those who had title but unpaid taxes, would be resettled with no compensation in one of two new settlements to be established in the municipality. Anyone who tried to stay on the land would be removed by force. And so, most families slowly moved away over the next year, leaving their homes behind. At some point, the municipality men moved in and lit the houses and other buildings on fire. Witnesses say they shot several dogs at the settlement.[56]

THE *PRAIRIE FARM ASSISTANCE ACT*

In 1939, the federal minister of agriculture introduced a motion to consider a new bill, the *Prairie Farm Assistance Act*, which would establish the Prairie Farm Assistance Administration (PFAA).[57] The measure allowed farmers to contribute to a fund controlled by the government based on 1 percent of their farm income. The fund could then become the source of payments in case of crop failure or emergency. The program was designed to provide stability and protection in what was often a precarious climate.[58] Fowke attributes government action such as the PFAA to a desire on the part of the federal Department of Agriculture to "demonstrate its interest in Canadian agriculture since the re-establishment and expansion of the Canadian agricultural frontier" was an abiding concern of "the federal government from Confederation till as late as 1930."[59] Although often thought of as a type of insurance program, a 1963 commission inquiry stated that the "*Prairie Farm Assistance Act* does not provide an insurance scheme for farmers as individuals. It is, in fact, a program helping where a general crop failure has occurred in a municipality or local improvement district."[60] It was clearly a stabilization measure.

CANADIAN WHEAT BOARD 2.0

When it took office, the Mackenzie King government faced several problems, not the least of which were the debates and controversies surrounding grain marketing and even the future of the CWB. One of the first actions of new government was to establish a cabinet wheat committee. To this end, in March 1936, W.D. Euler, minister of trade and commerce, introduced a motion to establish a special select committee to investigate and report on the marketing of wheat and other grains. The motion passed with virtually no debate.[61] The resulting committee concluded that the CWB was operating "consistent with the intention of Parliament in enacting the Wheat Board Act of 1935"; however, it recommended yet another Royal

Commission into the question of whether a body like the CWB was in fact preferrable to an open market.[62]

The 1936 Turgeon Royal Grain Inquiry Commission was charged with investigating several issues, by far the most important being the basic structure of the Canadian grain marketing system. The merits of compulsory versus voluntary pooling and compulsory versus voluntary wheat boards were the most vital issues it addressed. After extensive national hearings, the Turgeon Commission issued its lengthy report in May 1938. It addressed numerous aspects of the grain trade, both nationally and internationally. In terms of the central questions of the role of the CWB, the report recommended the resumption of the full operation of the Winnipeg Grain Exchange.

Despite the impact of drought throughout the 1930s on grain production, by the end of the decade surplus wheat had become a domestic and international issue. The CWB remained in place over the last years of the 1930s, but its main function by this point was to set minimum prices. However, as producers expanded production in anticipation of an increased wartime demand between 1938 and 1940, the government was faced with a mushrooming surplus of wheat.

When Parliament resumed in January 1939, the Throne Speech noted that the government would act on the issue: "Bills will be introduced to regulate the grain exchange along the lines laid down in the report of the royal commission on grain marketing, to revise the *Canada Grain Act*, and to assist further in the marketing of farm products."[63] The announcement was followed by legislative action. An amendment was made to the *Canada Grain Act* to establish an initial price for top-quality wheat rather than having the government establish it each year, it also limited the amount of grain each producer could market to the Wheat Board.[64] In May 1939, the *Grain Futures Act* was passed, providing for closer supervision and regulation of the operations of the Winnipeg Grain Exchange by the Board of Grain Commissioners.

The same year saw Gardiner introduce a resolution regarding "a measure to encourage cooperative marketing of wheat by guarantee and fund the initial payment by cooperative associations or elevator companies."[65] The act that followed, the *Wheat Cooperative Marketing Act*, facilitated the stabilization of producer pools via government guarantees of a minimum price for wheat marketed through such pools, although there may have been an ulterior motive in that successful co-operatives might allay the need for the CWB.[66] A related piece of legislation, the *Agricultural Products Cooperative Marketing Act*, extended these provisions to products other than wheat.[67] As C.F. Wilson points out, the measures were linked to the efforts of the Liberals to have the grain marketing system return to normal— that is, to an open grain market with futures-based commodity sales. The government hoped that the support of the pools and farmer co-operatives would take the pressure off in terms of maintaining the CWB; however, the value of the CWB to grain farmers had become firmly entrenched.[68]

THE SECOND WORLD WAR

How quickly and radically the world can change was indicated by two statements in two different Throne Speeches from 1939. The year began with a degree of optimism, reflected in the following comments from the governor general on January 12:

> The Government shared in the general sense of relief that the appalling disaster of war, which threatened Europe during the month of September last, was averted, and in the recognition which that crisis manifested of the widespread will of the peoples for peace. They are hopeful that the efforts now being made to find a solution for the specific differences which are causing friction will meet with success. They recognize, nevertheless, that time is required for these forces to work, and that the possibility of further tension in the meantime must be faced. In this situation, the Government have considered that the uncertainties of the future, and the conditions of modern warfare, make it imperative that Canada's defences be materially strengthened.[69]

Eight months later, as the inherent inhumanity, evil, and madness of fascism played out across Europe and much of the globe, on September 3, 1939, Canada did something it had never done on its own: it declared war on another nation, Germany. The second Throne Speech of the year, delivered on September 7, reads in part:

> As you are only too well aware, all efforts to maintain the peace of Europe have failed. The United Kingdom, in honouring pledges given as a means of avoiding hostilities, has become engaged in war with Germany. You have been summoned at the earliest moment in order that the Government may seek authority for the measures necessary for the defence of Canada, and for co-operation in the determined effort, which is being made to resist further aggression, and to prevent the appeal to force instead of to pacific means in the settlement of international disputes. Already the Militia, the Naval Service and the Air Force have been placed on active service, and certain other provisions have been made for the defence of our coasts and our internal security under the War Measures Act and other existing authority.[70]

Canada and Canadians were henceforth irrevocably changed.

While the problems of many Western farmers remained, a vast range of new imperatives now took precedence. Food supplies, always a fundamental issue in wartime, were something Canada was well placed to address, however, there were logistical hurdles to be overcome to ensure a smooth flow of grain from farms to those needing it. The problem of autumn elevator congestion required attention. It was caused by producers in need of income attempting to sell their recently harvested products and overloading the capacity of the grain-handling system. The Prairie pools were among those advocating a delivery quota system, which they said would be more equitable for all producers. A delivery quota system would allow each producer to deliver a specific quantity of grain based on an established number of bushels for every productive acre they farmed. For example, if the quota was fixed at 5 bushels, a producer with 100 acres of farmed land would be allowed to deliver 500 bushels, while a producer with 200 acres could deliver 1,000 bushels. Producers with 200 acres could deliver more grain, but their costs would be higher, as would be the producer's investment, thus requiring more income. Under the pressures of wartime, in 1940 the cabinet, through an Order-in-Council, introduced a delivery quota system. To ensure compliance, producers were required to sign a sworn declaration specifying their acreage, and they were issued an official permit book in which elevator agents and grain merchants recorded all deliveries.[71] In the same year, an amendment to the *Canadian Wheat Board Act* allowed the government to pay farmers for farm-stored grain, thereby compensating for the loss of markets in war-torn Europe, while eliminating the five-thousand-bushel maximum delivery amount. Royal assent for the bill, which came in August 1940, also approved the Order-in-Council dealing with delivery quotas.[72]

In April 1940, the government had taken the first action to address the surplus problem that at this stage still encumbered producers through another Order-in-Council, this one to pay compensation to producers for reducing their acreage. In February 1942, two trains carried over four hundred Western farmers to Ottawa; their goal was to seek higher prices for their grain since many argued the price did not meet the costs of production.[73] In anticipating the delegation, a member of the House of Commons from Saskatchewan, Mr. George Castleden, noted the seriousness of the situation facing Western farmers: "People do not come down here in wartime for pleasure; they are not coming here to cause trouble. These are patriotic Canadians of good character. They are people who have fought and suffered, people who have help build Canada. They are protesting the treatment of agriculture, and they would not be here if conditions were not desperate."[74] John Diefenbaker likewise addressed the desperation in the West: "They are coming, Mr. Speaker, to demand their rights. They come in no threatening mood, but rather as individuals who to-day find themselves in a position bordering on economic slavery."[75]

In spring 1943, Minister Gardiner addressed this concern by introducing a bill to put the matter into legislation that provided payments for farmers to reduce their wheat acreage. During second reading, he noted the expectation that the measure would increase prices and "give reasonable returns to farmers," whose production was vital to the war effort.[76] Later that year, Minister Gardiner introduced another amendment extending the program into 1943.[77]

Parallel with these legislative developments, the world cereal grain picture changed dramatically in 1943. Weather and wartime demand for wheat resulted in increases in the price of wheat. The war had forced Britain to create a centralized purchasing agent for cereal grains. This system required substantial stocks in the hands of the CWB; however, with the price of wheat rising, producers had the choice to either accept the Wheat Board's low initial price and later a final payment or going to the open market for a higher payment upon delivery. Many producers chose the latter option. In addition, the federal government was concerned that a rapid rise in the price of wheat would undermine its efforts to control inflation and hamper its commitment to use wheat in various mutual aid agreements. The question of the Western wheat crop was debated extensively in the House of Commons in the spring of 1943. Several members from Western Canada attempted to push the government to move to a compulsory wheat board by essentially eliminating trading of grain on the Winnipeg Grain Exchange.[78] Such was the explicit intent of a March 1943 amendment to a bill before the House by Mr. T.C. Douglas recommending that "steps should be taken to abolish trading on the Winnipeg grain exchange in order to prevent speculation and profiteering at the expense of the farmer." Douglas went on to argue that for eight years the Liberals had "deliberately sought to sabotage and discredit the wheat board in the eyes of the wheat producers of western Canada," and further, that "the Liberal party never wanted a wheat board."[79]

In late summer and fall 1943, continuing instabilities in the grain market forced the government to act. In September, acting under the wide powers of the *War Measures Act* and through an Order-in-Council, the government re-established the CWB as the compulsory and sole purchaser of Canadian wheat from farmers. Trading activities on the Winnipeg Grain Exchange were suspended, pleasing many farmers who had come to appreciate the benefits of an orderly marketing system offered by the CWB and its stable, year-round prices. It has been argued that the welfare of the farmers was not necessarily the primary motivation of the King Liberals.[80] Indeed, the prospect of rising wheat prices was not attractive and the federal government moved to make the Wheat Board the sole marketing agent for wheat. The irony of the board's re-establishment at this time has been noted: "The earlier theory had been that compulsory marketing would bring higher prices, but when it was actually established it was to keep prices under control."[81]

After September 1939, most Canadians were focused on the war effort. The logistics of developing an effective system for the production and distribution of foodstuffs for the Allied war effort sometimes proved challenging. On the agricultural front, the federal government worked to facilitate the production and distribution of food, as was noted above. Minor amendments were required to establish yearly prices to facilitate the operation of the CWB and certain agencies.[82] Even before the war ended, the Liberals were planning for the postwar recovery and readjustment period. Legislation was introduced to begin to look after returning veterans, and in a preview of things to come, family allowances were established in 1945.

POSTWAR LIBERAL KEYNESIANISM

By the end of the Second World War, Keynesian economics had been proven to work. Massive government spending—albeit on tools and weapons of destruction—along with a variety of interventionist and regulatory regimes had been instrumental in ending the Depression and producing high levels of growth and economic activity. The end of the war, the impact of a decline in government spending, and the return of soldiers to the domestic workforce were among the issues that confronted many Western nations. Returning to the economic conditions of the interwar era was, for most, simply not an option. It is not surprising that many Western nations undertook systematic action to prepare for peace. In Britain, the country's coalition government published a report into social services commonly known as the Beveridge Report. In Canada, a former researcher for Lord Beveridge, Leonard Marsh, was commissioned to head the Advisory Committee on Post-War Reconstruction, which subsequently generated the *Report on Social Security for Canada*, more commonly called the Marsh Report.[83]

In the United States, President Franklin D. Roosevelt's prewar New Deal set a certain tone for government action following the war. There were common elements to the philosophies, plans, and actions embraced by Britain, Canada, and the United States (and many other nations as well) as they approached the end of the war. This was quite different from the official ideology of classical laissez-faire liberalism. State spending, regulation, and direct and indirect involvement in economic matters were deemed to be in the national and public interests and had become, to various degrees, acceptable, understood as necessary, even desirable.[84]

Mackenzie King himself was inspired by an address by Lord Beveridge. Reginald Whitaker describes the orientation of the postwar King government as follows: "The logic of the new policies was provided by Keynesian economics which, through a new federal apparatus of fiscal and monetary control, guaranteed private sector capital accumulation through the maintenance of full employment and the protection of a stable environment to attract investment, especially American."[85] Canadian governments had always had an interventionist hue, but after 1945 this would rise to new levels.

ERODING THE NATIONAL POLICY

Even as governments sought to offer some measure of stability for the Western grain sector, important changes were occurring in the Canadian economy that would come to impact the position of Prairie farmers. As we have noted, between 1911 and the onset of the Depression, neither major party had seriously considered any substantive change to the protective tariff regime enshrined in Macdonald's National Policy. However, during the Depression both R.B. Bennett and his Liberal successor, Mackenzie King, feared, with good cause, the political implications of a prolonged economic slump, hence Bennett's willingness to tinker with reducing tariffs in exchange for access for Canadian products into imperial markets. Donald Creighton points out that King went even farther than Bennett, ending a trade dispute with the United States in 1935 and ultimately tying Canada even closer to the Americans.[86] Albeit under duress, the revisions marked a transition in the orientation of federal tariff policy away from the earlier focus on an east–west national trade and commerce to more of a north–south alignment in which the two countries' economies would come to be increasingly integrated. Continental drift was under way. Creighton sees the Depression as a watershed moment in this regard: "It was the Depression that brought an end to a great period of expansion which had begun with the settlement of the West; and there followed a long pause of ten bitter years. The Second World War marked a fresh beginning in the Canadian experience. The nation changed its direction and its pace. The next eighteen years brought an equally important alteration in its character."[87]

The alteration in the national character to which Creighton alludes was enhanced by Canada's wartime experience. In August 1940, President Roosevelt and Prime Minister King signed the Ogdensburg Agreement, creating a Permanent Joint Board on Defense composed of Canadian and American military and civil research personnel. As Creighton points out, the arrangement "bound Canada to a continental system dominated by the United States."[88] A subsequent economic agreement, the Hyde Park Declaration, stated that "each country should provide the other with the defense articles which it is best able to produce."[89] Creighton's portrayal of King's role in these events, and, indeed, in the overall conduct of the war, is less than flattering: "He behaved like a puppet which could be animated only by the President of the United States."[90] Commenting on King's relationship with Roosevelt, Creighton claims it "was not that of two equals, but of master and pupil, with the younger man as the acknowledged senior."[91]

The increasing integration of the US and Canadian economies was among the many economic impacts of the war effort. Under the leadership of C.D. Howe, the wartime Department of Munitions and Supply organized and coordinated production, using military Crown corporations when necessary.[92] A second major impact was the deliberate, coordinated, and co-operative integration of American and Canadian industrial capital and production. By the end of the war, many Canadian companies came to understand that such arrangements were advantageous, and as a result many Canadian companies sought to retain the benefits of continental integration after 1945. Capitalist industry requires expanding markets, and with the Canadian West essentially settled and agrarian expansion a thing of the past, a new approach was required. At the same time, Canada's neighbour and most important trading partner had assumed global economic, military, and political dominance through Marshall Plan reconstruction and global financial domination through the Bretton Woods Agreement, which made the US dollar essentially the standard global benchmark currency. Under these circumstances, the compelling logic of capital accumulation resulted in many Canadian companies seeing a southward turn as the surest way to future prosperity. This was a monumental change in direction for Canada, one that would see the Prairie cereal grain farmer assume an increasingly marginal place in the national economy.

Noting the intersection of commercial/business interests and the state during the Depression and the war, George Grant famously argued that

> After 1940 it was not in the interests of the economically powerful to be nationalists. Most of them made more money by being representatives of American capitalism and setting up branch plants. No class in Canada

more welcomed the American managers than the established wealthy of Montreal and Toronto, who had once seen themselves as the pillars of Canada. Nor should this be surprising. Capitalism is, after all, a way of life based on the principle that the most important activity is profit making. That activity led the wealthy in the direction of continentalism.[93]

As a result, Grant concludes, "Canada has ceased to be a nation, but its formal political existence will not end quickly"—in part, in his view, because the political absorption of Quebec would be too difficult for the Americans.[94] To cite the titles of a couple chapters from two important works on the subject, Creighton refers to the postwar era variously as "The Return to Colonial Status" and "The New Colonialism," the difference being, of course, a switch in colonial masters from the United Kingdom to the United States. We will consider some further implications of this change below, but for now it is worth dwelling on some of the agricultural issues and legislation that came to shape the postwar era. As we shall see, the first two decades after the end of the war saw the Canadian government take several legislative actions "in a Keynesian style," meaning they were aimed at stabilizing and maintaining the existing economic order and institutions.

THE AGRICULTURAL PRICES SUPPORT ACT

In 1944, with the war effort winding down, the government passed the *Agricultural Prices Support Act*. It established a board with the power (and a $200 million budget) to support farm prices in the transition from war- to peacetime by purchasing agricultural products or providing subsidies when prices fell below a designated level. Over its twelve years of operation, the board's activities were unimportant to grain growers, and according to one assessment, it had little impact overall.[95]

When Parliament opened in the fall of 1951, the Speech from the Throne carried a distinctive Keynesian postwar flavour. The results of the federal elections of 1945 and 1949 might be read as an indication that, after the crisis of the Depression and the role government spending had subsequently come to play in the creation of employment during the war, there was a willingness to consider a new approach. In 1945, the Liberals had won a reduced majority of only 5 seats, partly owing to the performance of the Co-operative Commonwealth Federation (CCF), which, with its social democratic and Keynesian approach to the market, gained 20 more seats than it had held in 1940. In 1949, the Progressive Conservative leader, former Ontario premier George Drew, promised lower taxes and less government, while the Liberals under Louis St. Laurent promised continued job creation, health insurance, expanded social programs, and greater rights for workers in the aftermath of a bitter strike by asbestos workers in Quebec. The Liberals' massive, 118-seat majority—and the CCF's loss of 18 seats—after the 1948 election might be interpreted as a swing on the part of moderate voters to a Keynesian-oriented party that had a better chance of governing.

Among the measures that followed were a more robust pension plan, negotiations with the Americans over improvements to the St. Lawrence Seaway, initial work on the South Saskatchewan River Project, and an Agricultural Products Marketing Board. Additionally, there was to be increased support for the Canadian Broadcasting Corporation, and more money for arts and culture, including for the National Gallery of Canada.[96] The following two decades would see universal old-age pensions and old-age security (1951–52); the *Unemployment Assistance Act* (1956); federal initiatives toward universal health care following the Royal Commission on Health Services (1961); the *National Housing Act* (1964); and the Canada Student Loans Plan (1964), which facilitated the expansion of the university sector.

In late fall 1951, the minister of agriculture introduced a resolution that illustrates the tendency of governments in this era to regulate aspects of various markets: "It is expedient to introduce a measure for the establishment of an agricultural products board, to prescribe the constitution and powers of the board, to provide for the establishment in the consolidated revenue fund of an agricultural products board account and for the payments out of the consolidated revenue fund for the buying, storing, transporting or processing of agricultural products."[97] When the matter was taken up a few days later, the minister noted that the new act to establish the Agricultural Products Board and replace the previous 1947 *Agricultural Products Act*, which had now expired, and that the government was now acting without the authority of the *War Measures Act*. The minister was clear that the new act was not going to be compulsory but merely authorized the government to buy farm products when it felt that was necessary. During the debate, members of the Official Opposition as well as the Social Credit Party and the CCF supported the bill in principle.[98] It passed relatively quickly, receiving its third and final reading on December 17, 1951. In an analysis of the evolution of agricultural support policies in Canada, Douglas Hedley notes that this act reflected a significant change in peacetime agricultural policy by virtue of its acceptance that the government has a role to play in supporting agricultural prices and farm incomes.[99]

THE POST–SECOND WORLD WAR CANADIAN WHEAT BOARD

The issue of grain marketing remained important as the war ended and the Twentieth Parliament opened. In the Commons, there were frequent demands for the retention of the CWB, as illustrated by the remarks of Mr. Robert Fair, who stated that "it has been operated as a gambling den in most cases to the detriment of the farmers of western Canada." In 1946, Mr. Fair's language was even stronger when speaking of the Winnipeg Grain Exchange: "So that again I say Remove this bloodsucker from the back of the farmers of Canada."[100]

While such rhetoric may not have resonated widely, even among Keynesian-influenced political leaders, in 1947 legislation to amend the

Canadian Wheat Board Act was passed. The legislation increased the powers of the CWB, extended its jurisdiction to 1950, and otherwise codified in legislation many of the actions and regulations that had been passed by Orders-in-Council during the war. The bill passed by a vote of 172 to 7, an indication of the overall political support for the continuation of orderly marketing.[101] In February 1948, C.D. Howe introduced a further amendment to the *Canadian Wheat Board Act* that, among other things, extended the power of the board to control the purchase and sale of oats and barley. In speaking to the measure, Howe cited what he called "strong representations" from various farm groups, including the national Canadian Council of Agriculture, and further claimed "that the government desires to meet the wishes of farm organizations in this regard."[102]

Throughout the early 1950s, Liberal governments regularly passed minor operational amendments to the *Canadian Wheat Board Act* dealing with payment schedules, storage fees for wheat holdings, and the like. One of the more notable was the five-year extension provided for in Howe's 1957 amendment, in which he praised the success and operation of the board. In speaking to the matter, John Diefenbaker noted, "We support the legislation continuing the wheat board. It is natural that we should do so, for we gave it birth and we have given it support throughout the years."[103]

The principle that the federal government should, when necessary, intervene to support farm incomes also informed a later bill. In 1957, D.S. Harkness, minister of agriculture, introduced a motion that the House consider a "Measure to Provide Guaranteed Prices for Certain Agricultural Commodities." He described the bill as far-reaching as it would create a board to oversee guaranteed prices for certain agricultural commodities and provide a fund of $250 million to support guaranteed prices for certain agricultural products.[104] Although the bill was not addressed particularly to the Prairies, during the ensuing debate one member from Saskatchewan, Mr. Louis Lewry, attempted to have Parliament address the cost-price squeeze in agriculture. The move was, however, ruled out of order.[105]

INTERNATIONAL WHEAT AGREEMENTS

Participation in international wheat agreements was another option available to governments that wished to stabilize and improve farm incomes, particularly during times when a variety of factors produced more chaos than normal in the international market. As was noted above, such a mechanism was unsuccessfully attempted in the early days of the Great Depression. Another effort was undertaken at the end of the war with the support of the newly created United Nations. "By early 1949 world wheat stocks were again accumulating, prices were beginning to slip as European agriculture recovered, acreage controls and price supports were once more being studied by governmental agricultural experts and most of the world was in a mood to seek cooperative stability in wheat."[106] In 1949, a four-year International Wheat Agreement came into effect that set ceiling (maximum) and floor (minimum) prices for wheat while also assuring wheat supplies for importing countries. Exporting countries agreed to quotas or limits on export amounts. The effect was to stabilize prices, provide assurance of sales for exporting countries (Canada, the United States, Australia, and France), and assure supplies for the thirty-seven importing countries. When the agreement was renewed for the period 1953–56, the United Kingdom refused to re-sign, resulting in downward pressure on wheat prices. A new agreement was reached in 1956 that expanded the exporting countries to include Argentina and Sweden. It was renewed, essentially intact, in 1959, 1962, 1967, and 1971, but thereafter the agreement began to unravel.[107]

Outside of these wheat agreements, nation-states undertook their own actions. In Canada, there was the perennial problem of overproduction and lagging sales. The United States dominated the world market; however, a reconstructed Europe, whose population remembered wartime food shortages and starvation, was focusing on self-sufficiency and export capacity. The situation meant that the CWB was selling Canadian grain in a difficult market.[108] Overproduction in a competitive world market meant unstable prices, low incomes, and economic insecurity. In order to attempt to address the situation, the Liberals introduced the *Temporary Wheat Reserves Act* in early 1956, at which time C.D. Howe noted the measure was being proposed to deal with what he called the "superabundance of production."[109] He argued that the problem of grain in storage and farmers without income could be solved by providing federal guarantees for farm loans based on stored grain. Howe rejected the option of wheat board advances since he noted the CWB was not a lending institution; however, subsequent debate saw the other parties indicate their support for cash advances over bank loans. Mr. Hazen Argue, for example, chastised the government for not assisting farmers and instead forcing them to pay interest to the banks the act was protecting.[110] The government passed legislation at the same time to cover the carrying costs incurred by the CWB for temporary wheat storage.[111]

CONTINENTAL DRIFT AND CANADIAN NATIONALISM

The postwar Louis St. Laurent Liberals had become pragmatic Keynesians, comfortable with significant state activity and planning. To ensure orderly economic growth after 1945, they appointed a Royal Commission led by Walter Gordon to study the long-term prospects of the Canadian economy. Among the important contexts the Royal Commission on Canada's Economic Prospects considered in its work was decades of significant American investment in most major non-agricultural sectors of the economy. The commission's five-hundred-page report was issued in 1956 and 1957.[112] Although it makes some interesting observations regarding agriculture, its key findings are to be found in chapter 18, "Domestic Savings and Foreign Investment." Here, the commission reviewed a massive amount of data on the Canadian economy, drawing the unassailable conclusion that the country was unique in the massive amount of foreign ownership, particularly American ownership, of its economy. Moreover, they note that "a big part of the foreign investment in Canada is concentrated in subsidiary companies controlled by non-residents in the resource and manufacturing industries."¹¹³ While recognizing the benefits of the economic activity such investment has generated, the authors also offer a cautionary note when describing some of the more negative consequences, including threats to political independence, the possibility of disjunction between a foreign shareholder's interests and Canada's national interest, price setting, and differences in export and wage policies.¹¹⁴ The questions that the Gordon Report raised regarding the potential impacts of American control of the Canadian economy would go on to play an important role in two political debates in the mid-1950s.

THE LAST NATIONALIST PRIME MINSTER?

In 1956–57, two major political developments in Canada signalled a dramatic shift in both international and domestic relationships and political priorities. Internationally, it was a geopolitical and military crisis over control of the French- and British-owned Suez Canal. To secure more revenue for its domestic programs, the Egyptian government nationalized the canal. In response, the British government assumed a belligerent position, going so far as to prepare for war. The Americans for their part urged restraint, even though this was during the Cold War and the Soviets supported Egypt. Despite centuries of imperial relations with Britain during which Canada had typically dutifully followed the lead of the metropole on such matters, Canada essentially sided with the United States. Lester Pearson, then minister of external affairs, proposed the formation of an international peacekeeping force. It would not be a stretch to argue that this was a decisive moment in Canada's history, one that had marked impact on its international alliances and its place within the Commonwealth.

Nationally, 1956–57 also saw the "great pipeline debate" in which the Liberals used every parliamentary tool available to pass a measure ensuring federal support for an American-controlled company to build a pipeline to carry Canadian natural gas to US markets. Donald Creighton describes the measure as sponsoring and assisting "the takeover of a great Canadian enterprise by a gang of American oil and gas companies," and as both a political blunder and a "dreadful political crime."[115] He summarized the wider geopolitical context as follows: "The Pipeline debate and the Suez crisis were the obverse and reverse sides of the same metal. The Liberal government's sponsorship of the pipeline project was an unmistakable sign of Canada's close identification with a continental North American economy dominated by the United States. The Suez crisis was an equally plain revelation of the disintegration of the postwar Commonwealth and submission of its members, including Canada, to American leadership in world politics."[116]

When the Liberals called an election in 1957, they had been in power since 1935, a total of twenty-two years. The new Progressive Conservative leader was John Diefenbaker, a one-time head of the Saskatchewan Progressive Conservative Party who was first elected to the House of Commons in 1940. Under Diefenbaker, the Progressive Conservatives utilized public concern with what they argued were the undemocratic tactics used in the pipeline debate, the turn away from traditional relationships and alliances with Britain, and the Liberals' apparent lack of a national vision for Canada. The Progressive Conservatives formed a minority government after the 1957 election but were swept to a historic victory in 1958. The party would subsequently pass several pieces of legislation geared at maintaining and supporting family farmers on the Prairies.

FACILITATING FARM CREDIT

The issue of farm credit was an important one throughout the postwar period as the pace of mechanization increased. In June 1959, under the leadership of D.S. Harkness, the Progressive Conservative minister of agriculture, the government repealed the *Canadian Farm Loan Act* and established a system of long-term credit for farmers. Minister Harkness indicated that this was a significant measure, telling the House that "from the point of view of the long-term welfare of agriculture I believe this is one of the most important bills which has been considered by the Canadian parliament. The importance of credit used by farmers as a supplement to their own capital had increased almost continuously during the last 50 years."[117] Further, he noted that farmers will have a voice through the "establishment of a farm credit corporation with an advisory committee, the majority of such committee to be composed of farmers or representatives of farm organizations."[118] The corporation would be authorized to make two types of long-term mortgages, such as those already allowed under the existing *Canadian Farm Loan Act*, but also longer-term mortgages that would be secured by the material possessions of the mortgage holder. The assets of the existing farm loan board would be transferred to the new corporation. The bill passed quickly with little debate.

THE AGRICULTURE AND RURAL DEVELOPMENT ACT

In 1958, Prime Minister John Diefenbaker spoke to the House regarding his government's agricultural policy. He noted the difficulties faced by Prairie grain farmers, particularly those who ran what he termed small farms, and acknowledged the considerable pressure from farmers for some form of deficiency payment, but he made clear this was not the approach the government would take. Instead, he proposed what he called a "far-reaching and comprehensive program" that would include the following: (1) funding to support the export of surplus grain; (2) a joint federal-provincial crop insurance program; (3) a feed and forage reserve program; (4) a review and improvement of farm credit; (5) a program to encourage the better use of land; and (6) a conservation conference.[119]

Three years later, Minister of Agriculture Alvin Hamilton would refer to the fifth item in this overall policy when he introduced a resolution authorizing the minister of agriculture to enter into agreements with provinces or agencies to jointly develop projects to facilitate the transformation of marginal lands, increase the income and employment in rural agricultural areas, and facilitate more research and investigation under the guidance of advisory committees. Hamilton noted the importance of assisting those farmers struggling on marginal land with low incomes, pointing out that in 1950, 26 percent of farmers in Saskatchewan had earned less than twelve hundred dollars in yearly income.[120]

During debate on the bill that established the *Agriculture and Rural Development Act*, the parliamentary secretary to the minister of agriculture noted that when it comes to agricultural development, some would claim that governments have two choices at their disposal: they could do nothing, allowing matters to take their own course, or they could attempt to manage and control the affairs and life of the farmer. The Progressive Conservative approach, by contrast, was to "provide an environment whereby people can take advantage of their own native abilities, initiatives and desires" in order to succeed. The parliamentary secretary made clear that that was the intent of the government's bill.[121] The member for Red Deer congratulated the government for understanding that "the independent family farm is the backbone of our economy as well as of our traditional democratic way of life."

The bill subsequently passed without a single negative vote. The years that followed saw a significant uptake by various provinces, in part, as a way to access federal funds.[122] The program remained in effect until the late 1970s. Diefenbaker himself saw the measure as a necessary step to address the complex problem of growing poverty in the rural West: "A larger percentage of farmers were handicapped in providing a satisfactory level of living for their families by a lack of productive resources resulting from unproductive land, uneconomical units and poor farming methods."[123]

CROP INSURANCE AND PRAIRIE GRAIN ADVANCE PAYMENTS

We typically think of insurance as compensation for a catastrophic loss of personal property, as when one's home is destroyed by fire. In the case of a business or commercial enterprise, insurance typically would cover the re-establishment of said enterprise. In the case of the crop insurance program introduced by the Diefenbaker government in 1959, the purpose had to do with maintaining and stabilizing farm income during periods of drought or in the wake of a natural disaster. To avoid any constitutional and jurisdictional issues, the measure involved agreements with the provinces. During committee debate, it was determined that the best route was a program of federal grants and loans in co-operation with the provinces to cover 50 percent administration, 20 percent premium, and loans for indemnity costs. The precise details of the program would vary from province to province, as would the crops covered, premium rates, and so on. The result, if not the explicit intent, of the program was to effectively stabilize the status quo.

The importance of keeping cash flowing into and then out of the hands of farmers was a concern early on as governments regulated the grain trade. That concern was addressed differently after the Second World War. In the fall of 1957, Gordon Churchill, minister of trade and commerce, introduced the *Prairie Grain Advance Payments Act* "to provide for making advance on account of initial payments for grain produced in designated areas," with the latter defined by CWB prior to delivery.[124] The essential logic of an advance payment can be gleaned from the term itself. For example, if a producer has grain but is for any number of reasons unable to sell it in the present, she can secure an advance payment; when the product is eventually sold, the advance payment is then subtracted from the amount the producer receives. The term "initial payment" refers to the CWB's practice of making an initial payment on delivery and later a final payment when the product is sold. During the committee debate, Churchill described the measure as a cash advance and not a handout, noting that it was necessitated by large surpluses since farmers could not wait for up to a year before getting cash.[125] On second reading, the minister noted virtually unanimous support for the concept of advance payments in difficult times. The bill was passed in a matter of days.[126] Judging from the take-up by Prairie farmers, the measure proved an important form of support. In 1968–69, for example, 113,491 advance loans totalling $151.8 million were proffered, followed by 122,080 loans for $272.8 million in 1969–70.[127]

Near the end of their term, the Diefenbaker Progressive Conservatives attempted to provide some measure of farm income stabilization, but their efforts missed the mark. In the fall of 1957, the minister of agriculture introduced a bill to establish guaranteed prices for certain agricultural commodities under the *Agricultural Stabilization Act*. The debate on the bill lasted for over three weeks and is recorded across hundreds of pages of *Hansard*. The aim of the bill was to establish a guaranteed price for certain commodities based on a three-year rolling average, with three primary intentions: price stabilization; production incentives; and protection from falling world prices. Yet the bill did not have a significant impact on the cost-price squeeze on the Prairies because it excluded wheat, oats, and barley produced in areas under the jurisdiction of the CWB.[128] Meanwhile, the Prairie pools continued to support deficiency payments.[129]

GRAIN TRANSPORTATION REVISITED: THE MACPHERSON COMMISSION

The question of transportation in Canada has never been a purely logistical and economic issue since it has always been connected to politics and public policy as far back as the construction of the CPR. The matter of freight rates constantly boiled to the surface, as it did in 1959 when the government moved to lower rates across the board. On March 9, 1959, George Hees, minister of transport, introduced a measure to reduce freight rates and provide a subsidy to carriers of up to twenty million dollars to compensate railroads for the lost revenue.[130] During the debate, the government came under pressure to appoint a commission to study all aspects of the issue, a suggestion it eventually accepted. To this end, in May 1959 M.A. MacPherson was once again tapped to lead a Royal Commission; his mandate was to consider the freight rate structure, the legal obligations of railroads, ways of increasing efficiency, and the provisions of the *Railway Act*.[131] MacPherson's far-reaching report began by noting that, in Canada, transportation, particularly railway transportation, is more than merely a question of hauling goods: "In addition to its economic function the railway has, of course, often played a more extensive role in the building of nations—a circumstance, which has been particularly apparent in the case of Canada. History records how the Canadian railways provided the means of meeting not only the demands of a developing economy but, also, the goals of national policy directed towards the establishment of national unity."[132]

The commission opened the door on a controversial issue whose impact was becoming apparent in the late 1950s: the abandonment of rail lines. Noting the historical importance of rail lines to many communities, the commission argued that "sober realism" suggests that in some cases, the decline in traffic resulting from declining farm numbers means that service reductions and line abandonment are entirely possible and economically logical.[133] When addressing the Crow's Nest Pass Agreement, the report notes that reduced rates for farmers in return for financial and land grants to the CPR had allowed the company access to the "rich mining area of southern British Columbia," and that the agreement was, therefore, a "quid pro quo." In spite of this, the majority of the commissioners concluded that in order to carry out its obligations in the national interest, the government should further assist the railroads and provide subsidies to bridge the difference between the statutory rates and the railroads' costs.[134] A dissenting view stated there should be no subsidy, and that "the Canadian Pacific Railway, having obtained very real advantages when it undertook—in perpetuity—to accept a ceiling on these grain rates, became party to a contract which is still in effect and which must be abided by."[135]

However, before any of the commission's recommendations could be acted upon, the Progressive Conservatives were defeated in the election of 1963.

GRAIN MARKET INSTABILITY

On the eve of the turbulent 1960s, the global grain market continued to experience instability. Although the Americans dominated the global market, accounting for over 40 percent of all sales and exports, for many

European nations war-time food shortages and starvation were still a vivid recent memory, and they were determined to move toward self-sufficiency and even export capacity.[136]

The CWB for its part was doing an admirable job of selling Canadian wheat and other grains on the international market. Indeed, an important event of the period was the CWB's sale in 1961 of nearly 1.4 million tonnes of wheat and barley to China. This caused considerable consternation in Washington, but it was important to the Diefenbaker government for several reasons, not the least of which was the aid it offered to Western farmers. Additionally, it illustrated Diefenbaker's desire to counter the growing integration of the Canadian and American economies. An analysis of the sale noted that Diefenbaker's vision of the Canadian economy was different from that of the Pearson Liberals, who thought that "Canada's postwar prosperity required the free flow of goods across the Canada-US border."[137] In the wake of the sale, Imperial Oil threatened to block fuel supplies for ships transporting the grain, and when Diefenbaker raised this with President Kennedy, he found his American counterpart to be rather unhelpful.

Diefenbaker would later recount in his memoirs the anger the Americans had felt upon learning that Canada had provided foodstuffs to a Communist country—which he gathered after President Kennedy discarded a speaking note to that effect in the Prime Minister's Office during a state visit.[138] Subsequent CWB sales to China and then to the Soviet Union further strengthened Canada's position on the international market, and eventually generated an American reaction in the form of export subsidies to make US grain more attractive to international buyers. The American decision was a factor in the collapse of the International Wheat Agreement. The subsequent dramatic decline in wheat and grain prices left the CWB in debt as the price drop meant it had to sell wheat for less than it had paid farmers for the grain.[139] A future Liberal government would have to address an ongoing crisis of overproduction.

WESTERN AGRICULTURE AND THE PEARSON LIBERALS

The Diefenbaker Progressive Conservatives entered the 1963 election campaign with a massive majority, but the political and social environment was increasingly unstable. Diefenbaker's reluctance to support the American demand that nuclear warheads be positioned on Canadian soil, plus Liberal promises regarding pensions, health-care reform, and the promise of a new flag, were among the factors that led to Diefenbaker's defeat. The Liberals formed a minority government in 1963 and then a majority in 1965, based, among other factors, on their restated promises for a Canada Pension Plan and medicare and assistance for the expanding number of "baby boomers" going to university. In 1967, Robert Stanfield replaced Diefenbaker as leader of the Progressive Conservative Party.

For George Grant and Donald Creighton, John Diefenbaker's political fate stood as one of the most poignant illustrations of Canada's status in North America in the decades after the Second World War. Both historians paint a picture of Diefenbaker as a nationalist outsider unable to grasp the full implications of an economy increasingly dominated by US-based multinational capital. Diefenbaker somewhat naively sought to restore Canada's ties with the Commonwealth so as to secure a larger measure of Canadian economic control and to "end its subservient acceptance of American foreign policy," but he was ultimately defeated (if not humiliated) by the multiple continental political and economic interests, including the political advisers of President Kennedy.[140] Going into the 1963 election, Kennedy invited Liberal leader Lester Pearson, Diefenbaker's main political rival, to a White House gala celebrating Nobel Peace Prize winners (Pearson's idea of a Suez peacekeeping force had earned him the award in 1957). Diefenbaker was annoyed at the resulting press coverage, which he saw as a form of election interference.[141] Diefenbaker himself recalls being approached by an American while visiting Egypt and being told, "I want to shake hands with the only Prime Minister of Canada who has ever been defeated by a President of the United States."[142] For Creighton, none of this was surprising; indeed, he described the Liberals, particularly King and St. Laurent, as thinking "instinctively in American continental terms."[143] Full integration would nonetheless take some time longer.

After the Liberals regained power in 1963, there was no immediate indication that they were anything but supportive of the CWB, as were most farmers producing cereal grains. In 1967, the minister of trade and commerce (responsible for the CWB) introduced a bill to amend the *Canadian Wheat Board Act*, noting that it dealt only with routine matters. The minister praised the activities and effectiveness of the board as he extended its operation, saying that "the board is now a permanent part of the Canadian scene and grain growers of the west wish it to be considered as such."[144] The amendments did just that, making the CWB a permanent institution in the Canadian grain marketing system by removing the five-year renewal clause. The subsequent debate saw no indication from any party that there was any concern with the operation of the CWB.[145]

In spite of the change in government, there was no change in philosophy regarding farm credit. In May 1964, Harry Hays, minister of agriculture, moved a resolution to increase the borrowing capacity of the Farm Credit Corporation (FCC) from $400 million to $600 million and the maximum borrowing capacity of a significant category of farmers from $20,000 to $40,000.[146] The extent to which the government appeared to be willing to provide loans to farmers was illustrated by a remark made by Minister Hays during final reading: "I can see the Farm Credit Corporation lending a total of $1 billion in the future."[147] The intended or unintended consequences in terms of farm consolidation and rising debt levels did not enter into the debates.

Among the perennial issues facing Prairie grain farmers were grain transportation and freight rates. Although Diefenbaker had lost power, the report of the MacPherson Commission, which his government had initiated, played a role going forward. In August 1966, the Liberal minister of transport, Mr. Pickersgill, moved first reading of a bill to "define and implement a national transportation policy for Canada," including amendments to the *Railroad Act*. The bill was introduced the same day as another bill to end a national railroad strike.[148] The complex, sixty-eight-page *National Transportation Act* contained a hundred clauses covering a vast array of issues, including the establishment of the Canadian Transport Commission, support for railroads to assist in adjusting to new rates, reducing other subsidies and financial assistance for railroads, and maintaining current grain freight rates.

The subsidies paid to railroad companies under the 1959 bill had risen fivefold by 1966. Pickersgill suggested that increased competition, an aim of the bill, would reduce the need for subsidies, thereby allowing the market to rule.[149] As the bill proceeded other issues emerged, however, such as the commitment to address the rationalization and abandonment of railway lines.[150] Mr. James Pickersgill raised another issue that was to become a major controversy when he noted that the MacPherson Commission had determined that the Crow Rate were "not remunerative" for the railways. As is often the case, any debate over transportation and freight rates was bound to be controversial and this was the case when the House of Commons Standing Committee on Transport and Communications debated the act. Although the Keynesian view that government intervention in the market could be positive was soon to fall out of favour, the act still adhered to the notion that, on matters such as transportation policy, it was important to put the national interest first: "The new Clause is a re-assertion of transportation policy objectives congruent with the central issue of Canadian historical development. Nowhere is this more evident than in the statement "the responsibility of governments [is] to attend to the provision of the transportation system. Those are words that John A. MacDonald, or Wilfrid Laurier, or C.D. Howe would most assuredly endorse."[151] The mere mention of the Crow Rate was, however, enough to attract attention, and one parliamentarian suggested that the government is proceeding to "ruin" the rate—a statement denied by the minister, who indicated that as long as he stay in that role, so, too, would the Crow Rate remain.[152] The bill was in fact somewhat prophetic, but the government had larger immediate issues on its plate.

MACHINERY: THE BARBER COMMISSION AND CORPORATE CONCENTRATION

The issue of farm machinery, and especially the costs of acquiring and maintaining such equipment, was a persistent source of anxiety for many farmers even before the First World War, but the increased mechanization of production after 1945 only exacerbated these concerns as the cost-price squeeze intensified. These issues had become so acute that in 1966 the federal government appointed Dr. Clarence Barber to a one-person commission of inquiry to look into the financing, distribution, and cost of farm machinery.[153] The six-hundred-page Barber Report began with a historical overview of the farm machinery industry in Canada and data relating to its major firms. It also contained many recommendations covering a range of aspects of the farm machinery sector.[154] Barber addressed the question of the industry's concentration in the hands of fewer and fewer corporations, noting that his recommendations were "designed to make the farm machinery industry adopt policies oriented more towards lower costs and lower prices." More specifically, he argued that "Mergers that are likely to significantly lessen competition in the farm machinery industry should be prohibited, unless it can be shown that they have important cost-saving effects. In the latter case, they might be allowed if there is reasonable assurance that the cost-saving effects would be passed on, in substantial measure, to the farmer."[155]

Elsewhere Barber recommended the adoption of a policy that farm organizations had long advocated—namely, some form of free trade in farm machinery.[156] On the matter of industry profits, he did not find these to be excessive, but he noted that "the industry has followed a policy of pricing its products at a high level in relation to manufacturing costs and has developed an expensive distribution system which has effectively concealed the high profits earned at the manufacturing level."[157] He did not foresee any reduction in the pace of farm mechanization; indeed, he anticipated quite the opposite, pointing to a continuing reduction in the number of farms and an increase in average farm size.[158] In the House of Commons, the government was repeatedly questioned as to the implementation of Barber's recommendations, but it made no commitments.[159] By October 1971, a member could claim that the "commission reported and made several good recommendations, but the government has done absolutely nothing to implement them," and when asked again, Pierre Trudeau, Liberal leader since 1969 and now prime minister, merely said, "I shall take note of the questions."[160] Little followed other than the establishment of a machinery testing institute.[161]

In a subsequent scholarly article, Commissioner Barber reflected on his experience heading the one-person commission as well as some of its conclusions. Among other points, he offered the following observation of corporate behaviour: "Major companies avoid price competition for fear of provoking retaliation and lower profits for all concerned. These firms concentrate instead on various forms of nonprice competition such as the development of improved products, an increased number of sizes, options, and models for each major product line, better repair parts service, more emphasis on quality reflected in improved warranty provisions, and on the extension of customer credit."[162]

In the decades that followed the release of the Barber Report, the dynamics of capital concentration and centralization continued unabated in the industry. Indeed, some of Barber's comments regarding mergers exhibited a degree of prescience in the face of the ongoing restructuring of the farm machinery industry in subsequent decades. Although Barber had recommended some form of regulation, the growing size of these enterprises, it could be argued, rendered them beyond the regulatory capacity of most nation-states. A 1978 study of the organization, structure, and control of Canadian agriculture noted, in congruence with Barber's findings, that the input environment of the agricultural machinery industry was by this time largely oligopolistic. The study further noted that "economies of scale are extensive for a number of these industries (e.g., some farm machinery items, fertilizers, and agricultural chemicals) and have been a factor encouraging the development of multinational giants, most of which are foreign-based."[163] A cursory examination of some of the leading producers of farm equipment, contained in chapter 5, will suffice to illustrate the transformation that some of these companies underwent in the postwar decades.

FARMERS IN A COST-PRICE SQUEEZE

A key issue for our purposes relates to the fate of the Western family farmers amid these large structural changes. Parliamentary representatives from the West had long called on the federal government to do something to address rising costs and falling or unstable commodity prices. Speaking in July 1955, Mr. Bryson argued that the House should move into committee to discuss the serious difficulties cereal grain producers and other farmers faced in trying to survive in "an economy which arbitrarily administers both costs and prices." Using the sex-specific language of the day, Mr. Scott Bryson outlined the situation as follows: "The Agricultural producer is the only producer in this country who has no control over his costs of production or the prices he receives for his product." The relationship "between cost of production and the prices received for the commodity produced" are the "greatest single problem" facing farmers. In the debate that followed, the cost-price squeeze was extensively discussed, as were several ways of addressing it. These included parity prices that would link prices to costs, bartering Canadian wheat internationally, establishing a floor price for wheat, creating a two-price system for domestic and international sales, and support prices (subsidies) and/or price controls on inputs.[164] In the end, however, no measures were forthcoming. Table 3.2 illustrates the extent to which farm costs on several necessary items rose every year from 1945 to 1961.

Table 3.2. National Farm Input Costs, 1935–61

Year with 1935 base index of 100	Farm machinery	Equipment & material	Taxes & interest rates
1935	100	100	100
1945	115.1	125.9	113.4
1946	118.8	128	117.2
1947	126.3	139.5	125
1948	141.6	173.1	131.3
1949	158.3	180.3	138.7
1950	165.1	189.9	144.3
1951	186.8	206	151.8
1952	195.4	215.8	161.4
1953	196.7	207.4	168.2
1954	197.9	203.3	174.6
1955	198.8	204.6	177.2
1956	209.4	208.8	184.7
1957	223.8	211.3	191.9
1958	236.7	213	196.7
1959	248.4	219.1	204.7
1960	254.2	222.7	214.5
1961	261.4	226.7	220.6

National cost increases for farm machinery, equipment, material, taxes, and interest between 1935 and 1961, with 1935 as the basis. *Source: Statistics Canada, Historical Statistics of Canada, General Statistics (Series M1-248), "Table M221-227: Price Index Numbers of Commodities and Services Used by Farmers, Canada, 1913 to 1961," https://www150.statcan.gc.ca/n1/pub/11-516-x/sectionm/4057754-eng.htm.*

If we compare the trends in terms of costs with income trends, the picture farmers were facing becomes clear. Table 3.3 uses 1961 as the benchmark year indexed at 100 for an estimate of composite farm income. While there is growth, the variable income picture as opposed to the steady cost data illustrate the predicament farmers faced.

Table 3.3. Composite Index of Farm Prices of Agricultural Products, and Realized Gross Farm Income, Saskatchewan, 1945–61

Year	Farm price index Sask.	Realized gross farm income
1945	75.8	448,057,000
1946	85.5	442,604,000
1947	89	485,918,000
1948	97.3	602,632,000
1949	97.9	627,160,000
1950	99	466,214,000
1951	105.8	682,361,000
1952	96.8	754,771,000
1953	90	781,473,000
1954	82.2	511,315,000
1955	80.1	486,026,000
1956	82.1	634,182,000
1957	79.6	575,366,000
1958	84.2	649,108,000
1959	86	618,138,000
1960	89	636,469,000
1961	100	664,809,000

Farm price index and realized gross farm income for Saskatchewan during the immediate post–Second World War period, 1945–61. *Source: Statistics Canada, Historical Statistics of Canada, General Statistics (Series M1-248), "Table M186-195: Composite Index of Farm Prices of Agricultural Products, Canada and by Province, 1935 to 1974," and "Table M99-108: Realized Farm Gross Income, Canada and by Province, 1926 to 1974," https://www150.statcan.gc.ca/n1/pub/11-516-x/sectionm/4057754-eng.htm#1.*

It is quite easy to understand the structural reason why Prairie farmers faced a cost-price squeeze for decades. Family farms typically produce products and commodities that are sold on international markets and whose prices are therefore subject to international competition. In terms of world markets, there are hundreds of thousands, indeed millions of grain producers. Even though Canadian farmers sold their products through the CWB as a "single desk seller" on the world market, Canada and its producers had relatively little capacity to impact world prices. The same is true of the country's participation in international grain agreements, which were helpful to some degree but only in a limited fashion. In short, on the output side, prices, and thus returns and incomes, fluctuate significantly as the farm price data in table 3.3 illustrates.

On the input side, as we saw when we looked at farm machinery companies, the normal dynamics of the concentration and centralization of capital were already at work. One of Fowke's main claims is that the creation of an agrarian population that would serve as a market for Canadian industry was one of the National Policy's core goals. That fewer and fewer enterprises in any given field of production do not tend to enhance price competition is not a particularly radical conclusion so much as a simple fact. The immediate postwar period was characterized by intensive mechanization. Between 1946 and 1951, the number of farm tractors in Saskatchewan increased from just over 66,000 to over 90,000, grain combines from 21,851 to 41,215, and farm trucks from 26,674 to 49,277—all this in just five years![165]

Politicians regularly heard the stories of individual farmers. In 1958, a Western farmer wrote to the minister of agriculture: "Being a small farmer of a half a section, I find myself in a cost price squeeze which is gradually worsening. Trying to pay for my land, taxes, machinery, groceries, repairs, etc. it is impossible with prices as they stand today." Another farmer provided more detail, noting that things were worse than they had been during the Depression: "I have accumulated 640 acres of land worth $20,000, machinery worth $10,000, buildings another $10,000. I have 10,000 bushels of wheat stored on hand and after taking the advance on my 1959–60 crop and paying my expenses, I find myself left with $88 to live on for a very indefinite period."[166] The advance of which this farmer speaks was a program that allowed farmers to receive an advance payment for grain in storage that had to be paid off when the grain was sold. This meant, in essence, that such farmers were pawning the grain they had on hand!

Reduced to brutally simple terms, all this resulted in the producer being squeezed on the input side by costs that tended always to escalate, while on the output side was characterized by fluctuating and variable prices. As a result, there were times when input costs rose faster than output prices. During these periods, farmers would lose money, and indeed many would leave agriculture altogether, as the chart below indicates.

Figure 3.1. Number of Saskatchewan Farms, 1921–71

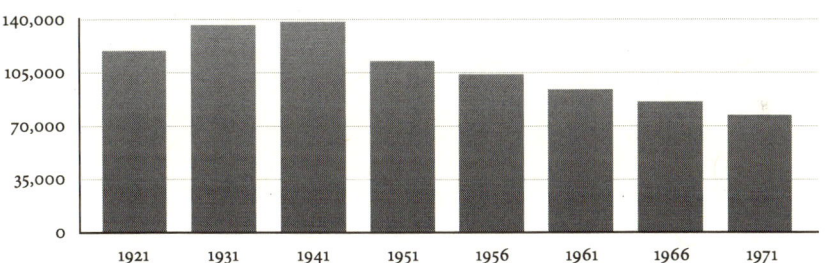

The bar graph represents the changing number of farms in Saskatchewan in ten- and then five-year intervals starting in 1921. *Source: Statistics Canada, Historical Statistics of Canada, General Statistics (Series M1-248), "Table M1-11: Farm Population, Census Data, Canada and by Province, 1931 to 1971," https://www150.statcan.gc.ca/n1/pub/11-516-x/sectionm/4057754-eng.htm#1.*

Put another way, only 56 percent of the Saskatchewan farms that had existed in 1941 remained in operation in 1971. That means that nearly half of the farms in Saskatchewan were lost over the course of these three decades. In population numbers, the Saskatchewan farm population dropped from 564,012 in 1931 to 514, 677 in 1941 before decreasing steadily to 233,792 in 1971.[167] In the past, when Western farmers were faced with adversity and what they saw as the injustice of the system, they tended to act collectively by protesting, lobbying governments, starting their own co-operative grain companies, organizing new political parties when they felt the mainstream parties did not represent them, organizing mass delegations to Ottawa, and so on. Likewise, the crisis of overproduction and the ever-present cost-price squeeze served to once again ignite Prairie protest from the late 1950s through to the 1960s. In 1959, armed with a petition with 320,000 signatures supporting deficiency payments, 1,100 farmers and farmers' delegates met with various government and Opposition representatives on March 5, 1959.[168] The government, however, refused to adopt deficiency payments.[169]

Although it was not tasked with addressing the specific issue of the cost-price squeeze in agriculture, the 1956 Royal Commission on Price Spreads of Food Products was nevertheless relevant to the issue as its mandate was, among other things, to "inquire into the extent and the causes of the spread between the prices received by producers of food products of agricultural and fisheries origin and the prices paid by consumers."[170] To this end, the Royal Commission investigated several changes in the food distribution industry during the 1950s. While this was an era of growing prosperity, it was also an era in which corporate domination of the food distribution system was becoming apparent. Among the commission's findings was a noticeable growth of corporate chain stores: "Sales of corporate chain stores as a proportion of total retail food sales rose from 29.5% in 1930 to 44.0% in 1958." And it further noted that these large chain stores were very profitable, with total sales having increased from an average per store of $60,000 in 1930 to $946,000 in 1958.[171]

As for the issues facing agricultural producers, the commission looked at the rising costs of farm machinery but did not make any significant recommendations. It noted that a discrepancy between the returns to producers and the returns to those processing and selling farm products: "It is evident that, during the period, the returns from the marketing of food have been more substantial than the returns from the production of the food materials." Having noted this, the commission did not see a structural problem between a highly competitive output and an emerging oligopolist input sector but instead concluded that the gap was "due to a considerable extent to the particular conditions of the period." The commission's tepid "solution" was for the federal government to provide for the incorporation of co-operatives—a measure that was in fact already in place![172]

ALTERNATE FORMS OF PRAIRIE AGRICULTURE

Although beyond the scope of this volume, it is worth noting the importance of alternate modes of organizing agricultural production on the Prairies, such as those employed at Hutterite colonies. Statistics Canada reports that there were seventy such colonies in Saskatchewan in 2016.[173] Sometimes controversial, sometimes misunderstood, sometimes welcomed, and sometimes threatened, by most conventional economic standards Hutterite colonies are host to various forms of successful agricultural production.[174] Hutterites are pacifist Anabaptists who hold productive property in common, typically employ the latest technology, and sell some of the commodities they produce communally in public markets. The economic stability and success of many Hutterite colonies on the Prairies has been attributed to their members' commitment, their hard work, and the cost savings stemming from communal ownership. As one observer noted, "By working together for the good of all, they reduce costs....Whereas 10 non-Hutterite farms would require 10 full lines of equipment, the Hutterite willingness to share equipment and labour significantly reduces the machinery investment."[175] The average size of a Hutterite colony in Western Canada is about 8,000 acres, which is about the same size as the farm one Alberta colony bought near Tisdale, Saskatchewan, in 2016 for $26.5 million.[176]

An interesting development after the Second World War was a Saskatchewan experiment with alternative organization and property relations in the form of co-operative farms. An active Department of Co-operation and Co-operative Development was created in Saskatchewan after the left-wing CCF formed a provincial government in 1944. As veterans returned from the war, many governments developed policies and programs to assist their reintegration into the postwar economy. Rather than just providing individual land grants—a common approach—the Saskatchewan government made it possible for individuals to pool or combine their land grants and start co-operative farms. In 1945, the first co-op farm was incorporated near Sturgis. Sixteen other co-ops were established, perhaps the best known being the Matador Co-op at Kyle.[177]

Over the years that followed, the various co-op farms disbanded, their assets either sold off or divided among members. Historian Bill Waiser attributes their decline in part to physical location (poor soil and climate), while another assessment notes the lack of a unifying commitment such as in the case of Hutterites: "Some [members] were high-minded while others were opportunistic; some were revolutionaries while others were simply interested in government aid. And the commitment to co-operative living varied from person to person. Consequently, there was no coherent, unified body of thought to guide the experiment and build loyalty. In addition, there was no indigenous secular utopian tradition to relate to, so participants were isolated in their pioneering activities."[178] Other, more detailed analyses of the co-operative farm model note the importance of equity for most independent commodity producers, for whom the sale of farmland is often the basis of one's retirement plan. In the case of a co-op farm in which members hold equity together, the intergenerational transfer of assets and retirement planning prove to be thorny issues.

STORM CLOUDS

As the turbulent 1960s proceeded, frustration grew as the cost-price squeeze continued to wear family farmers down. The federal government reacted in September 1967 by appointing a task force to assess the agricultural industry and make the necessary recommendations. The summer before the task force's report was released, in December 1969, Prime Minister Trudeau embarked on a tour of the West. On July 16, 1969, he was confronted by a crowd in front of Regina's storied Hotel Saskatchewan, some on their tractors, others holding unflattering signs. The farmers brought spoiled wheat, some of which was thrown at the prime minister. In the angry exchange that followed, Trudeau is reported to have said that he did not get into politics to be disrespected. Referring to the significant capital value of many farms (capital value of land and machinery being different from income), he said, "We can't give money away to the rich." The crowd booed loudly. A day later in Saskatoon, speaking to over eight hundred farmers in front of the Bessborough Hotel, he indicated that it might make sense for the government to assist farmers who want to leave agriculture.[179] A year later, in April 1970, a demonstration by an estimated seven thousand Saskatchewan farmers and their supporters again rallied in Regina, this time in front of the Saskatchewan Legislative Building.[180]

By 1970, it was beginning to feel as though the famous Bob Dylan song "The Times They Are A-Changin'," released in 1964, was perhaps a prescient description of the uncertain future awaiting the family farm.

CHAPTER 4

PHASE 3— UNLEASHING the MARKET

Neoliberalism and Family Farming, 1970–2014

NEOLIBERAL GLOBAL CAPITALISM, 1970–2008

THE ERA THAT BEGAN IN THE 1970s HAS BEEN CLEVerly described as one in which the "Keynesian chickens...[came] home to roost" as a series of structural economic problems began to emerge.[1] Japan and parts of western Europe, rebuilt with American aid, now possessed new and more efficient technologies and consequently were able to produce high-quality consumer and other products more efficiently. Consumers in North America increasingly bought these less expensive and often superior goods. The infrastructure expenditures aimed at accommodating the postwar baby boom (highways, suburban expansion, schools, and universities) stimulated the economy but also drove up deficits. The expanding range of social services provided by the welfare state also created both jobs and greater government debt. In the United States, spending associated with the Cold War, the so-called space race, and the Vietnam War increased deficits and debt. The postwar prosperity of the Western world was based on very inexpensive petroleum energy; however, the

Organization of Arab Petroleum Exporting Countries, founded in January 1968, began to control the supply of oil, significantly raising the international price. At the same time, while the Fordist/welfare-state era of global capitalism had provided a period of relative stability and diminished inequality, some began to argue that the welfare state was out of control, that taxes were too high, and that there was too much state regulation.

The value of the American dollar, which was the unquestioned postwar international currency, became less stable, more so after President Nixon moved it off the gold standard in early 1971. Monetary instability, a growing money supply, declining sales of many consumer goods, and rising personal debt levels generated a new phenomenon characterized both by inflation and increasing unemployment (generated by overproduction as well as mechanization of production), resulting in the popularization of a new word—stagflation.[2]

The issues that were driving the changes that began in the 1970s were not just economic; they were political, and indeed cultural, as well. While it might be argued that massive government spending during and after the Second World War was partly responsible for the prosperity of the era, critics of Keynes and his allies were getting louder. Among the most ardent was Austrian-born British economist and philosopher Friedrich August von Hayek, whose earlier work informed the thought of University of Chicago economist Milton Friedman. Friedman, a free-market fundamentalist, was one of the most persistent critics of Keynesian economic thought throughout the 1950s and '60s, someone who argued in favour of free markets and against the monetary policies of the era.[3] Of particular concern for Friedman and his fellow monetarists (as they are commonly called) was the increase in the postwar money supply, which they saw as the cause of the increasing inflation. Just as Keynesian economics had seemed to offer a panacea during the crisis of the Depression, Friedman's ideas were seen by some as a way out of burgeoning state and individual debt, inflation, regulatory regimes, and unemployment during the early 1970s.

As is often the case, economic ideas in a time of turbulence can translate into political change. Friedman and his disciples were not just champions of a certain kind of monetary policy, they were also evangelical free-market fundamentalists. What emerged in the 1970s was the gathering of various related ideas and ideals into an overarching economic and political approach often called neoliberalism. The concept of neoliberalism has been subject to much debate, but for our purposes a short definition will suffice. Neoliberalism can be understood as "a set of economic reform policies that...are concerned with the deregulation of the economy, the liberalization of trade and industry, and the privatization of state-owned enterprises."[4] Elizabeth Martinez and Arnoldo Garcia identify five essential tenets of neoliberalism: (1) rule of the market; (2) curbing of social service expenditures; (3) deregulation; 4) privatization; and 5) an emphasis on individual responsibility over the common or community good.[5]

The neoliberal monetarist critique of postwar state capitalism was at its essence a call for a return to laissez-faire free market capitalism and individualism of the classical liberal type. British prime minister Margaret Thatcher exemplified the ideology by musing that there was really no such thing as society, only individuals.[6] Neoliberals deemed the welfare state was responsible for sapping individuals of their work ethic, for costing hard-working taxpayers too much, and for empowering the state and its bloated, bureaucratic apparatus, resulting in intolerable and counterproductive state regulation. The market, by contrast, was deemed to be the supreme and ultimate decision maker for economic matters, with so-called market rationality used to direct the operations of many non-economic social institutions, including education, social services, and health care. Neoliberals argued that the proper role of the state was to provide a minimal degree of economic oversight, acting essentially as a referee to make sure that all sides obeyed the rules of the market. The private sector, competition, and the rule of the market were endowed with the exalted status of common sense and a kind of natural order of things, while government, public service, and the public sphere were denigrated and ridiculed as inherently inefficient, costly, a waste of taxpayers' hard-earned money.

The implementation of Keynesian and welfare-state spending, regulation, and taxation were never without controversy. As might be expected during times of crisis, such as the Great Depression and the global fight to defeat fascism, consensus was easier to come by, especially when compared to the postwar era, when Western economies were prosperous. From the perspective of the corporate stock owner, the post-1945 boom had been good for business; but for some, high-income tax rates and power sharing with unions and governments were becoming a problem. As one economist writes, "Corporate profits were relatively high throughout the late 1940s and 1950s and fell throughout the 1960s and 1970s to reach a low in 1982."[7] It is this context that allows the economic geographer David Harvey to argue that neoliberalism was nothing less than a revolution: "My view is that it refers to a class project that coalesced in the crisis of the 1970s. Masked by a lot of rhetoric about individual freedom, liberty, personal responsibility and the virtues of privatisation, the free market and free trade, it legitimised draconian policies designed to restore and consolidate capitalist class power."[8]

The late 1960s also brought other forms of social discontent and transformation. A neoconservative counter-revolution was fermenting, one that sought to restore what it saw as order, civility, respect, and family values amid an era of so-called hippie-inspired counterculture, anti-war protests, and calls for more democracy in many institutions. As control of major countries such as the United States, Britain, and Canada passed into the hands of conservative, neoliberal-oriented political parties, an era of deregulation, reduced government spending, program cuts, and privatization of public assets ensued. The change in economic policy was accompanied and bolstered by the popularization of neoconservative ideologies emphasizing individual freedom and responsibility, traditional family values (i.e., support for the traditional, patriarchal nuclear family), less state involvement (except in the military), and individual responsibility.

While international capital had always been highly mobile—a fact demonstrated as early as 1670 by the activities of the HBC—the late 1900s ushered in qualitative changes in this regard. International trade agreements overseen by global financial institutions and the geographic mobility of manufacturing and processing operations seeking the least costly labour zones transformed parts of the industrial heartland of North America into what has since become known as the Rust Belt. Electronic monitoring of production made it possible to have components and finished products transported anywhere by fleets of super-sized container ships. In addition, consumption and cultural patterns changed too, becoming more diverse as international foods and other commodities became more readily available, marking a shift away from traditional Western industrial domination. An additional characteristic of the era was the enormous growth of national and international financial markets and of the banking industry more broadly. Growth spurred by economic deregulation and the revolutions in electronics and computing and the growth of Internet and technology companies resulted in several worrisome economic downturns, as in 2000, when the NASDAQ benchmark lost about 46 percent of its value following the bursting of the so-called dot-com bubble.[9] The initial years of the twenty-first century were likewise marked by a housing boom in the United States, continued growth and deregulation of the financial and banking sectors, and the ever-increasing concentration and centralization of capital via corporate mergers and takeovers.

We now need to examine legislation related to agriculture and its impact on the family farm during this new stage of capitalism, covering the period from about 1970 to 2008.

THE TROUBLE WITH NORMAL

Although it would not come out until 1983, Canadian singer-songwriter Bruce Cockburn's song "The Trouble with Normal" contained a refrain rich in prescience for many family farmers in the 1970s: "The trouble with normal is it always gets worse." In the late 1970s, while watching the evening news on CBC Television, my mother asked a simple question: "When are things going to get back to normal?" Although the postwar period through to the late 1960s saw Western family farmers contend with fluctuating incomes and steadily rising prices, and although many of my parents' neighbours had held auction sales and left farming and moved to cities or out of the province, she was thinking back to an era of "happy days." As her children grew up during the 1950s and '60s, she felt many reasons to be thankful, including a measure of security that resulted from the social programs and prosperity noted above. Many of these programs did not impact her family directly, but she had a sense that the postwar Keynesian era was on of relative social stability and prosperity in the West. Although not her "cup of tea," Canada had been swept up in a wave of "Trudeaumania" in 1968, when the Liberals won a forty-six-seat majority in the House of Commons. The party's campaign theme of a "just society" resonated with her, and while she may not have paid attention to the new government's Speech from the Throne, she would have approved of the claim that it was "deeply and irrevocably committed to the objectives of a just society and a prosperous economy in a peaceful world."[10] When the Trudeau government brought down its first budget on October 22, 1968, this sense of optimism was leavened with some words of caution as it noted the need for a "severe restraint" on government spending and, further, that "We shall have to resist requests by members on both sides of the house, and from groups and individuals outside, to spend money for worthy purposes which we cannot afford to do along with the other things we are doing."[11] The Trudeau government's second budget, delivered in spring 1969, spoke in a worrisome fashion about faster-than-anticipated increases in federal spending in the form of transfers to provinces for health, welfare, and education, and the growing worries about increasing prices and inflation in general.[12]

THE 1970 TASK FORCE ON AGRICULTURE

The 1967 Speech from the Throne had seen the government call for the creation of "a Special Task Force under the Minister of Agriculture...to be charged with projecting agricultural goals for the future and recommending policies to meet these goals."[13] Before the speech, the cabinet had already decided that just such a task force "be appointed to make a comprehensive assessment of agricultural goals and policies, on the understanding that its terms of reference would be submitted to the Cabinet after the head of the Task Force had been appointed."[14] John Diefenbaker expressed disappointment that this was the government's only announcement regarding agriculture: "So far as agriculture is concerned it is a wonder that seconder of the address in reply said everything is well. All that is going to be done for the farmer, with prices falling and the cost of things he has to purchase rising, is a task force for agriculture, as if agriculture is not in enough difficulties now."[15] Following discussions with provincial ministers of agriculture, the terms of reference for the task force were established. The minister of agriculture outlined these in the House of Commons in March 1968; they included a comprehensive assessment of Canadian agriculture with attention to the income and welfare of farmers, technology, necessary adjustments, and policy recommendations.[16]

Unlike many Royal Commissions in the past, the task force did not hold any public hearings but instead contracted out a number of research projects and used existing research data. Minister of Agriculture Bud Olson received the final report in February 1970; however, it was not tabled until May.[17]

The nearly 475-page report ticks many boxes in the definition of neoliberalism noted above by advocating and recommending market dominance, restraints on government expenditures, deregulation, privatization, and an emphasis on individual responsibility. In introducing its key recommendations, the report lays out the philosophical principles that inform them:

> The obvious keynote that permeates all our recommendations is that the government should intelligently assist an orderly and planned transition that will encourage agricultural adjustment to achieve the largest possible gains at the lowest possible tangible and intangible costs. Another theme running through all our recommendations is that governments should

reduce their direct involvement in agriculture thereby encouraging farmers, farm organizations and agribusiness to improve their management and leadership functions and stand more self-sufficiently on their own. We assume that agriculture should be operated much as any other industry. If this is not feasible, the agricultural industry invites a degree of government paternalism that agriculture may not want.[18]

At the same time, in making suggestions for government involvement in the transformation of farming and agriculture, the report also disavowed any adherence to what it called a "simplistic laissez-faire system." Indeed, under the task force's recommendations, the government would play an active role in achieving several of the report's key recommendations, including the following:

1. The surpluses must be controlled and reduced to manageable proportions by reducing production drastically, if necessary. Where alternatives exist, production resources must be shifted to more promising market opportunities. Where such alternatives cannot be found, land and other resources must be retired.

2. Governments should provide temporary, limited programs of assistance for the crop switching and land retirement, necessary to cut surplus production. At the same time this Report emphasizes programs to expand demand, particularly on the international scene.

3. Agricultural subsidies and price supports that are not effective and efficient in achieving worthwhile high priority objectives should be phased out.

4. Younger non-viable farmers should be moved out of farming through temporary programs of welfare, education, and provision

of jobs in other sectors of the economy. Older farmers should be given assistance to ensure that they have at least a "livable" standard of living.[19]

The report, finally, lauded the history and accomplishments of the family farm—but it is worth noting that such praise was by no means unqualified:

> The family farm has given valuable service in opening up and settling the country and has been the backbone of rural society. In addition, it has been credited with being the most efficient unit for agricultural production. There is no doubt that interested and dedicated management and work by the operator and his family have wrought wonders. As we have suggested before, perhaps these contributions were part of the "subsidy" given by rural people to agricultural production; a "subsidy" that is now fast declining and bringing increased costs of production despite handsome improvements in labour productivity. Moreover, while the average farm operator could operate a small farm business at reasonably low costs, given hard work, dedication, long hours, low returns and a little luck, the situation alters with rapid technological change, low and unstable prices, rising input costs and improving off-farm opportunities for members of the farm family. Inflation and the cost-price squeeze imply that individual farm enterprises must continuously expand and improve efficiency in order to maintain or increase incomes. Unfortunately, many farmers have too small earnings to be able to save or to justify borrowing sufficient amounts to finance the required expansion. They fall further behind in the competitive race, even though they make some improvements in productivity. Those who fall behind tend to receive declining real and relative incomes and may either become part of the rural poor with economically "unviable" farms or be forced out of agriculture altogether.[20]

On the question of the fate of many farmers, the task force viewed a radical restructuring as inevitable. Indeed, it accepted the predictions of the Department of Agriculture regarding the future number of farms. The department estimated that this would drop nationally from 623,091 in 1951 to 315,310 in 1980, a reduction of about 50 percent. Not all farms would be equally impacted by these trends, however, as the expectation was that the cohort of large farms (at that time this was defined as farms whose annual sales were over $10,000) would increase from 21,243 to 189,186, an approximately ninefold increase. The cohort of small commercial farms (with annual sales between $2,500 and $4,999) would drop from 144,828 to 15,765, slightly more than a ninefold decline. The report euphemistically referred to the increasing number of large farms and the decline in the number of small farms as the "scissors effect."[21] Yet as the report made clear, the situation for small farms was even worse than this data would suggest: "The Task Force is of the opinion that the projections of the CDA [Canadian Department of Agriculture] in regard both to numbers and 'scissors effect' are conservative. If the recommendations of the Task Force are implemented, changes would be more rapid than projected by CDA and it is likely that by 1980 there will be fewer than 315,000 farms in Canada. Corresponding to this accelerated rate of change will be an even larger proportion of farms in the largest size category."[22] If the recommendations of the task force were to be implemented, it would mean a radical restructuring of Canadian agriculture, including Prairie family farming.

Given the report's radical recommendations, the reception it received in the House of Commons was somewhat surprising. In answer to one question, Minister Olson indicated that the government would not ignore the report; indeed, he noted that if one were to look carefully, one would see "a great deal of similarity the between the contents of the report and measures before the House."[23] The report was mentioned in a debate on the cost of living in September 1973, with Mr. Les Benjamin of the New Democratic Party (NDP)—which had succeeded the CCF after its dissolution in 1961—noting in passing that the task force had recommended "at least one-third of the farmers in this country had to go," while Mr. Jack Horner of the Progressive Conservatives quoted the report's call for assistance to younger farmers as they transitioned out of agriculture as part of a criticism of excessive government spending.[24] The lack of a systematic government response was related to the fact that the report was really recommending an end to state support for agriculture, and "Governments did not view as politically viable the Task Force recommendations that would have set agricultural policies in such a direction."[25] With hindsight, this observation may have been premature, because what was to unfold, more by stealth than according to any explicit articulation, were a series of measures that would in fact lead to the very outcomes the task force had advocated. If the government were to undertake actions to implement the recommendations of the task force after October 1972, it would have had to do so as a minority government dependent on the NDP and its strong Western base.

FIGHTING INFLATION

By the end of the 1960s, it was becoming apparent that not all was well in the global capitalist system. Canada was no exception. Between 1960 and 1964, the country's consumer price index had risen an average of 1.4 percent per year; between 1970 and 1974, that figure rose to 7.9 percent, spurred by an increase of 12.4 percent in 1974.[26] The question of food prices was discussed extensively in the House of Commons in the spring of 1973 before the government announced the establishment of the Food Prices Review Board later that year.[27] In its final report for 1976, the board noted that the consumer price index had increased by 14.6 percent in 1973, 16.3 percent in 1974, and 12.9 percent in 1975. In October 1975, Prime Minister Trudeau met with provincial premiers before addressing the entire nation to announce a system of mandatory wage and price controls aimed at curbing inflation.[28] Minister of Finance Donald Macdonald formally introduced Bill C-73, the *Anti-Inflation Act*, that same month, and soon after the government created the Anti-Inflation Board.[29] The irony of this announcement was that Trudeau had campaigned in the 1974 election against wage and price controls, giving the Progressive Conservatives an opportunity to point out what they saw as a Liberal about-face.

The issues of inflation and the cost-price squeeze were of obvious concern to all farmers, and yet in the rancorous debate that followed, much of the public conversation tended to centre on what was being controlled—whether prices or wages. Remarks by Saskatchewan member Lorne Nystrom's illustrate the NDP's position at the time: "This bill is one that will adequately control the wages and salaries of workers. On the other hand, it will have very little effect in controlling prices, profits, dividends and professional fees and incomes of people derived from investments and corporate profits." The nation was split on the issue, with support for controls coming from organizations such as the Canadian Chamber of Commerce and the Canadian Bar Association, while the Canadian Labour Congress, representing 1.9 million workers, was opposed.[30] The Liberal majority nonetheless assured the bill's passage in the House.[31]

WHOSE CANADA, ANYWAY?

We previously noted that the Royal Commission on Canada's Economic Prospects, helmed by Walter Gordon in the 1950s, indicated a concern with the levels of foreign investment in Canada. In the early 1960s, Gordon withdrew from formal politics to become involved in another study of the future of Canadian industry.[32] The Task Force on the Structure of Canadian Industry was chaired by University of Toronto economist Mel Watkins, who later noted that "the task force shifted the debate on foreign ownership toward more interventionist policy, leading, in due course, to the creation of the Canada Development Corporation and the Foreign Investment Review Agency."[33] The issue of Canadian nationalism and control of the Canadian economy was, at this moment in history, was of greater concern to members of the Left; however, as we have noted, conservatives such as George Grant and Donald Creighton were also concerned about the political implications of American domination of the Canadian economy.

TOO MUCH GRAIN?
LOWER INVENTORIES FOR TOMORROW

As the 1970 Task Force on Agriculture was doing its work, farmers continued to be plagued by low prices and surplus product. In the fall of 1970, the Speech from the Throne announced that "the LIFT program has removed a substantial portion of the accumulated wheat surplus, which was inhibiting the international wheat market, and has encouraged a healthy diversification of agricultural activities." It also noted that more programs will be introduced to "assist in the adjustment to changes in this vital sector of our economy."[34] The one-time, $100 million LIFT, or Lower Inventories for Tomorrow, program, which sought to make acreage-based payments to encourage farmers to take some land out of wheat production to help reduce the wheat surplus, had been enacted without legislation. Since there was no legislation, farmers were notified by a bulletin explaining the program.[35] Information about the one-year program was duly sent to all permit book holders indicating that the payment would be $6 per acre for converting wheat to summer fallow and $10 for converting wheat acreage to perennial forage, thus keeping it out of production longer.[36] The program was controversial from the start; indeed, even before the announcement was made, Mr. John Burton correctly noted that in actuality a number of massive international grain transactions, including a huge purchase of US grain by the Soviet Union, had raised wheat prices and enhanced international demand resulting in the surplus being drawn down.[37] Nevertheless, in the fall of 1970 the minister of agriculture, Otto Lang, reported that 94,525 farmers had participated, receiving about $27.5 million, though he indicated that the government had no plan to carry the program into 1971.[38]

The LIFT program's effectiveness, and indeed its very purpose, were ultimately called into question by events external to Canada. As conditions changed, the government was not spared the wrath of politicians like John Diefenbaker, then still a member of the House of Commons, who referred to it as a "complete farce" that ended up costing Western farmers between $350 and $500 million in lost wheat sales. Minister Lang, for his part, defended the program as a specific remedy for a specific problem, but with the changed conditions he now hoped an additional nine million acres of wheat, barley, and rapeseed would be planted to ensure sufficient supply.[39]

THE *FARM PRODUCTS MARKETING AGENCIES ACT*, 1970–71

The Liberal government of Pierre Trudeau was accused of ignoring or misunderstanding family grain farmers in the West, but the same cannot be said for the overall Canadian agricultural sector. In October 1970, the government introduced a bill facilitating the establishment of national marketing agencies for a wide range of farm products. The bill, essentially the same as a similar one in the previous parliamentary session that was never passed, was wide in its application, as the minister of agriculture explained on second reading, geared to "the establishment of national marketing agencies for farm products." [40] The bill's final passage has been described as a "marathon debate, extending over twenty-one months and culminating in two all-night sessions of the House of Commons."[41] The resulting act established the National Farm Products Marketing Council, which would eventually oversee, in the words of the minister, both a council and "hopefully marketing agencies" for many commodities.[42]

The debates and controversies that surrounded the bill illustrated emerging ideological differences among the political parties on the relationship between the government and the agricultural sector. For example, Progressive Conservative Jack Horner argued that the bill would facilitate the establishment of marketing boards across many commodities, noting that Prime Minister Trudeau and his government were a "power-hungry government: and determined to interfere in the market." Others, such as the NDP's A.P. Gleave, worried about the possibility that farmers' interests would lost in the mix when agribusiness, processing interests, and consumers sit down to control production and pricing.[43] The matter was the subject of an extensive, thirty-seven-day-long debate in front of the Standing Committee on Agriculture; this included a national tour and a full committee's report containing thirty amendments.[44] The bill eventually returned to Parliament on December 28, 1971. There were multiple votes on amendments before it passed at 6:42 a.m. on December 30, 1971.[45]

Why, one might ask, was the federal government so prepared to burn political capital to have this measure passed? One reason has to do with what has been called a potential national unity crisis caused by a "chicken and egg war."[46] This was the result of producers of eggs and broiler chickens in various provinces competing for markets beyond their provincial boundaries, particularly producers in Ontario and Quebec. The ensuing conflict saw Manitoba seize eggs coming into the province from British Columbia, an action that was eventually subject to a Supreme Court ruling that a province could not restrict products from another province entering its markets. Nurse and Muirhead, having analyzed the various actors and interests involved, concluded that, "despite their differences, most egg and poultry farmers were eventually able to find consensus in order to establish a national marketing scheme."[47] In her article focusing on the *Farm Products Marketing Agencies Act*, Grace Skogstad offers an assessment of the circumstances that allowed the government to take action:

> If generalizations from one case study are possible, the lessons of the FPMAA [*Farm Products Marketing Agencies Act*] are that the CDA [Canadian Department of Agriculture] and the Minister of Agriculture will be dominant in formulating agricultural policy under the following circumstances: when the federal government enjoys a strong public mandate; the federal cabinet itself is united behind the federal Minister of Agriculture; the policy proposed is one that most provincial governments support or one that the provinces of Quebec and Ontario both commend; the provinces themselves are not in conflict with one another; the role of the public and the consumer are minor, and consequently, that of other government

departments (such as Consumer Affairs) is as well; and the policy is a response to a crisis.[48]

THE *PRAIRIE GRAIN ADVANCE PAYMENTS ACT*, 1971

Other efforts were undertaken to throw lifelines to Prairie producers in the early 1970s. One was advance payments on grain before it was sold to provide income when it was needed. In April 1971, Otto Lang introduced an amendment to the *Prairie Grain Advance Payments Act*.[49] Lang noted the amendment sought to extend the advance payments to cover rye, flax, and rapeseed, removing what he called "the ancient special bias toward wheat compared with other grains" and thereby allowing producers to make more direct, market-condition-based decisions and diversify their production. In addition, the bill—under the title *Amendments Respecting Rate per Bushel, Emergency Payments, Extension and Application to Rye, Flaxseed and Rapeseed*, or Bill C-239 for short—provided for government interest charges on farmers who had secured an advance and who paid it back in cash, as opposed to a deduction from their returns on delivery of grain. Although the debate was rather subdued, Mr. Stanley Korchinski, of the Progressive Conservatives, suggested that the bill was about trying to control what farmers produce by paving the way for the inclusion of rye, flax, and rapeseed under the CWB.[50] The question of extending the Wheat Board's powers was once again raised by Mr. Horner: "The concept that flax, rye and rapeseed should be under the jurisdiction of the Wheat Board is wrong." He went on to note that farmers were losing money on the barley they sold through the CWB. This turned out to be an important comment as it suggested a shift in the Progressive Conservative Party's historical support for orderly marketing under the CWB. On the other hand, the NDP had different concerns relating to changes to the way CWB quotas were to be used in determining payment and the possible negative implications for small farmers.[51]

FEED GRAINS AND THE
CANADIAN WHEAT BOARD, 1973

For most of the twentieth century, commodity specialization was a major trend in Canadian agriculture as a whole and certainly among Western family farmers. As the Prairies were settled, wheat and cereal grain production in Ontario and Quebec declined, but beef production grew in both provinces. Initially, it seemed that the Prairies would dominate wheat, cereal grain, and livestock production, but a series of factors, including periodic ferocious winters and the inappropriateness of large-scale, Texas-style open range ranching, meant that cattle production did not become the dominant form of agriculture in the region. By 1910, most of the largest ranches had been broken up as settlement expanded and homesteads came to occupy the open range, forcing ranchers to buy land to remain in operation.[52] In subsequent years, however, while cattle production and ranching did continue to grow in the West, factors such as population concentration and market demand resulted in the growth of the beef, pork, dairy, poultry, and egg industries in Ontario and Quebec. Feed grain is a necessary input for these industries. In the early 1970s, feed grain from Western Canada was marketed through the CWB, whose mandate it was to maximize revenues for grain producers, although in the West farmers could sell grain privately (called off-board sales) to each other and feed mills. In the early 1970s, in the face of the grain glut and the drop in prices, some livestock and dairy producers outside the Prairies began to agitate for access to more and less costly Prairie feed grain outside of the CWB, since the Wheat Board used international prices. The issue was raised in the House of Commons on numerous occasions, with claims that Central Canadian farmers were being discriminated against.[53] It even threatened to destroy a venerable farm lobby group, the Canadian Federation of Agriculture, as it attempted to reconcile regional differences.[54] The resulting rancour seemed to be splitting the country along regional lines, as a Quebec member of Parliament claimed feed grains selling for forty-five dollars a tonne in Manitoba cost eighty in Quebec, while a Western member later argued that the CWB had served Quebec farmers well.[55]

The minister in charge of the CWB, pressed to act, promised in the fall of 1973 an "equitable relationship in feed grain prices."[56] In so doing, he was echoing a similar commitment contained in the Speech from the Throne earlier that year. For some Western grain growers the announcement confirmed their fears that the Liberals, official statements to the contrary notwithstanding, were prepared to undermine the powers of the CWB. The announcement was first made outside the House but tabled in mid-September 1973. The action removed restrictions on interprovincial sales of feed grains and the power of the CWB to set prices for feed grains. Prices for domestic grains would be set by the market, although the CWB would still control international sales. The announcement was made at a low-profile event in Regina, leading supporters of the CWB to suggest that the measure was indeed an attempt to undermine the Wheat Board. Some argued that the changes would cost Western farmers income, while others saw it as an indication that the Liberals, accounting for only seven of sixty-eight Western members of Parliament, were out of touch with the region.[57] Manitoba's provincial minister of agriculture called the action a "sell-out to the producers in Eastern Canada," while the National Farmers Union called Minister Lang the Benedict Arnold of Western farmers.[58]

Two small amendments were made to the *Canadian Wheat Board Act* in the years that followed. The first came from the Senate and dealt with the date of the final payment. Mr. Horner, speaking for the Progressive Conservatives, still indicated support for the CWB, his earlier comments notwithstanding. He repeated what he said was a common rhetorical question in western Canada—that is, "whether the Wheat Board works for farmers, and the reply to that question is yes, its job is to serve farmers."[59] The later amendment, coming in 1976, had to do with the process for electing the CWB advisory committee and the pooling of different grades.[60] A more controversial amendment came in 1977 with Bill C-34, which would allow a voluntary pool for canola (then called rapeseed). The bill, introduced by Mr. Otto Lang, who by now had assumed the role of minister of transport, was supported by Mr. Alvin Hamilton, speaking for the Progressive Conservatives, but opposed by Mr. Lorne Nystrom, speaking for the NDP, the latter arguing that the bill would diminish the capacity of the CWB to act for all farmers.[61] An important issue was clearly in the making.

AGRICULTURE ON THE BACK BURNER

The 1960s and early 1970s are often remembered as a period of cultural, social, and political change. A focal point of attention in Canada was Quebec, where years of political repression under the auspices of provincial governments headed by Maurice Duplessis in collaboration with the Catholic Church were blown away by the Quiet Revolution and a radical reawakening of an always-present Québécois nationalism. A variety of militant political action groups emerged in the province during this period, culminating in the Front de libération du Québec, and the infamous October Crisis of 1970 involving the kidnapping of a British trade commissioner and the murder of a provincial cabinet minister. Although not germane to the topic at hand, it is important to keep the issue of national unity in mind as a major focal point, if not an obsession, of Ottawa's as we examine some federal actions at the time.[62] In such an environment, one can imagine that the concerns of Prairie family farmers might take second seat at best.

Prime Minister Trudeau opened the thirtieth session of the Parliament of Canada in 1974 with a substantial agenda including stabilizing incomes for farmers and fishers and "the establishment of Petro-Canada, the national petroleum corporation."[63] On introducing a bill to create Petro-Canada, the government stated that its purpose was to ensure for Canadians adequate and reliable supplies of petroleum at reasonable prices, while the Progressive Conservatives immediately attacked the proposal, calling it inappropriate government involvement in the economy.[64] Mr. T.C. Douglas gave perhaps the definitive statement on his party's position: "I want to make it perfectly clear that we in the NDP not only do not object but we welcome the wide powers and financial investments which are authorized by the passage of this legislation."[65] With the support of the NDP, Petro-Canada was born on July 10, 1975. However, not all was well down on the farm at the beginning of the 1970s.

The era was also one of pending economic crisis as inflation soared, oil prices increased, and government deficits grew. In his 1995 budget, Minister of Finance Paul Martin noted that, while staying the overall "fiscal course," "it is essential that the government should exercise greater restraint over its own spending." Rather than just relying on budget cuts, the government introduced legislation in the form of the *Government Expenditure Restraint Act*. In the debate that followed the bill's introduction, Max Saltsman noted that it should be called "a Tory conversion bill" since it contained the measures for which the Progressive Conservatives had "been asking for a long time." He suggested that since the Liberals are "bowing to Conservative pressure," people may as well vote Conservative and get the real thing.[66] These comments were perhaps informed by recent discussions about potential privatizations, including of Air Canada and the CBC. A member from Saskatchewan warned that the overall direction of the government would result in a scaling down of the Crow Rate to the detriment of farmers.[67]

THE *AGRICULTURAL STABILIZATION ACT*, 1975

Even as the federal Liberals struggled with deficits and inflation, and as a consequence moved in the direction of increased fiscal restraint, they sought to stabilize farm incomes. Back in 1958, the Diefenbaker government had created the Agricultural Stabilization Board to determine the amount of government subsidies that should be paid when prices fell below a certain benchmark. In winter 1975, the Liberals amended and updated the legislation.[68] While debating the measure, the minister of agriculture, Mr. Ed Whelan, spoke of the need for price guarantees in the form of floor prices that would be calculated based on a specific formula (i.e., 90 percent of the average price over five years for certain commodities). At the time the minister noted that the new legislation was required in the face of rapidly increasing input costs, but that the limited scope of the bill was appropriate since many products were covered by other protection measures, such as butter and cheese under the Canadian Dairy Commission and eggs under the Farm Products Marketing Agencies. The measure added industrial milk and cream, corn, soybeans, oats, and barley outside CWB areas.[69] The bill was extensively debated and passed in the summer of 1975.[70]

THE ONSET OF RESTRAINT: EARLY DAYS

In November 1976, James Faulkner, then president of the Treasury Board of Canada, introduced Bill C-19 "to amend or repeal certain statutes to enable restraint of government expenditures." During the subsequent debate, Robert Andres (who had subsequently replaced Faulkner as president of the Treasury Board) referred to actions taken the previous year to reduce government expenditures and eliminate some government activities, including salary freezes for members of Parliament, judges, and some civil servants. The measure also eliminated programs such as Opportunities for Youth, Information Canada, and Company Young Canadians, while ending the indexing of family allowances. Crown corporations were required to seek financing in the private sector. Included in the expenditure-restraint bill were changes to funding for the *Western Grain Stabilization Act* and amendments to the *Railway Act*, including the removal of the 1960 cost ceiling for moving grain east and the 1966 ceiling on flour transport shipped east through Atlantic ports.[71] The era of neoliberalism was dawning in Canada, and the attacks on the Keynesian welfare state and associated social and economic programs would soon inform agricultural legislation.

THE CROW'S NEST PASS AGREEMENT IN QUESTION: THE SNAVELY COMMISSION, 1975

With grain transportation the perennial issue in the West and fiscal restraint now on the agenda, it was no surprise that in spring 1975 an Order-in-Council established yet another commission "to conduct an inquiry to determine the costs and revenues of grain traffic and the relationships of such costs and revenues."[72] The purpose of the Snavely Commission was to investigate total costs and revenues, examine railway practices, develop a cost profile, and study the impact of railway spending under different grain-handling and transportation systems.[73] Given the commission's mandate, it necessarily investigated the impact of the Crow Rate on railroad operations and revenues. While the subsequent report did not outright recommend that the Crow Rate be abandoned, it concluded that the Crow Rate (also called the statutory rate) had resulted in the railroad companies losing money and had hampered efficiency in the entire system.[74] A comment in the report illustrates how close Snavely came to recommending elimination of the Crow Rate altogether: "While fully aware that the following comments may be construed by some to be outside my terms of reference, I am compelled to note that present rail rate structure for statutory grain is virtually devoid of monetary incentives for efficient use of the transportation resource and, perhaps even worse, monetary penalties for inefficient use of that resource."[75]

The Snavely Commission also addressed the issue of rail system rationalization. Its report suggested that the Crow Rate was hampering the loading and use of longer trains composed of railcars carrying identical commodities (known as unit trains). Unit trains can be more efficiently loaded through larger handling facilities, allowing the railroads to spend less time and resources picking up and shuttling railcars from different locations. A move in this direction, however, would require a restructuring of existing rail networks: "Thus, line abandonment will cause a significant reduction in the line-related costs per carload and per ton—particularly if the grain dependent lines retained in the system experience an increase in density as a result."[76] The report was tabled in December 1976, and while it is difficult to identify an immediate and specific legislative outcome, Ralph Goodale later noted that the document was favourably received and would play a role in policy and action.[77] Perhaps the most important point is that the issues of rail line abandonment and the future of the Crow Rate were raised as matters of public and legislative debate.

THE *WESTERN GRAIN STABILIZATION ACT*, 1976

In 1974, Otto Lang had introduced the *Western Grain Stabilization Act*, a measure that allocated $250 million to stabilize net proceeds from the production and sale of Western grain.[78] Lang had acknowledged the "grave difficulties" facing Western farmers as far back as 1968 and 1969 and explained that the government had been studying the entire industry, including grain handling and transportation. He noted that Prairie grains face unique problems due to the fact that a high proportion of the product is exported and that other stabilization measures were therefore ineffective. Western grains were no longer to be covered by the *Agricultural Stabilization Act*.[79] The bill operationalized a voluntary 2 percent levy paid by farmers on the sale of grain, which would be matched by government to create a fund out of which payments were to be made. The fund would be self-sustaining based on the contributions of producers and the initial government allocation, with payments to individual producers limited by their contributions over the previous three years. The measure initially had an 80 percent participation rate.[80] The 1976 bill is important because it signalled a different approach to farm support: "The WGSA [*Western Grain Stabilization Act*] was introduced in Canada in 1976 as a way of reducing the income instability facing prairie grain producers. The WGSA is distinguished from many other stabilization programs in that, instead of trying to stabilize prices, it attempts to stabilize grain producers' net cash flow."[81] The bill was also important because it was in large part financed directly by producers.

THE FUTURE OF RAIL LINES:
THE HALL COMMISSION, 1975–77

As was noted above, one of the major physical and economic changes on the Plains during the first three decades of the nineteenth century was the tremendous expansion of railroad networks across the Prairies. The cost of maintaining this extensive network and the likelihood that railroads might start to abandon rail lines was already an issue in 1933 when the minister of railways and canals introduced a bill, subsequently passed without debate, requiring railway companies to get the approval of the Board of Railway Commissioners before they could abandon any railroads.[82] As the rural population continued to decline in the 1960s, and some rail lines were consequently abandoned, the government felt it necessary to address this issue head-on. To this end, it presented the *National Transportation Act* in 1967. Following the passage of that act, the federal government used Orders-in-Council to prevent massive rail line abandonment by allowing the railways to jettison only 1,800 miles of track.[83] As the issue continued to simmer, in 1974 the government took further action by protecting over 12,000 miles, shielding a further 6,282 miles from abandonment until 1977, and allowing just 525 miles to be put up for abandonment.[84]

In the meantime, the government established a Royal Commission headed by the eminent Supreme Court justice Emmett Hall. The word "eminent" is to be taken seriously in this case, because before he was appointed to the highest court in 1973 Hall had led a Royal Commission on Health Care in Canada, whose report was largely responsible for the implementation of a national system of public health care in Canada. For his work concerning the railways, Justice Hall was aided by five commissioners, a large research staff, and commission council. The commission received 37 briefs from companies, governments, and farm organizations, held 77 local hearings and 14 regional hearings, and reviewed nearly 1,200 submissions.[85] Its final report is far-ranging, covering the history of the grain trade and transportation, producer characteristics, the elevator network, the overall shipping system, transportation costs, the railway network, and more. Especially relevant for our purposes are the commission's recommendations regarding the retention and abandonment of rail lines. It was clear that abandonment would occur, but not at the whim of the rail companies. Volume 1, chapter 13 contains a summary of the commission's recommendations, including allowance for "the abandonment in stages to the year 1981 of 2,165 miles of grain-related branch lines" while "1,813 miles of prairie branch lines become part of the basic rail network, guaranteed to the year 2000." Further, the report recommended "that the remaining 2,344 miles of prairie branch lines be placed under a new body, the Prairie Rail Authority. Continuance of lines in this category would be conditioned on need."[86] If implemented, these recommendations would mean a radical restructuring of grain transportation and handling on the Prairies.

Regarding the costs of grain transportation, the report states that "the railway must be compensated for the cost of moving grain by rail. The railways must be then responsible for the adequate maintenance and any upgrading of lines now within the basic network or subsequently added to the basic network, guaranteed to the year 2000." In turn, the new Prairie Rail Authority would have the power to use general revenue funds from the federal government to operate and maintain branch lines not part of the basic network.[87] On an issue that was becoming contentious, freight rates and the statutory Crow's Nest Pass Agreement, Hall was clear: "Regardless of what rate may be set for the transport of grain to export position that rate must be statutory, not variable. Anything else would be a violation of promises made to the producers of Western Canada. How the difference between the new rate and the Crow's Nest Rate will be apportioned between the Government and the producer is, of course, a matter for Government decision."[88] The report was nonetheless clear about the CWB remaining the core marketing agency: "Throughout the hearings there was almost universal support for the Canadian Wheat Board. There is probably no single institution in Western Canada which affects the daily lives of farmers more than the Canadian Wheat Board. In some cases, there was mild criticism of some board practices in the areas of selling, car allocation, application of quotas, etc. However, there is no doubt that the board is accepted as the producers' friend."[89]

The day after the report was tabled by Minister Lang, in May 1977, a member of the Progressive Conservative Party moved to commend Hall for the recommendation regarding the retention of the Crow Rate, and to direct the minister of transport to have the CWB make a statement about implementation. Another Progressive Conservative, Alvin Hamilton, stated that the Hall Report will go down as a sort of Magna Carta for Western Canada. The prime minister replied that he could not comment on the implementation of the complex report but agreed Judge Hall should be commended. Otto Lang seconded that commendation while noting he would shortly be putting forth proposals related to various recommendations.[90] In the days and months that followed, the House heard a lot of back and forth on implementation, worries about the future of the Crow Rate, and the details of rail line abandonment. At one point, Minister Lang stated that the Crow Rate would not be abandoned and then repeated the statement when challenged.[91] Minister Lang was pressed on the issue again when he was asked, "Is it the Minister's policy to abandon the Crowsnest Pass freight rate as set out in statute and as it applies to the export of grain?" Lang answered, "No, Mr. Speaker," but then equivocated by stating that it is a complex issue that must be settled in the West.[92] At another point, John Diefenbaker pushed Lang on remarks that had been in the press about the abandonment of the Crow Rate, to which Mr. Lang responded that he had been misquoted.[93] The Hall Report continued to be the topic of questions in the House, with Mr. Lang noting again that it was a complex report, and that he would be coming back with details.[94]

The theme of government restraint was becoming prominent as the 1970s closed, including in the 1978 Speech from the Throne, which indicated $500 million in government spending cuts along with a further $2 billion the following year. It was claimed that this was all in the interests of a leaner government and "to encourage a more vigorous expansion of the private sector by reducing government's share of the national wealth."[95] In the subsequent debate, the leader of the Opposition, Joe Clark, criticized the government for apparently its timid approach to both restraint and dealing with what the Progressive Conservatives saw as an excessive government presence in the economy. Clark noted the existence of 385 Crown corporations, which he claimed amounted to a "statist government," since governments should only intervene in the economy as a last resort when the private sector cannot function.[96]

Before much action could be taken on the budget that followed, the House was dissolved, and an election called for spring 1979. As a result of the election, a new minority Progressive Conservative government led by Prime Minister Joe Clark opened Parliament on October 9, 1979. In the Speech from the Throne, the new government promised to improve federal-provincial relations and stimulate the economy by reducing "the burden of government on the economy by better controlling expenditures." Additionally, the size of the civil service was to be reduced, and there was a commitment "to offer for private purchase and ownership Crown corporations operating in areas where direct government intervention is no longer necessary."[97] The House reconvened on a sombre note with many tributes to the recently deceased John Diefenbaker.

The question of the Crow Rate remained an issue on which there was some apparent confusion regarding the new government's position. For example, Les Benjamin asked about members of the Progressive Conservative Party recently musing about eliminating the Crow Rate and about a related task force on the issue the party had set up. Mr. Don Mazankowski, a member of the new government, simply said he had not seen the report, but when questioned later, he indicated his party would conduct further consultation on the question.[98] The president of the Treasury Board, questioned about a report on the Crow Rate, answered that such a study had occurred, but said that he would need the permission of those participating before releasing it. The minister of transportation used an interesting phrase in answer to one member's question when he said, "it is the intention of the Department of Transport to preserve for farmers the *value* of the Crowsnest rates" (emphasis added).[99] In November 1979, during an Opposition day in the House, NDP leader Ed Broadbent introduced a motion that the House condemn the government for not supporting farmers in a number of ways, including the apparently impending abandonment of the Crow Rate.[100] In November 1979, the prime minister was pressed regarding his party's commitment to maintaining the Crow Rate given the benefits of such a system, but after a testy exchange he would commit only to seeing that farmers continued to enjoy those benefits.[101]

The Clark government's first budget was tabled on December 11, 1979, by Finance Minister John Crosbie. It indicated that the government was set to embark in a clear fiscal direction: "The fundamental objective of our fiscal plan is to bring about a steady reduction in our deficits."[102] In order to accomplish this, expenditures were to be reduced to the tune of $1.75 billion per year until 1983–84, an excise tax on gas and diesel would be introduced, private-sector growth encouraged through a variety of tax measures, and trade stimulated through multinational trade agreements. Before any of the promised measures could be enacted, however, the Clark government went down in a vote of confidence on the budget on December 14. In the subsequent February 1980 election, the Liberals were returned with a majority government.

The first Speech from the Throne following the Liberal victory in 1980 contained an ominous question: "Will Canada still exist as a country at the end of this decade or will it have been broken up by the tensions of our past and recent history?"[103] The context was an ongoing debate and referendum campaign in Quebec over the province's sovereignty and possible separation from Canada. The result of that referendum, held in May 1980, was reasonably reassuring, although Quebec nationalism and potential sovereignty would remain on the national agenda for years to come. The Throne Speech also announced the continuation of expenditure restraint and deficit reduction, as well as plans to create a new agricultural export corporation and address issues in the transportation and handling of Prairie grain. There was also a pledge regarding co-operation in the context of concerns about inadequate Western representation in government. In the budget that followed, the word "restraint" figured more prominently than in previous budgets, as when the Liberals promised "the maintenance of government expenditures within the rate of growth in the economy to ensure that the federal government does not take up an ever-growing proportion of the flow of income," or pledged, "over the period to fiscal 1983–84, a steady reduction in the government deficit and financial requirements."[104] The next budget, a little over a year later, saw the finance minister return to a set of similar themes: "The first is the need for restraint on the part of the government and restraint on the part of all Canadians. For our part, I believe we must reduce our deficit and our borrowing requirements substantially, even more than I proposed a year ago."[105]

In terms of the impact on agriculture, the main budget item was a commitment to keep the borrowing costs for loans from the Farm Credit Corporation five percentage points below the normal borrowing rate, and at a "special rate of 11 and ¾ percent." This was in the context of 1981, when the Canadian mortgage rates hit 21.46 percent in September.[106]

If these Liberal budgets paid little attention to agriculture, the same cannot be said for the oil and energy sector in Canada. Amid rising world oil prices, the April 1980 Speech from the Throne announced the government's intention to develop a "program of action" that, among other things, was designed "to achieve security of energy supply at a fair price for all Canadians" and "increase Canadian ownership and control of our economy."[107] The speech noted that the objective of the new policy would be 50 percent Canadian ownership in the energy sector. The details were provided in the budget speech in which the National Energy Program (NEP) was introduced.[108] While the budget spoke of security of supply, greater opportunity for Canadian participation, and fairness in price and revenue sharing, the NEP was to become a dominant political issue for several years, pushing any number of other important issues to the side.

In what is surely an understatement, the response of Canada's main oil producing province, to say nothing of the oil industry writ large, has been described as follows: "These measures—aimed at shifting control of Canada's oil resources away from the provinces and private industry, and toward the federal government—irked Alberta and its oil industry players and workers."[109] The response included a massive anti-NEP ideological campaign, production cuts in Alberta, a virtual investment strike by multinational oil capital, and increased Western alienation, the latter exemplified by the popularity of bumper stickers emblazoned with the phrase "Let the Eastern Bastards Freeze in the Dark." At the Supreme Court, Alberta successfully argued that the federal government could not tax provincial resources.[110] After its victory in 1984, the new Progressive Conservative government headed by Brian Mulroney would quickly set about dismantling the NEP.[111] For our purposes, it is enough to simply note the shifting priorities of federal governments increasingly and decisively away from Prairie agriculture as a priority in favour of matters relating to continental and global economic matters. Given the uproar that surrounded the NEP, it is small wonder Western agriculture was not a particular priority in the years that followed.

In the 1981 budget, an additional $50 million was allocated to the FCC to allow it to offer reduced interest rates on loans. The measure was essentially a lifeline to farmers facing the exorbitant interest rates of the day.[112] In terms of farming, the next year's budget again focused more on emergency measures. An additional $100 million was allocated to farmers in difficulty and an increase made to the loan fund for the FCC, allowing it to offer an additional $200 million in loans at a rate 4 percent below the bank rate.[113] In 1983, the tune was the same in that the agricultural sector was to "benefit" from an additional $100 million for FCC loans, again at lower than prevailing interest rates. In the words of the finance minister,

> In recognition of the exceptional financial difficulties being faced by many farmers, the government is also extending tonight the Special Farm Financial Assistance Program administered by the Farm Credit

Corporation. An additional $100 million will be made available this year for these special FCC loans to farmers in financial distress, bringing the total available in 1983–84 to $150 million. Eligible recipients will be entitled to interest rebates of four percentage points for the first two years. As in the past, I expect that these loans will enable the recipients to remain in agriculture and to become commercially viable contributors to Canada's agricultural economy.[114]

The steady increase in the availability of funds for farmers through the FCC is surely related to one of the dominant trends we have noted in the Western family farm sector, growing capitalization, which in turn is linked in a market-based system to the increasing concentration and centralization of capital. An important research question not addressed here is the extent to which this was understood and therefore intentional, or whether this was a classic unintended consequence of government decisions.

From late 1981 through 1982, finally ending on June 29, 1983, the Liberals worked to establish a new Crown corporation called Canagrex. The measure was introduced in December 1981 by Eugene Whelan, perhaps one of the most colourful ministers of agriculture in Canadian history. Often decked out in a green Stetson hat, Whelan was an unabashed supporter of orderly marketing and marketing boards at a time when some members of the Progressive Conservative Party were becoming more explicit in their public calls for more free market policies. Canagrex was primarily designed to market Canadian agricultural products both domestically and internationally. The protracted debate in the House of Commons over Canagrex lingered over the entirety of the year 1982, and the legislation only passed after the Liberals imposed closure in late 1982. The debate was surely among one of the most raucous in Canadian history, involving months of name-calling, largely from the Progressive Conservatives since the NDP supported the bill in principle. The accusations included support of communism, of fascism, and government control of every aspect of citizens' lives, the government having been branded as pocket dictators. From the perspective of Western Canada, ideological name-calling aside, the bill had a negligible impact on the operation of the CWB, then the central agent for marketing Western grain.[115]

The remaining budgets of the Trudeau and then Turner governments focused on economic recovery, fiscal restraint, and job creation with an emphasis on the private sector; as the pre-election 1984 budget explicitly stated, "The private sector must be the main creator of jobs."[116] While all the assistance that was provided to the FCC in these years was surely appreciated, without doubt allowing some farms to expand, the fact is that such support was also allowing them to buy out their neighbours, and in some cases to fall further and further into debt. There was, however, an ongoing issue between some farmers and the railroads.

THE GILSON TASK FORCE, 1982

The question of the future of the Crow Rate continued to occupy the House, but by 1982 there was a noticeable shift in the Liberals' position on the subject. In February 1982, when questioned about the government's position by the leader of the NDP, the prime minister indicated that it was a complex question lacking unanimity in the West while labelling the NDP's unadulterated support for the Crow Rate as "reactionary."[117] The next day, the Progressive Conservatives and the NDP attempted to introduce motions seeking clarification, noting that the minister of transport, Jean-Luc Pépin, had announced an important policy change outside of Parliament.[118] The work to be undertaken would not be a public investigation, but rather private discussions about a matter that Minister Pépin quipped would point toward "negotiations on the subject," though he later stated that he hoped to bring legislation forward.[119] The Liberals decided to appoint a well-known agricultural economist from the University of Manitoba, Dr. Clay Gilson, to study the issue. In the period that followed, the government was questioned on the Crow Rate virtually daily, with Gilson's work only a small part of the debate. The topic of "freight rates" occupies three pages of the *Hansard* index for that session of Parliament. Among the approaches adopted by the NDP were frequent calls for a producer referendum on any changes.[120] Gilson's report was tabled in August 1982, following which a dispute arose regarding the fact that members of Parliament were unable to secure a copy.[121]

The report covers some of the same ground that Hall and others had covered in terms of explaining the structure and organization of the Western grain-transportation system and its impact on various commodity groups, railway costs, and prospective increases in costs. The crux of its recommendations was the effort to calculate the cost of the Crow Rate for railroads and options for a compensatory approach that would provide the railroads with revenue streams to motivate performance and infrastructure maintenance. The report did not explicitly recommend abandoning the Crow Rate, but rather sought a new method of financing what would become known as the Crow Benefit. The difference between the Crow Rate and full compensatory costs would become a $685 million subsidy paid in perpetuity at first to the railroads; over time, this would shift to a payment to farmers.[122]

The study was released and extensively discussed, with Minister Pépin indicating that cabinet had already made a decision in early 1983 and that he would be making an announcement within a week, albeit in Winnipeg and not the House.[123] Pépin was criticized in Parliament for making important announcements outside the House, thereby denying members a chance to respond, particularly on important matters such as the Crow Rate, which was again referred to as the Magna Carta of the Western farmer.[124] In defending the legislative direction his government was taking, the prime minister declared, "I think it is fair to say that just about everyone in the West agreed that the Crow Rate should be reopened and that the question should be looked at."[125] The government was about to take drastic action that would continue to impact many farmers for many years.

THE *WESTERN GRAIN TRANSPORTATION ACT*, 1983

In May 1983, Minister Pépin introduced the *Western Grain Transportation Act* so as "to facilitate the transportation, shipping and handling of western grain," along with various amendments to other related bills.[126] He declared, "I am proud, today, because of the historical impact of this legislation which is aimed at replacing the equally historic Crow rate." He noted, "I also feel some trepidation, Mr. Speaker, because the subject is a complex one." Speaking to farmers' fear of change, he noted that they would be protected in several ways, including by receiving the Crow Benefit payment "in perpetuity," the phasing in of increased costs, and a link between freight costs and the price of grain.[127] In essence, the bill abrogated the grain rates outlined in the Crow's Nest Pass Agreement, which had been established in perpetuity as part of an important trade-off involving major government support and benefits that facilitated the future success and growth of the CPR. It seems that perpetuity does have an end point after all!

Instead of being based on the historic statutory Crow Rate, freight rates would be increased to ensure adequate compensation for the railroads. This increase was to be borne by producers, though they were to be aided by the federal government through the Crow Benefit, a $658 million fund to subsidize the railroads. The Crow Benefit pool would increase in the next few years, but farmers were now going to pay at least 30 percent of transportation costs.[128] The bill also provided for the creation of the Senior Grain Transportation Committee, composed of industry representatives, to provide advice to the minister.

The bill was met with range of criticisms and proposed amendments. The NDP opposed outright most aspects of the legislation.[129] Progressive Conservative Ray Hnatyshyn addressed the particular difficulties the changes would impose on smaller farmers, who cannot afford to haul grain to larger, more distant elevators, and the negative impact on local communities as grain handling is centralized in larger centres. He noted that a farmer with a thousand acres would see freight charges increase from about $4,800 to $24,800.[130] Others spoke of the threat to national unity resulting from the remarks the prime minister had allegedly made about the West not voting Liberal, the unfairness in the face of increasing transportation subsidies offered by the US government to American farmers, and even the impact on the farm implement manufacturing industry when farm income drops.[131]

In mid-May, as the debate carried on and criticism mounted, Minister Eugene Whelan gave notice of the government's intention to impose closure to limit the debate on second reading, generating condemnation from most members of the Official Opposition and the NDP.[132] Castigating the government for using closure, most members unsuccessfully attempted to introduce amendments while presenting petitions—including one with thirty thousand signatures—opposing the bill.[133] On October 19, 1983, the minister of transportation indicated that there would be only two more days of debate under second reading and one for third reading, imposing closure; this set off a period of raucous "debate" that resulted in the expulsion from the House of an NDP member.[134] On third reading, the debate grew even more acrimonious, with interjections of "shame" and name-calling ("snake" and "communist") and one member concluding that "this is indeed a very sad day for Parliament."[135] The Senate passed the bill without amendment.

While the bill may not be the most controversial or most debated in Canadian history, it must come close. From its introduction to its receiving royal assent in November, the bill clearly occupied more time in that parliamentary session than any other matter. After the *Western Grain Transportation Act* was passed and the Crow Benefit was lost and freight rates skyrocketed—doubling, and even tripling, for some farmers—short-term compensation was offered in the form of a onetime payment to the provinces under the Western Grain Transition Payment Program.[136] In the subsequent 1984 election, the Liberals were shut out in Saskatchewan, with the Progressive Conservatives taking nine seats and the NDP the remaining five.[137]

A NEW GOVERNMENT AND MORE BITTER WINE: MULRONEY BUDGETS

There may have been high hopes for better times in the West after the 1984 election, with Prairie voters having largely supported the winning party; however, the first Speech from the Throne hinted at what would become the mantra of the Mulroney Progressive Conservatives. Two sentences stand out. The first spoke to the future actions of the minister of finance: "He will announce a plan designed to reduce the deficit in an orderly, balanced and fair manner, and to control the growing burden of the public debt." The following sentence made clear "that we must deal urgently with the deficit is beyond dispute."[138] Other priorities were restoring "a spirit of goodwill and true partnership between Canada and the United States, ensuring public safety, consensus building and economic renewal."[139] A better indication of the government's intentions and direction can be found in its budget speeches. Michael Wilson delivered the first budget of the new government on May 23, 1985, in which he identified two major problems—unemployment and national debt. On the debt side, he noted that the government had already begun to reduce spending, and that within the next year, more than $8 billion would have to be cut. Encouraging private initiative through deregulation and privatization was seen as the primary route to more jobs. Agriculture warranted one mention, in a list of economic programs that aimed to bring about improvement through greater efficiencies.[140]

On the agricultural front, the government was not yet prepared to fully unleash the forces of the free market, particularly in light of a political base in the West that still included a number of typical small and medium-sized family farms. Hence several established programs serving Western grain growers were maintained, revised, and even enhanced. We find a series of small amendments made to ensure that various established pieces of legislation were appropriate for the times. For example, in 1984 the *Farm Products Marketing Act* was amended to address a crisis in the tobacco industry; the change received support from all parties and was passed quickly.[141] Amendments were made in June 1985 by all-party agreement to amend the *Farm Improvement Loan Act* to allow the minister to guarantee loans for an eighteen-month period, important given the ever-increasing capital-intensive nature of farming. The bill passed the same day.[142]

In 1985, amendments were also made to the *Western Grain Stabilization Act*, a bill that the minister of agriculture noted had its roots in the Diefenbaker Progressive Conservatives of the 1950s. The measure was largely supported by the other parties and passed in two days.[143] In April 1985, Mr. Mazankowski, minister of transport, introduced an amendment to the *Western Grain Transportation Act*. This was largely a holding pattern: the amendment would freeze freight rates pending a full review of the act, remove a cap on grain haulage, and place a moratorium on branch line abandonment until the full implications of the Hall Report were understood. The Opposition claimed mixed feelings, but the bill passed as members waited for more action on the Hall Commission's findings.[144]

Following the fall opening of the 1986 Parliament, a new Throne Speech indicated that deficit reduction remained a first principle in an economic renewal strategy that included increased trade with the United States and deregulation without compromising on social justice. Notable is a statement about the agricultural sector in general: "In meeting its commitment to Canadian agriculture, my government will spare no effort in seeking to protect the interests of Canada's farming community in the face of unfair pricing and subsidy practices conducted beyond our borders."[145] In the debate over the speech in October 1986, the prime minister provided more detail. Noting the conflict over agricultural subsidies and the fact that farmers needed help, he announced his government's commitment to enhancing the cash flow of Canadian grain farmers through the injection of a billion dollars. While welcoming the measure, the Opposition worried that it seemed to contradict the government's previous criticism of subsidies, and that officials in the Ministry of Agriculture seemed not to know about the program.[146] The announcement in the House was not accompanied by any details about policies or programs that might be forthcoming.

A small bill amending the *Farm Improvement Loan Act* was passed in 1986 extending the life of the FCC, given that it had a sunset clause. During the debate, the minister of agriculture noted the provisions of the bill were relatively minor given the FCC's role in providing farm credit.[147]

In line with what we know about government privatization initiatives, Minister of Agriculture John Wise introduced a bill to dissolve Canagrex, a Crown corporation to market agricultural and food products, in October 1986. Minister Wise noted that this was partly about cutting costs and partly about the government deeming the public corporation unnecessary.[148] Members of the Opposition who philosophically supported what Canagrex stood for disagreed, arguing that it was another case of the government putting "the screws to small producers." Mr. Althouse summarized the position of the NDP as follows: "Unfortunately it did not fit in with the philosophy of the current Government so it had to die the same death as the Avro Arrow had to suffer."[149] The bill was passed and Canagrex was dissolved.

While debating the Speech from the Throne in the fall of 1986, Prime Minister Mulroney noted the difficulty that the ongoing subsidy trade war was causing grain farmers and indicated that he was working with Saskatchewan premier Grant Devine on a relief program in the amount of a billion dollars. The money for the Special Canadian Grains Program was earmarked for a variety of grain, oilseed, and soybean producers, not just Western grain farmers, with the payment amount based on a formula that considered seeded acreage, productivity, the value of the product, and regional yields. Farmers were required to provide the necessary information, which was then verified by the records of those holding grain permit books.[150]

In 1986, an important program based on the *Prairie Grain Advance Payments Act* was slightly amended. Agriculture Minister Mayer noted that subsidies provided by the European Economic Community and the US Farm Bill had serious implications for agriculture. He noted that the stabilization bill was another measure that dated to the Diefenbaker government's actions in 1957, and that his amendments would allow cash advances either based on a producer's quota or acres farmed, provide interest relief for those in default, help those renting land, and make emergency aid easier to secure. There was no serious opposition.[151] The following year, 1987, the minister of state (grains and oilseeds), Charles Mayer, introduced an amendment to the *Wheat Board Act*. The minister heaped praise on the historic importance and effectiveness of the CWB and indicated the amendments were merely six in number and meant to bring the act up to date. The amendments brought changes to the quota system, a name change from rapeseed to canola, car delivery technicalities, and authority for the CWB to borrow from private banks, plus matters relating to advisory board compensation. The Opposition Liberals indicated no intention to take much time on the bill.[152] In June 1988, Doug Lewis, by now minister for state (grains and oilseeds), introduced a further amendment to the *Western Grain Stabilization Act* allowing a write down of part of the Western Grain Stabilization Fund and making it easier to enrol.[153] A minor amendment to the *Canada Grain Act* in 1988 saw members of the Canadian Grain Commission agree to seven-year terms.[154] The overall future orientation was clear; however, assistance would tend to be in the form of expanded credit, advanced repayable payments, and programs whose costs were shared among producers.

Perhaps one of the most controversial legislative changes in this period had to do with the administration of advance payments of grain introduced by Doug Lewis, minister of agriculture, in September 1989. *The Advance Payments for Crops Act* amended the previous advance payments act and the *Prairie Grain Advance Payments Act*. On second reading, Mr. Mazankowski noted that the advance limit would be increased from $30,000 for individual producers to $250,000 and that interest-free advances would be eliminated, with the interest on advances henceforth to be negotiated by the CWB. As the debate grew more intense, Mr. Mazankowski acknowledged the change: "Yes, the producers will have to pay interest, but the guarantees offered them through their producer organizations will allow them to get the cash they need at a better rate." The debate became so intense and difficult for the government that it was forced to enact closure in order to facilitate the bill's passage. The importance of the measure in the context of the restructuring of farming then under way related to the increased ceiling that allowed greater debt accumulation and the tendency of smaller producers to rely on advances.[155]

THE *NATIONAL TRANSPORTATION ACT*, 1987

The Speech from the Throne in the fall of 1986 referred to the importance of agriculture and of the need to work with provincial governments and farm organizations to assist those in financial difficulty as well as to improve the transportation system. The latter was in reference to an issue that was going to begin to change the physical and economic face of the Prairies, particularly Saskatchewan.[156] To that end, the minister of transportation, John Crosbie, introduced the *National Transportation Act* in the fall. Minister Crosbie, engaging in his trademark witty banter, explained that bill was far-reaching, covering a variety of modes of transportation and increasing competition in the sector; however, for Western grain farmers a key provision dealt with branch line abandonment. The bill replaced the Canadian Transport Commission with the National Transportation Agency.[157] Both the Liberals and the NDP focused on the negative impact of deregulation on various industries, including agriculture, but for Western grain growers, the spectre of massive rail line abandonment was the most worrisome part of the bill.

The parliamentary secretary to the minister of transport made it clear that the new National Transportation Agency was to oversee rail line abandonment: "These new provisions ensure a more flexible and balanced approach to branch line abandonment and allow for the best possible use of taxpayers' dollars in providing adequate transportation services." His commitment to protect those lines designated as part of the permanent system was met with a sarcastic "You want to bet?" from one member.[158] As the debate dragged on, the common theme from the Opposition was the extent to which the bill mimicked failed attempts in the United States to deregulate, would jeopardized safety, and would lead to the elimination of many services. The debate carried on, occupying much of Parliament's time between February and June 1987.

On June 15, 1987, the Progressive Conservative government took the drastic action of limiting the debate through closure.[159] The government majority ensured the bill's passage, whose final wording reflected its explicit neoliberal basis, as can be seen in the following excerpt:

(a) competition and market forces, both within and among the various modes of transportation, are the prime agents in providing viable and effective transportation services;
(b) regulation and strategic public intervention are used to achieve economic, safety, security, environmental or social outcomes that cannot be achieved satisfactorily by competition and market forces and do not unduly favour, or reduce the inherent advantages of, any mode of transportation.[160]

Wilson's second budget had been delivered in February 1986. It summarized what he saw as the government's accomplishments, with a promise of more cuts to come: $22 billion over the next five years through program cuts, fifteen thousand job losses in the civil service, cuts to Via Rail and the CBC, and selling and eliminating a number of Crown corporations. The only mention of agriculture was a plan to assist tobacco farmers. The words "west" and "grain" are not to be found.[161] In March 1986, the deputy prime minister tabled a twenty-one-volume report of the Task Force on Program Review in the House of Commons. It labelled government spending as out of control, attacked a range of subsidy programs, and suggested selling off between $40 and $60 billion worth of government assets.[162]

In December 1986, the prime minister made what some observers called "a surprise appearance" at the Agricultural Outlook Conference in Saskatchewan to re-announce a $1 billion aid package for farmers caught up in the burgeoning grain trade war.[163] During debates in the House of Commons over the next year, the details of this spending grew clearer. For example, Mr. Bill Gottselig noted that the funding in the prime minister's December announcement the day before would assist with fuel tax rebates, provide an additional $100 million for each of the following three years in FCC funding, help write off $750 million in Western Grain Stabilization

Fund debt, and help with PFRA soil degradation work.[164] It would seem that a significant portion of the funds were already allocated or required for ongoing programs.

Finance Minister Wilson's third budget was something of a rerun, with new dates and numbers, of the familiar themes of how badly the previous government had performed and how the current government's actions of deficit reduction, privatization, deregulation, and support for the private sector was working. The budget did, however, offer sector-specific spending increases: "Our fiscal situation in 1987–88 will continue to be affected by low prices for oil and grain. For example, additional support to grain farmers through ongoing federal programs will be $1.5 billion higher than I anticipated in my February 1986 budget."[165]

February 10, 1988, marked the last budget of the Thirty-Third Parliament, again delivered by Finance Minister Michael Wilson. The budget announced that the deregulated private sector had been revitalized, fiscal responsibility had been restored, privatizations had reduced government intrusion in the marketplace, and a new trade deal with the United States had been signed; however, more spending reductions were in order. This budget did specifically address agriculture and the issues facing the farm community in the face of international market disruptions. Assistance to the agricultural sector to support income and assist with debt was necessitated by international developments: "These actions have been made necessary in large part by falling grain prices caused by the continuing export subsidy war between the United States and the European Economic Community and by the lack of effective international rules governing agricultural subsidies."[166]

Following their victory in the so-called free trade election of 1988, the Mulroney Conservatives took the unusual step of opening the Thirty-Fourth Parliament with an abbreviated Speech from the Throne that amounted to just six short paragraphs and addressed a single item—the free trade agreement then being negotiated with the United States.[167] The government pushed the free trade bill through and offered another Speech from the Throne in April identifying the ratification of the Meech Lake Accord, deficit reduction, and further privatizations of Crown corporations as foci.[168] The 1989 budget was all about debt and deficit reduction ($5 billion in 1989 with a further $9 billion to follow), cuts to provincial transfer payments, privatization, and a new goods and services tax. In terms of explicit mentions of agriculture, the budget called for the "encouragement of a productive and economically viable agriculture sector," while branch line rehabilitation was almost eliminated, dropping from $46 million to $2 million. Payments stemming from the *Prairie Grain Advance Payment/Advance Payments for Crops Act* remained at $27 million.[169]

THE MARKET RULES: *GROWING TOGETHER*

It is clear, then, that as the twentieth century drew to a close the realities of a globalized economic order were more and more apparent in all sectors of the economy. One of the consequences of globalization in a regionalized economy such as Canada is increased inequality. As provincial governments endeavoured to secure some of the economic benefits of globalization for their provinces, the notion of a one-size-fits-all, national-level policy was increasingly under strain. Owing to the unique jurisdictional position of agriculture, federal and provincial ministers of agriculture had been meeting occasionally since at least the 1930s.[170] It was therefore no surprise when the federal minister of agriculture organized a meeting with his provincial and territorial counterparts in 1989. The meeting resulted in the establishment of two working groups to address concerns about differences in legislation and the impact of legislation across the country and the need for a national safety net for agricultural producers.[171] Such meetings have since become annual events.

By the end of the twentieth century, virtually all provincial governments had adopted some version of a neoliberal policy framework, a key element of which was reduced government expenditures and a growing reliance on market forces. When the ministers of agriculture met in 2001 in Whitehorse they agreed to what became known as the Whitehorse Accord, which indicated provincial and territorial acceptance of the importance of five broad policy areas: risk management, renewal, environment, food safety and quality, and science.[172] From the perspective of a Western Canadian cereal grain or oilseed producer, this heralded a new focus on the agri-food sector as a whole. Western farmers had long since lost their central role in the national economy and had become a relatively small cog in a growing continental and global machine.

In November 1989, Minister of Agriculture Don Mazankowski released an important policy document. The seventy-page *Growing Together: A Vision for Canada's Agri-Food Industry* outlined a new direction in agricultural policy in Canada.[173] The Minister's Message section made this new direction crystal clear: "Our action plan must be guided by some clear principles that give us a sense of direction. Our vision of the future is a *more market-oriented agri-food industry*." The message goes on to note that the industry will be provided "with a framework of consistent and predictable government programs that encourage *a more self-reliant sector*" (emphasis in original). The theme of self-reliance is underlined in a section titled "Choosing a New Vision," where the phrase "greater self-reliance" is repeated six times. In the following passage, we see a linkage asserted between self-reliance and the marketplace: "Farmers expect to depend on the marketplace to earn their long-run return. Effective support programs can cushion farmers against sudden changes in the markets or weather. But continuing subsidies, with little expectation of improved market prospects should signal the need to work out a plan for the transition to a more self-sufficient basis of operation."[174]

As for how to address market-related problems: "The objective should be to assist producers to organize in such a way that they can solve market problems themselves, learn to be more market-responsive and more self-reliant."[175] The policy document was, however, silent on actual programs or specifics.

1990s NEOLIBERALISM, MULRONEY-STYLE

The 1990 budget continued the Mulroney Progressive Conservatives' neoliberal onslaught on public spending and the privatization of public institutions and services. The budget notes that the public service had been reduced by twelve thousand jobs and program spending had been cut from $16 billion to $9 billion, with a further saving of $19 billion over the next five years, resulting in a $31 billion surplus by 1994–95. Privatization continued unabated, such that Petro-Canada and Telesat Canada were now on the block.[176] In the years that followed, Wilson found even more and more ways to cut government spending and programs. In 1991, provincial-based programs that relied on federal assistance for funding took a beating with caps and freezes on transfers and reductions in housing and money for the environment. The budget notes that agricultural-related subsidies, including funding under the *Western Grain Transportation Act*, had been rising at 4 percent annually, while reforms had been made to several important programs.[177]

The Progressive Conservative budgets of the late 1980s and early 1990s come close to a textbook form of neoliberalism. Year after year there were government spending cuts, privatization of public resources and services, and deregulation. Don Mazankowski promised further cuts, privatization, deregulation, and the elimination of even more public services, agencies, regulatory bodies, and advisory committees. By that year, to mention just a few casualties, gone were the Canadian Institute for International Peace and Security, the Law Reform Commission, the International Centre for Ocean Development, the Veterans' Land Administration, the Agricultural Products Board, the Science Council of Canada, the Economic Council of Canada, the Canadian Environmental Advisory Council, the National Advisory Committee on Development Education, the Canada Employment and Immigration Advisory Council, and the Advisory Committee on La Francophonie.[178] The 1993 budget promised "more than $30 billion in spending cuts and other measures" building on previous actions, all in the name of streamlining. It also boasted of "the elimination, wind-up or merger of 41 agencies and advisory boards."[179] While spending cuts were the mantra, governments took in a considerable amount of revenue from the privatization frenzy. The sell-off included De Havilland, Canadair, Teleglobe Canada, the Canada Development Corporation, Air Canada, Petro-Canada, Nordion International, and Telesat Canada. A Bank of Canada review indicates the total, one-time revenue generated from these sales was about $3,639,000,000.[180] Another study of privatization in Canada covering the period 1985–97 calculated the total proceeds at $11,968,000,000.[181]

The fall of 1990 brought discontent and worry across the Western grain sector, exacerbated by the collapse of the General Agreement on Tariffs and Trade negotiations over the issue of farm subsidies in the United States and the European Union. Kevin Wipf describes the impact as follows: "The federal government had been banking heavily on a GATT agreement, both for the wellbeing of its agriculture sector and the success of its reforms." He notes that various farm groups had been counting on relief from the subsidy war but that, "upon hearing that negotiations had ended,...[they] immediately began calling for emergency aid."[182] An additional trade-related matter of concern to different farmers was the future of the CWB. There was a persistent sentiment in the United States that the CWB was an impediment to fair and free trade, particularly as Canadian-US free trade negotiations were drawing to a successful conclusion. As we saw, the Mulroney Progressive Conservatives had opened the Thirty-Fourth Parliament with a short session with essentially one item on the agenda—the Canada–United States Free Trade Agreement.[183] In spite of the praise that Minister Mayer had expressed for the CWB earlier in 1987, in 1989 he used an Order-in-Council to remove oats from the Wheat Board's jurisdiction.[184] In 1992, he attempted to remove the CWB's jurisdiction over barley sales to the United States, but the decision was overturned by a court ruling that the *Canadian Wheat Board Act* would have to be amended before the action was legal.[185]

A major revision of agricultural support programs occurred in 1991 with the *Farm Income Protection Act* introduced by Pierre Blais, minister of state (agriculture), in spring 1991.[186] The bill enabled the creation of a number of new programs, including the Gross Revenue Insurance Plan, the Net Income Stabilization Account (NISA), the Crop Insurance Program, and the Revenue Insurance Program.[187] It built on the existing *Crop Insurance Act* and *Agricultural Stabilization Act*, but with its passing, both acts plus the *Western Grain Stabilization Act* were repealed. Under the new legislation, farmers could choose crop insurance, revenue insurance, or both and set aside money in NISA accounts for payouts when income decreased beyond a certain point. The ensuing debate saw the Opposition make various and sundry political points with support for the idea of a comprehensive program as opposed to mere ad hoc programs. Opposition parties also questioned the legitimacy of the consultation process and the degree of provincial co-operation because only Saskatchewan had agreed to participate.[188] Under the Gross Revenue Insurance Plan (GRIP), producers received money when their market revenue fell below a certain target level. Under NISA, producers paid into a fund (no more than 3 percent of what were termed eligible net sales on specified commodities) to be matched by the governments (both federal and participating provincial). A producer could withdraw money when the income from a particular commodity fell below a five-year average of income from all sources.[189] While these measures provided some support for agricultural producers, the overall focus of government involvement was increasingly the national agricultural industry as a whole and tripartite funding—that is, shared funding responsibilities among the federal government, provinces, and territories and producers themselves.

MORE LIBERAL NEOLIBERALISM

The first half of the 1990s brought momentous political changes to Canada. The Progressive Conservatives found themselves challenged by a new political party, the Reform Party, based out of Western Canada. The Reform Association of Canada (as it was formally known) was led by a popular and articulate spokesperson, Preston Manning, the son of a former conservative

Alberta premier, Ernest Manning. The Manning name provided instant political credibility in Alberta, the elder Manning having been the province's Social Credit premier for more than twenty years. While the new party's supporters were opposed to some of the policies of the Mulroney Conservatives, they certainly did not support the Liberals or the NDP. In 1989, the Canadian political landscape changed when Ms. Deborah Grey, representing the Reform Party, won a federal by-election in Alberta.

The income crisis on many farms continued despite the various programs under *Farm Income Protection Act*. The fall of 1991 brought numerous rallies across the country, including seven thousand farmers in front of the Manitoba Legislature and twelve thousand in Saskatoon at a Saskatchewan Wheat Pool–organized rally. The government response was disappointing to many as Minister Bill McKnight "responded to the request for new money by declaring that the federal government could not provide any more aid."[190] In February 1993, Mulroney announced his resignation as leader of the Progressive Conservatives and prime minister. He was replaced by Ms. Kim Campbell, who became the first female prime minister in Canadian history. Ms. Campbell called an election for September 8, 1993. The unpopularity of the Mulroney Conservatives resulted in the party being effectively wiped off the map as it won just two seats. Many small *c* conservative voters opted instead for the Reform Party, while in Quebec, many Progressive Conservative voters moved to the Bloc Québécois. The Liberals once again had a majority government under Jean Chrétien.

On assuming power in 1994, the Chrétien Liberals used the Speech from the Throne to speak in generalities of job creation, fiscal discipline, sustainable development, health care, and support for First Nations.[191] An interesting change in the cabinet was the appointment of Ralph Goodale as minister of agriculture and agri-food, rather than just minister of agriculture. The government's first budget reflected a change in tone compared to previous Conservative efforts, with a focus on the new economy, jobs, fiscal restraint, and tax and social security reform. This was perhaps partly the result of an impending second Quebec sovereignty referendum. Such political considerations notwithstanding, in February 1994 the financial outlook had not markedly changed when Paul Martin introduced the first of a two-part budget plan for 1994 and 1995 promising a "fundamental reform of programs in most policy areas to enhance their impact on growth and job creation, to raise their efficiency and to secure the government's interim target of a three percent deficit-to-GDP ratio by 1996–97."[192] Deficit reduction was very high on the agenda: "The measures in this budget, which reduce the deficit, result in gross savings of $3.7 billion in 1994–95, rising to $13.6 billion by 1996–97. Over the three-year period, the gross savings total $28.6 billion." The word "agriculture" appears twice in the budget document, once regarding Agriculture Canada labelling and the other noting that grants to agriculture would steadily decrease from $2.9 billion in 1992–93 to $2.2 billion in 1995–96. Evidently, neoliberalism is neoliberalism, regardless of the party in power!

As was noted, the Progressive Conservative Party was virtually wiped off the electoral map in 1993, not because there were no small *c* conservative voters, but because the Reform Party increasingly represented such voters in the West. The presence of the Reform Party soon led to conservative-minded Canadians across the country engaging in conversations about a united right-wing alternative to both the Liberals and the NDP. Out of those discussions came a new party, the Canadian Reform Alliance, more commonly called the Canadian Alliance. The Progressive Conservatives recovered somewhat in 1997, winning 20 seats in that year's federal election, but the Reform Party won 60. In 2000, the Progressive Conservatives saw their seat count fall back to 12 while the Canadian Alliance went up to 66, including 10 of 14 seats in Saskatchewan. Internal party dissent and intrigue resulted in leadership changes to both conservative parties, with Stephen Harper taking over the Canadian Alliance and Peter MacKay replacing Joe Clark as the leader of the Progressive Conservatives. In 2003, the two parties merged, and, dropping the "progressive" label, the Conservative Party of Canada was born.

KILLING THE CROW

The 1995 budget, part two of Martin's plan, announced that the government had been able to reduce its budget deficit by $4.4 billion more than previously expected.[193] The budget promised to continue cutting (perhaps "gutting" is a more appropriate verb) a range of programs; in the celebratory language of the document, "that means that over the next three fiscal years, this budget will deliver cumulative savings of $29 billion, of which $25.3 billion are expenditure cuts."[194] The word "agriculture" does not appear in the document, although "western" is found once; nevertheless, the budget radically changed Western grain farming with a single sentence: "subsidies under the *Western Grain Transportation Act* are being eliminated effective in 1995–96, resulting in savings of $2.6 billion over the next five years." Martin went on:

> This subsidy evolved from the Crow Rate established in 1897. It has played a pivotal role in the development of the prairie economy, but in more recent years it has come to restrict the ability of prairie farmers and industry to adapt and compete.
>
> The elimination of this subsidy will encourage crop diversification, the development of value-added production and a more efficient and effective transportation system, while also being consistent with our international trade obligations.
>
> To facilitate this change:
>
> - we will make a one-time payment of $1.6 billion to prairie farmland owners, to be provided for in this fiscal year, 1994–95;
> - we will invest a further $300 million over several years to facilitate a more efficient grain handling and transportation system;
> - and we will provide new credit guarantees to help Canadian farmers sell to non-sovereign buyers abroad.[195]

The death of what was left of the Crow Rate, the so-called Crow Benefit, would result in a major restructuring of Western farming, some would say for the better, some for the worse. Writing in *Maclean's*, Peter C. Newman, one of Canada's most prolific business writers, summarized the impact of these changes in the following terms:

> Saskatchewan Premier Roy Romanow has forecast that in his province alone net farm income will drop by a calamitous $320 million a year. As farmers go bankrupt and branch lines disappear, the reason for the existence of many Prairie elevator towns will disappear, turning them into ghost communities. One reason there hasn't been more of an outcry is that along with killing the Crow, Martin announced a one-time, tax-free payment of $1.6 billion to affected farmers, as well as $300 million for improvements to western railroads. Farm organizations, well aware that in an age of drastically reduced government expenditures the Crow might not survive, had been lobbying for transitional payments of $7 billion, but at least they got something.[196]

Following the passage of the *Canada Transportation Act* and the repeal of the *Western Grain Transportation Act* in 1995, the government continued to regulate freight rates by setting a maximum rate. Justice Willard Estey was charged with studying the issue with an eye to determining the appropriate maximum rate cap and address ongoing transportation issues. The complexity of this task is illustrated by the fact that Mr. Estey held nearly 150 meetings with over 1,000 participants.[197] Estey eventually accepted a proposal from the CPR that would involve removing the rate cap to make the grain-transportation system more competitive. He adopted the railroad's very words, that "greater efficiency and competition inherent in a commercial system make it less expensive."[198] In May 1991, the government announced the agreement, but another investigation was required to oversee and guide the implementation of the new commercially oriented system. Arthur Kroger was charged with setting up a series of working groups to sort out the details, but the controversy continued. The government eventually passed Bill C-34, an act to amend the *Canada Transportation Act*, over the objections of the NDP, who argued it was a Trojan Horse that would dilute the power and authority of the CWB over grain transportation.[199]

During this same period, two slight amendments to the *Canadian Wheat Board Act* were passed. The first, in 1994, was based on a proposal from Minister Goodale to utilize a voluntary "check-off," or contribution, from final payments to fund research and development in areas of interest to the CWB. While the measure passed with relatively little debate, a Saskatchewan member of the Reform Party, Elwin Hermanson, spoke disparagingly of the CWB, describing it as "out of date and unresponsive to the needs of producers," and accusing the minister of practising housekeeping rather than genuine reform.[200] A second amendment to the *Canadian Wheat Board Act* dealt with freight rate pooling in the aftermath of the 1995 budget destruction of the Crow Rate.[201] Perhaps one of the most important outcomes of the Liberal-majority Thirty-Fifth Parliament was the privatization of the Canadian National Railroad (CN). If there was any doubt about the neoliberal credentials of this cohort of Liberals, the killing of the Crow Rate and the privatization of the storied CN Railroad, into which the public had invested countless millions of dollars, presented a clear signal. The bill was called the *CN Commercialization Act*, leading one to wonder if the so-called commercialization of a successful commercial enterprise reflected neoliberal ideology, sarcasm, or just ham-handedness.[202]

THE 1990s: INDUSTRY-WIDE REFORM AND UNCERTAINTY

In 1994, the Department of Agriculture underwent a name change to become Agriculture and Agri-Food Canada. During the debate over the change, Minister Goodale noted that the new name reflected the important transformation the agri-food industry had undergone in recent years and the need to recognize the important economic activity taking place beyond the farm gate; Mr. Elwin Hermanson for his part took the opportunity to attack the CWB as "unresponsive to the needs of producers."[203] In May 1996, Minister Goodale introduced the *Agricultural Marketing Programs Act*, "an act to establish programs for the marketing of agricultural products," which repealed a number of existing acts, including the *Agricultural Products Board Act*, the *Agricultural Products Cooperative Marketing Act*, the *Advance Payments for Crops Act*, and the *Prairie Grain Advance Payments Act*.[204] The measure was designed to provide equal treatment for all commodity producers, reinstate cash advances, facilitate the activities of co-operatives, and address defaults on advance payments. The two advance payments acts were together rolled into a single program, with the exception that the Canadian Wheat Board continued to operate an advance for board grains in Western Canada. A representative of the Reform Party did not see the bill as a major issue, referring to it as a diversion from the important issue of reforming or changing the *Canadian Wheat Board Act*.[205] A month later, Minister Goodale introduced an act to provide for mediation between insolvent farmers and their creditors, to amend the *Agriculture and Agri-Food Administrative Monetary Penalties Act*, and to repeal the *Farm Debt Review Act*. The measure was generally supported by the Opposition and was quickly passed.[206]

THE CWB: ON THIN ICE

As the Canadian and American economies adjusted to the effects of the Canada–United States Free Trade Agreement, the issue of the CWB remained a matter of concern, although now for diverse reasons among an increasingly fractured "community" of agricultural producers. After the Liberal victory in 1993, Minister of Agriculture Ralph Goodale established the Western Grain Marketing Panel to address issues of grain marketing in the changing environment created by free trade agreements and GATT. Another body was also studying the issue as the Canada–United States

Joint Commission on Grains attempted to address some perennial issues. The commission's report, issued in 1995, addressed several topics, including the impact of different support programs, the effect of Canadian shipments to the United States on local prices, and limits on US access to Canadian markets. Among the many recommendations was one pointing to the need for Canada to deregulate the rail transportation system.[207]

The report appeared in the middle of a growing controversy in Canada over the CWB. In 1990, the CWB itself instigated a study of its future and threats and possibilities in the global wheat market. The resulting publication, known as the Steers Report, made several recommendations, including a significant restructuring of the CWB's governance. To make the CWB more accountable to producers and its workings more democratic, the report recommended that the commissioners overseeing the board's operations be elected by farmers, as opposed to the existing situation in which they were appointed by the government.[208] Perhaps the notion of "when in doubt, study" is more appropriately applied to several further developments in the 1990s. In January 1996, the nine-person Western Grain Marketing Panel toured Western Canada, holding fifteen public hearings.[209] It issued a report in July 1996 that elicited strong reactions from many corners. Its thirty-three recommendations included removing the CWB's barley sales monopoly and creating a farmer-elected board of directors to replace the government-appointed board.

Goodale's call for feedback illustrated the fractured nature of farm-based organizations. The Western Canadian Wheat Growers Association and the Manitoba-based Keystone Agricultural Producers thought the report did not go far enough, while the National Farmers Union, the Canadian Federation of Agriculture, the Saskatchewan Wheat Pool, the NDP government in Saskatchewan, and the Family Farm Foundation opposed many of the recommendations, particularly the removal of barley from the CWB.[210] True to his fundamentally democratic ethos, Goodale decided to hold a plebiscite among Western producers to gather opinions on the question of continuing the CWB's barley monopoly. The results were in by February

1997, with 63 percent of voters supporting retaining CWB control over barley (except domestic sales), while 37 percent favoured an open market.[211] In the meantime, the CWB received further support in the form of a Federal Court ruling against a claim made by the Alberta Barley Commission and the Western Barley Growers Association that the CWB monopoly was a violation of the *Canadian Charter of Rights and Freedoms*. The court ruled that the state has the right to regulate trade, something it has been doing in the case of the CWB since 1947.[212] The decision was upheld on appeal. The Supreme Court subsequently refused to hear a further appeal.

While this debate was occurring, a group of farmers seeking the end of the CWB decided to undertake certain forms of illegal protest. Beginning in April 1996, some farmers began to engage in civil disobedience by transporting grain to the United States without CWB authority. As a result, a number were arrested and charged with failure to provide a CWB export licence. In one case, an individual served 155 days in the Brandon Correctional Institution, in the process becoming a hero for the cause.[213] A new organization called Canadian Farmers for Justice held rallies to publicize the protest and to support those farmers who had been charged and arrested. In August 1997, over four hundred supporters held a rally in Regina that included the dumping of wheat at the door of Ralph Goodale's office.[214] In a much-publicized incident in 2002, thirteen farmers appeared in a Lethbridge court and were subsequently taken to jail after refusing to pay their fines. An estimated five hundred farmers from across the West attended the event and a subsequent rally at which Alberta premier Ralph Klein spoke.[215]

There was, thus, fireworks when Minister Goodale introduced an amendment to the *Canadian Wheat Board Act* in December of 1996; however, the changes did not come until the next year.[216] Jerry Pickard, parliamentary secretary to the minister of agriculture and agri-food, noted that the bill empowered farmers by creating a farmer-dominated board of directors, thereby making the CWB more accountable to them. The bill also changed some of the CWB's financial operations and altered how the board's mandate could be changed in the future. The new board of directors was to be composed of five government appointees and ten farmer-elected directors, making, Mr. Goodale argued, giving farmers the majority voice in the CWB's major decisions. Additionally, the amendments meant that any future changes to the Wheat Board's mandate would require approval of the board of directors and the Canadian Grain Commission, and that "if the proposed change is significant or fundamental, then an affirmative vote among farmers would need to be a prerequisite."[217] The bill substantially reduced the power of ministers to change an important part of the CWB's operation by regulation:

> The Minister shall not cause to be introduced in Parliament a bill that would exclude any kind, type, class or grade of wheat or barley, or wheat or barley produced in any area in Canada, from the provisions of Part IV, either in whole or in part, or generally, or for any period, or that would extend the application of Part III or Part IV or both Parts III and IV to any other grain, unless:
>
> a. the Minister has consulted with the board about the exclusion or extension; and
> b. the producers of the grain have voted in favour of the exclusion or extension, the voting process having been determined by the Minister.[218]

In the debate that followed, the Reform Party's hostility toward the CWB was manifest in full force. Mr. Hermanson led off: "The minister has made absolutely no progress on reforming grain marketing under the Canadian Wheat Board, just like he has made no permanent progress to reduce transportation inefficiencies in the movement of prairie grain, and just like he has made no progress in correcting the wrong-headed approach to cost recovery."[219] The vitriol that followed was sometimes fanciful, as when one member of Parliament implied that indemnification for the board of directors "tells me there is a problem with the financial statements," or when another claimed that "when we add all that up what do we get? There seems to be conspiracy to cover up around here. There seems to be some doubt being cast on the integrity of this government and on the management of the Canadian Wheat Board." Reform Party members decried the fact that the CWB still held a monopoly without giving farmers a choice. On final reading of the bill, Mr. Hermanson summarized his points as follows: "I want to make clear that the bill is a haywire and baler twine attempt to reform a terribly outdated Canadian Wheat Board."[220] It was now the Liberals' turn to circumvent democratic principles, and they announced the use of time allocation on February 11, 1997, although the bill did not pass until June.

The Thirty-Seventh Parliament made some important changes to the *Farm Credit Corporation Act*, including giving it a new name, Farm Credit Canada (thereby conveniently leaving the abbreviation intact). In addition, amendments introduced in the spring of 2001 allowed the FCC to engage in lease financing arrangements, offer equity financing to producers and farm-related businesses, and provide financial services to farm-related businesses.[221] Mr. Howard Hilstrom was generally supportive, but he was concerned that the FCC might be brought into competition with the private sector, while others worried about extending FCC beyond farming activities.[222]

SHIFTING POLITICAL SANDS

Even as the Liberal governments of Prime Ministers Jean Chrétien and (after 2003) Paul Martin presented a series of balanced budgets, not all was well in Ottawa. The seemingly ever-present issue of Quebec nationalism and potential sovereignty remained in the background, and at times seemed to occupy the foreground as well. For some years, the federal government had sought to promote its presence and the advantages of federalism in Quebec, but in the early 2000s some apparently questionable and even potentially illegal activities were disclosed in the press and raised in Parliament. The federal auditor general investigated, and the government itself established a Royal Commission to study the matter. To oversimplify a complex story, the entire affair was a major blow to the Liberal Party, ultimately resulting in its electoral defeat in 2006 at the hands of the new Conservative Party of Canada (born, as we will recall, of the merger of the Canadian Alliance and the Progressive Conservatives).[223]

There is no doubt that the leader of the new party was ideologically conservative. Stephen Harper had made a speech at the founding convention of the Reform Party and was first elected under that party's banner. He left politics for a brief period to head the National Citizens Coalition, a right-wing advocacy group, but then returned to lead the Canadian Alliance, and ultimately to play a leading role in the formation of the new iteration of the Conservative Party. As one political observer has noted, "The consistent thread throughout all this is Harper's fidelity to ideology."[224]

In the 2004 election, the Conservative Party increased its standing to ninety-nine seats, reducing the Liberals to minority status, but the Conservatives were on the upswing and found themselves in the position of a minority government two years later. After another two years, the Conservatives were, once again, elected as a minority in 2008, albeit with nineteen more seats. In 2011, the Harper Conservatives swept to power with a twenty-four-seat majority.

HARPER'S NEOLIBERALISM

In 2006, the new Conservative minority government used the Speech from the Throne to announce a cautious agenda that, among other things, promised a return to accountability, respect for tax dollars, and fiscal responsibility. On agriculture, it stated that "this Government recognizes the unique challenges faced by those who make their livelihood from our land and oceans in our vital natural resource and agriculture industries. It will take action to secure a prosperous future for Canadian agriculture, following years of neglect. It will respond to short-term needs, create separate and more effective farm income stabilization and disaster-relief programs and work with producers and partners to achieve long-term competitiveness and sustainability."[225]

As might be expected from a minority government, the second Speech from the Throne was general and cautious, with themes such as strong leadership, strengthening the federation, public safety, and fiscal responsibility.[226] In 2007, Mr. Gerry Ritz, minister of agriculture and agri-food and minister for the Canadian Wheat Board, unveiled a new vision for agriculture in Canada titled *Growing Forward*. It was the first systematic policy outline since 1989. He noted that the document was the result of extensive consultations with provincial and territorial ministers, and that the new policy framework would replace the existing Canadian Agricultural Income Stabilization Program. *Growing Forward* has been described as "a bold market-driven vision for Canada's agriculture, agri-food and agricultural-based products industry on every region of the country."[227] Several program areas, the costs for which were shared with provinces and territories, were identified, including the need for producer savings accounts, margin-based support when prices fall below a certain point, crop insurance, and disaster and recovery relief.

After the 2008 election, which brought the Conservatives a larger minority, the November Throne Speech focused a little more on fiscal management, jobs, and private-sector partnerships, with only one mention of farmers: "Our Government will continue to support Canada's farmers by ensuring freedom of choice for grain marketing in Western Canada and strongly supporting our supply-managed sectors at home and in international negotiations."[228] In the face of the 2008–09 economic collapse, a very short Throne Speech in 2009 spoke of uncertain times and the need for an economic stimulus plan that would involve government action on investments in infrastructure, protecting the financial sector, supporting all industries, and "encouraging private expenditure."[229]

In the aftermath of winning a majority on May 2, 2011, the Conservatives' June Throne Speech, while announcing that the government's economic action plan had worked, noted that it was now time for fiscal restraint and balanced budgets:

In order to accelerate the return to a balanced budget and to eliminate the deficit one year earlier, over the next year we will undertake a Strategic and Operating Review of government spending led by a new Cabinet sub-committee established for this purpose. This review will be focused on reducing the cost of government, while keeping taxes low and preserving transfers to individuals and provinces for essential things like pensions, health, and education. Our Government will also complete its stimulus package as promised and continue specific measures to restrain the growth of government expenditures.[230]

Of particular importance for Western farmers was this sentence: "It [the government] will also introduce legislation to ensure that western farmers have the freedom to sell wheat and barley on the open market."[231]

THE HARPER CONSERVATIVES AND AGRICULTURE

The minority Harper government was able to get some routine and largely inconsequential agricultural measures passed during its first term. The Conservatives moved quickly to amend the *Agricultural Marketing Programs Act* by consolidating several programs, increasing coverage, and adding livestock to the commodities covered. Minister Strahl acknowledged the need to recognize the growing costs of running large farms by increasing "the overall limits on advances from $250,000 to $400,000" as well as enhancing emergency cash advances. The minister estimated the cost of the measure at $100 million.[232] The Liberal Opposition congratulated the government, and the bill passed the same day. In February 2008, the government was able to pass amendments to the *Agricultural Marketing Programs Act* that provided cash advances for hog and beef producers, disease prevention, assistance to the temporary foreign workers program, and other emergency funding, but most of this was inconsequential for grain farmers. The bill was generally supported and endorsed by all parties and passed quickly.[233]

During the 2009 session the government continued to have some measures easily passed, such as increases to the availability of agricultural loans and the repeal of the *Farm Improvement Loan Act*. The act was meant, Mr. Pierre Lemieux indicated, to address the issue of intergenerational transfers of farms since he estimated that "over the next 15 years, Canadian farmers, operating almost 84,000 farms, are expected to retire. I say 'expected' because we know some will work beyond the age of 70." The legislation was intended to provide loans to assist farm transfers to future generations. This would allow a beginning farmer to borrow up to 90 percent of the purchase price with a loan limit of $500,000 for property and $350,00 for other loan purposes. The bill made about $600 million per year available to agricultural producers.[234] While the Liberals supported the bill, Wayne Easter asked, "Will the parliamentary secretary just answer these two simple questions? What is this bill really about? It is not about providing money to farmers. It is about providing debt. Who is guaranteed under this bill? Is it not the banking sector? There is a 95% guarantee to the banks. Is that not correct, parliamentary secretary? When is the government going to actually deal with what the problem really is, which is sustainable farm income?"[235] Mr. Lemieux responded, "We are talking about taking the loan rate for beginning farmers from 80% to 90%, so that they can borrow up to 90% in order to allow for the transfer of farms among generations. This is good legislation for our farmers."[236] One thing was clear: under these provisions, farmers' debt would rise.

TERMINATING THE CWB

As we have seen, the role and value of the CWB was never a matter on which all Prairie farmers and grain producers agreed; however, from its inception during the First World War through its role in the crisis of the Depression and in the decades after 1945, the majority of Western farmers and grain producers found the CWB a useful and necessary instrument for Canadian wheat marketing and sales in a world market increasingly dominated by an ever smaller number of increasingly larger private grain companies.[237]

As early as 1971, members of the Progressive Conservative Party were expressing concern about extending the jurisdiction of the CWB to flax and rapeseed.[238] Some within the party, however, voiced concern that it was the Liberals who were eroding the CWB, as when John Diefenbaker pressed Otto Lang for assurance that the CWB would not be weakened by removing feed grains. Lang responded that he thought there was concern in the West about the role of the CWB, prompting Diefenbaker to play off the so-called Auto Pact, the 1965 automobile trade deal between Canada and the United States, which was important for Ontario manufacturers, and ask for an "Ottopact," with an assurance that the minister would protect the CWB.[239] In 1973, changes to the feed grain legislation were seen by supporters of the CWB as a first step in the direction of the Wheat Board's full erosion. The Hall Commission had strongly supported the CWB, but as we saw, concerns were expressed that the 1983 *Western Grain Transportation Act* might further weaken the board. In 1986, Progressive Conservative Charles Mayer still heaped praise on the CWB while granting it more borrowing power. The tone began to change with the emergence of the Reform Party, as we saw with Elwin Hermanson's claim that the CWB was "out of date and unresponsive to the needs of producers" and the Reform Party's opposition to a bill that would make it more difficult to radically change the CWB's mandate.

In March 2008, Gerry Ritz introduced an act to amend the *Canadian Wheat Board Act*; however, Liberal Wayne Easter raised a point of order suggesting that the bill was illegal since it contravened the original, which had specified that nay amendments required consultation with the CWB's board of directors.[240] The Speaker ruled the bill in order; however, it did not proceed. In May 2008, Ritz introduced two more bills, one to allow the government to remove barley from the CWB by proclamation, the other to change the eligibility requirements for those voting for CWB directors.[241] Neither bill went anywhere in the minority Parliament.

The Harper Conservatives were determined, and after securing a majority in the 2011 election, Minister Ritz introduced a bill with an ideologically loaded name, the *Marketing Freedom for Grain Farmers Act*.[242] The theme of freedom was to be the mantra of the government, as when Prime Minister Harper claimed that "Western Canadian farmers have long been looking for the freedom to market their grain, just like farmers in Quebec and other parts of eastern Canada have. We are going to give them that freedom."[243]

The controversies that surrounded the eventual demise of the CWB have been extensively covered in academic studies and the popular press. André Magnan's account of the role of the CWB in the transformation of the global wheat market identifies key actors in terms of those "for" and "against" the CWB in the 1990s. In the "for" column, he identified the CWB leadership, the National Farmers Union, the wheat pools, the Saskatchewan NDP, and the federal Liberals. The "against" forces were the Western Canadian Wheat Growers Association, Western Barley Growers Association, Farmers for Justice, private grain companies, the Government of Alberta, and the federal Conservatives.[244] In September 2011, a plebiscite was held on the future of the CWB. About four hundred thousand farmers voted (55 percent of those eligible to vote), with 62 percent opting to retain the CWB as the single desk seller.[245] The 2011 vote followed an earlier 2007 ballot containing three alternatives (retain the CWB as is, eliminate it altogether, or maintain it on a non-compulsory basis), none of which received a majority.[246]

The debate over the elimination of the CWB covered many of the same points that had been heard in previous years in terms of who would benefit, who would be counted in the category of "farmers," whether another plebiscite was appropriate, and so on. In a move that surprised many, Peter Van Loan moved to limit further debate to just two days on second reading, creating mild chaos in the House.[247] The matter was taken up and passed, given the Conservative majority, when debate resumed on October 20, 2011. The debate on the proposed act continued as various parties stated and restated their views that the CWB was either a bedrock of Western Canadian agriculture or the bane of Canadian farmers.

Debate resumed on October 24, 2011, with each side again stating and restating their positions and identifying support from one side or the other.

On the side of those advocating abolition of the CWB were many groups representing the private sector, such as the Business Council of Manitoba. Twenty witnesses appeared before the legislative committee before the bill came back to the House in late November. That same month the Conservatives again invoked closure.[248] The Opposition were immediately on the attack, noting that this was the eighth time the Conservatives had used closure, to which Gerry Ritz retorted, "Madam Speaker, it is precisely because the bill is so important that we need to move it through."[249] Speaking to the charge that the Conservatives were stifling debate, Tom Lukiwski was adamant: "Our intentions have always been clear. We are acting on those intentions. We will get the job done and we will get it done tonight."[250]

So determined was the government that it ignored a December 2011 Federal Court ruling that it was required to hold a vote before changing the *Canadian Wheat Board Act*, as per the provisions of the act itself.[251] Earlier, the prime minister had declared, like a true partisan, his disinterest in further dialogue on this important issue: "This train is barrelling down a Prairie track. You're much better to get on it than to lie on the tracks, because this is going ahead."[252] Without explaining his rationale, Minister Ritz dismissed the earlier plebiscite, in which 62 percent of producers supported the CWB, as a mere "non-binding survey," despite calls from Goodale to honour the outcome.[253] Get it done they did, and, with royal assent in December 2011, the train rolled on and the CWB was essentially killed.

A *Globe and Mail* article summarized the winners and losers this debate in the following manner:

Potential Winners
- Big grain-handling companies: Richardson International, Viterra and Cargill will be able to exploit their financial and supply-chain muscle.
- Big grain farmers: By making their own deals, many believe they will prosper.
- Farmers close to US markets: They will find it easier to sell and move their wheat and barley.

- Free-market advocates: They have never liked the board's monopoly power.
- Trade lawyers: If Canadian grain swamps US markets, expect more trade tensions.

Potential Losers
- Small producers who lack clout, resources, and expertise to make their own deals.
- Grain companies that lack easy port access.
- Farmers who rely on their own producer rail cars, now allocated by the Canadian Wheat Board.
- Farmers in remote areas who depend on the board's marketing and distribution.
- Prairie traditionalists who worry about the loss of support institutions.[254]

What is interesting about this list is the fact that both the big and the small farmers mentioned here were required to engage in marketing their own grain or to engage experts to do so for them. An important part of the grain trade is futures markets, which involve producers signing a legally binding contract to provide a specific amount of a commodity at a specific time for a predetermined price. While this may seem to provide a measure of security for a producer, it also assumes that the producer can deliver. Such contracts can leave a producer vulnerable in the event of a crop failure. A headline in a Saskatchewan paper recently read, "Farmers in 'Dire Straits' over Unfulfilled Grain Contracts." The story quotes a leader of the Agricultural Producers Association as saying that "farmers are facing, in some cases, a very significant financial penalty [for] contracts that—through no fault of their own—they're not able to fill due to the unprecedented drought."[255] The freedom that unfettered markets provide have always amounted to a double-edged sword.

CWB: FINAL PASSAGE

The CWB did not last long after the so-called freedom bill. In 2015, a partnership involving the large American company Bunge and an investment firm based in the Kingdom of Saudi Arabia, SALIC, purchased the assets of the former CWB and, along with the Farmers Equity Trust, created G3 Canada Limited. Farmers were able to receive "trust units" in the Farmers Equity Trust in return for signing a contract and delivering grain to G3 through one of its seventeen Prairie delivery points. The total number of shares farmers as a group could hold in G3 was limited to 49,900 Class B shares, thereby ensuring Bunge and Salic retained control.[256]

True to his rather fundamentalist neoliberal ideological proclivities, Harper subsequently pardoned all the farmers against whom charges had been laid for the illegal export of grain and who had been convicted.[257] In class-structured societies, the notion of freedom is mediated by the fact that freedom for one class may not necessarily entail freedom for another. The end of the CWB meant the end of the concept of producers pooling their grain to provide a greater degree of equity in the form of returns for all producers, regardless of the size of their operations. Also lost was equal access to all markets (regional, national, and international) for all producers, again regardless of size, and access to the resources necessary to organize and arrange the marketing of their grain. Lastly, lost was the single desk that sold all producers' grain in an orderly manner, as opposed to multiple producers scrambling and competing for markets as best they can.

RESTATING NEOLIBERAL POLICY FRAMEWORKS

In 2013, *Growing Forward 2*, a five-year, market-oriented agricultural policy framework, was released; like its predecessor, it was based on a few stand-alone federal programs and a variety of provincial-federal cost-share programs. Explaining the underlying philosophy and orientation of *Growing Forward 2*, the minister of agriculture and agri-food, Gerry Ritz, argued that it "will help deliver...transformative change for the industry. By shifting the focus from reactive to more proactive investments in innovation, competitiveness and market development, *Growing Forward 2* will give Canada's food producers and processors the tools they need to compete at home and abroad." Additionally he spoke of "a new suite of programs in innovation, competitiveness and markets."[258]

In December 2013, Minister Ritz introduced an omnibus bill, *An Act to Amend Certain Acts Relating to Agriculture and Agri-Food* (commonly referred to as the *Agricultural Growth Act*), that proved to be quite controversial. When the bill returned to the House in March 2014, the minister used explicitly neoliberal language to describe the bill's ostensible purpose: "Farmers want to earn their money from the marketplace, and they can beat the competition hands down if we are playing on a level playing field. Our government continues to work with industry to level that playing field, open new markets for our farmers, and sign new free trade agreements."[259] As an omnibus bill, it changed and amended a number of pieces of legislation, including the *Feeds Act*, the *Fertilizers Act*, the *Seeds Act*, the *Health of Animals Act*, the *Plant Protection Act*, the *Agriculture and Agri-Food Administrative Monetary Penalties Act*, the *Agricultural Marketing Programs Act*, and the *Farm Debt Mediation Act*. Among the most contentious issues addressed by the bill were the rights of plant breeders, with the Liberal, NDP, and Green Party members all arguing that it would limit the rights of farmers to produce their own seed while granting extended rights to commercial and corporate breeders. The bill was debated extensively in the House in March, May, and June 2014, and then in the Standing Committee on Agriculture and Food in October and November 2015, finally receiving royal assent in February 2015. Ritz later expressed pleasure on the extension of plant breeders' rights in the bill, noting that "Bill C-18 is almost as important as the last Bill C-18 we passed," and that there was significant consultation "with industry, like-minded people, forward thinking producers."[260] The "last Bill C-18" referred to here was the bill that abolished the CWB.

EXIT HARPER

Even as he seemed to achieve some of his policy goals, the Harper Conservatives nonetheless accrued the costs of their tendency to engage in prolonged political debates, their disregard for Federal Court rulings, their strident ideological positioning, and their single-minded attachment to the tenets of neoliberalism. In addition, the Conservatives faced several scandals and missteps as Canadians went to the polls in 2015. The legitimacy of an appointed Senate had been a bugaboo for the party dating back to the Reform days, when the conservatives tended to demand an elected Senate, but Harper had carried on with business as usual, and was rewarded with several scandals involving his Senate appointees. There were also controversies over election spending after 2008, issues with the treatment of veterans, and a scandal relating to one of Harper's Supreme Court nomination. Then there was the double prorogation of a single Parliament, a move that seemed to be geared toward avoiding further debate over the war in Afghanistan. Ongoing issues with fighter jet replacement contracts, complaints about government-sponsored political advertisements, and the lingering impact of the 2008 economic crisis helped a young and dynamic new Trudeau gain a majority in 2015.

DECADES OF CHANGE: A SUMMARY

We began this chapter with my mother's reflections on returning to normal, when her normal turned out to be a rather abnormal era of postwar growth and prosperity. By the late 1960s, there were signs of the breakdown of postwar "happy days." The first warnings came in the form of the 1966 amendments to the *Railroad Act* that spoke of the potential need to rationalize and abandon rail lines, along with concerns about the Crow Rate and rising subsidies. While Prairie grain farmers produced more grain than could be sold, national governments faced important continental and global questions over things like control of the Canadian economy, the influence of international oil cartels, Quebec nationalism, and ever-rising consumer prices. Discontent on the Prairies was one trigger in the establishment of a major study of agriculture in Canada that essentially concluded there was not just too much grain, but too many grain farmers as well. It was clear that the class that had once formed the centrepiece of the National Policy had lost its position in the era of continentalism and emerging globalization.

The radical recommendations contained in the report of the 1970 Task Force on Agriculture were not immediately implemented, but a variety of short-term, piecemeal measures were introduced to address lower inventories of wheat, while federal policy increasingly addressed the national agricultural and food production system writ large, with less of a focus on any one region. Some lifelines were thrown to Western grain farmers in the form of advance payments on grain (that would have to be paid back), while changes to feed grain policies helped farmers outside the West. Stabilization of farm incomes had been an issue for decades, but it received new attention in the mid-1970s, although now partly funded by farmers themselves. Farm credit did not seem to be a problem even as debts increased.

The early 1970s brought an end to the postwar boom as global instability—an international recession, the end to inexpensive petroleum, government debts and deficits, and international trade disruptions, to give a few examples—marked a transition away from the era of the postwar Keynesian welfare state to one marked by the ascendence of neoliberalism. Smaller government, spending restraint, privatization of public assets and services, and deregulation came to Canada. The Crow's Nest Pass Agreement and the associated rates came under sustained examination and criticism. Rail line abandonment was placed firmly on the agenda. Government after government, regardless of political affiliation, sang from the same song sheet. The Crow Rate was replaced by the Crow Benefit, and then that, too, was abolished. Some governments used short-term funding to placate a Western rural base, but nothing in the extension of credit through a refurbished FCC or one-time assistance seemed to deflect the relentless march of market rationalization. New visions were unveiled premised on the unquestioned and seemingly unquestionable wisdom of the market.

One unassailable outcome of the operation of a relatively unencumbered market is a reduction in the number of producers in any given sector or arena. That tendency has been apparent among cereal grain farmers since the end of the Second World War; however, the qualitative changes that accompany these quantitative changes were not apparent until the postwar boom subsided. Nowhere was this more apparent than in the debate that ended with the elimination of the CWB. Enacted by an explicitly right-wing Conservative Party, the *Marketing Freedom for Grain Farmers Act* announced the arrival of a new class of agricultural producers: no longer independent commodity producers, these were commercial, incorporated enterprises increasingly reliant on wage labour and espousing entrepreneurial individualism over community. We will now turn our attention to the changing environment faced by this new generation of agricultural entrepreneurs and the remaining elements of the classical mixed family farm.

CHAPTER 5

A TENUOUS LOCATION in the FOOD CHAIN

THE AGE OF UNCERTAINTY, 2008–PRESENT

THE ACTIVITIES OF CERTAIN PLAYERS IN THE largely unregulated banking, insurance, finance, and housing sectors saw the emergence in 2008–09 of a major financial crisis that, while perhaps less dramatic than that resulting from the crash of 1929, was nevertheless hugely impactful. This crisis brought with it a significant number of bankruptcies, a collapse in many housing markets, bank failures in some countries, and, of course, rising unemployment and growing poverty. Although most Western governments had been committed to neoliberal deregulation and cuts in state spending for nearly forty years, the events of 2008–09 demanded action. Hence the return of some state intervention as many Western democracies rushed in with bailout packages for a variety of economic sectors, from the banks and insurance industries to the automotive companies. Direct grants and loans to private industry were accompanied by a spate of infrastructure spending to create construction jobs. In Canada, for example, the Conservative government, previously diehard anti-Keynesians, announced a $47 billion stimulus package in its 2009 budget.[1] In the United States, millions of jobs were lost as unemployment doubled to 10 percent, home prices dropped by 30 percent, and key stocks lost more than 50 percent of their value.[2] Unlike the shift to Keynesian economics in the 1930s, states' post-2008 efforts to stabilize global capitalism did not change the dominant ideological stance of most governments. Indeed, it seemed as if many were prepared to accept high levels of unemployment, unstable labour markets, and growing poverty so long as their major corporate sectors did not collapse. The prevalence of neoliberal thinking meant that deficits and debts were subsequently addressed through continued cuts in government spending and services and without substantial increases to government revenue.

In this penultimate chapter, we will look at the current circumstances or situation of Western independent commodity producers engaged in cereal grain and oil production in an era of considerable uncertainty. Part of the uncertainty for producers has to do with the vulnerable positions they occupy in a food chain composed of input providers, commodity buyers, and processors, who make up some of the largest corporate enterprises on the planet. Family farmers are structurally and literally "in the middle" of the input-output nexus, but increasingly distant from the major processors and the consumer service industry. On the input side, in order to produce commodities for sale, they must enter market relationships with providers of machinery, fertilizer, seeds, chemicals, technology, repair services, business advice, and information services. On the output or income side, in order to access markets for their commodities, they must engage in relationships with those providing transportation services, grain and commodity buyers, or brokers providing marketing services and expertise. Additionally, agricultural producers typically require the services of banks and the brokers of insurance and other financial products to secure inputs and market their commodities. But before we consider in more detail the input, output, processing, and retail elements of this food chain, we must return to developments within the agrarian independent commodity producers as a class.

FAULT LINES

Beginning with the arrival of white settlers on the Canadian Plains, a measure of economic inequality has prevailed among family farmers. This has resulted from a variety of factors, including differential amounts or access to start-up capital, the productivity of given section of land, innovation and entrepreneurial drive, market conditions, geographical location, and sometimes just good or bad luck in terms of weather, storms, and fires. As the processes described in the previous chapters unfolded, the early class homogeneity that existed was eroded as several variables facilitated differentiation and the emergence of internal class divisions or fractions. These variables included the following:

- Commodity specialization results in some producers concentrating on particular commodities (wheat, canola, barley, livestock, dairy, etc.), while others remain traditional family farms producing multiple cereal grain or plant oil commodities, often also including beef, pork, poultry, or dairy, typically on a small scale.

- Landholding size differentiation creates a range of diverse and sometimes conflicting interests and concerns, with the economic and social needs and interests of a traditional small family farm operating perhaps 640 acres—quite different from that of a multi-generation enterprise operating many thousands of acres.

- Incorporation status often distinguishes traditional family operations using non-wage family labour from an incorporated (even if family-based) or shareholder enterprise employing hired labour or contract services to conduct core operations such as planting, spraying, or harvesting.

- Capitalization differences create a distinction between traditional family farms, often employing relatively small-scale machinery repaired and kept functional by owners themselves, and large, highly capitalized enterprise employing their own or leasing large, new machines, and thereby utilizing the latest technologies and innovations.

- Administration and financial planning regimes are very different for the unincorporated small family farm, with in-house "bookkeeping" and maintenance of accounts and records (typically by spouses and partners), as opposed to those engaging professional legal, accounting, and consultancy services.

- Income streams of the traditional farm family typically relied on the immediate sale of relatively small quantities of cereal grain, plant oil, or livestock sold through agents and brokers and perhaps supplemented by some family members' off-farm income. This is quite different from operators of large, incorporated enterprises operating at volumes that make self-marketing impossible, generating substantial gross income often from a limited range of mass-produced, specialized commodities frequently produced by non-family wage labour.

- Locale and geography have always been an important factor impacting commodity specialization, operational size and growth opportunities, the suitability of a region or locale for certain cereal crops or livestock grazing, and market access.

The inevitable result of these mostly market-related dynamics is differentiation among the agrarian producers in a region such as Saskatchewan or the Prairies as a whole. In an analysis of the structural differentiation among farmers as a class, Bob Stirling and John Conway proceed from the assumption that Western farmers are best understood as representing merely a section of the broader petite bourgeoisie.[3] Of this section, they further identify at least three main subdivisions: small producers who relied on off-farm labour and income to survive; a middle cohort of traditional family-farm operators; and larger farms increasingly operated with the regular employment of wage labour and the deployment of significant capital, in this sense more akin to a capitalist enterprise than independent commodity producers.

In another, more recent study of the stratification of Canadian farms, Al Mussell notes the existence of three cohorts of farmers, each experiencing the changing structure of farming differently. One is small farms that are not reliant on farm cash receipts as their primary source of income, and who are therefore isolated from many of the factors impacting other farmers; essentially, these are households living on farms but not farming. The second group is composed of middle-sized farmers, many of whom are increasingly dependent on off-farm income yet earn enough through farming that it "remains a sufficient share of household income [such] that these farms are threatened by economic downturns in agriculture." Mussell does not use the term, but I would suggest this is a *precarious* cohort of agrarian independent commodity producers trying to hang on to their class status. Finally, he notes a much smaller but important group of large and very large farms that are growing in number and whose primary source of income are farm cash receipts. Of this cohort he remarks, "It is likely that the farm is, or at least was, an extension of the household on these farms—but either way the size and sophistication of these farms could serve to sever the apparent connection between the household and the farm."[4] I take the notion of severing the household-farm connection to suggest that the farm has become a fully-fledged business with a growing cadre of specialized employees rather than family labour. Given the definition of independent commodity producer/family farm used here, this marks a change in class position.

In 2001, Statistics Canada created its own typology of farmers largely based on income levels derived from farming. It was revised in 2013. The

Statistics Canada typology distinguishes seven different types of farms, with the first based on gross farm income (GFI): (1) low-income farms (GFI less than $9,999 and total family income below Statistics Canada's low-income measure); (2) small farms (GFI $10,000–$99,999); (3) medium farms (GFI $100,000–$249,999); (4) large farms (GFI $250,000–$499,999 and 50 percent of total family income from the farm); (5) very large farms (GFI over $500,000); (6) pension farms (GFI $10,000–$249,999 and oldest operator over sixty and receiving pension income); and (7) lifestyle farms (GFI $10,000–$49,999 and whose operators are not full-time farmers and with off-farm family income equal to or more than $50,000 and who do not fall into the pension category).[5] These categories, using a nominal definition of class such as that referred to in the introduction, illustrate divisions within and among agricultural producers, but they do not get to the core issue of social relations in the economic order.

A CLASS IN TRANSITION

Regardless of how we understand the divisions among and within the class we are studying—agrarian independent commodity producers in Western Canada—it is a class in transition. Before we examine the changing environment in which both input and output relationships and market engagements occur, some statistics might better illustrate the changing characteristics of agrarian producers, particularly cereal grain and oilseed producers in Saskatchewan. Although much of the data we have considered relates to Saskatchewan, one could argue that many of the impacts of the political and economic changes considered here apply equally well to the smaller numbers of cereal and plant-oil producers in Manitoba, Alberta, and elsewhere.

In 2017, Statistics Canada released a snapshot of Saskatchewan agriculture entitled, perhaps somewhat romantically, "Saskatchewan Remains the Breadbasket of Canada." We will begin our statistical profile with figure 5.1 below, which shows a simple graphic representation of the agricultural operator numbers in Saskatchewan.

Figure 5.1. Agricultural Operations in Saskatchewan, 1921–2016

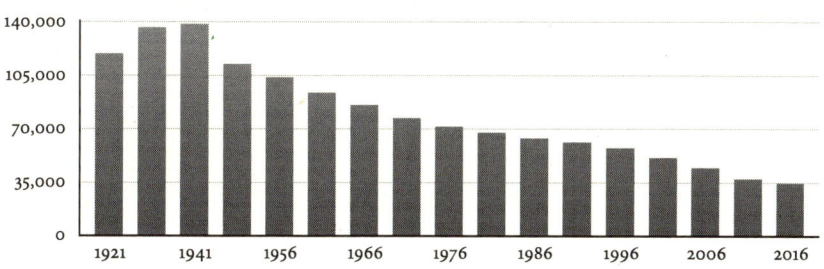

Table showing the number of farms operating in Saskatchewan between 1921 and 2016. Source: "Saskatchewan Remains the Breadbasket of Canada," Statistics Canada, May 10, 2017, https://www150.statcan.gc.ca/n1/pub/95-640-x/2016001/article/14807-eng.htm.

If we delve into these numbers, some trends are apparent. Commodity specialization is among the most important changes in Saskatchewan over the last fifty years, as is apparent from the significant dependence on a small number of commodities, with three commodity types prevailing. In 2016, Statistics Canada reported that of the 34,523 farms in Saskatchewan, the primary products of 21,505 of these operations, or 62 percent, was oilseed and grain, while for 21 percent it was beef production, 10 percent other crops, and 5 percent other animals.[6]

As for farm size, in Saskatchewan there is a definitive trend. The farm sizes reported by Statistics Canada do not precisely match the historical division of the land based on the survey system of quarter sections (160 acres) and sections (640 acres); however, a slight revision of the categories suggested by Stirling, Conway, and Mussell (and noted above) using acreage data illustrates the concentration and centralization of production with a decline in traditional family farms and an increase in the number of what we call very large farms. In the context of the restructuring currently under way, the typology or classification schema suggested in table 5.1 here must be understood as a work in progress.

Saskatchewan farms are increasingly highly capitalized, with the total value of livestock, land, and machinery/equipment continually rising. As

Table 5.1. Twenty Years of Change in the Types of Saskatchewan Farms, 2001–21

Farm size (acres)	Type of farm	# qtrs	2001 Total farms: 50,598		2006 Total farms 44,329		2011 Total farms 36,972		2016 Total farms 34,523		2021 Total farms 34,128	
			# farm	% farm	# farm	% farm	# farm	% farm	# farm	% farm	# farm	% farm
<399	Hobby/ acreage	<2	5,633	28	4,698	29	3,969	29	3,664	30	3,629	33
400–759	Small	2–5	8,775	17	7,210	16	5,563	15	5,081	15	5,026	15
760–1,599	Average/ middle	6–10	14,239	28	9,116	25	8,821	24	7,011	20	6,556	19
1,600–2,879	Middle/ large	11–18	8,518	17	8,049	18	6,673	18	5,876	17	5,171	15
2,880–3519	Large	19–22	1,647	3	1,795	4	1,724	5	1,595	5	1,544	5
>3,520	Very large	+23	2,819	4	3,592	8	4,112	11	4,495	13	4,644	14

Using fare acreage data, this table illustrates a twenty-year pattern of declining middle-sized farms with a steady increase in the largest enterprises and a growth in very small holdings (which must be understood as largely hobby farms or acreages with the holders not primarily involved in farming). Source: Statistics Canada, "Table 32-10-0156-01: Farms Classified by Total Farm Area, Census of Agriculture Historical Data," https://doi.org/10.25318/3210015601-eng.

seen in table 5.2, statistics on farm capital provide data on three combined categories, livestock and poultry, land and buildings, and machinery and equipment.

Table 5.2. Estimated Value of Major Productive Assets on Saskatchewan Farms, 1981–2021

Year	Estimated value livestock and poultry	Estimated value land and buildings	Estimated value machinery and equipment
1981	$1,390,182,000	$25,048,160,000	$4,916,910,000
1986	$1,249,912,000	$20,773,520,000	$6,144,308,000
1991	$1,823,279,000	$17,588,836,000	$6,360,633,000
1996	$1,813,595,000	$20,615,848,000	$7,545,166,000
2001	$2,977,295,000	$21,858,071,000	$8,158,809,000
2006	$2,645,228,000	$25,136,763,000	$8,341,635,000
2011	$2,165,889,858	$38,453,701,674	$10,907,659,705
2016	$5,297,666,085	$74,536,288,036	$14,907,659,705
2021	$4,053,363,776	$108,282,477,359	$17,073,006,955

This table shows the estimated values in land, buildings, machinery, equipment, and farm animals on Saskatchewan farms for a forty-year period beginning in 1981. Sources: Statistics Canada, Value of Farm Capital: Agriculture Economic Statistics, Catalogue No. 21-013-X (Ottawa: Minister of Industry, November 2011), 10–15, https://www150.statcan.gc.ca/n1/pub/21-013-x/21-013-x2011002-eng.pdf. Data for 2011 and 2016 comes from Statistics Canada, "Table 32-10-0437-01: Farm Capital, Census of Agriculture, 2011 and 2016, Inactive," https://www150.statcan.gc.ca/t1/tbl1/en/tv.action?pid=3210043701, and Statistics Canada, "Table 32-10-0237-01: Farm Capital, Census of Agriculture, 2021," https://www150.statcan.gc.ca/t1/tbl1/en/tv.action?pid=3210023701.

If we look at the percentage change in total farm capital, shown in table 5.3 below, the same distinct pattern is apparent, with only the largest two categories increasing and the very largest increasing at a significant rate while all others decline.

Table 5.3. Classification of Saskatchewan Farms Based on Total Capitalization

Farm classified by total farm capital ($)	2011 number of farms	2016 number of farms	% change
< 100,000	1,013	586	−42
100,000–199,999	2,605	1,434	−45
200,000–349,999	4,522	2,666	−41
350,000–499,999	4,183	2,580	−38
500,000–999,999	9,159	6,863	−26
1,000,000–1,499,999	5,148	4,259	−17
1,500,000–1,999,999	3,050	2,961	−3
2,000,000–3,499,999	4,334	5,276	+22
> 3,500,000	2,938	7,898	+168

This table illustrates the dramatic growth in Saskatchewan farms with the highest level of total capital. *Source: Statistics Canada, "Table 32-10-0435-01: Farms Classified by Total Farm Capital, Census of Agriculture, 2011 and 2016, Inactive," https://www150.statcan.gc.ca/t1/tbl1/en/tv.action?pid=3210043501&pickMembers%5B0%5D=1.1548.*

The relationships between owners and operators in Saskatchewan are also changing rather dramatically. In 2001, approximately 66 percent of farms were listed as sole proprietorships. In 2021, that number had decreased to 58 percent. Those operating as partnerships dropped from 23 percent to 14 percent. Many family farms were operated as family corporations, with that number increasing from 9 percent to 26 percent. Finally, non-family corporations increased from less than 1 percent in 2001 to 1.5 percent in 2021.[7]

An important criterion for identifying the persistence of independent commodity production is the amount of paid labour that is utilized, because, by definition, independent commodity production in agriculture is based on the use of the farmer's own and unpaid family labour. According to 2016 census data, a total of 3,823, or 11 percent, of all farms reported paying full-time workers on a year-round basis, while 1,917 (6 percent) employed wage labour year-round on a part-time basis. Finally, 6,430 farms representing 19 percent of farms employed hired labour on a seasonal or temporary basis. The categories used by Statistics Canada were not mutually exclusive; therefore, the total number of farms reporting the use of wage labour amounted to 27 percent of all farms (not the sum of the previous three categories). The total number of employees was 25,927, 26 percent of whom were paid family members.[8]

A further defining characteristic of independent commodity production is reliance on income from commodity sales rather than the sale of wage labour by household members. An indicator of the capacity of producers to sustain their class position and reproduce their operations based on commodity sales is the amount of non-farm paid labour in which they engage. The 2016 census reported that 42 percent of farm operators in Saskatchewan (note there can be more than one operator per farm) engaged in non-farm work. As table 5.4 below indicates, the number of hours of non-farm work varied, with a total of 28 percent of operators working for wages for more than thirty hours a week.

Table 5.4. Hours of Paid Non-farm Work by Saskatchewan Farm Operators, 2016

Average weekly hours non-farm paid work	Number operators 2016	% of operators 2016
Total number operators	45,350	100
No paid non-farm work	26,320	58
Less than 20 hours	3,955	9
20–29 hours non-farm work	2,415	5
30–40 hours non-farm work	6,190	14
More than 40 hours non-farm work	6,470	14

This table documents the number of farm operators and the type and volume of non-farm paid work they performed in 2016. *Source: Statistics Canada, "Table 32-10-0445-01: Characteristics of Farm Operators: Other Paid Work, Census of Agriculture, 2011 and 2016, Inactive," https://www150.statcan.gc.ca/t1/tbl1/en/tv.action?pid=3210044501&pickMembers%5B0%5D=1.1548.*

We noted in chapter 2 Cecilia Danysk's work on farm labour in the earlier settlement phase and the extent to which many who worked for wage labour on farms did so with the intention of securing sufficient funds to establish their own farms. Given the significant capitalization of contemporary farming, it would be nearly impossible to use the income from agricultural wage labour, which is typically non-union and not particularly high paying, to enter farming, meaning agricultural wage labour would realistically be either a career or supplementary income. Other opportunities for paid income in rural Saskatchewan might include the potash industry and oil and gas extraction. The Saskatchewan potash industry employs over five thousand workers, and while many of them may also own and operate farms, no data is available on the number of farmer-workers there are in the sector.[9] Emily Eaton has studied the oil industry as a source of high-pay employment in rural regions. In addition to the industry's significant negative impact on the rural environment, she notes that, while wage labour in the sector pays well, it is also subject to the ups and downs of international oil prices, can be dangerous and physically demanding, and often involves workers being away from home, a situation that places strains on a variety of relationships.[10]

One final aspect of this statistical picture relates to farm income and debt, a key element in understanding the sustainability of an enterprise. As we have seen, farm income is highly variable and largely dependent on international commodity prices. Between 2015 and 2018, for example, the total cash receipts received by Saskatchewan farmers went down by over $450,000,000, to just over $14 billion. While $14 billion in income sounds like a lot (and in some sense it is), total operating costs were over $10 billion. When depreciation and the costs of inventory changes are subtracted, total net income was about $1.8 billion.[11] Again, while this may lead us to assume that all is well, in just four years, between 2015 and 2019, the total farm debt in Saskatchewan increased by 37.6 percent, rising from $12,863,784,000 to $17,701,182,000.

In terms of lenders, in 2019, $4,290,037,000 was owed to chartered banks, $6,449,855,000 to federal agencies such as FCC, and $3,484,507,000 to credit unions. An additional $1,980,664,000 was owed to private individuals and supply companies, the remaining to provincial governments, insurance companies, and other lenders and advance payment agencies.[12] In short, having received a total net income of $1.4 billion in 2018, the overall sector had a total debt of $17.7 billion!

We have highlighted the growth of large farms in Saskatchewan using Statistics Canada data, meaning that all large farms over 3,520 acres are lumped together. Recall that this cohort of farmers increased by 119 percent between 1996 and 2016. An argument can be made that this does not fully illustrate some important developments in agriculture. When one examines just how large some farm operations are, the full extent of the transformation of independent commodity production in some quarters becomes clear. While there is no easily accessible data on the largest farms in Saskatchewan, stories in the media and the websites of some of these enterprises allow a glimpse.

Saskatchewan is home to some very large agricultural enterprises, such as Monette Farms, headquartered in Swift Current and with holdings near Regina, Prince Albert, and Havre, Montana.[13] The Monette website does not provide specific public information regarding the size of the company's holdings, but an April 2020 story from CTV News on delays in the movement of migrant workers speaks of Monette operating 100,000 acres.[14] Although specifics of the size of the company's workforce are not provided, a video tribute to Monette's workers ends by naming over thirty employees to whom the video is dedicated. The video also contains an impressive picture of fourteen large combine harvesters in formation moving down a field and another showing seven large tractors pulling seeding equipment. Another significant Saskatchewan agricultural producer is Delage Farms at Indian Head.[15] Delage operates 28,000 acres producing largely wheat, peas, and lentils. Their website shows eight large combines running in formation against a Saskatchewan flatland field. Again, no public information is available, but the website includes a team photo of over twenty-five people beside a large vehicle; they are decked out in green clothing bearing the insignias of the Saskatchewan Roughriders football club.

Other large enterprises in Saskatchewan include Kambeitz Farms, which operates near Sedley. The website describes Kambeitz as a fifth-generation enterprise now operating 70,000 acres with a million-bushel grain storage capacity and its own rail siding allowing access to international markets.[16] Another major Saskatchewan agricultural producer with roots in the homestead era is Carefoot Farms of Swift Current. Descendants of John Carefoot now farm about 18,000 acres in addition to operating agricultural services and an aerial application business.[17] Judging from the photos on their website, Carefoot's operation would be typical of many of the very large farms that practise high-input farming, but that is not true of Travis Heide's 40,000-acre organic farm based near Waldron, Saskatchewan. The Heide farm does not have a website, but as it edges toward becoming the largest organic farm in Canada, if not North America, it has garnered much media coverage.[18]

The scale of these operations is made more notable in the context of the average farm size in Saskatchewan, which was 1,784 acres in 2016. A study of farmland ownership patterns in Saskatchewan by André Magnan and Annette Aurélie Desmarais found that, despite changing ownership restrictions over the years, in 2014 private investors, corporations, investment companies, and partnerships owned significant blocks of land, with the two largest private blocks comprising 160,858 and 113,723 acres, while the combined holdings of thirteen others (whose owners are mostly based outside Saskatchewan) amounted to more than 278,000 acres.[19] And finally there is Andjelic Land, which owns more than 225,000 acres in ninety-two rural municipalities on which about two hundred and fifty farmer-tenants operate.[20]

Several scholars have analyzed and commented on the consequences of the changes in the nature and structure of farm operations and operators and their implications for the future. Two experts in the field of Canadian agriculture, Al Mussell and Douglas Hedley, studied national trends in farm size; they noted that small and middle-size farms often struggle to grow or even to hang on, while large and very large farms can use their competitive advantage to grow and expand. They argue that capital-intensive large farms can exploit the advantages of economies of scale, including the capacity to exercise bargaining power when purchasing inputs. They conclude that the historical pattern of step-by-step or incremental growth among relatively homogenous farms has given way to a situation in which larger and more capital-intensive farms are able to operate and earn income on a different scale. The result is differentiation or stratification within agriculture that follows a familiar pattern in market economies—the big get bigger and small or medium units disappear.[21]

In his 2017 Fellows Address to the Canadian Agricultural Economics Society, Alfons Weersink looks at the growing heterogeneity of the farm sector. He begins by noting what we have thus far been discussing: "Farm units used to be relatively similar. There was a single farm operated by a single farmer that supported a single farm family. The operator worked full-time on the farm, which tended to be diversified with multiple crops and/or livestock species."[22] He shows that the contemporary scene is changing, with the number of small and large farmers growing while the number of middle-size farmers is declining. He notes that many of the farms in the small farm group are new entrants to the sector who typically are seeking to find a niche in the complex food-and-beverage marketplace. An important characteristic of the changing agricultural production scene, Weersink argues, is the increasing share of total production attributed to larger farmers. He notes that the sector's heterogeneity has to do with more than just size: "In addition to size, farms are differentiated by attributes such as specialization, focus, ownership structure, and markets."[23] While Weersink is addressing the national picture here, his analysis has important implications for the Saskatchewan-specific data we have been considering.

Regardless of the commodity produced, landholding size, legal incorporation status, capitalization, scale, administration and operating agreements, income stream varieties, or geography and locale, all agricultural producers require a variety of industrially produced inputs and access to markets for their commodities. We have paid some attention to both the input side of Western family-based farming from the dawn of the National Policy through the to the post–Second World War boom and the emergence of a continental economy. On the output side, likewise we have noted the emergence of an infrastructure and of various forms of marketing arrangements involving both co-operatives and private grain traders throughout the nineteenth century. It is now time to catch up on the key developments on the input and output sides that have become fully apparent since the 1970s.

INPUT ENVIRONMENT, 1970–2020

In chapter 2, Darrin Qualman's concept of high-input farming provided an appropriate tool for understanding contemporary Prairie grain farming. The core elements of high-input farming (more complex and ever-larger machinery, continually expanding electronic and other technology, and more fertilizers, herbicides, and pesticide chemicals) have increased decade by decade since the end of the First World War. In this section, we will take a look at some of the key developments over the past half century in the structure and organization of those enterprises providing inputs, such as machinery, implements, chemicals, and fertilizers. As we will see, the input sector is both very important and highly concentrated—indeed, so much so that the information available on the sector paints a picture of multinational enterprises so large that they almost literally defy description. To avoid having the reader drown in endless detail, what follows are mere capsule summaries of a few of the leading producers and providers of farm machinery, agricultural chemicals, and fertilizers.

During the last half of the twentieth century, John Deere underwent significant growth and expansion; the result is the industrial behemoth we know today, with its twenty-three owned and leased factories across North America producing agriculture, turf, construction, and forestry equipment.[24] The company also owns, operates, or leases factories in Argentina, Brazil, China, Finland, France, Germany, India, Israel, Italy, Mexico, the

Netherlands, New Zealand, Russia, and Spain.[25] John Deere Capital Corporation is the company's global financial services subsidiary. In 2018, the company's revenue was US$33.3 billion.[26]

A competitor of Deere is CNH Industrial, incorporated in the Netherlands with its head office in London, England. The company's 2018 income of US$25.7 billion derived from established brands such as Case IH and New Holland, Steyr tractors, and agricultural equipment and products sold under the Kongskilde, Överum, and JF monikers. CNH produces light, medium, and heavy trucks, and commercial vehicles under its Eurocargo, Trakker, and IVECO ASTRA brands, as well as mining and construction vehicles and busses. The company has 167 consolidated subsidiaries operating 66 manufacturing facilities globally, including a financial services operation.[27]

The next giant is AGCO, whose 2018 revenue of US$9.4 billion came through the sale of "a full range of agricultural equipment, including tractors, combines, self-propelled sprayers, hay tools, forage equipment, seeding and tillage, implements, and grain storage and protein production systems."[28] Over three thousand dealers in 140 countries distribute its Challenger, Fendt, GSI, Massey Ferguson, and Valtra products. It operates its own financial services through Babobank. Among its major holdings are the American operations of German company Deutz-Allis, the Hesston Corporation, Massey Ferguson, Fendt, Valtra, Farmer Automatic, KG, Intersystems Holding, and Precision Planting. Along the way, AGCO also absorbed White Farm Equipment, a corporation that had previously bought out Oliver Farm Equipment.[29]

In addition to these big three, several other major multinational corporations produce agricultural machinery and equipment. Kubota is a Japanese-based multinational with sales of US$13.9 billion in 2018. The company produced a range of products used in agriculture, including irrigation equipment, small tractors, steel pipe, and a variety of precision equipment. Kubota has manufacturing subsidiaries, affiliates, and offices in thirty-one countries, ranging from Australia to Vietnam.[30] Italian-based SDF Group, with eight factories in Europe, China, and India, had sales of

US$1.6 billion under brand names SAME, Lamborghini Trattori, Deutz-Fahr, and Gregoire in 2018. German manufacturer CLAAS, focusing on combines, balers, forage equipment, mowers, and tractors, had a 2018 revenue of US$4.3 billion.[31]

While these titans dominate global production and trade, some Canadian- and Saskatchewan-based companies have carved out a notable presence in the sector. In 1996, the late Rob Stenson along with Art Stenson and Gary Anderson founded a manufacturing company in Swift Current. After several acquisitions, including Westfield Industries, Ag Growth International (AGI) went public in 2004. AGI acquired Westeel in 2015 along with other companies, including FRAME, Europe's leading designer and manufacturer of steel silos. By 2019, AGI had acquired over forty brands in five business platforms: the seed, fertilizer, grain, feed, and food industries. AGI operates in North America, Asia, Australia, Europe, Africa, and South America. During the first six months of 2019, AGI's sales were nearly C$510 million.[32]

It is important to note that not all the machinery inputs bought by grain and other producers are produced by multinational enterprises. Prairie farmers have always been pioneering and innovative when it comes to inventing, developing, and improving farm machinery.[33] Likewise, local entrepreneurs have developed specialized equipment and machinery for Prairie conditions; in recent years, these same companies have taken advantage of the establishment of greater free trade across North America to expand production and sales of a variety of specialized agricultural machines and equipment for both local and international consumption. A variety of Saskatchewan-based producers have established continental and global niches in seeding machinery, grain-handling and -transportation equipment, cultivators, tractor attachments of various sorts, stone pickers, and livestock-handling equipment, to name just a few. Saskatchewan-based industry has played an important role in the transition to no- and zero-till farming in recent decades, as Michael Gertler notes: "Canada's Prairie region has been a leader in the development and adoption of no-till/zero-till

(ZT) systems. With firms such as Bourgault, Morris, Friggstad, Flexi-Coil, Conserva Pak, Seed Hawk and SeedMaster, Saskatchewan has been an important centre for the design and production of air seeders and air drills."[34]

Among the most successful Saskatchewan-based companies is Brandt Industries. From its origins as Brandt Electric in 1932, the company went on to produce one of the first grain augers in Saskatchewan. It has grown to be a major multinational force in a few agricultural, construction, and industrial sectors. The Brandt Group of Companies includes Brandt Agricultural Products, Brandt Developments, Brandt Engineered Products, Brandt Equipment Solutions, Brandt Finance, Brandt Positioning Technology, Brandt Road Rail, and Brandt Tractor. In 2021, Brandt acquired Cervus Equipment, giving it equipment dealerships in several Saskatchewan centres, including Melfort, Nipawin, Prince Albert, Rosthern, Saskatoon, and Watrous, as well as 15 in Alberta, 1 in British Columbia, 9 in New Zealand, and 10 in Australia.[35]

The innovations and novel technologies that characterize virtually all contemporary new farm machinery undoubtedly enhance performance and efficiency as well; however, it is rare to see any significant lowering of costs due to price competition. Indeed, an assessment of the impact of the international economic instabilities that characterized the end of the 2010s points to the opposite trend, with farm costs seeming only to rise regardless of the available policy alternatives.[36] In 2019, Alberta combine sales were down 19 percent while tractor sales dropped 4 percent, but one observer found that the impact was not what one might expect: "Five years ago, the average new Class 7 combine ran right around $380,000. Today, that same combine is closer to $540,000, a 42 percent increase." And further, "Tractor prices have also jumped, from around $120,000 five years ago to about $180,000 today for a front-wheel-drive tractor and $330,000 five years ago to $425,000 today for a four-wheel-drive tractor."[37]

Although there is no comprehensive or systematic data showing the number of farm machinery dealers in Saskatchewan at any given moment, after 1945 many towns and some villages in the province had local machinery dealers. This was an era when local dealers were increasingly franchised, which in turn helped to enhance the dramatic mechanization that took place during the postwar period.[38] While we may not have decade-by-decade data on the reduction in the number of machinery dealers across the province, we do know that there was a decline as towns and villages lost various business in the face of a declining population. Saskatchewan people tend to be fond of their local and community history. Many Prairie towns and villages have produced local histories that indicate the presence of machinery and farm implement dealers as core businesses.[39] A search for implement dealers in Saskatchewan in 2020 (excluding cities) indicates a total of 40 towns with machinery dealers, 21 of them with only a single dealer.[40] In 2017, a major restructuring of farm equipment and machinery distribution in Saskatchewan occurred when Pattison Agriculture announced the merger of two of its Saskatchewan dealerships, Maple Farm Equipment and JayDee AgTech. The president of Pattison Agriculture is quoted as saying the deal, which involved 157 dealerships employing 440 workers and serving producers operating over 18 million acres, "creates one of the largest agriculture-focused equipment companies in Canada."[41] As a result, Pattison Agriculture now operate John Deere dealerships throughout Saskatchewan in Yorkton, Wynyard, Balcarres, Moosomin, Foam Lake, Preeceville, Humboldt, Kelvington, Swift Current, North Battleford, Kindersley, Maple Creek, Shaunavon, Leader, Kyle, and Unity, as well as in Russell, Manitoba.[42]

Chemicals including herbicides and pesticides as well as fertilizers are key elements of high-input agriculture. In Saskatchewan, 79 percent of farmers reported using pesticides in 2013, the highest number in any province in Canada.[43] In a 2017 Statistics Canada survey, 94 percent of Saskatchewan farms used herbicides, 26 percent used insecticides, while 37 percent used fungicides.[44]

As is the case in equipment manufacturing, this industry is controlled by a relatively few very large firms. (The fact that all the figures quoted in this paragraph are in US dollars illustrates the scale of these enterprises.)

Among the largest is the Syngenta Group: operating in more than a hundred countries, the company saw its 2021 sales exceed $28 billion with its offering of more than a hundred brands of post- and pre-emergence herbicides.[45] Bayer Crop Science chalked up sales of over $21 billion in 2020, while BASF SE had $6.76 billion in revenue. The Bayer Group represents 420 consolidated companies.[46] Along with its seed division, it has several other major divisions, including pharmaceuticals, consumer health, and animal health. In 2016, Bayer purchased US-based Monsanto for $63 billion, after which it continued to produce and sell original Monsanto products absent the Monsanto name.[47] Bayer Crop Science Canada offers a wide range of fungicides (16), insecticides (7), herbicides (19), as well as seeds and seed treatments.[48] Another major actor is the 150-year-old German firm BASF, one of the largest chemical companies in the world. Its 12 divisions manage 58 global and regional business units that together produce over 75 products, including fungicides, herbicides, insecticides, and biological crop-protection products, as well as seeds and seed-treatment products.[49]

In 2016, two large and established American chemical companies, Dow Chemicals and Dupont, merged to become DowDuPont; however, in 2019 the company split into three conglomerates. Dow Chemical specializes in material sciences (plastics and silicones) and DuPont Corteva Agriscience focuses on agricultural products and services.[50] Other chemical and fertilizer companies include Corteva, which operates in more than 140 countries, has more than 150 research and development facilities, and owns more than 12,000 patents for products produced in over 100 production and manufacturing facilities.[51]

Omnipresent on the Prairies is Nutrien, one of the leading global producers of fertilizers. Nutrien boasts more than 1,700 retail facilities across the United States, Canada, Australia, and key areas of South America, servicing more than 500,000 grower accounts.[52] Its direct-to-grower sales in 2018 were over US$12 billion, including revenue from its subsidiaries the Potash Corporation of Saskatchewan, Agrium Potash, and Cominco Fertilizer Partnership. Nutrien produces 22 percent of the world's potash output, in part through its Saskatchewan mines at Allan, Cory, Lanigan, Patience Lake, Rocanville, and Vanscoy.[53]

The lesson to be drawn from this rather mind-numbing set of data concerning groups of companies so large that their revenues dwarf those of many governments is quite simple: regardless of whether you are a traditional family farm, or an incorporated family enterprise, or a large investor-funded commercial agribusiness corporation, when you enter the marketplace to purchase various inputs you have no choice but to confront some of the largest corporations in the world. What about the sale of agricultural commodities?

FARM GATE TO TABLE IN A GLOBAL MARKET

Beyond the ideological attraction of owning your own land, supposedly freeing you of the control of others and making a better future for you and your family, the hours, days, and years of back-breaking work that occupied settlers on the Prairies were typically geared to one activity—producing commodities such as cereal grain for sale. As we noted in chapter 2, owing in part to the actions of the private grain trade and to farmers' determination to get a fair deal, for at least the first half of the 1900s the most significant organizations devoted to grain handling and sales were farmer-owned co-operatives—namely, the Prairie wheat pools and the United Grain Growers (UGG). The pools emerged in the aftermath of the first iteration of the CWB, when farmers realized the value of collective versus individual competitive selling. The UGG was a farmer-owned co-operative that dated from 1917, when the Grain Growers' Grain Company and the Alberta Farmers' Co-operative Elevator Company merged.[54]

Although owned by its farmer-patrons, the UGG did not pay dividends like other co-operatives, opting instead to retain earnings and steadily expand its operations and purchasing companies such as McGabe Grain and Midland and Pacific. During the 1960s and '70s, the leadership of the UGG shifted the ideological stance of the company toward more deregulated, market-oriented policies, culminating in the decision to allow shareholders to own more than one share at the same time it moved to sell shares on the Toronto Stock Exchange—a decisive move away from typical co-op principles. In 1992–93, the company began a radical reorganization, offering producers who had delivered grain to the UGG during the last six years an opportunity to buy shares.[55] Then, in 1998 the Alberta Wheat Pool and Manitoba Pool Elevators merged to form a new company, Agricore, which subsequently merged with the UGG in 2001, ending Agricore's days as a farmer-owned co-operative.[56]

As the UGG was expanding and restructuring, the Saskatchewan Wheat Pool (SWP) was itself on the verge of a change that would see the disappearance of the last major producer co-operative. An important financial presence in the Canadian grain market and an iconic physical presence with its many local elevators across the Prairie landscape, the SWP had been a success story. In 1975, for example, it returned over $12 million in cash payments to members in addition to allocating resources for construction of facilities. The world was changing, however, and by the 1990s the SWP was facing an ever more difficult situation, as Brett Fairbairn explains: "The cooperative could not...escape the dominant agricultural trends. Low farm incomes created pressure to operate on low margins; rural depopulation left the pool with fewer and aging members. Pool managers and leaders became concerned in the late 1980s with the cooperative's debt burden, resulting from an aging membership entitled upon retirement to share payouts. At the same time, they saw a need for investment and expansion to meet the challenges of transnational competitors and new agricultural markets."[57]

Laureen Gatin's study of the SPW illustrates how the co-operative, which was also once a model of democratic governance and participation in a complex organization, was transformed from a co-op into a joint-stock company. The death knell for the last co-operative alternative to private grain enterprises came via a private member's bill in the Saskatchewan legislature. Farming members of the restructured SWP were eligible to have a portion of their ownership shares converted to one Class A voting share, with their remaining equity converted to Class B shares. There was extensive member opposition to the privatization, most systematically from a group calling themselves the Cooperating Friends of the Pool.[58]

The commencement of share trading in spring 1996 marked a historic shift, but more change was still to come. In 2007, the new SWP acquired Agricore United and subsequently changed its name to Viterra, meaning even the Saskatchewan Wheat Pool name would pass into history. A representative of the National Farmers Union, which opposed the privatization of the SWP, commented on the change as follows: "In some ways it's putting the last nail in the coffin so that people aren't confused anymore....It hasn't been a farmers' co-operative for many years. So, I guess they're trying to lay that in the ground."[59] In January 1996, a group opposed to the transformation of the SWP picketed the pool's head office in Regina bearing placards with such phrases as "Who let the sharks into the pool?" while others carried a makeshift coffin containing share-offering plans.[60] A month later, the president of the SWP felt it necessary to use a half-page ad in an important regional paper to name and criticize opponents of the change, whom he accused of "making frivolous and vexatious allegations."[61]

It turns out that the webs of interconnection in the corporate world are thick as Viterra soon bought ABB Grain, a very large Australian-based company that included in its pedigree the remnants of the privatized Australian Wheat Board. But further consolidation was to come when, in spring 2012, Viterra was purchased for C$6.2 billion by Glencore International.[62] Glencore has been described as "one of the world's leading integrated producers and marketers of commodities, headquartered in Baar, Switzerland, and listed on the London and Hong Kong Stock Exchanges. Glencore has worldwide activities in the production, sourcing, processing, refining, transporting, storage, financing and supply of metals and minerals, energy, and agricultural products."[63]

The demise of farmer-owned and -controlled grain-handling co-operatives was part of a grand restructuring of the entire Prairie grain-handling system that also involved the loss of a significant number of rail branch lines and the concomitant loss of many grain elevators. The expansion of an intricate network of rail lines and grain-handling sites was an essential element of the settlement process. As the Canadian economy became more closely tied to a north–south commercial, trade, finance, and integrated manufacturing axis in the aftermath of the Depression and the Second World War and farm numbers began to decline, not only did rail line expansion cease, but decline set in as well. We saw this as early as 1966 with changes to railroad legislation, but it was the Snavely Commission followed by the Hall Commission and then the 1987 changes to the *National Transportation Act* that resulted in wholesale abandonment. The Canadian Transportation Agency provides information on rail line abandonment, including the names of the seventy communities impacted by this process between 1997 and 2018, during which time nearly 1,150 miles of track were abandoned.[64]

The loss of rail lines necessarily means the abandonment of many local elevators. The drop in the number of grain elevators since the 1960s is even more pronounced, as we see in table 5.5.

Table 5.5. Decline in Primary Elevators in Saskatchewan, 1962–2019

Year	Number of elevators	Year	Number of elevators
1962	2,878	1995	709
1965	2,842	2000	437
1970	2,732	2005	191
1975	2,309	2010	162
1980	1,805	2015	173
1985	1,031	2019	180
1990	834		

This table illustrates the steady decline in the number of primary elevators in Saskatchewan between 1962 and 2019. Source: Canadian Grain Commission, "Primary Elevators in Saskatchewan from 1962 to 2019," Government of Canada, last modified December 4, 2018, https://www.grainscanada.gc.ca/application/geicoweb/geicohistorysearchreport-en.

The obvious question is, where, given all of these disruptions, is a cereal grain producer to sell her or his grain? In a move that harkens back to the turn of the twentieth century, the private grain trade has returned in force, now represented by some of the largest multinational enterprises in the sector. Although not yet a major presence in Canada, Archer-Daniels-Midland (ADM) ranks as one of the largest grain-handling companies in the world, with 2019 sales of over $74 billion and an income of $1.4 billion (all figures in this paragraph are US dollars).[65] Another mammoth grain-handling company, Bunge, is not yet a major operator in Canada, but it is a world power nonetheless. Bunge's 2018 income was $456 billion from a portfolio that "includes 32 port terminals, 51 oilseed processing plants, more than 160 grain silos and 119 production facilities." Bunge also has "relationships with more than 70,000 farmers spanning over 60 countries."[66] Another growing presence on the Prairies is Cargill, with 2021 sales and other revenue of $134.5 billion from operations in 125 countries.[67] Lastly, Glencore International's three divisions (metals and minerals, energy, and agriculture) with assets worth $128.7 billion, reported revenue of $219.75 billion in 2018, generating $3.41 billion.[68]

ADM, Bunge, Cargill, Glencore, and Louis-Dreyfus are the largest global players. Many of these companies date back to the 1800s and are involved in a range of activities beyond the buying and selling of grain. A study of the sector notes that these firms trade in "a host of other agricultural and non-agricultural commodities, while they also undertake a range of activities from finance to production to processing and distribution."[69] Further, "New entrants into this space have also taken on complex structures and activities in a bid to stay competitive."[70] That seems to be the case with some long-established, large Canadian corporations.

There are several important contemporary Canadian firms buying and selling grain; we first encountered some of them in chapter 2, including Richardson International. Now over 150 years old, that company operates as Richardson Pioneer and provides grain marketing, agronomic services, seed supply, crop protection, fertilizer and nutrient products, and financial services.⁷¹ Since Richardson is a privately owned company, no information on income or earnings is available. Likewise, Paterson Grain, founded in 1908, is a privately held company marketing grain that also provides business planning, crop nutrition and seed products, and various chemicals. Income and profit information are not available to the public.⁷² Founded a year after Paterson, Parrish & Heimbecker remains family owned and describes itself as operating at more than 60 locations and as "growth-oriented, diversified and vertically-integrated with operations spanning across grain trading, handling and merchandising, as well as crop inputs, flour milling and feed mills."⁷³ As a private company, Parrish & Heimbecker also withholds revenue and profit data.

Perhaps the next logical question is, who is buying grain in Saskatchewan these days? Railroad data shown in table 5.6 indicates that in Saskatchewan in 2013 there were only 146 elevators and inland terminals capable of spotting twenty-five cars or more.

Table 5.6. Major Inland Terminal Operators in Saskatchewan

Company	Number of SK elevators and terminals	Company	Number of SK elevators and terminals
Cargill	12	Viterra	39
CWB (Bunge)	5	Legumex Walker	3
Louis-Dreyfus	5	Saskcan Pulse Trading	3
Parrish & Heimbecker	11	Simpson Seeds	2
Paterson Grain	14	Various Independents	64
Richardson Pioneer	29		

This table lists the major inland terminal operators in Saskatchewan from largest to smallest. *Source: Canada Pacific, Canadian Grain Elevator and Terminal Directory (Calgary: Grain Marketing Department, Canadian Pacific, 2015), https://www.cpr.ca/en/customer-resources-site/Documents/canada-grain-directory.pdf.*

Rather than just thinking in terms of producers, inputs, and outputs, perhaps we might think in terms of the entirety of the food chain. If we consider the land base and input sectors as linked to the producer on one side, and the commodity markets and marketers a link on the other side, the grain merchants and handlers are not the end of the chain. Food production is, and always has been, about consumption: food is produced for people to consume, satisfying a prerequisite for life. A full understanding of the complexities of what has happened and continues to happen on the Prairies requires a brief consideration of two more links in the food chain, those enterprises focused on food processing and grocery distribution.

As is the case with agricultural inputs and increasingly the export and sale of grain and most agricultural products, the food processing industry is increasingly dominated by a relatively small number of very large multinational corporations. The sector has been subject to a significant amount of scholarly attention and examination by various agencies.[74] Just to provide a flavour of this aspect of the food chain, here is a small of sample of some of the major actors in the processing sector.

Among global companies is Swiss-based Nestlé, which has been active in Canada since 1918. Through mergers and acquisitions, some of Nestlé's brands include Nescafé, Maggi, Taster's Choice, Carnation, Nestlé Quik, Stouffers, MJB Coffee, Rowntree Mackintosh, Perrier, and Alpo pet food. Nestlé's total 2017 sales were over $91 billion (all figures in this and the next paragraph are in US dollars).[75] It has partnerships with another giant, General Mills and its vast range of products, including Betty Crocker, Yoplait, Bisquick, Ralston Purina, Pillsbury, and Green Giant.[76] Then there is Kraftco, owned by Philip Morris. In 2003, Philip Morris changed its name to the Altria Group. In a deal worked out by 3G Capital and Warren Buffett's company Berkshire Hathaway, in 2015 Kraft merged with Heinz Foods, making the new company the third-largest in the United States.[77] In 2019, its sales were about $25 billion, with an array of products under both Kraft and Heinz brands.[78] After accidentally discovering how to make cornflakes in 1898, the Kellogg family introduced a new corn-based breakfast cereal to Canada in 1914 and never looked back. The company produced a lot of food for the United States Armed Forces during the First World War and breakfast food for Apollo 11's famous moon landing.[79] In addition to a wide range of breakfast cereals, Kellogg's owns Eggo Company Foods, Kashi, and RxBar, which generated a combined $13.54 billion in sales in 2018.[80] Kellogg's sold Keebler to Nutella for $1.3 billion in 2019.[81]

Among the other processing giants is PepsiCo. In 2018 it employed nearly 270,000 people worldwide and garnered an operating profit of over $10 billion and net revenue of over $64 billion. PepsiCo's North American operations include Frito-Lay North America (whose products include name brands such as Cheetos, Doritos, Fritos, Lay's, Ruffles, and Tostitos Tortilla); Quaker Foods North America (including name brands like Pearl Milling [previously Aunt Jemima], Cap'n Crunch, Life cereal, Quaker Chewy granola bars, Quaker grits, Quaker oat squares, and Quaker oatmeal, rice cakes, granola, and Rice-A-Roni products); and North America Beverages (whose products include Pepsi, Aquafina, Mountain Dew, Gatorade, Propel, Sierra Mist, and Tropicana). PepsiCo is involved in third-party agreements and joint ventures with Unilever (under the Lipton brand name) and Starbucks. Through another agreement with Keurig, the company also produces Dr Pepper, Crush, and, through an agreement with the Dole Food Company, Ocean Spray cranberry products.[82]

PepsiCo's main competitor is Coca-Cola, the world's largest beverage company. It is also organized into what it calls operating segments; these cover Eurasia and Africa, Europe, Latin America, North America, and Asia-Pacific, as well as the company's bottling, investments, and corporate divisions. Coca-Cola produces a wide range of brand names, in North America and across the globe; these include various Coca-Cola products, Minute Maid, Aquarius, Bonaqua/Bonaqa, Powerade, Dasani, Fanta, Sprite, Schweppes, and Glacéau Vitaminwater.[83] The last link in the chain is, of course, the retail consumer.

The local merchant was an important element in the development of Prairie towns and villages. Prior to the First World War, it was common for these settlements to have at least one general store. The early general stores were typically over-the-counter operations of the type you might see depicted in Western movies and in which many products were literally behind the counter and served personally by proprietors and staff. In many towns and villages, family-run independent stores provided a broad range of retail services on the Prairies in the post–Second World War era. It was common for the local grocery or hardware store to offer their regular customers short-term credit, either for convenience or out of temporary need. In his essay "The Golden Age of the General Store: Life before Malls" R.B. Fleming noted that "the credit system was a delicate balancing act, for the merchant had to be careful not to offend a recalcitrant customer while at the same time making certain that the store collected enough money to pay accounts at wholesale houses in nearby cities."[84]

As Prairie towns grew, many local grocery stores became associated with the US-based Independent Grocers Alliance (IGA). Operating in Canada since 1955, IGA provided franchise owners with a name brand and promotions as well as an assured supply chain that included a few IGA-branded products.[85] After a series of ownership changes, in 1964 IGA became part of a major Central Canadian food retail and wholesale operation called the Oshawa Group. In 1999 it was purchased by Sobeys.[86]

Co-operative purchasing and retail sales activities on the Prairies date from at least 1899.[87] John Archer has documented the existence of what was a typical formal co-operative purchasing and sales organization with 600 members dating from as early as 1908.[88] The development of local co-operative stores providing a wide range of products, including food, resulted in the formation of a Prairie-wide purchasing organization in 1928; since 1947, it has formally been known as Federated Co-operatives Limited.[89] Larger supermarket-style food stores grew in importance amid the 1950s baby boom. In the United States, several mergers and acquisitions resulted in the creation of Safeway, with its open-store format and mass inventory.[90] By the early 1950s, many Safeway stores offered more than six thousand products in large, twenty-thousand-square-foot stores. Safeway

Canada acquired its own dairy company and added in-house pharmacies before being bought out by Sobeys in 2013.[91]

One of Safeway's major competitors in larger markets was Loblaws, a company in Toronto in 1919 under the name Loblaw Groceterias. These stores were volume-based, allowing them to offer lower prices on a cash-and-carry basis. Garfield Weston bought a controlling interest in the Loblaws in the early 1950s. George Weston Ltd. was already an established presence in the Canadian food industry, having introduced mechanized bakery-production methods to lower production costs and allow the company to expand into the United Kingdom. Weston bought out Western Grocers in 1944. Perhaps the company's Superstores are the most obvious face of Loblaws today, but it also acquired the Shoppers Drug Mart Corporation for C$12.4 billion in cash and stock in 2014.[92] Loblaws' current CEO, Galen Weston, is a member of Canada's second-wealthiest family, whose wealth *Forbes* magazine estimates at US$8 billion.[93]

In 2017, George Weston Ltd. and Loblaws admitted to a widespread bread-price-fixing scheme running from 2001 to 2015. In the end, they "cooperated with the Competition Bureau in exchange for immunity, which protected both companies from any fines or other penalties, including jail time. To assuage consumer outrage, Loblaws offered shoppers $25 gift cards. In late 2017, two $1-billion class-action lawsuits were filed against Weston, Loblaws and several other companies believed to be part of the scheme."[94]

By the first decades of the twenty-first century, the external environment in which Western Canadian farmers and other agricultural producers operate had changed radically. The normal dynamics of market concentration and centralization in the input sectors had reduced the number of producers to a relatively small number of very large enterprises. Likewise, in the output sector, market competition, innovation, entrepreneurial shrewdness, and sometimes luck had reduced the number of competitors, resulting in fewer but larger enterprises involved in the national and international grain trade. In one of his last ruminations on the dynamics of the market and of capitalism more broadly, Heilbroner insightfully notes that "Nowadays one does not hear much about the Invisible Hand, Adam Smith's marvellous metaphor for the market system."[95] He attributes this to the operation of a non-competitive market dominated by giant multinational corporations, the latter creating demand and needs and then catering to them through largely non-competitive pricing. This was not what Smith had envisioned.

FROM UNITY TO DIVISION

We noted the relative homogeneity of family farmers and their economic and political concerns through the end of the 1920s. Even though most were vitally interested in the production and marketing of grains, commodity specialization began to erode the notion of common economic interests among producers. As a result, producer associations and organizations promoting particular commodities, products, and livestock breeds had emerged even before the First World War. While it is safe to say that through the 1910s and '20s, most of these organizations would agree on general issues, such as the tariff, the need to regulate the grain trade, and even support for the CWB and grain pooling, after the Second World War such consensus would be harder to find. The rapid mechanization of agricultural production after 1945, the embrace of new crops and market opportunities, and the growing size of many producers were bringing about a changed political and economic landscape. By the time the turbulent 1960s had passed, there were open and even antagonistic differences between and among sectors and groups of cereal grain producers, particularly over such fundamental issues as the Crow Rate, the CWB, and rail transportation restructuring.[96] An illustration of these dynamics is in order.

As the debate over the Crow Rate intensified, a group of farmers interested in changing, if not eliminating, the rate met in Regina in January 1970. Among the organizers was an agricultural machinery dealer from Avonlea, Saskatchewan, Mr. Walter "Wally" Nelson, who was instrumental in organizing those opposed to the Crow. The result was a new agrarian organization, the Palliser Wheat Growers Association. Mr. Nelson was committed to free markets and "a more market responsive regulatory environment for the grain industry."[97] Palliser Wheat Growers subsequently became the Western Canadian Wheat Growers Association (WCWGA).[98] Whereas one might argue that the agrarianism of the 1920s emphasized co-operation and government regulation, and even occasionally ownership of grain handing facilities, the WCWGA is avowedly pro–private enterprise and pro-market in all its advocacy. Among the initiatives the WCWGA were supporting in early 2020 were "open and competitive markets, greater operating freedom to manage our farm businesses in a profitable and sustainable manner and removal of barriers to market access."[99]

The WCWGA proudly ties itself to a group of sponsors that includes some of the giant agricultural-related multinationals discussed above, among them Bayer, BASF, John Deere, Nutrien, Case IH, New Holland, Corteva, Richardson, and Viterra. In 2020, the association's website featured an excerpt from a speech the premier of Saskatchewan, Scott Moe, delivered to a WCWGA conference. After beginning by addressing those gathered only as "Gentlemen," he thanked the members for being willing to "mix it up every now and again, to throw off the gloves and defend market-oriented solutions in our province and in our nation." He noted that "for many years you have been the voice of reason in this debate and for many years you have served as a deep repository of common sense." As an example, he cited the debate over grain marketing, and went on to praise the organization's stance on issues such as the carbon tax.[100] (He did not otherwise explain who the voice of *un*reason belonged to.)

At about the same time as the Palliser Wheat Growers was emerging, another farm organization was reorganizing. In 1921, a group of farmers split from the Saskatchewan Grain Growers Association over the issue of a compulsory wheat pool; the result was the formation of the Farmers Union of Canada (Saskatchewan Section).[101] A national organization was not forthcoming at the time, and the Saskatchewan organization was nearly defunct by the late 1940s, but producer unrest and a new leader resulted in the formation of the Saskatchewan Farmers Union. The new organization did well at attracting members and it became an active voice in policy advocacy on such matters as crop insurance and agricultural stabilization. Amid the agricultural crisis of the 1960s and '70s, various national farmers unions decided to form a national organization, and the National Farmers Union (NFU) duly emerged out of a 1969 meeting of the groups in Winnipeg.

From its inception, the NFU was clear that its major concern was the health and wellness of the traditional family farm. In line with this orientation, any member over fourteen years of age belonging to a farm family enjoys full voting rights.[102] It is organized according to a regional structure, with its eight sections representing all parts of Canada. Regional conventions elect regional board members, and the national board is elected annually. The NFU's "Statement of Purpose" articulates an orientation and approach quite different from that of the WCWGA, with its commitments to family farming, environmental sustainability, gender equality, and vibrant rural communities. On its website the NFU continues to hold up the original 1969 Statement of Purpose, which reads in part: "We are learning that the pursuit of only individual self-interest leads inevitably to self-destruction. We are learning that the society in which we live and toil is exploitive in nature and the power of abundance we possess is widely subjected to economic exploitation to our disadvantage."[103]

While much more could be said about both the WCWGA and the NFU, the point here is to highlight the fragmented voices representing agriculture. There are, of course, a great many other national and provincial organizations and associations speaking for particular agricultural interests. Associations from virtually every sector and region are members of the Canadian Federation of Agriculture, as are provincial umbrella associations such as the Agricultural Producers Association of Saskatchewan. The latter was formed in 2000 as a result of a decision by the Saskatchewan Association of Rural Municipalities to establish an organization "aimed at giving Saskatchewan producers more of a voice and say in policy making."[104] While the association works with many agricultural and corporate partners, specialized commodity groups also play a very important role in its operations.

In Saskatchewan alone, the list of farm associations includes representatives for about every agricultural commodity from livestock (including breed-specific organizations) through poultry, virtually all crops, organics, and biotech, not to mention dozens of commercial developments and research facilities.[105] In 1987, Dr. Grace Skogstad identified nearly thirty major Canadian farm organizations.[106] Little wonder that in 1967, after a major farm demonstration in Ottawa, the minister of agriculture, Joe Green, mused on the difficulty of dealing with farm issues when confronted with so many disparate voices.[107]

The title of this chapter invokes farmers' *tenuous* position in the agricultural food chain, and we began by identifying the current era of global capitalism as an "age of uncertainty." Given what we know about the dynamic and ever-changing nature of capitalism, perhaps tenuousness and uncertainty aptly describe a society in which social classes are a primary reality. However, history tells us that what is tenuous or uncertain for one class may not be so for another. An emerging theme in this volume has been the changing positions of Western independent commodity producers—especially those trading in grain and oilseed—in the emerging and evolving global capitalist order and in the Canadian economy particularly. Between Confederation and the Great Depression, the overall structural position of the Western grain farmer was, leaving aside the vagaries of weather and individual malfeasance, anything but tenuous owing to the beneficial nature of the National Policy. To be sure, the normal tendencies of the market to concentrate and centralize production, coupled with the transition of the Canadian economy toward continental integration, introduced an element of tenuousness and uncertainty, but governments were prepared to offer a substantial degree of support to largely maintain the status quo. It was the full force of the so-called free market and the emergence of a fully globalized capitalist economic order, along with the hegemony of neoliberal political economy, that introduced a definite element of tenuousness into the positions of Western family farmers. Henceforth, they would become one quite small and indeed shrinking piece of the global economy.

So much of uncertainty described in this chapter stems from the confusion that seemed to reign after the onset of the 2008–09 financial crisis. It was as if the unfettered and deregulated market promulgated by so many powerful economic and political interests since the 1970s was incapable of functioning, at least without generating unprecedented levels of domestic and global inequality. If the market, as the be-all and end-all of human affairs, necessarily concentrates and centralizes wealth to generate unsustainable inequality, which in turn erodes the capacity of the market to function, then surely we have entered an age of uncertainty.

CHAPTER 6

MEANWHILE, BACK on the FARM

UNABATED NEOLIBERALISM

A LTHOUGH WE HAVE FOCUSED ON THE PERIOD PRIOR to 2015, the trends and tendencies outlined in previous chapters continue to inform the current direction in federal agricultural legislation. Just as both major political parties in Canada came to accept the National Policy as the foundation for their agricultural policies before the Great Depression, so, too, in the decades since have they adopted the world view first systematically articulated in the 1989 policy statement *Growing Together: A Vision for Canada's Agri-Food Industry*. The essential message of that document—that farming is a business essentially like any other—was more or less retained with the publication over a similar policy statement, 2007's *Growing Forward*; this has continued with *Growing Forward 2* (2013) and the *Canadian Agricultural Partnership* (2018), which announced a new government policy under that name. In announcing the Canadian Agricultural Partnership (CAP), Lawrence MacAulay, minister of agriculture and agri-food, stated that "our goal is to help Canadian farmers, ranchers and processors compete successfully in markets at home and around the globe, through this strong collaboration between provincial, territorial and federal governments."[1] The CAP framework offered easier and streamlined access to services with "key enhancements to programs that help farmers manage significant risks that threaten the viability of their farm and are beyond their capacity to manage."[2] The Canadian Federation of Agriculture identified three familiar priorities: "Growing trade and expanding markets. Innovative and sustainable growth of the sector. Supporting diversity and a dynamic, evolving sector."[3]

Hidden in all this rhetoric are some fundamentally important assumptions, not just about farming and agriculture but about how the world works, and indeed how life is to be lived. In "Neoliberalism: The Idea that Swallowed the World," Stephen Metcalf describes neoliberalism as "a way of reordering social reality, and of rethinking our status as individuals." He reminds us that the market is a human institution, and that humans must be decision makers and not just decision *takers*, as that would suggests a loss of agency. Although he is not speaking about farming and farmers, Metcalf's words help us to understand Western agriculture as presented here: "You see how pervasively we are now urged to think of ourselves as proprietors of our own talent and initiative, how glibly we are told to compete and adapt."[4]

QUESTIONS AND CONSEQUENCES

Our final task is to address some of the social, cultural, political, and economic implications of the transformation of the class structure of the Prairies and of Saskatchewan especially. The first of these relates to how we understand agriculture and family farming. Is farming and food production a calling involving the satisfaction of a fundamental human need in a socially conscious manner, or is it a business whose primary objective is generating a return on investment? The second relates to the fate of the various communities that are a part of, and have served the needs of, the agricultural sector. How have various local communities been impacted by the declining number of family farms? The third set of implications we want to explore brings our analysis back to the level of the individual, in this case how the changes explored here have impacted people's health and well-being. The last implication we will consider relates to the political dimensions of the structural changes we have been describing. This must also include some reflection on the implications of our narrative for truth and reconciliation.

FROM COMMUNITARIAN AGRARIANISM TO ENTREPRENEURIAL CORPORATIZATION

For decades, sociologists have been studying the emergence of different world views and ideological perspectives regarding the nature and character of farming and food production. One academic article, whose title—"The Great Agricultural Transition: Crisis, Change, and Social Consequences of Twentieth Century U.S. Farming"—resonates with the theme of this volume, albeit from the American perspective, begins like this: "The exodus of Americans from farming is one of the most dramatic changes in the U.S. economy and society in the past century."[5] Based on a definition of class similar to the one used here, the authors identify an emerging corporatist model of farming, essentially pro-industrial or high-input agriculture, based on "global production chains in which family farmers themselves play a relatively small part of the sociological story which centers largely on the actions of agribusiness, the state, and increasingly, non-governmental organizations concerned with trade and environment."[6] Caroline Tauxe has studied the contradictions between the ideologies and mythologies of family farmers, on the one hand (with their firm belief in a pioneer-rooted self-sufficiency, individualism, free enterprise, and the sanctity of the land), and the decline of the family farm as the dominant economic institution and the concomitant increase in corporate power, on the other.[7]

Studies of farmers' attitudes and approaches to agriculture in Washington State and Nebraska document the emergence of clear-cut ideological and behavioural differences between two different agricultural paradigms—the new environmental paradigm and the conventional or industrial paradigm. The latter has been described as "capital-intensive, large-scale, highly-mechanized agriculture with monocultures of crops and extensive use of artificial fertilizers, herbicides and pesticides, with intensive animal husbandry."[8] The new environmental paradigm, by contrast, emphasizes the protection of the environment, balance, co-operation as opposed to the domination of nature, smaller farm sizes, and various sustainable agricultural practices that might be described as natural, organic, regenerative, bio-dynamic, agro-ecological, and/or low-input farming.[9] Other scholars have differentiated between conventional agriculture and alternate agriculture, with the former entailing high-input agriculture practices, monoculture production, the domination of nature, high levels of capital input, and self-interest, all driven by a singular focus on the profit motive. Alternate agriculture, meanwhile, refers to lower capital needs, local and regional production and processing, community preservation, diversity of products, and an embrace of long-term values over short-term profit.[10]

Academics have also examined the ideological and other fissures that have developed among North American farmers. A study of gender—specifically masculinities among farm men—identified differences between practitioners of conventional and alternative farming in terms of how they performed masculinity. In particular, it found that the conventional farmer is increasingly depicted in advertising material as the "white business-class manager who operates the farm operations without getting his hands dirty."[11]

The notion of "The Entrepreneurial Self" is invoked in the title of a study of farmers' self-identity in the American Midwest. Tracking the transformation of what has been called the "yeoman family farmer" through a series of interviews with Minnesota farmers, the author documented the increasing salience of an entrepreneurial self-conception as opposed to an earlier emphasis on one's interpersonal and social responsibilities in a larger community. Such an attitude tends to see individuals as the sole authors of the economic difficulties they encounter. In the words of one farmer interviewed for the study, "A farmer who lost his farm is a lousy manager. Where in the world can you be a lousy manager and keep your job?" Another described his colleagues like this: "Farmers are competitive. We've got a better barn; we got better cows; we got better horses; we got everything better. They're competitive and sometimes they don't even like each other very well."[12]

Three Saskatchewan sociologists, by contrast, offer a slightly more nuanced picture of contemporary farming, distinguishing between conventional and neo-conventional and organic.[13] While Gertler, Jaffe, and Beckie refer to the "duelling discourses" between neo-conventional and organic producers, neo-conventional or high input has powerful supporters in Saskatchewan. Saskatchewan premier Scott Moe's comments to the 2020 WCWGA convention, noted above, were less diplomatic and inclusive than one might expect of a leader with the responsibility of representing all the citizens of a province. But Moe's predecessor, Brad Wall, has been even more belligerent. In remarks made at a breakfast panel at the Canadian Western Agribition in 2018, he attacked those who would question the high-input commercial model: "Let's not take a knife to a gun fight...we ought to learn from what happened in oil in general, the energy sector, and the agriculture sector. We ought to be ready to put resources and effort and effect into countering what is already out there, and what's probably coming from groups that want to have a run at modern agriculture."[14] Wall is also reported to have referred to unnamed non-governmental agencies and environmentalist as the apparent opponents at this gun fight.[15]

Those who threaten whatever it is that Mr. Wall and Mr. Moe think is threatened are not explicitly named; however, the high-input model has long been the object of criticism. As early as the 1980s, Canadian philosopher and environmentalist Alan Drengson, the author of multiple books, including *The Practice of Technology*, criticized the industrial paradigm for "fail[ing] to create a sustainable agriculture" and for "undermin[ing] the culture of agriculture and the rural communities that make farming possible as a way of life."[16] Perhaps those who would voice these concerns, like the writer and activist Wendell Berry, are the opponents to "modern agriculture" that Moe and Wall worry about.[17] Or perhaps they have in mind those engaged in the sustained opposition to genetically modified wheat, whom Emily Eaton describes in *Growing Resistance*. She documents a number of factors—including the organized actions of consumers fearing negative health consequences, producers fearing market loss, and environmentalists fearing ecological catastrophe—that succeeded in pressuring Monsanto into withdrawing its genetically modified wheat project. However, she also warns that future action against similar proposals will face even stiffer resistance.[18]

COMMUNITY VIABILITY

In 1938, Thornton Wilder won a Pulitzer Prize for his play *Our Town*. With its nostalgic and romantic portrayal of life in small-town North America, the play quickly became a classic. One need not embrace the entirety of Wilder's vision to appreciate that there was an element of civility, comfort, and security in the towns and villages that served the rural population of Saskatchewan and the Prairies. As was noted above, between 1900 and 1945 the number of villages in Saskatchewan grew from 28 to 394, while the number of towns increased from 7 to 90. Ironically, by the time the Canadian economy entered the postwar boom, many small towns and villages were reaching their apex. Jack Stabler and Rose Olfert have been studying the changing character of Saskatchewan cities, towns, and villages, for several decades.[19] According to their own classification system, the number of urban centres offering a significant range of commercial services declined significantly between 1961 and 2001.[20] The 2016 Saskatchewan census confirms the trend of falling numbers of small towns and villages, having reported only 16 cities, 150 towns, and 258 villages.[21] Between 1991 and 2008, no less than 56 villages in Saskatchewan restructured to become organized hamlets, meaning residents became part of the rural municipality in which their hamlet is located. A further marker of the changing physical and political landscape is the fact that between 1993 and

2007, 15 of these organized hamlets restructured and disappeared as formal entities altogether, with their territory and population absorbed into the rural municipality in which they are situated.[22]

Each of these communities, no matter their size, represented people's homes or businesses, their place of employment, their future opportunities and dreams. The class structure of these towns and villages would have been interesting and complex, characterized by small retail and service businesses, often operated by family labour or a small number of paid employees, as well as a variety of professionals, such as doctors, teachers, pharmacists, lawyers, and accountants. Additionally, there would have been a variety of employees working for banks, elevator companies, machinery dealerships, municipal governments, local utilities, school boards, plus various members of the clergy. As towns and villages disappear, so, too, do local merchants, implement parts dealers, mechanics, bank tellers, local characters pontificating over coffee in the café, teachers, barbers, lumber yards, hardware stores, pharmacies, post offices, schools, elevators, hospitals, theatres, dance halls, pool rooms, and everyone and everything else that populated these places. When Saskatchewan reached its centenary in 2005, dozens of villages and hamlets existed in name only, with fewer and fewer people remembering them each year. These places are marked by lone, boarded-up brick school buildings, weathered churches, a dilapidated building or two, or sometimes just a bend in the highway. Imagine having your postal address in Expanse, Reward, Stalwart, Sovereign, Bounty, Plato, Amulet, Sanctuary, Hossier, Hitchcock, Summerberry, or Orkney—*imagine* is all you can do because they are gone, many of them now existing only in local histories, plaques, stone monuments, and fading memories.

HEALTH AND WELLNESS ON THE FARMS

We now turn our attention to the individual level and the health implications of the restructuring of Prairie agriculture. Here, too, the picture is not encouraging. It is a fact that one of the key determinates of health is income and social status. The pattern is clear and illustrates that those in lower socio-economic positions exhibit patterns that result in various kinds of negative health outcomes.[23]

A study of agricultural injuries in Canada began with this ominous statement: "Farming has been recognized as one of the most dangerous occupations in Canada with respect to work-related injuries."[24] Another documented nearly two thousand deaths from agricultural injuries between 1990 and 2008, the vast majority of them (92 percent) occurring among men, with those between forty and sixty-nine suffering the most fatalities.[25] In Saskatchewan, men accounted for the majority of farm-related fatalities between 1990 and 2013, with the number peaking in 1996 at thirty-six but falling with the decline in the farm population. Not surprisingly, the most dangerous months were May (planting) and September (harvest), when the work pressure and stress of getting the crop "in and off" are directly related to the yearly income of the family or enterprise.[26]

The Canadian Centre for Health and Safety in Agriculture, based at the University of Saskatchewan, partnered with 213 rural municipalities to create the Agricultural Health and Safety Network.[27] The network has studied the difficulties of rural people with respiratory conditions who need to access specialized health care as well as the relationship between insecticide exposure and diabetes, concluding that "there is increasing evidence for a cause-effect link between environmental toxicants and diabetes that is related to adipose tissue accumulation and reported effects on insulin production/resistance." Another study by some of the same authors of the health risks associated with what we are calling high-input agriculture found that "workplace exposure to insecticides and fungicides together were statistically significantly associated with the prevalence of prostate cancer."[28]

A significant health risk for individuals who are under various forms of stress is suicide. A 2017 CBC News report highlighting the prevalence of suicide in the agricultural sector quoted a tweet from one farmer emphasizing that "Farm stress is real, suicide is real." The tweet was prompted by the suicide of another farmer and a subsequent statement from the president of the Agricultural Producers Association of Saskatchewan indicating that a conversation on the topic was long overdue.[29] Indeed, he problem is neither new nor isolated to one geographical region or even nation, as studies conducted in Australia and India illustrate.[30] Dr. Mike Rosmann, an American farmer turned clinical psychologist and agricultural commentator, knows farmers well. Describing the situation of one male farmer, he succeeds in painting a much more widely applicable portrait of the independent commodity producer in a patriarchal society facing the loss of his land, machinery, and livelihood:

> The farmer felt he let his family down, his wife and children said, for he claimed that he had made poor business decisions and blamed only himself.... This distressed farmer also was reluctant to let other relatives (his mother and siblings) outside of his immediate family, or any neighbors know of his financial and emotional plight.... He was unable to accept help from his neighbors or anyone. All he could focus on was his perceived failure in comparison to their success.... Intense desire to succeed on their own is characteristic of many farmers. Farmers want to be responsible for their successes and failures and they may isolate themselves emotionally and socially from assistance, even when desperately needed.[31]

In 2019, CBC News reported a significant increase in farm-stress-related emergency calls in Saskatchewan: "Regina-based Mobile Crisis Services said it received 447 calls during those months [April to September] that year, compared to 257 calls over the same quarter in 2018. From July to September 2019 alone, there were 225 calls received, up from 141 over the same months last year—a 60 percent increase."[32] Between June 2018 and January 2019, the House of Commons Standing Committee on Agriculture and Agri-Food studied the mental health challenges faced by Canadian agricultural producers. One Saskatchewan farm operator told the committee the following: "In February, I sat in a room full of 400 producers. We were asked to stand up when a question asked applied to us. The first question was, 'Have you ever lost a family member or friend to suicide?' Ninety percent of the room stood up, and that broke my heart."[33] The resulting report, *Mental Health: A Priority for Our Farmers*, issued in May 2019, begins with this statement: "Farming is hard work: debt, long days, loneliness, and stress. Farmers have to deal with many factors outside their control, such as unpredictable weather, government regulation and market volatility and which are often major stressors. As a result, many farmers struggle with depression or other mental health problems. Some even go as far as suicide."[34]

POLITICAL LOYALTIES

When C.B. Macpherson studied Alberta farmers in the middle of the twentieth century, he was struck by what he described as an oscillation between conservatism and radicalism on the part of the province's petite bourgeoisie.[35] He referred to their inability to adopt or break from conservatism and to make common cause with what he saw as the two other main classes, capitalists and workers. Part of Macpherson's explanation for the "oscillation and confusion" resided in the family farm's simultaneous "dependent and subordinate position in the economy," which he claimed had given rise to an agrarian rather than a class-based consciousness.[36] While Macpherson's analysis is essentially correct, I would offer a minor clarification. The understanding of class and class interests that informs this work would suggest that in Saskatchewan the agrarian petite bourgeoisie tended to vote based on what they perceived as their class interests as agrarian independent commodity producers. In short, traditional family farmers belonged to an agrarian-based class and were therefore endowed with an agrarian class consciousness and an understanding of what they wanted and needed from governments, and in turn which governments they would support. Their outlook, to use Macpherson's term, was based on their class position as well as the agrarian modes of production in which they engaged.

While recognizing the issue of ecological fallacy—or more correctly, the ecological correlation—an examination of political support for various federal parties in Saskatchewan over the last 120 years still reveals some interesting patterns.[37] In the first federal election after Saskatchewan became a province, the Liberals dominated with 9 seats and only 1 for the Conservatives. The 1911 election was fought over an issue of major importance for farmers—the protective tariff. The Liberals were proposing some reduction in tariffs in an agreement with the Americans. The result was national decimation of the Liberals while in Saskatchewan they again took 9 out of 10 seats. The 1917 election was a wartime contest that produced a Unionist Government, all 15 Saskatchewan seats went in support of the coalition. By 1921, grain marketing and the tariff returned to the fore and the newly formed Progressive Party, based on the Farmers' Platform of lower tariffs, won 15 seats, with the Conservatives holding 1 and the Liberals none. Notwithstanding the Progressives' failure to accommodate their identity problems to the party system, in Saskatchewan the 1925 and 1926 elections were largely a contest between the Progressive Party and Liberals.[38] While the Liberals had failed to act meaningfully on tariff reform, for many farmers this paled in comparison to the Conservatives' insistence on the sanctity of tariffs, and when coupled with King's promotion of the notion of old-age pensions, the Liberals came out on top of the fading and flailing Progressives with 16 seats to the latter's 5.

As the Depression began, it seems that most of the Saskatchewan population did not buy Bennett's promised to use tariffs to blast Canada's way into world markets because the province once again went against the grain and elected 12 Liberals compared to 7 Conservatives, who won a majority nationally. The dominance of the Liberals in Saskatchewan was not challenged until 1953, when the provincial popularity of the CCF saw that party elect 11 members compared to 5 Liberals and 1 Progressive Conservative. Support for the CCF and their brand of Keynesianism held strong until 1958, when John Diefenbaker, himself a meeker Keynesian, carried all but one of the province's constituencies. In 1961, the Progressive Conservatives again dominated, electing 16 members to the Liberals' sole seat. A rebranded CCF, now known as the NDP, contested seats in 1963. Many of the legislative initiatives discussed in chapter 3 were of direct benefit to family farmers, the majority of whom overwhelmingly supported the Diefenbaker and Progressive Conservatives through to 1968. But as we have seen, despite the best efforts of the Diefenbaker and his party to support and maintain family farmers, as a class they were fragmenting, and the number of traditional independent commodity producers was in steady decline.

The fragmentation of this class, the pressures of the cost-price squeeze, instabilities in the international wheat markets, and the Progressive Conservatives' move to replace Diefenbaker in 1967—each of these developments did its part to erode support for the party in 1968, when only 5 Progressive Conservatives were elected as compared to 6 members of the NDP. Saskatchewan politics at the federal level throughout the 1970s and '80s somewhat mirrored the many changes that were happening to the class composition of the farming community and many small rural communities. Federal elections were hotly contested with the numbers of Progressive Conservatives and NDP members varying dramatically from election to election. The constant missing element during this period was the Liberal Party. The emergence of the Reform Party and then the Canadian Alliance as the representative of the political Right represented a superficial change, but it did not alter the content of the debate. The fundamental economic issues continued to revolve around questions of transportation, rail rates (the so-called Crow debate), grain marketing and the role of CWB, rail line abandonment, producer subsidies, and a variety of other regulatory regimes.

A new group of agrarian independent commodity producers was emerging who were inclined much more to a vision of agriculture as an opportunity to demonstrate entrepreneurial aplomb rather than a calling. For such producers, an increasing number of whom were small employers, the regulatory regimes associated with the Crow Rate and state intervention in the marketing of grain through the CWB were a restriction instead of a form of assistance. The neoliberal veneration of the market and deregulation, coupled with an emphasis on competition, individualism, and entrepreneurship, seems to have struck a chord with many in Saskatchewan. The manoeuvring on the right of the political spectrum that eventually led to the formation of the Conservative Party of Canada in 2003 set the stage for a dramatic change in the federal political landscape in Saskatchewan and much of the West. From 2004 to the present, the Conservatives have dominated every federal election in Saskatchewan, variously winning 12 or 13 of the 14 seats in 2019 and 2021 winning all the seats.

Although this study has focused largely on the federal level, it is interesting to note that there was also a consolidation of provincial right-wing political forces. The 1999 Saskatchewan provincial election saw the NDP reduced to minority status, while a new right-wing party, the Saskatchewan Party—formed in 1997 by Reform Party supporters along with some former Liberals and Progressive Conservatives—won 24 seats. In 2003, under new leader Lorne Calvert, the NDP held on to a thin, 2-seat majority over the Saskatchewan Party, and the Liberals again disappeared from the legislature. In 2007, the Saskatchewan Party under leader Brad Wall gained a 19-seat majority over the NDP. The Saskatchewan Party increased its seat count in what is in effect a two-party legislature in each election from 2007, to 2016, only going down three in 2020 still winning 48/13.[39]

Without wanting to be flippant, it is undoubtedly true that the end of a class (or a substantial fraction of a class), or a class under threat or facing an existential crisis, tends to generate a mess. In his powerful treatise *The Age of Anger*, Pankaj Mishra employs the French word ressentiment to characterize the current world view of many who find themselves in crisis. The concept describes a complex mix of feelings—including resentment, anger, envy, humiliation, and powerlessness—that accompanies the loss of one's bearing, stability, and sense of place and meaning.[40] The current decade has witnessed the emergence of a number of new political organizations in Saskatchewan, including the Saskatchewan United Party, the Buffalo Party, True North Saskatchewan, and Unified Grassroots.[41] Although some of the grievances and issues these organizations and movements articulate are related to the recent pandemic, it would be more accurate to use the title of Nik Nanos's survey of Canadians' opinions of our major institutions—"Losing Faith"—to describe what is happening.[42]

FAMILY FARMS?

At our present juncture in the twenty-first century, the class of Western agrarian independent commodity producers (family farmers) created by the National Policy and maintained until the 1970s is now coming undone, restructured and transformed by internal and external forces and pressures. The history of capitalism is in large part a history of the transformation of class structures—their emergence and fracturing and eventual disappearance, followed by their reorganization and recomposition. Perhaps the classic account of such a transformation is E.P. Thompson's analysis of the complex history of the English working class. He describes the making, remaking, and unmaking of a class as anything but clear and simple. We know that when new classes and class fractions emerge, or when existing classes become restructured or fade in importance or disappear, the results can include a paradoxical mix of confusion, uncertainty, conflict, realignment, disorientation, and perplexity for some, but also feelings of self-assurance, reassurance, clarity, confidence, certainty, conviction, and buoyancy for others.

The situation facing Saskatchewan farmers involved in grain and oilseed production contains elements of this paradoxical mix. The trend over the past fifty to seventy years is clear—the number of grain and oilseed farms in Saskatchewan continues to fall decade after decade while the size of the remaining farms, in terms of land base, capitalization, and the employment of wage labour, continues to increase. If we understand the family farm as an enterprise operated by a class of independent commodity producers, then its future is cloudy at best. As more farmers and farm families become reliant on off-farm income, their structural position and identity erode. The question of establishing criteria for membership in a class is, and always has been, notoriously difficult. While some formerly independent commodity producers transition into wage labour and salaried careers, others assume the role of employers reliant on wage labour, as opposed to family-based labour, to produce commodities. Given the growing importance of wage labour for this cohort, we must ask: At what point does an agricultural producer become, in structural and subjective terms, an employer, which is to say a capitalist using wage labour to produce commodities? And what of the composition, residency, and lifestyle of the expanding wage labour agricultural workforce? Is this labour force a permanent element of rural communities, purchasing groceries and services at the local businesses, or are they transient and seasonal, with their families residing outside the communities in which they work?[43]

Attempts to answer these types of questions invariably draw us into a definitional and normative discussion of what we mean by "the family farm" in an era of significant class restructuring. A recent article with the tantalizing title "The Canadian Family Farm, in Literature and in Practice" undertook a meta-review of how the concept has been used, supplemented by interviews with self-identified family farmers. Having reviewed the literature, the authors offer the following definition of the family farm: "i) the farm is a business controlled by family members; ii) the business ownership and managerial control are transferred within the family over different generations; iii) a majority of the labor is provided by the operator and his/her family; iv) a substantial part of the capital is furnished by the operator and his/her family."[44] The results of their interviews indicated a more normative understanding. Some participants in the study suggested a family farm is "a farm owned by members bound by kinship or marriage; a small farm; a farm whose material practices reflect community values; a farm which contributes to a local economy and to rural social cohesion; a farm whose material practices grow wider food justice and environmental sustainability."[45] However, they further note it is not always this clear-cut: "Indeed, there was one farmer who implied that there is such incredible diversity in farm strategies and labour arrangements among family farmers he knows that a coherent definition would be too closed to be inclusive of what he called a 'dynamic.'"[46]

This notion of a dynamic situation informs a study on consolidation and concentration of farmland in Saskatchewan that focuses on what the authors refer to as "mega-farms" (those operating more than thirty thousand acres), many of which, they note, have their roots in family farms. They describe the difficulty of defining a family farm in the rapidly changing arena of agricultural production, stating that they prefer a definition of family farm "that includes operations of different sizes, with varying amounts of family versus hired labour, and where farming contributes to some, most, or all of the family's income."[47] They note that the changing structure of agriculture we have documented has produced a variety of conceptual debates, if not conceptual confusion, with some scholars developing new terminology such as "family farm entrepreneurs," "multi-family farms," and "multi-family farm entrepreneurs." Having reviewed the literature, and considered the difficulty of distinguishing a family from a corporate farm, they offer a definition that focuses more on what a family farm is *not*: "For our purposes... we suggest that a farm ceases to be a 'family farm' when one or both of the following are true: 1. the majority of full time operators or employees are not members of the same (extended) family; 2. Family members have less than a 50% controlling interest in the business."[48] They go on to document an important trend in Saskatchewan landholding toward ever larger, highly capitalized agricultural production enterprises based on wage labour that, while it may not appear to be particularly materially significant at this time, is an important trend in line with what this book argues.

RECONCILIATION AND INDIGENOUS AGRICULTURE

There is perhaps no single defining geophysical, economic, cultural, political, ideological, spiritual, and social concept or reality in Saskatchewan and the West more powerful than the notion of "the land." All of the land that encompasses Saskatchewan is covered by treaty. The bulk of agricultural land is covered by Treaties 4 and 6; Treaties 2, 5, and 7 cover, respectively, the province's southeast corner, a small section near the Manitoba border, and another small area near the Alberta border; and Treaties 8 and 10 cover a vast northern area. This is why the banner that runs along the top of the website of the Saskatchewan Office of the Treaty Commissioner states unequivocally, "We Are All Treaty people."[49]

It is a tragedy of Canadian history that these treaties have not been honoured, and that successive governments have instead sought to ideologically and legally legitimize actions such as the implementation of the *Dominion Lands Act* and the subsequent granting of millions of acres of Prairie land to non-Indigenous white settlers. Even the briefest mention in these pages of the many insurmountable barriers that were created not just to discourage but to actually prevent Indigenous people from taking up family and commercial farming serve to illustrate why addressing economic injustice and land rights must be a priority. Indeed, injustices such as these partly explain why it was so necessary to establish the Truth and Reconciliation Commission of Canada in 2008. In its historic and groundbreaking final report, the commission laid out ninety-four Calls to Action, including Call to Action #45, which partly deals with land:

> We call upon the Government of Canada, on behalf of all Canadians, to jointly develop with Aboriginal peoples a Royal Proclamation of Reconciliation to be issued by the Crown. The proclamation would build on the Royal Proclamation of 1763 and the Treaty of Niagara of 1764, and reaffirm the nation-to-nation relationship between Aboriginal peoples and the Crown. The proclamation would include, but not be limited to, the following commitments:
>
> i. Repudiate concepts used to justify European sovereignty over Indigenous lands and peoples such as the Doctrine of Discovery and terra nullius.

ii. Adopt and implement the United Nations Declaration on the Rights of Indigenous Peoples as the framework for reconciliation.
iii. Renew or establish Treaty relationships based on principles of mutual recognition, mutual respect, and shared responsibility for maintaining those relationships into the future.
iv. Reconcile Aboriginal and Crown constitutional and legal orders to ensure that Aboriginal peoples are full partners in Confederation, including the recognition and integration of Indigenous laws and legal traditions in negotiation and implementation processes involving Treaties, land claims, and other constructive agreements.[50]

We are in dire need of a path forward. In 1992, the provincial and federal governments and twenty-five First Nations signed the Saskatchewan Treaty Land Entitlement Framework Agreement as an important step in addressing some of the past injustices relating to treaty land entitlements, land claims, theft, and misappropriation. Some additional First Nations later signed on. The agreement provided both federal and provincial financial assistance to First Nations to expand their agricultural activities. Land purchases and transfers were on a "willing seller/willing buyer" basis.[51] Coupled with some specific land claim settlements, the agreement has had some success, making possible a 2015 federal government announcement declaring "Saskatchewan's One Millionth Acre," which refers to the amount of land that has been returned to Indigenous people under the Treaty Land Entitlement and Specific Claims agreement.[52] According to Statistics Canada, in 2016 there were 15,765 self-identified Indigenous Canadians among the over 590,000 people identified in the agricultural population. At the time, Indigenous people comprised 4.9 percent of the total Canadian population but only 2.7 percent of the agricultural population. The agricultural population includes all people living in agricultural households, which means that not all members of the agricultural population are identified by Statistics Canada as agricultural operators. Indigenous agricultural producers make up 1.9 percent of the total number of agricultural producers in Canada. That figure represents a more than 50 percent increase since 1996, while the total number of agricultural operators declined by about 30 percent. Clearly, Indigenous agriculture is, in spite of all of the earlier obstacles and challenges, becoming more important.[53]

A further indication of the importance of agriculture for many Indigenous people was demonstrated by a December 2018 event called the Forum on Indigenous Agriculture in Saskatchewan, held at Wanuskewin Heritage Park near Saskatoon. The forum brought together elders, chiefs, councillors, land managers, economic development officers, and farm, ranch, and land managers from twenty-four First Nations, as well as farmers, academics, and students.[54] Attendees heard that "agriculture is practiced on 3–4 million acres of First Nations reserve lands in the Saskatchewan Prairies, but predominantly by non-Indigenous farmers."[55] Delegates discussed some of the historical obstacles and impediments to Indigenous agriculture and farming as well as various programs and initiatives, including the Saskatchewan Indian Agriculture Program, which had significant potential before funding was terminated. They also expressed their commitment to a collaborative approach and the co-creation of information. Additional commitments were made to address a number of themes, including the central role of Indigenous knowledge and traditional relationships to the land, capacity building and education, building equitable and effective relationships, farm financing, and the necessity of ensuring that research would result in policy and legislation.[56]

Some First Nations have engaged very successfully in agriculture and farming. For example, Cowessess First Nation has a long history of agricultural activity and a concern with food sovereignty. Chief Cadmus Delorme notes that "there are policy implications as to why Indigenous Peoples don't farm their own land and an explanation for why the agriculture industry currently has minimal Indigenous involvement." Cowessess First Nation has over 200 head of Angus cattle and farms 4,500 acres, with the potential of expanding to 32,000 acres. Chief Delorme is optimistic: "Cowessess First

Nation wants to be part of the growth [in agriculture] as a First Nations-led business. Our end goal is to be farm leaders, and good neighbours who want to work together, grow together, and better understand one another. Agriculture can be that connection between all of us."[57]

Success stories such as this notwithstanding, racism had been a perennial issue in rural Saskatchewan. Numerous reports document how Indigenous people in the province are still subject to explicit as well as implicit racism, whether that takes the form of being followed around a retail outlet, encountering racist graffiti, being called derogatory names, or physical violence. Premier Moe has acknowledged that racism is a problem in Saskatchewan.[58] A notorious example is case of Colten Boushie, a Cree man who was shot and killed by Gerald Stanley, a Saskatchewan farmer, in August 2016. At the time of his death, the twenty-two-year-old Boushie was returning from swimming with several friends when they stopped their car at a farm. During the ensuing interaction, Stanley shot Boushie in the head as he sat in the car, killing him. At his trial, Stanley was acquitted of second-degree murder by a jury that did not have any Indigenous members. In addition to the mistreatment of Mr. Colten Boushie's mother by the RCMP, the case continues to raise fundamental questions. In commenting on the case, Indigenous scholar Brenda Macdougall, who grew up in Saskatchewan, noted the racist reaction to the killing and the larger picture of contemporary Prairie society that it suggested: "In the context of the Canadian West, this narrative is rooted in the historical myth of settlement, which tells us that hardy pioneers made productive unoccupied, unused, and unencumbered lands. This mythology was partly constructed for settlers by their government, then embellished by a citizenry who have excised from historical memory the contributions of indigenous people to their prosperity."[59]

There are, however, some more positive examples of how the land has been shared for non-agricultural purposes. The notion of sharing the land and rights related to hunting, harvesting, gathering medicine, and holding traditional ceremonies are important to some Indigenous people. A group composed of farmers, ranchers, and Indigenous people have come together in Saskatchewan to establish the Treaty Land Sharing Network with the goal of affirming treaty rights and to provide a safe setting in which Indigenous people can engage some of their traditional practices on land that they do not otherwise own.[60] But these sorts of efforts notwithstanding, some groups and individuals in Saskatchewan are concerned that the provincial government is continuing to sell off Crown lands, which has implications for treaty settlements and land claims. Over twenty organizations, including the Office of the Treaty Commissioner, Nature Saskatchewan, the Saskatchewan Federation of Labour, and the National Farmers Union have issued a statement calling for a halt to the sales. By the National Farmers Union's estimation, over two million acres of Crown land have already been sold.[61] In what might be a "one step forward, two steps back" situation, the Government of Saskatchewan has enacted the highly restrictive *Trespass to Property Amendment Act, 2019*, and the *Trespass to Property Consequential Amendments Act, 2019*, both of which came into effect on January 1, 2022.[62]

It is clear that there are tremendous opportunities for Indigenous farming and farmers in Saskatchewan, but at the same time there are also significant challenges, both in terms of Indigenous access to land and resources and the attitudes and behaviour of the larger Saskatchewan population.

EPILOGUE
UNANSWERED QUESTIONS

Given the many upheavals and transitions we've charted throughout this book, and the centrality of agriculture in the development not only of individuals families but of whole societies, we need to ask fundamental questions about food production. We humans need food, but what is not determined by our biological needs are the types of food we consume, how it is produced and prepared, and the social, cultural, and political implications of the decisions we make about how and by whom that food is produced. Given the various threads mapped out in this volume, it is legitimate to ask what the social, political, and environmental implications of high-input agriculture are. Is all the land in the world necessarily and unquestionably subject to private ownership and exploitation by its owners? Desmarais and colleagues make an important distinction between the ownership of and/or investment in farmland as a social good and its being pursued merely for financial gain.[1] Much of our food comes from farms, and farmers are enmeshed in a very complex agri-food industry dominated by some of the largest economic enterprises on the planet. The concentration of power in the sector became more apparent during the spring of 2020, when a global pandemic led to massive economic dislocation, including the temporary closure of several meat-packing plants in Canada and the United States, global supply chain disruptions, and widespread product shortages, which, added to the ongoing negative impacts of climate change, resulted in heightened concerns about food supplies. One particularly worrisome area was the highly concentrated red meat industry, in which "Tyson Foods Inc., and its top two rivals—JBS and Cargill Inc.—today control about two-thirds of America's beef, and the large bulk of it gets processed in a few dozen giant plants. Pork and chicken are similarly dominated."[2]

There are those who would take an unequivocal stand on the merits and apparent productivity of high-input or industrial agriculture, but is the matter really that clear-cut? Some farmers, consumers, and environmentalists were able to thwart the introduction of genetically modified wheat, but what are the long-term implications of our continued dependence on high levels of chemical fertilizers, pesticides, and herbicides? The short-term benefits of higher yields might be obvious, but what are the long-term impacts of such intensive agricultural practices on the land itself? A key element of the contemporary Prairie agricultural landscape, regardless of the commodity being produced and sold, is the high level of corporate concentration among producers. Regardless of whether one operates a large corporate farm, an incorporated "family enterprise," a medium-sized operation employing some wage labour, or a traditional family farm, all buy machinery, equipment, chemicals, fertilizer, and other inputs in what can only be called an oligopolistic market. On the other hand, many of those buying, exporting, and processing the producers' commodities also rank among the largest multinational enterprises. What are the results of the economic power differentials within this sector?

In the introduction, we noted a number of areas where this account might have provided a deeper analysis. It's worth singling out several of these here. The first is the book's exclusive focus on federal legislation and its concomitant neglect of provincial policies and actions. The second is the absence of an adequate consideration of the implications of Western settlement for Indigenous people, as well as the dearth of attention to issues relating to sex and gender. To this we must add a third. In a sense, this book is about economic and political power. We have examined a variety of federal legislative actions, programs, and policies, whether it was in phase 1 (e.g., the *Dominion Lands Act*, the creation of the CPR, the *Manitoba Grain Act*, etc.), phase 2 (e.g., PFAA, the PFRA, and the FCC, etc.), or phase 3 (e.g., the elimination of the Crow Rate and the CWB, the CAP regime, etc.). These were all political decisions. We described some of the outcomes and implications of government legislation and actions, but the crucial questions of why and how a particular action or decision was taken at a particular time has not been broached.

Elsewhere, I have argued that states, governments, and official agencies, as institutional structures, do not make decisions themselves; rather, it is the human agents within these institutions who make decisions. I have also argued that in a liberal democracy such as Canada, there are mechanisms of power through which individuals, classes, groups, and organizations can attempt to influence or impact the actions, policies, and the decision-making processes of governments and the state.[3] An important project not addressed in this volume is the investigation and analysis of how different individuals, classes, and interests engaged various mechanisms of power to influence the sort of policy and legislative actions described in previous chapters. While such a task is obviously beyond the limits of this study, it remains an important undertaking.

The final missing element relates to one of the most important concepts in the entire volume, the operation of the market. In the introduction, we noted that a robust understanding of Macpherson's notion of the market as the site for the "net transfer of power" opens our understanding of a fundamental element of market relations. We know something of the various mechanisms through which "powers" are transferred in the agricultural sector. Even before 1900, Prairie farmers understood that when they took their grain to the local grain buyer there was a net transfer of power. When they sensed that it was not what they believed to be a fair transaction, they organized protests and began to replace the private grain trade with their own co-operatives, hoping to recapture some of the wealth they believed was being appropriated. The same farmers understood that when they purchased their agricultural inputs, there was a net transfer of power to the producers and distributors of those inputs. Farmers also understood that when they borrowed money from banks and other financial institutions, and paid interest on that money, there was yet another net transfer of power.

Given the complexity of contemporary grain production, in recent years scholars have turned their attention to other mechanisms through which wealth is extracted from agriculture through what has been called the financialization of Prairie agriculture.[4] The sector is increasingly complicated by the presence of specialized technicians—previously called "mechanics"—whose job it is to repair computerized farm machinery, real estate agents, consultants, and advisers of every ilk, transportation specialists, human resource agents, to name a few. In each case there is a market transaction, so obviously much more work is required to understand the different mechanisms through which wealth is transferred in the sector. Recent research out of Australia documents the difficulties some farmers have in handling the complexities of a large enterprise in a complex market situation, while in Canada the debate concerns what some have called the "right to repair" debate.[5] The agricultural press has been busy offering advice to producers so they can avoid "futures contracts" committing them to deliver a specified quantity of a given product at a specified date, only to find that, for any number of reasons (including drought), they are unable to fulfil their legal obligation. Stories with titles such as "The Most Common Grain Marketing Errors," "Four Things to Know about Grain Contracts," and "Grain Contracts a Dilemma for Farmers This Year" illustrate the dire situation many a producer has found themselves in.[6]

There can be no doubt that in a complex society such as Canada, the market is a necessary and powerful contrivance for making economic decisions. The paradox of the unfettered market, however, is its inherent tendency to concentrate and centralize economic power and resources in increasingly fewer but larger enterprises. In a sector such as food production, which is fundamental to human existence and survival, if we take the longer view (centuries instead of mere decades) important questions inevitably come to the fore about how humanity is to ensure food sustainability, quality, quantity, and accessibility for all. Do we simply allow all parties along the food chain to engage in whatever form of competition marks their location in complex markets, and in the end sink or swim? Do we worry about the behemoths of the food industry, whose sole interest is their shareholders' bottom line, and who control as commodities the produce that is literally our lifeblood, or do we envision alternate models of production, processing, marketing, and distribution? These are fundamental questions that every human should consider and have the right to play a role in answering.

And so, we are left contemplating the future of family farming and agricultural production in Saskatchewan and the West more broadly. The hopes and aspirations of my grandparents and their neighbours, as first-generation white settlers, were at least partially realized, albeit in the face of a challenging geophysical, economic, social, and political environment and at an immeasurable cost to many Indigenous people and nations. The fate of subsequent generations will almost certainly follow a similar uneven path involving opportunities and setbacks, prospects and obstructions, potentials and impediments. Those family farmers who benefited from the homestead laws could not in their wildest imaginations have entertained the possibility of a farm of ten thousand acres, never mind fifty thousand. As we contemplate some of the questions raised above, we might play with words and ask "whether or wither" the family farm.

ACKNOWLEDGEMENTS

It is difficult to properly acknowledge important sources of support, encouragement, and criticism when a book takes fifty years to produce, but I must try. I was fortunate to study in a department in which faculty members including James N. McCrorie, Bob Stirling, Mary Jo Kinzel, and John Conway made sure that students encountered Canadian scholars such as Vernon Fowke and Harold Innis, whose work is essential to understanding this province and the wider West. As teachers, colleagues, and friends, their understanding of the special role of the Prairies in the political economy of Canada connected what I was learning to the joys and pains experienced by my parents and their friends.

As I finished my dissertation in the 1980s, I already knew that I would one day have to write this book, and I was blessed with an opportunity to return to Saskatchewan, where the project could ultimately be fulfilled. Amid the follies and foibles of life, work, play, and family, the book continued to ferment and take shape in talks, papers, and essays.

About a decade ago, a chance conversation about "that man Partridge" with a distant relative of his, Karen Clark at University of Regina Press, did much to sharpen my feeling that this was a viable project. A spell living in Ontario further heightened my interest in reintroducing Canadians to Fowke's analysis of Prairie agriculture and the deepening crisis facing the family farm. I thank Ms. Clark for her continued interest and her subsequent counsel, which eventually led to a formal proposal and ultimately a manuscript.

As the project evolved and developed, I was lucky to receive encouragement from friends and colleagues, among them Phillip Hansen. I thank Bryan Hillis for invaluable commentary on an initial draft, and Ms. Debby Adair for some early and excellent editorial assistance. I acknowledge and thank the members of the Sociology Department at Brock University who offered a recovering senior administrator an environment that allowed me to get back to important tasks.

I am grateful to Kelly Laycock at University of Regina Press, who took the reins as the project neared completion, and Shannon Parr for bringing the project home with expert and professional guidance. It is a truism, but the absolute truth, that the essential element in every book of this ilk is the copy editor. By whatever good fortune, Ryan Perks agreed to take on this manuscript, and it is the case that words defy my gratitude for his expertise in style and content (if I had the words, he would surely improve them anyway). I also wish to thank the anonymous reviewers at the press, whose input improved the manuscript in many ways. Peer review is an essential element of all academic endeavours, and I acknowledge and thank the anonymous reviewers for their assistance. Having said that, I alone am responsible for all errors, omissions, and what has been misconstrued.

I remain eternally grateful for the love, support, and guidance of Wendee Kubik, Erin, Lee, and their families.

NOTES

INTRODUCTION

1   C.W. Mills, *Sociological Imagination* (New York: Oxford University Press, 1959), 6–9.
2   Vernon C. Fowke, *Canadian Agricultural Policy* (Toronto: University of Toronto Press, 1946), vii; Paul Phillips, "Vernon Clifford Fowke," *Canadian Encyclopedia*, last modified December 15, 2013, https://www.thecanadianencyclopedia.ca/en/article/vernon-clifford-fowke.
3   Paul A. Baran, "Commitment of the Intellectual," in *The Longer View: Essays toward a Critique of Political Economy* (New York: Monthly Review Press, 1969), 8–9.
4   Periodization as an analytical tool has been the topic of much intellectual discussion. As Dietrich Gerhard notes, "the historian knows that any division of time into definite periods is artificial." Gerhard, "Periodization in European History," *American Historical Review* 61, no. 4 (1956): 900. Even with this qualification, periodization is still a useful analytical tool, thus the question becomes the criteria that we use to establish periods or epochs. Peter N. Stearns notes that "periodization, when it works best and most dynamically in history, involves real (and hopefully explainable) alterations in characteristics." Stearns, "Periodization in World History Teaching: Identifying the Big Changes," *History Teacher* 20, no. 4 (1987): 563. See also Adam McKeown, "Periodizing Globalization," *History Workshop Journal*, no. 63 (Spring 2007): 218–30; A. Gangatharan, "Warnings and Cautions: The Problem of Periodization in History," *Proceedings of the Indian History Congress*, no. 69 (2008): 862–71; Herbert Heaton, "Criteria of Periodization in Economic History," *Journal of Economic History* 15, no. 3 (1955): 267–72; William Green, "Periodizing World History," *History and Theory* 34, no. 2 (1995): 99–111. Cognizant of these warnings, we will proceed.
5   This schema draws from several sources, including S.B. Clough and C.W. Cole, *Economic History of Europe* (Boston: D.C. Heath and Co., 1967); Broadus Mitchell, *Postscripts to Economic History* (Totowa, NJ: Littlefield, Adams, and Co., 1967); E.K. Hunt, *Property and Prophets: The Evolution of Economic Institutions and Ideologies* (Grand Rapids, MI: Harper and Row, 1990); Robert Heilbroner, *The*

Making of Economic Society (Englewood Cliffs, NJ: Prentice Hall, 1968). Also see Jeffrey Sklansky, "The Elusive Sovereign: New Intellectual and Social Histories of Capitalism," *Modern Intellectual History* 9, no. 1 (2012): 233–48.

6   The periodization schema used here focuses on the most important sites for the emergence and development of capitalism, first Britain and then the United States. Two important developments during the 1770s are indicative of the transition that was then under way. First was the American Revolution, which signalled the extent to which the state regulations associated with mercantilism were becoming onerous to emerging entrepreneurial classes; second was the publication of a significant critique of mercantilism in the form of Adam Smith's *The Wealth of Nations* in 1776.

7   See Pankaj Mishra, *Age of Anger: A History of the Present* (London: Allen Lane, 2018), and *Bland Fanatics: Liberals, Race, and Empire* (New York: Farrar, Straus and Giroux, 2020).

8   I have utilized a variation on this approach consistently over the last several decades. The material here is also presented in my "From the National Policy to Continentalism and Globalization," in *Fighting for the Farm: Rural America Transformed*, ed. Jane Adams (Philadelphia: University of Pennsylvania Press, 2003), 47–74, as well as in "Globalisation, Neoliberalism and Rural Decline: Australia and Canada" (co-authored with Ian Gray and Geoffrey Lawrence), in *Writing Off the Rural West*, ed. Roger Epp and Dave Whitson (Edmonton: University of Alberta Press, 2001), 89–105. I do not claim originality for the notion. Several scholars have adopted the technique of identifying phases or periods of agricultural policy in Canada. While none of them use the exact schema I have adopted, my approach nonetheless follows from their work. See D. Berthelet, "Agricultural Canada Policy and Expense Patterns, 1868–1993," *Canadian Farm Economics* 19, no. 1 (1985): 5–15; Douglas Hedley, "Governance in Canadian Agriculture," *Canadian Journal of Agricultural Economics*, no. 65 (2017): 523–41, and "The Evolution of Agricultural Support Policy," CASE Fellows Paper 2015-1 (2015), https://caes-scae.ca/wp-content/uploads/2018/11/2015-Hedley-Evolution-Ag-Policy-Fellows-Paper-RI.pdf. See also Grace Skogstad, "Agriculture and Food Policy," *Canadian Encyclopedia*, last modified July 31, 2014, https://www.thecanadianencyclopedia.ca/en/article/agriculture-and-food-policy; "The Two Faces of Canadian Agriculture in a Post-Staples Economy," *Canadian Political Science Review* 1, no. 1 (June 2007): 26–41; and *The Politics of Agricultural Policy-Making in Canada* (Toronto: University of Toronto Press, 1987).

9   James Daschuk, *Clearing the Plains: Disease, Politics of Starvation, and the Loss of Aboriginal Life* (Regina: University of Regina Press, 2013).

10 The definitive description of the complexities of class when viewed not as a static category or abstract structural position in an economic order but as a historically located and culturally impacted lived experience is found in E.P.

Thompson, *Making of the English Working Class* (Middlesex, UK: Penguin Books, 1968). Among those who have explored the complexity of class is the late Eric Olin Wright. Wright constantly revised his understanding of class, adding new classes and fractions. See his *Classes* (London: Verso, 1989). The interested reader might want to compare Henry Veltmeyer, *Canadian Class Structure* (Toronto: Garamond Press, 1986), and Stewart Clegg, Paul Boreman, and Geoff Dow, *Class, Politics and the Economy* (London: Routledge and Kegan Paul, 1986). As it is used here, the concept of class fraction owes something to the famously complex picture of class found in the work of Nicos Poulantzas; see his *Political Power and Social Classes* (London: NLB and Sheed and Ward, 1973). The term is also used by Pierre Bourdieu, but in a different way given his complex understanding of class and its relationship to various forms of capital. See, for example, his essay "The Forms of Capital," in *Handbook of Theory and Research for the Sociology of Education*, ed. John Richardson (New York: Greenwood, 1986), 228–55.

11 Aage Sørensen, "Symposium on Class Analysis: Toward a Sounder Basis for Class Analysis," *American Journal of Sociology* 105, no. 6 (2000): 1523–58; John Gubbay, "A Marxist Critique of Weberian Class Analysis," *Sociology* 31, no. 1 (1997): 73–89; Steven Vallal and Emily Cummins, "Relational Models of Organizational Inequalities: Emerging Approaches and Conceptual Dilemmas," *American Behavioural Scientist* 58, no. 2 (2014): 228–55.

12 See, for example, Daniel W. Rossides, *The American Class System* (Toronto: Prentice Hall, 1968).

13 See Phillip Hansen, *Reconsidering C.B. Macpherson* (Toronto: University of Toronto Press, 2015), especially chap. 2.

14 Hansen, 93.

15 Hansen, 93.

16 The terms "petite bourgeoisie" or "petty bourgeoisie" are often used; however, since there is a danger that such a designation tends toward a simplistic property or ownership understanding of class, we will use the term "independent commodity producers" (with some variations) to identify the class. Over the past decade, there has been an ongoing debate regarding the nature of independent commodity production as opposed to or alongside peasant production. See Harriet Friedmann, "World Market, State, and Family Farm: Social Bases of Household Production in an Era of Wage Labor," *Comparative Studies in Society and History*, no. 20 (1978): 545–86; "Household Production and the National Economy," *Journal of Peasant Studies*, no. 7 (1980): 158–84; "The Political Economy of Food: The Rise and Fall of the Post-War International Food Order," *American Journal of Sociology*, no. 88 (1982): 248–86; and "Agriculture and the State System: The Rise and Decline of National Agricultures, 1870 to the Present," *Sociologia Ruralis*, no. 29 (1989): 93–117. See also Susan A. Mann, *Agrarian Capitalism in Theory and Practice* (Chapel Hill: University of North Carolina

Press, 1990); Mann and James M. Dickinson, "Obstacles to the Development of a Capitalist Agriculture," *Journal of Peasant Studies*, no. 5 (1978): 466–81; Frederick Buttel and Philip McMichael, "New Directions in the Political Economy of Agriculture," *Sociological Perspectives* 33, no. 1 (1990): 89–109. For a good summary, see Henry Bernstein, "Capitalism and Petty Commodity Production Social Analysis," *International Journal of Anthropology*, no. 20 (December 1986): 11–28; Barbara Harris-White "Capitalism and the Common Man: Peasants and Petty Production in Africa and South Asia," *Journal of Political Economy* 1, no. 2 (2012): 109–60; B.R. Roberts, "Peasants and Proletarians," *Annual Review of Sociology*, no. 16 (1990): 352–77.

17 Max Weber identified what he called the infinite complexity of reality and the necessity of selecting specific elements to focus on if we want to, using our finite minds, understand it. See his "Objectivity in the Social Sciences," in *Methodology of the Social Sciences* (New York: Free Press, 1949). For the use of abstraction, see Theotonio Dos Santos, "The Concept of Social Class," *Science and Society* 34, no. 1 (1970): 166–93.

18 For a definition of patriarchy as a gender order, see Knuttila, *Paying for Masculinity: Boys, Men, and the Patriarchal Dividend* (Halifax: Fernwood Publishing, 2016), 29–30.

1. CONFEDERATION TO DEPRESSION

1 Harold A. Innis, *The Cod Fisheries: The History of an International Economy* (New Haven, CT: Yale University Press, 1940); Innis, *The Fur Trade in Canada* (Toronto: University of Toronto Press, 1956); and *Essays in Canadian Economic History* (Toronto: University of Toronto Press, 1962).

2 Sophus A. Reinert and Robert Fredona, "Merchants and the Origins of Capitalism," Harvard Business School Working Paper No. 18-021 (September 2017), https://www.hbs.edu/ris/Publication%20Files/18-021_b3b67ba8-2fc9-4a9b-8955-670d5f491939.pdf; Carlos and Nicholas, "Giants of an Earlier Capitalism: The Chartered Trading Companies as Modern Multinationals," *Business History Review*, no. 3, (1988): 398–419.

3 Arthur J. Ray, "Hudson's Bay Company," *Canadian Encyclopedia*, last modified January 19, 2023, https://www.thecanadianencyclopedia.ca/en/article/hudsons-bay-company.

4 William Schooling, *The Governor and Company of Adventurers of England Trading into Hudson's Bay during Two Hundred and Fifty Years, 1670–1920* (London: Hudson's Bay Company, 1920), https://archive.org/details/governorcompanooscho/page/n9/mode/2up.

5 Schooling, *Governor and Company of Adventurers of England*; Ray, "Hudson's Bay Company."

6. See "Upper Canada & Loyalists (1785 to 1797)," Statistics Canada, last modified August 26, 2015, https://www150.statcan.gc.ca/n1/pub/98-187-x/4151286-eng.htm.
7. "Progress of population, 1700 to 1825," Statistics Canada, last modified November 4, 2010, https://www65.statcan.gc.ca/acyb02/1867/acyb02_1867001803-eng.htm.
8. James Daschuk, *Clearing the Plains: Disease, Politics of Starvation, and the Loss of Aboriginal Life* (Regina: University of Regina Press, 2013), 62.
9. Amanda Robinson, "Manifest Destiny," *Canadian Encyclopedia*, last modified December 19, 2019, https://www.thecanadianencyclopedia.ca/en/article/manifest-destiny.
10. Kenneth Norrie and Douglas Owram, *A History of the Canadian Economy* (Toronto: Harcourt Brace Jovanovich, 1991), chap. 6.
11. Norrie and Owram, chap. 10.
12. Vernon C. Fowke, *The National Policy and the Wheat Economy* (Toronto: University of Toronto Press, 1957), 7–8.
13. Gérald A. Beaudoin, "Distribution of Powers," *Canadian Encyclopedia*, last modified April 24, 2020, https://www.thecanadianencyclopedia.ca/en/article/distribution-of-powers.
14. Beaudoin.
15. "The Quebec Resolutions, October 29, 1864 (The 72 Resolutions)," Macdonald-Laurier Institute, August 13, 2017, https://macdonaldlaurier.ca/the-quebec-resolutions-october-29-1864-the-72-resolutions/.
16. Canada, *House of Commons Debates*, November 7, 1867 (governor general's speech), 6.
17. Canada, *House of Commons Debates*, November 8, 1867 (Tupper), 10.
18. Canada, *House of Commons Debates*, November 29, 1867 (McDougall), 159. He noted that section 146 of BNA Act made provision for the action and that Britain was prepared to agree.
19. Canada, *House of Commons Debates*, December 6, 1867 (Harrison), 194.
20. Canada, *House of Commons Debates*, December 4, 1967 (McDougall), 182. See also December 5, 1867, (Parker), 190; December 5, 1867 (Connell), 192; and December 5, 1867 (Harrison), 194.
21. Canada, *House of Commons Debates*, December 6, 1867, 200.
22. Shirlee Anne Smith "Rupert's Land," *Canadian Encyclopedia*, last modified August 18, 2022, https://www.thecanadianencyclopedia.ca/en/article/ruperts-land.
23. See "Rupert's Land and North-Western Territory Order," Canadian Constitutional Documents: A Legal History, last modified April 11, 1997, https://www.solon.org/Constitutions/Canada/English/rlo_1870.html.
24. Smith, "Rupert's Land."
25. Canada, *House of Commons Debates*, June 7, 1872 (Morris), 461, and June 14, 1872, 517. The speed with which the matter was handled was quite astounding, with second reading and details provided on June 7, 1872, and final assent on June 14.

26 Vernon C. Fowke, *Canadian Agricultural Policy* (Toronto: University of Toronto Press, 1946), 163. See also Chester Martin, *Dominion Lands Policy*, ed. Lewis H. Thomas (Montreal: McGill-Queen's University Press, 1973), where he explains how the *Dominion Lands Act* of 1872, modelled on homestead legislation in the United States (1862), was a federal law that provided the legal authority under which the Crown granted lands to individuals, colonization companies, the HBC, railway construction, municipalities, and religious groups. The act also set aside land for First Nations reserves.
27 J.M. Bumsted, "Red River Colony," *Canadian Encyclopedia*, last modified March 25, 2015. https://www.thecanadianencyclopedia.ca/en/article/red-river-colony.
28 Canada, *House of Commons Debates*, March 28, 1871 (Tilley), 280. The necessity of hanging on to the Western lands figured prominently the House on May 28, 1869; see March 28, 1871 (A.P. McDonald and Harrison), 472–84.
29 Canada, *House of Commons Debates*, April 20, 1883. The bill to formally incorporate the CPR seems to have not been particularly controversial, receiving royal assent on June 14, 1872.
30 Canada, ParlInfo, *Speeches from the Throne*, 2nd Parliament, March 11, 1873, 22.
31 Canada, *House of Commons Debates*, April 2, 1873, 179, for the non-confidence motion. For a summary, see Gord McIntosh, Eli Yarhi, and Andrew McIntosh, "Pacific Scandal," *Canadian Encyclopedia*, last modified January 14, 2021, https://www.thecanadianencyclopedia.ca/en/article/pacific-scandal; Pierre Berton, *The National Dream: The Great Railway, 1871–1881* (Toronto: Anchor Canada, 1970); Den Otter, "Nationalism and the Pacific Scandal," Canadian Historical Review 69, no. 3 (1988): 315–39; W.L. Morton, *The Critical Years: The Union of British North America, 1857–1873* (Toronto: McClelland and Stewart, 1964), 245–77.
32 Canada, *House of Commons Debates*, November 5, 1873 (Macdonald's resignation), 169.
33 Hans Rosenberg, "Political and Social Consequences of the Great Depression of 1873–1896 in Central Europe," *Economic History Review*, no. 13 (1943): 58–73; Samuel Bernstein, "American Labor in the Long Depression, 1873–1878," *Science & Society* 20, no. 1 (1956): 59–83; O.V. Wells, "The Depression of 1873–79," *Agricultural History* 11, no. 3 (1937): 621–33.
34 P.B. Waite, *Canada 1874–1896: Arduous Destiny* (Toronto: McClelland and Stewart, 1971), 57–9.
35 Lewis Thomas, *The North-West Territories, 1870–1905* (Ottawa: Canadian Historical Association, 1970), 4–5.
36 Canada, *House of Commons Debates*, March 12, 1875, 653–8.
37 David Hall, "North-West Territories (1870–1905)," *Canadian Encyclopedia*, last modified August 18, 2022, https://www.thecanadianencyclopedia.ca/en/article/north-west-territories-1870-1905.
38 Canada, *House of Commons Debates*, March 3, 1870 (J. Howe), 209.

39   The treaty-making process is an important and complex one, and beyond scope of this volume. For a glimpse of some of these complexities, see "Aboriginal Treaties: An Introduction to Treaties in BC and Canada, and Métis Settlements," University of British Columbia Library, last modified July 11, 2022, https://guides.library.ubc.ca/aboriginal_treaties. Also see Arthur J. Ray, Jim Miller, and Frank Tough, *Bounty and Benevolence* (Montreal: McGill Queens Press, 2000); Daschuk, *Clearing the Plains*; Anthony J. Hall, "Treaties with Indigenous Peoples in Canada," *Canadian Encyclopedia*, last modified September 11, 2017, https://www.thecanadianencyclopedia.ca/en/article/aboriginal-treaties; Gretchen Albers, "Treaties 1 and 2," *Canadian Encyclopedia*, last modified August 5, 2021, https://www.thecanadianencyclopedia.ca/en/article/treaties-1-and-2; Michelle Filice, "Treaty 4," *Canadian Encyclopedia*, last modified November 1, 2016, https://www.thecanadianencyclopedia.ca/en/article/treaty-4, and "Treaty 6," *Canadian Encyclopedia*, last modified October 11, 2016, https://www.thecanadianencyclopedia.ca/en/article/treaty-6.
40   William A. Dobak, "Killing the Canadian Buffalo, 1821–1881," *Western Historical Quarterly* 27, no. 1 (1996): 35.
41   Candace Savage, *A Geography of Blood: Unearthing Memory from a Prairie Landscape* (Vancouver: Greystone Books, 2012), 90.
42   Norrie and Owram, *History of the Canadian Economy*, 359.
43   Waite, *Canada 1874–1896*, 78–9.
44   Canada, *House of Commons Debates*, March 7, 1878, 854.
45   Donald Creighton, *Canada's First Century* (Toronto: Macmillan of Canada, 1970), 33.
46   Norrie and Orwam, *History of the Canadian Economy*, 238.
47   Donald Creighton, *John A. Macdonald: The Young Politician, the Old Chieftain* (Toronto: University of Toronto Press, 1955), 120–1, 203, 208.
48   Donald V. Smiley, "Canada and the Quest for a National Policy," *Canadian Journal of Political Science/Revue canadienne de science politique* 8, no. 1 (1975): 12.
49   K.A. MacKirdy, J.S. Moir, and Y.F. Zoltvany, *Changing Perspectives in Canadian History* (Don Mills, ON: J.M. Dent and Sons, 1971), 227.
50   Fowke, *National Policy and the Wheat Economy*, 8.
51   Canada, *House of Commons Debates*, introduced by Sir John A. Macdonald May 3, 1873, 434.
52   Andrew Woolford, "Ontological Destruction: Genocide and Canadian Aboriginal Peoples," *Genocide Studies and Prevention* 4, no. 1 (2009): 85.
53   Ray, Miller, and Tough, *Bounty and Benevolence*, chap. 6; Daschuk, *Clearing the Plains*, 181–3.
54   Canada, *House of Commons Debates*, February 13, 1879, 5. Several decades ago there was an academic debate between those who argued that the actual intent of the tariffs was to draw foreign investment to Canada, which had thus far been quite low owing to a financially conservative or risk-averse attitude

within the Canadian business elite that prevented domestic capital from industrial investments. See, for example, R.T. Naylor, "Rise and Fall of the Third Commercial Empire," and his two-volume *History of Canadian Business, 1867–1914*. Naylor argued that the emerging Canadian capitalist class was too conservative and cautious to risk investing in industry, preferring instead to use tariffs to attract foreign investment. The alternate view that I am presenting tends to be informed by analyses summarized in L.R. Macdonald, "Merchants against Industry: An Idea and Its Origins," *Canadian Historical Review* 56, no. 3 (1975): 263–81. These debates have been reviewed more recently by Bruce Smardon in "Rethinking Canadian Economic Development: The Political Economy of Canadian Fordism, 1880–1914," *Studies in Political Economy*, no. 85 (Spring 2010): 179–208, and "Shifting Terrains of Accumulation: Canadian Industry in Three Eras of Development," *Studies in Political Economy*, no. 87 (Spring 2011): 143–72. See also Norrie and Owram, *History of the Canadian Economy*, 446–7.

55 Canada, *House of Commons Debates*, March 14, 1879, 409.
56 Lord Dufferin is quoted in Waite, *Canada 1874–1896*, 85.
57 Waite, 103.
58 The Conservatives won 123 seats, compared to 92 for the Liberals.
59 Canada, *House of Commons Debates*, February 13, 1879, 4.
60 Canada, *House of Commons Debates*, April 13, 1879, 1886–7.
61 Omer Lavallé, "Canadian Pacific Railway," *Canadian Encyclopedia*, last modified July 15, 2021, https://www.thecanadianencyclopedia.ca/en/article/canadian-pacific-railway. The creation and early days of the CPR are among the most covered, even in Canadian history. Perhaps the most widely read is Pierre Berton, *The Last Spike* (Toronto: Anchor Paperback, 2001). See also Harold A. Innis, *History of the Canadian Pacific Railway* (Toronto: McClelland and Stewart, 1923); Robert Chodos, *The CPR: A Century of Corporate Welfare* (Toronto: James Lorimer and Company, 1973).
62 Creighton, *Canada's First Century*, 83.
63 Canada, *House of Commons Debates*, July 15, 1880 (Tupper), 1424–5.
64 Quoted in Michael Bliss, *Canadian History in Documents, 1763–1966* (Toronto: Ryerson Press, 1966), 202–3.
65 MacKirdy, Moir, and Zoltvany, *Changing Perspectives in Canadian History*, 203–4.
66 See "The Canadian West: Anticipation, Contact, Accommodation," Library and Archives Canada, accessed May 2, 2019, https://www.collectionscanada.gc.ca/canadian-west/052902/05290202_e.html.
67 Canada, *House of Commons Debates*, May 26, 1869, 480. Royal assent was granted on June 22, 1869.
68 Ninette Kelley and Michael Trebilcock, *The Making of the Mosaic: A History of Canadian Immigration Policy* (Toronto: History of Toronto Press, 2000), 63.

69 Reginald Whitaker, *Canadian Immigration Policy since Confederation* (Ottawa: Canadian Historical Association, 1991), 4.
70 Canada, *House of Commons Debates*, September 24, 1896 (Tupper), 1937–8, and (Davin), 1939–1940.
71 Kelley and Trebilcock, *Making of the Mosaic*, 118, 188; Laura Detre, "Canada's Campaign for Immigrants and the Images in *Canada West* Magazine," *Great Plains Quarterly* 24, no. 2 (2004): 115–16.
72 Canada, *House of Commons Debates*, April 23, 1897 (Foster), 1202.
73 J.M.S. Careless, *Canada: A Story of Challenge* (Toronto: Macmillan, 1963), 312.
74 James N. McCrorie, *In Union Is Strength* (Saskatoon: Centre for Community Studies, 1964), 19.
75 Paul Sweezy, *The Theory of Capitalist Development* (London: Dennis Dobson, 1952), chap. 14. See also Robert Heilbroner, *The Nature and Logic of Capitalism* (New York: W.W. Norton & Co., 1985), 163–5.

2. PHASE 1—ACTIVIST GOVERNMENT

1 Arthur J. Taylor, *Laissez-faire and State Intervention in Nineteenth-Century Britain* (London: Macmillan, 1972), 48.
2 Karl Polanyi, *The Great Transformation* (Boston: Beacon Press, 1944), 250.
3 Sheldon Krasowski, *No Surrender: The Land Remains Indigenous* (Regina: University of Regina Press, 2019), 4.
4 Krasowski, 1.
5 Krasowski, 272.
6 Krasowski, 158–60, 272–3.
7 James Daschuk, *Clearing the Plains: Disease, Politics of Starvation, and the Loss of Aboriginal Life* (Regina: University of Regina Press, 2013), 90–5.
8 For the full text of Treaty 4, see "Treaty Texts: Treaty No. 4," Government of Canada, accessed January 13, 2022, https://www.rcaanc-cirnac.gc.ca/eng/1100100028689/1581293019940.
9 See Sarah Carter, "Indigenous Reserve Agriculture to 1900," *Indigenous Saskatchewan Encyclopedia*, University of Saskatchewan, accessed February 19, 2021, https://teaching.usask.ca/indigenoussk/import/indigenous_reserve_agriculture_to_1900.php; *Aboriginal People and Colonizers of Western Canada to 1900* (Toronto: University of Toronto Press, 1999); and *Lost Harvests: Prairie Indian Reserve Farmers and Government Policy*, 2nd ed. (Montreal: McGill-Queens University Press, 2019). See also Helen Buckley, *From Wooden Ploughs to Welfare: Why Indian Policy Failed in the Prairie Provinces* (Montreal: McGill-Queens University Press, 1992), 52.
10 Peggy Martin-McGuire, *First Nation Land Surrenders on the Prairies, 1896–1911* (Ottawa: Indian Claims Commission, September 1998), xiii, http://specific-claims.bryan-schwartz.com/wp-content/uploads/docs/FNLS_summary_eng.pdf.

11　Drew Bednasek, "Remembering the File Hills Farm Colony," accessed March 23, 2021, https://d2cu82y6e07f22.cloudfront.net/2020/01/15211238/04HG37-Bednasek.pdf. See also Stefanie Davis "'The Untold Story': Effects Of Sask. Experimental Colony Still Felt on Peepeekisis Cree Nation," CTV News, August 5, 2021, https://regina.ctvnews.ca/the-untold-story-effects-of-sask-experimental-colony-still-felt-on-peepeekisis-cree-nation-1.5534504.

12　Dave Bedard, "Feds Apologize for Saskatchewan Farming Colony Scheme," *Manitoba Co-operator*, August 10, 2022, https://www.manitobacooperator.ca/daily/feds-apologize-for-saskatchewan-farming-colony-scheme/.

13　Morris Zaslow, *The Opening of the Canadian North, 1870–1914* (Toronto: McClelland and Stewart, 1971), 14.

14　Canada, *House of Commons Debates*, April 27, 1883 (Macdonald), 860; May 2, 1883 (Charlton), 937. Macdonald introduced further amendments via Bill 138, which he had mentioned on second reading on April 16, 1883; see April 7, 1884, 1428–9.

15　Canada, *House of Commons Debates*, March 31, 1886, 426; on the further modification, see April 9, 1886 (While), 600.

16　Shirlee Anne Smith "Rupert's Land," *Canadian Encyclopedia*, last modified August 18, 2022, https://www.thecanadianencyclopedia.ca/en/article/ruperts-land.

17　Omer Lavallé, "Canadian Pacific Railway," *Canadian Encyclopedia*, last modified July 15, 2021, https://www.thecanadianencyclopedia.ca/en/article/canadian-pacific-railway.

18　Ninette Kelley and Michael Trebilcock, *The Making of the Mosaic: A History of Canadian Immigration Policy* (Toronto: History of Toronto Press, 2000), 120–1.

19　D.J. Hall, "Clifford Sifton: Immigration and Settlement Policy, 1896–1905," University of Calgary Libraries and Cultural Resources Collection, accessed June 21, 2020, http://contentdm.ucalgary.ca/digital/collection/p22007coll8/id/41509/.

20　See Canadian Museum of History, "The Last Best West: Advertising for Immigrants to Western Canada," https://www.historymuseum.ca/cmc/exhibitions/hist/advertis/ads7-09e.html; and Graham Chandler, "Selling the Prairie Good Life," *Canada's History*, September 7, 2016, https://www.canadashistory.ca/explore/settlement-immigration/selling-the-prairie-good-life.

21　Clifford Sifton, "The Immigrants Canada Wants," *Maclean's*, April 1, 1922, 16 and 34.

22　Bill Waiser, *Saskatchewan: A New History* (Calgary: Fifth House, 2005), 5–7.

23　Laurier's much-used phrase see Canada, *House of Commons Debates*, February 21, 1905, 1421.

24　Canada, *House of Commons Debates*, February 21, 1905, 1432.

25　Canada, *Census of Canada, 1931, vol. 1, Summary* (Ottawa: King's Printer, 1936), 66, https://publications.gc.ca/collections/collection_2017/statcan/CS98-1931-1-eng.pdf.

26　G.I. Trant, "General Statistics (Series M1-248)," *Historical Statistics of Canada* (Ottawa: Agriculture Division of Statistics Canada, 2015), https://www150.statcan.gc.ca/n1/en/pub/11-516-x/pdf/5220015-eng.pdf?st=ZmxR88Cd.

27 T.D. Regehr, "Canadian Northern Railway," *Canadian Encyclopedia*, last modified March 4, 2015, https://www.thecanadianencyclopedia.ca/en/article/canadian-northern-railway.
28 Canada, *Report of the Royal Commission into Railways and Transportation in Canada, 1931–1932* (Ottawa: King's Printer, 1932), xvi, xix.
29 W.A. Mackintosh, *Economic Problems of the Prairie Provinces* (Toronto: Macmillan Company of Canada, 1935), 37–8.
30 See Canada, *House of Commons Debates*, 4011–12.
31 George Parkin de Twenebroker Glazebrook, *A History of Transportation in Canada* (Toronto: Ryerson Press, 1964), 156–7.
32 Glazebrook, 166.
33 Canada, *Grain and Rail Transportation in Western Canada: Report of the Grain Handling and Transportation Commission, vol. 3* (Ottawa: Grain Handling and Transportation Commission, 1977), 1.
34 Canada, *House of Commons Debates*, January 30, 1884 (George Gigault), 74.
35 Canada, *House of Commons Debates*, appendix 6, February 19, 1884, 5.
36 Canada, *House of Commons Debates*, April 30, 1886 (Carling and various speakers in support), 960–7. For approval of experimental farm bill receiving royal assent, see Canada, *House of Commons Debates*, May 11, 1886, 1146. See also T.H. Anstey, "The Formation of the Experimental Farms," *Prairie Forum* 11, no. 2 (Fall 1986): 185–94.
37 Stephen Morgan Jones, "Agricultural Research Stations," *Canadian Encyclopedia*, last modified March 4, 2015, https://www.thecanadianencyclopedia.ca/en/article/agricultural-research-stations.
38 Canada, *House of Commons Debates*, April 29, 1913.
39 Donald Creighton, *Canada's First Century* (Toronto: Macmillan of Canada, 1970), 75.
40 Canada, *House of Commons Debates*, September 14, 1896, (Davin), 1194, refers to grain dealer fraud and excessive transportation costs. Mr. Oliver (September 24, 1896, 1953–6), addressed the negative impact on immigration more directly.
41 Canada, *House of Commons Debates*, March 26, 1897 (Foster, and Mr. Davin's questions), 73–80. On March 31, 1987, Mr. McLean reported that the CPR had indicated a plan to build a rail line through the Crow's Nest Pass region; see the testy exchange between Mr. Maclean and the Minister of Railways and Canals Blair on April 7, 1897. Canada, *House of Commons Journals*, April 7, 1897, 436 and 494.
42 Ken Norrie and T.D. Regehr, "Crow's Nest Pass Agreement," *Canadian Encyclopedia*, last modified January 24, 2014, https://www.thecanadianencyclopedia.ca/en/article/crows-nest-pass-agreement.
43 John Gallagher, *To Kill the Crow* (Moose Jaw, SK: Challenge Publishers, 1983), 67–8.
44 A.W. Currie, *Canadian Transportation Economics* (Toronto: University of Toronto Press, 1967).

45 Currie, chap. 4.
46 K.S. Kearns, "Winnipeg Commodity Exchange," *Canadian Encyclopedia*, last modified March 4, 2015, https://www.thecanadianencyclopedia.ca/en/article/winnipeg-commodity-exchange.
47 Gordon Goldsborough, "Memorable Manitobans: William Linton Parrish (1860–1949)," Manitoba Historical Society, last modified June 22, 2020, http://www.mhs.mb.ca/docs/people/parrish_wl.shtml. For information on the Richardson empire, see "About Us," Richardson International, accessed February 22, 2023, https://www.richardson.ca/about/, and Goldsborough, "Memorable Manitobans: James Armstrong Richardson (1885–1939)," Manitoba Historical Society, last modified December 26, 2021, http://www.mhs.mb.ca/docs/people/richardson_ja.shtml.
48 Brett Fairbairn, "United Grain Growers (Agricore United)," in *Encyclopedia of Saskatchewan* (Regina: Canadian Plains Research Centre, 2005), 968–9. Paterson's history can be found in Goldsborough, "Memorable Manitobans: Norman McLeod Paterson (1883–1983)," Manitoba Historical Society, last modified October 4, 2022, http://www.mhs.mb.ca/docs/people/paterson_nm.shtml.
49 Canada, *Grain and Rail Transportation in Western Canada*, 3:1.
50 Canada, 3:39.
51 Gary Storey, "Grain Handling and Transportation System," in *Encyclopedia of Saskatchewan*, 407.
52 See Glen C. Larson, "The Alphabet Line," *Prairie Fiddler* (blog), September 28, 2018, https://glenclarson.com/2018/09/28/the-alphabet-line/, and the detailed map in Bill Berry, *People Places: Saskatchewan and Its Names* (Regina: Canadian Plains Research Center, 1997), 60.
53 K. Murray Knuttila, "The Saskatchewan Agrarian Movement, 1900–1930: A Case Study of Populism" (master's thesis, University of Regina, 1975), especially chap. 5, which focuses on dockage and other sources of conflict.
54 Allan Levine, "Bawlf, Nicholas," in *Dictionary of Canadian Biography*, vol. 14, University of Toronto/Université Laval (2003–), accessed March 8, 2023, http://www.biographi.ca/en/bio/bawlf_nicholas_14E.html.
55 Hopkins Moorehouse, *Deep Furrows* (Toronto: George McLeod, 1918), 39–41.
56 Levine, "Bawlf, Nicholas."
57 Canada, *House of Commons Debates*, March 17, 1898, 2059, and March 29, 1899, 618.
58 Canada, *House of Commons Debates*, April 4, 1900 (M. Sutherland), 3224.
59 Harold S. Patton, *Grain Growers' Cooperation in Western Canada* (Cambridge, MA: Harvard University Press, 1928), 30.
60 C.F. Wilson, *A Century of Canadian Grain: Government Policy to 1951* (Saskatoon: Western Prairie Producer Books, 1978), 32–3.
61 For the 1902 amendments, see the remarks by Scott in Canada, *House of Commons Debates*, March 10, 1902, 920–1. See Sifton's comments in the House regarding the 1903 amendments, August 4, 1903, 7989–90.

62 Wilson, *Century of Canadian Grain*, 28.
63 Canada, *Report of the Royal Commission on the Grain Trade of Canada, 1906* (Ottawa: King's Printer, 1908), 17, https://publications.gc.ca/collections/collection_2016/bcp-pco/Z1-1906-4-eng.pdf.
64 The literature is truly voluminous. Among the many dissertations and theses are Knuttila, "Saskatchewan Agrarian Movement," and "The Impact of the Western Canadian Agrarian Movement on Federal Government Policy, 1900–1930: An Assessment and Analysis" (PhD diss., University of Toronto, 1982). Among the classics are Moorhouse, *Deep Furrows*; Patton, *Grain Growers' Cooperation in Western Canada*; S.M. Lipsett, *Agrarian Socialism* (Berkley: University of California Press, 1971); C.B. Macpherson, *Democracy in Alberta: Social Credit and the Party System* (Toronto: University of Toronto Press, 1953); James N. McCrorie, *In Union Is Strength* (Saskatoon: Centre for Community Studies, 1964); and W.L. Morton, *The Progressive Party in Canada* (Toronto: University of Toronto Press, 1950).
65 Canada, *House of Commons Debates*, July 10, 1908, 12560.
66 See unsigned editorial in *Grain Growers' Guide*, 1, no. 7 (January 1909): 14–15.
67 *Grain Growers' Guide* 2, no. 24 (January 1910): 8.
68 *Grain Growers' Guide* 3, no. 2 (August 1910): 8.
69 In Saskatchewan, for example, a provincial Royal Commission in 1909 resulted in the formation of the Saskatchewan Co-operative Elevator Company. See Patton, *Grain Growers' Cooperation in Western Canada*, 102.
70 For a full description, see Knuttila, "Impact of the Western Canadian Agrarian Movement," chap. 3.
71 Canada, *House of Commons Debates*, December 5, 1911, 794, 869.
72 Canada, *House of Commons Debates*, January 30, 1912, 2174.
73 The definitive treatments are to be found in Morton, *Progressive Party in Canada*, and his "The Western Progressive Movement, 1919–1921," *Report of Annual Meeting Canadian Historical Association* 25, no. 1 (1946): 41–55.
74 Brett Fairbairn, "Grain Growers' Grain Company," in *Encyclopedia of Saskatchewan*, 406.
75 For the full details, see Wilson, *Century of Canadian Grain*, chaps. 4, 5, 6, and 7. For a summary, see André Magnan, *When Wheat Was King: The Rise and Fall of the Canada–UK Grain Trade* (Vancouver: UBC Press, 2016), 46–9.
76 *House of Commons Debates*, June 28, 1920, 4346.
77 Canada, *House of Commons Debates*, October 9, 1919, 916. For the benefits, see Patton, *Grain Growers' Cooperation in Western Canada*, 197–8.
78 "1921 Federal Election in Canada," Re:Politics, October 1, 2005, https://repolitics.com/election/1921-federal-election-in-canada/.
79 See Garry Fairbairn, *From Prairie Roots: The Remarkable Story of Saskatchewan Wheat Pool* (Saskatoon: Western Producer Prairie Books, 1984); Samuel W. Yeates, *The Saskatchewan Wheat Pool: Its Origin, Organization and Progress, 1924–1935*

(Saskatoon: United Farmers of Canada, 1947); Kathy Lang, "Saskatchewan Wheat Pool," in *Encyclopedia of Saskatchewan*.

80 Canada, *House of Commons Debates*, June 12, 1922 (J.A. Robb), 2834, and June 19, 1922. For further debate on Bill 176 in the context of a new wheat board, see June 22, 1922, 3174–91. The bill was passed on June 22, 1922, but not implemented. Wilson, *A Century of Canadian Grain*, notes the non-proclamation at 228 and 467.

81 Appointed by Order-in-Council May 1, 1923. See Canada, *Report of the Royal Grain Inquiry* (Ottawa: King's Printer, 1925), https://publications.gc.ca/collections/collection_2016/bcp-pco/Z1-1923-2-2-1-eng.pdf. Meighen subsequently noted the commission was being very quiet in its work. See Canada, *House of Commons Debates*, June 29, 1924, 4711.

82 Canada, *Report of the Royal Grain Inquiry*.

83 Canada, 7.

84 See the quick passage of the 1928 amendments introduced on April 10 in Canada, *House of Commons Debates*, April 10, 1928, 1869.

85 Vernon C. Fowke, "Royal Commissions and Canadian Agricultural Policy," *Canadian Journal of Economics and Political Science* 14, no. 2 (May 1948): 175.

86 Fowke, 164.

87 For a summary of some of the different perspectives and approaches to Prairie history, see Royden Loewen, "On the Margin or in the Lead: Canadian Prairie Historiography," *Agricultural History* 73, no. 1 (Winter 1999): 27–45.

88 Canada, *Census of Prairie Provinces, 1926: Manitoba, Saskatchewan, Alberta* (Ottawa: King's Printer, 1931), xv, https://archive.org/details/1926981926F1931engfra/mode/2up.

89 My calculations are based on data provided in Cecilia Danysk, *Hired Hands: Labour and Development of Prairie Agriculture, 1880–1930* (Toronto: University of Toronto Press, 1995), 178.

90 Danysk, 15.

91 Lyle Dick, "Estimates of Farm-Making Costs in Saskatchewan, 1882–1914," in *Agricultural History*, ed. Gregory Marchildon (Regina: Canadian Plains Research Centre, 2011), 114.

92 E.I. Chicanot, "Women Pioneers in the Canadian West Have Made Good in Many Varied Lines of Endeavor, Involving Even 'Hard Labor,'" *Maclean's*, November 1, 1923.

93 Ann Leger-Anderson, "Women of Saskatchewan—Historical Overview," in *Encyclopedia of Saskatchewan*, 1026.

94 Quoted in R.W. Sandwell, *Canada's Rural Majority: Households, Environments, and Economies, 1870–1940* (Toronto: University of Toronto Press, 2016), 136.

95 Bruce R. Shepard, "Tractors and Combines in the Second Stage of Agricultural Mechanization on the Canadian Plains," *Prairie Forum* 11, no. 2 (Fall 1986): 260, 262.

96 Waiser, *Saskatchewan*, 273.
97 Shepard, "Tractors and Combines," 206.
98 Canada, *House of Commons Debates*, March 19, 1930, 752.
99 David Monod, "The End of Agrarianism: The Fight for Farm Parity in Alberta and Saskatchewan, 1935–48," *Labour/Le Travail*, no. 16 (Fall 1985): 117.
100 Monod, 117.
101 See Mr. Robb's comments in Canada, *House of Commons Debates*, February 10, 1927, 173, and February 11 1927, 217.
102 W.G. Phillips, *The Agricultural Implement Industry in Canada: A Study of Competition* (Toronto: University of Toronto Press, 1956), especially chart at 12–13.
103 Canada, *House of Commons Debates*, March 25, 1930 (Evans), 941.
104 See House of Commons Committees, 18th Parliament, Special Committee on Farm Implement Prices, 1937, vol. 1, 1296 ("Recommendation/Conclusion"), https://parl.canadiana.ca/view/oop.com_HOC_1802_4_1/11.
105 Quoted in Donald Wetherell and Elise Corbet, *Breaking New Ground: A Century of Farm Equipment Manufacturing on the Canadian Prairies* (Saskatoon: Fifth House, 1993), 19.
106 Canada, *House of Commons Debates*, May 16, 1923 (Steedsman), 2835–7, May 17, 1923 (Tolmie), 2861–70, and May 21, 1923 (Morrison), 2928–31.
107 Fertilizer Canada and the Canadian Fertilizer Institute both seem to promote and represent the fertilizer industry, but their websites do not have any historical data. D.A. Rennie, J.D. Beaton, and R.A. Hedlin, *The Role of Fertilizer Nutrients in Western Canadian Development* (Calgary: Canada West Foundation, 1980), contains a lot of information but not much early history.
108 For debates on Bill 101 as it was introduced on and first reading, see Canada, *House of Commons Debates*, March 19, 1909, 2910, and discussed further on April 16, 1909, 4446–69.
109 Canada, *House of Commons Debates*, April 1, 1921 (Caldwell), 1497. The bill was debated April 19, 1921; second reading is at 2231.
110 See "Table M525: Expenses for Fertilizer, Canada, 1926 to 1976," Statistics Canada, last modified July 2, 2014, https://www150.statcan.gc.ca/n1/pub/11-516-x/sectionm/4057754-eng.htm.
111 Sandra Rollings-Magnusson, *The Homesteaders* (Regina: University of Regina Press, 2019), 1–3.
112 Allan Anderson, *Settling Saskatchewan* (Regina: University of Regina Press, 2013), 8.
113 Ebele Mogo, "A Brief History of Saskatchewan's Pioneer Settlers of African Descent," Saskatchewan History and Folklore Society, August 5, 2020, https://www.skhistory.ca/blog/a-brief-history-of-saskatchewans-pioneering-settlers-of-african-descent.
114 Canada, *Census of the Prairie Provinces* (Ottawa: King's Pinter, 1918), xxxxvii.
115 Canada, 280.

116 Canada, *Census of Saskatchewan, 1916: Bulletin* (Ottawa: Department of Trade and Commerce, Census and Statistics Office, 1916), http://publications.gc.ca/collections/collection_2017/statcan/CS98-1916P-1-eng.pdf.
117 See "Table R783-794: Number of Establishments and Gross Value of Production, by Size of Establishment, Measured by Gross Value of Production, Selected Years, 1900 to 1959," Statistics Canada, last modified July 2, 2014, https://www150.statcan.gc.ca/n1/pub/11-516-x/sectionr/4147443-eng.htm#6.
118 See "Wilfrid Laurier: Canada's Century, 1904," *Canadian Encyclopedia*, last modified July 12, 2017, https://www.thecanadianencyclopedia.ca/en/article/wilfrid-laurier-canadas-century-1904.
119 Canada, *Census of Canada, 1911*, vol. 1 (Ottawa: King's Printer, 1912), 548–53.
120 Canada *Census of the Prairie Provinces [1918]*, xix.
121 Canada, *Census of Canada, 1941*, vol. 2 (Ottawa: King's Printer, 1944), 187.
122 Canada, *Census of Prairie Provinces*, xi. For definitions, see "Population (Series A1-247)," Statistics Canada, last modified July 2, 2014, https://www150.statcan.gc.ca/n1/pub/11-516-x/sectiona/4147436-eng.htm#1.
123 Canada, *Census of Canada*, 1931, 1:181–8.
124 Canada, 1:181–8.
125 Deryck Holdsworth and John Everitt, "Bank Branches and Elevators: Expressions of Big Corporations in Small Prairie Towns," *Prairie Forum* 13, no. 2 (Fall 1988): 176.
126 Holdsworth and Everitt, 176.
127 David B. Danbom, "Romantic Agrarianism in Twentieth-Century America," *Agricultural History* 65, no. 4 (Autumn 1991): 1.
128 Danbom, 1.
129 Michael Dalecki and C. Milton Coughenour, "Agrarianism in American Society," *Rural Sociology* 57, no. 1 (1992): 49–50.
130 The literature on Canadian Prairie settlement defies summary, articulation, or comment here. For an excellent sampling, see the selections from *Prairie Forum* complied and edited by Gregory Marchildon under the *History of Prairie West Series: Immigration and Settlement, 1870–1939* (Regina: Canadian Plains Research Centre, 2009); *The Early Northwest* (Regina: Canadian Plains Research Centre, 2008); *Agricultural History* (Regina: Canadian Plains Research Centre, 2011); and *Business and Industry* (Regina: Canadian Plains Research Centre, 2012). Also see Marchildon and Wendee Kubik, eds., *Women's History* (Regina: University of Regina Press, 2015).
131 Quoted in Jeffrey Taylor, "The Language of Agrarianism in Manitoba, 1890–1925," *Labour/Le Travail* 89, no. 23 (Spring 1989): 100.
132 *Grain Growers' Guide* 1, no. 4 (October 1908): 40–2.
133 E.A. Partridge, "Address of Mr. E.A. Partridge at Annual Meeting of Grain Growers' Grain Co.," *Grain Growers' Guide* 1, no. 4 (October 1908): 6.
134 *Grain Growers' Guide* 3, no. 21 (December 1910): 4.

135 Richard Hofstadter, "The Myth of the Happy Yeoman," *American Heritage* 7, no. 3 (April 1956), https://www.americanheritage.com/myth-happy-yeoman.
136 The Saskatchewan working class has a rich history of struggle to establish and maintain its basic rights and proper share of the province's wealth, though this is beyond this volume. The following are recommended readings on this topic: Danysk, *Hired Hands*; James Warren and Kathleen Carlisle, *On the Side of the People: A History of Labour in Saskatchewan* (Regina: Coteau Books, 2005); John F. Conway, *The Rise of the New West* (Toronto: James Lorimer, 2014); Doug Taylor, *For Dignity, Equality and Justice* (Regina: Saskatchewan Government Employees Union, 1984); and Glen Makahonuk, *Class, State and Power: The Struggle for Trade Union Rights in Saskatchewan, 1905–1997* (Saskatoon: Self-published, 1997).
137 Howard Leeson, ed., *Saskatchewan Politics: Crowding the Centre* (Regina: Canadian Plains Research Centre, 2008), appendix A, 407–10.
138 Quotes from Richard Allen, "Social Gospel," *Canadian Encyclopedia*, last modified March 4, 2015, https://www.thecanadianencyclopedia.ca/en/article/social-gospel. See also Allen, *The Social Passion: Religion and Social Reform in Canada, 1914–1928* (Toronto: University of Toronto Press, 1971).
139 Jeffrey Taylor, *Fashioning Farmers: Ideology, Agricultural Knowledge and the Manitoba Farm Movement, 1890–1925* (Regina: Canadian Plains Research Centre, 1994), 7. Taylor identifies Prairie farming in the period as a form of simple commodity production. As opposed to subsistence production, simple commodity producers "depend on the capitalist market for the disposition of their produce and the purchase of all of their inputs other than labour." Such a view is quite similar to the one adopted here.
140 Jeffrey Taylor, "Theoretical and Practical Ideologies in the Making of Early Twentieth-Century Manitoba Farm Men," *Prairie Forum* 17, no. 1 (Spring 1992): 13–31.
141 "Prime Ministers of Canada," ParlInfo, accessed October 28, 2019, https://lop.parl.ca/sites/ParlInfo/default/en_CA/People/primeMinisters.
142 Darrin Qualman, "The 100th Anniversary of High-Input Agriculture," DarrinQualman.com, January 9, 2018, https://www.darrinqualman.com/high-input-agriculture/.
143 Kenneth Norrie and Douglas Owram, *A History of the Canadian Economy* (Toronto: Harcourt Brace Jovanovich, 1991), 447.
144 Norrie and Owram, 470, 447. See 458 on the ending of the boom.
145 Norrie and Owram, 470.
146 Norrie and Owram, 481.
147 Broadus Mitchell, *Postscripts to Economic History* (Totowa, NJ: Littlefield, Adams, and Co., 1967), 172.
148 Robert Heilbroner, *The Making of Economic Society* (Englewood Cliffs, NJ: Prentice Hall, 1968), chap. 7.

3. PHASE 2—CRISIS AND STABILITY

1. E.K. Hunt, *Property and Prophets: The Evolution of Economic Institutions and Ideologies* (Grand Rapids, MI: Harper and Row, 1990), 154–5.
2. James Struthers, "The Great Depression in Canada," *Canadian Encyclopedia*, last modified August 13, 2021, https://www.thecanadianencyclopedia.ca/en/article/great-depression.
3. Lorne Brown, *When Freedom Was Lost: The Unemployed, the Agitator, and the State* (Montreal: Black Rose Books, 1987).
4. Gregory Marchildon, "The Prairie Farm Rehabilitation Administration: Climate Crisis and Federal–Provincial Relations during the Great Depression," *Canadian Historical Review* 90, no. 2 (June 2009): 276. See also H. Blair Neatby, "William Lyon Mackenzie King," *Canadian Encyclopedia*, last modified October 10, 2019, https://www.thecanadianencyclopedia.ca/en/article/william-lyon-mackenzie-king.
5. Doug Owram warns against the danger of "portraying Keynesian theory as bursting upon the mid-depression as a revelation out of nowhere." See his "Economic Thought in the 1930s: The Prelude to Keynesianism," *Canadian Historical Review* 66, no. 3 (1985): 355. Terry Cook argues that the use of the state by conservative parties was often related to nationalist projects and the need to ward off excessive American influence. See Cook, "The Canadian Conservative Tradition: An Historical Perspective," *Journal of Canadian Studies/Revue d'études canadiennes* 8, no. 4 (November 1973): 31–9.
6. See Paul Baran and Paul Sweezy, *Monopoly Capital* (New York: Monthly Review Press, 1966), and Sweezy, "Why Stagnation?," *Monthly Review* 34, no. 2 (June 1982): 1–10.
7. As mentioned, I've borrowed this term from the ABC sitcom of the same name (1974–84) that represented the comforts of middle-class life in much of the West in the 1950s and '60s. For an analysis of Fordism and post-Fordism, see Bob Jessup, "The Welfare State in the Transition from Fordism to Post-Fordism," in *The Politics of Flexibility: Restructuring State and Industry in Britain, Germany, and Scandinavia*, ed. Bob Jessop, Hans Kastendiek, Klaus Nielsen, and Ove K. Pederson (Cheltenham, UK: E. Elgar, 1991), 82–104. Also see Jessop, "The Regulation Approach, Governance and Post-Fordism: Alternative Perspectives on Economic and Political Change?," *Economy and Society* 24, no. 3 (1995): 307–33; David Harvey, *The Condition of Postmodernity* (Cambridge: Blackwell, 1990); and Harvey, A Brief *History of Neoliberalism* (Oxford: Oxford University Press, 2005).
8. Terry Marsden, "Exploring a Rural Sociology for the Fordist Tradition," *Sociologia Ruralis* 32, nos. 2–3 (August 1992): 211.
9. Harvey, *The Condition of Postmodernity*, 135.

10   Armine Yalnizyan, "Income Inequality and the Pursuit of Prosperity," Canadian Centre for Policy Alternatives, Walter Gordon Massey Symposium, March 10, 2009, p. 1, https://policyalternatives.ca/sites/default/files/uploads/publications/National_Office_Pubs/2009/Walter_Gordon_lecture_on_income_inequality-1.pdf.
11   *Constitution Act, 1930*, 20–21 George V, c. 26 (U.K.), https://www.solon.org/Constitutions/Canada/English/ca_1930.html.
12   Canada, *House of Commons Debates*, introduced March 31, 1930, debated in committee on April 9, 1930, with second and third reading May 1 and May 2 with passage on May 2, 1930.
13   Norman Hillmer, "Statute of Westminster, 1931," *Canadian Encyclopedia*, last modified April 29, 2020, https://www.thecanadianencyclopedia.ca/en/article/statute-of-westminster.
14   Marchildon, *The Heavy Hand of History: Interpreting Saskatchewan's Past* (Regina: Canadian Plains Research Center, 2005), 56.
15   Marchildon, 56.
16   John H. Thompson and Allan Seager, *Canada, 1922–1939* (Toronto: McClelland and Stewart, 1985), 207; Donald Creighton, *Canada's First Century* (Toronto: Macmillan of Canada, 1970), 197–9.
17   Quoted in Michael Horn, *The Great Depression in Canada* (Ottawa: Canadian Historical Association, 1984), 17.
18   Quoted in Peter B. Waite, *The Loner: Three Sketches of the Personal Life and Ideas of R.B. Bennett, 1870–1947* (Toronto: University of Toronto Press, 1992), 82.
19   Canada, *House of Commons Debates*, April 17, 1931 (Donnelly), 703.
20   Canada, *House of Commons Debates*, bill introduced on July 29, 1931, 4275–7; Thompson and Seager, *Canada, 1922–1939*, 208 and 217. On Bennett's fear of radicalism, see Creighton, *Canada's First Century*, 201.
21   See Bill Waiser, *Saskatchewan: A New History* (Calgary: Fifth House, 2005), chap. 14.
22   Ian M. Drummond, "Ottawa Agreements," *Canadian Encyclopedia*, last modified October 9, 2015, https://www.thecanadianencyclopedia.ca/en/article/ottawa-agreements.
23   Kenneth Norrie and Douglas Owram, *A History of the Canadian Economy* (Toronto: Harcourt Brace Jovanovich, 1991), 503–5.
24   Canada, *House of Commons Debates*, introduction and first reading, March 15, 1934, 1498.
25   Canada, *House of Commons Debates*, second reading April 18, 1934, 1498, and finally passed June 7, 1934, 3781.
26   Creighton, *Canada's First Century*, 225.
27   Canada, *House of Commons Debates*, May 16, 1934, 3093.
28   Canada, *House of Commons Debates*, June 4, 1934, 3639.
29   Canada, *House of Commons Debates*, June 4, 1934, 3655.

30 See "Supreme Court Judgments: Reference re legislative jurisdiction of Parliament of Canada to enact the Farmers' Creditors Arrangement Act, 1934, as amended by the Farmers' Creditors Arrangement Act Amendment Act, 1935," Supreme Court of Canada, accessed February 23, 2023, https://scc-csc.lexum.com/scc-csc/scc-csc/en/item/8632/index.do. Also see Virginia Torrie, "Farm Debt Compromises during the Great Depression: An Empirical Study of Applications Made under the Farmers' Creditors Arrangement Act in Morden and Brandon, Manitoba," *Manitoba Law Journal* 41, no. 1 (2018): 377–433, and R. McQueen, "The Farmers' Creditors Arrangement Act," *Canadian Journal of Economics and Political Science/Revue canadienne d'Economique et de Science politique*, no. 1 (February 1935): 104–8.

31 Canada, *House of Commons Debates*, May 1, 1939, 3386. It is safe to assume the majority were in the West.

32 Quoted in McQueen, "Farmers' Creditors Arrangement Act," 104.

33 Canada, *House of Commons Debates*, original motions introduced February 22, 1934, 224.

34 Canada, *House of Commons Debates*, June 28, 1934 (Woodsworth), 4381–4.

35 Mark S. Bonham, "Bank of Canada," *Canadian Encyclopedia*, last modified May 3, 2018, https://www.thecanadianencyclopedia.ca/en/article/bank-of-canada; Ross A. Eaman, "CBC/Radio-Canada," *Canadian Encyclopedia*, last modified August 4, 2015, https://www.thecanadianencyclopedia.ca/en/article/canadian-broadcasting-corporation." For the paper corporation comment, see Cook, "Canadian Conservative Tradition," 34.

36 Canada, *House of Commons Debates*, initial resolution April 8, 1935, 2604, with details on April 10, 1935, 2604–18.

37 Marchildon, "Prairie Farm Rehabilitation Administration," 291–2.

38 Canada, *House of Commons Debates*, April 28, 1936, 2232. Gardiner (at 2234) refers to the act as having been passed in 1935 with $750,000 being the amount associated with the 1935 bill.

39 Second and third reading took place on April 11, 1935. See Marchildon "Prairie Farm Rehabilitation Administration."

40 Canada, *House of Commons Debates*, April 6, 1939 (C. Dunning), 2653.

41 Alvin Finkel, *Business and Social Reform in the Thirties* (Toronto: James Lorimer and Co., 1979), 59, 60–1; C.F. Wilson, *A Century of Canadian Grain: Government Policy to 1951* (Saskatoon: Western Prairie Producer Books, 1978), 416–17.

42 Canada, *Report of the Commission to Enquire into Trading in Grain Futures* (Ottawa: King's Printer, 1931), http://epe.lac-bac.gc.ca/100/200/301/pco-bcp/commissions-ef/stamp1931-eng/stamp1931-eng.htm; Finkel, *Business and Social Reform*, 61; André Magnan, *When Wheat Was King: The Rise and Fall of the Canada–UK Grain Trade* (Vancouver: UBC Press, 2016), 50–1; Wilson, *Century of Canadian Grain*, chap. 15.

43 Wilson, *Century of Canadian Grain*, chaps. 18 and 19. Argentina, Australia, Canada, and the United States all agreed to limit exports to increase wheat prices.
44 Canada, *House of Commons Debates*, May 21, 1935, 2927.
45 Canada, *House of Commons Debates*, June 12, 1935, 3573–4.
46 Canada, *House of Commons Debates*, July 4, 1935, 4275.
47 Finkle, *Business and Social Reform*, 67, and Robert Irwin, "Farmers and 'Orderly Marketing': The Making of the Canadian Wheat Board," *Prairie Forum* 26, no. 1 (2001): 85–105.
48 Speaking to the matter in February 1939, Gardiner made it clear that this was seen as a temporary act. See Canada, *House of Commons Debates*, February 16, 1939, 1032–7. Later, while speaking to the PFRA, he repeated the position: *House of Commons Debates*, April 5, 1939, 2612–13.
49 Creighton, *Canada's First Century*, 216–17.
50 Brown, *When Freedom Was Lost*, 30.
51 Canada, *House of Commons Debates*, Gardiner's motion February 8, 1937, 637; February 9, 1937, 720–30; February 11, 1937, 765–801; February 1, 1937, 813–48. The amended bill passed on February 26, 1937, 1295–1300.
52 Canada, *House of Commons Debates*, May 29, 1941, 3307. See also Gardiner on June 3, 1941, 3424.
53 These activity summaries come from Robert A. Halliday, "Looking Back at the Prairie Farm Rehabilitation Administration," Forum For Leadership on Water, October 2020, https://www.flowcanada.org/looking-back-at-the-pfra.
54 Brian Noble and Surendra Kulshreshtha, "Saskatchewan Community Pastures," in *Saskatchewan: Geographical Perspectives*, ed. Bernard D. Thraves, Marilyn L. Lewry, Janis Dale, and Hansgeorg Schlichtmann (Regina: Canadian Plains Research Centre, 2007), 361.
55 Dave Phillips, "PFRA Pastures Transition Study," Frogworks Consultants, January 7, 2015, https://www.naturesask.ca/rsu_docs/pfra-final-report.pdf. See also Katherine Arbuthnott and Josef K. Schmutz, "PFRA Community Pastures: History and Drama of a Prairie Commons," Canadian Centre for Policy Alternatives, *Saskatchewan Notes* (April 2013), https://policyalternatives.ca/publications/reports/sasknotes-pfra-community-pastures.
56 Trevor Herriot, *Towards a Prairie Atonement* (Regina: University of Regina Press, 2016), 68.
57 Canada, *House of Commons Debates*, April 5, 1939, 2611.
58 Canada, *House of Commons Debates*, introduced May 5, 1939, 3636, passed on May 10, 1938, 3841. For more details, see Wilson, *Century of Canadian Grain*, 603–5.
59 Vernon C. Fowke, "Royal Commissions and Canadian Agricultural Policy," *Canadian Journal of Economics and Political Science* 14, no. 2 (May 1948): 158.
60 Canada, *Report of the Prairie Farm Assistance Administration Commission of Inquiry Established under Order-in-Council P.C. 1963–1896 of 21st December, 1963*

(Ottawa: Queen's Printer, 1964), https://publications.gc.ca/site/eng/9.818833/publication.html.
61 Canada, *House of Commons Debates*, March 18, 1936, 1207.
62 Canada, House of Commons Special Committee on the Marketing of Wheat and Other Grains, *Minutes and Proceedings and Evidence No. 1*, 331–2.
63 Canada, ParlInfo, *Speeches from the Throne*, 18th Parliament, January 12, 1939, 7.
64 Canada, *House of Commons Debates*, May 10, 1939, 3841–2.
65 Canada, *House of Commons Debates*, April 6, 1939, 2635.
66 D.A. MacGibbon, *The Canadian Grain Trade, 1932–1951* (Toronto: University of Toronto Press, 1952), 26. On the notion of co-ops replacing the CWB, see Wilson, *Century of Canadian Grain*, 604.
67 Wilson, *Century of Canadian Grain*, 606.
68 Wilson, 606–9.
69 Canada, ParlInfo, *Speech from the Throne*, 18th Parliament, January 12, 1939, 2.
70 Canada, ParlInfo, *Speech from the Throne*, 18th Parliament, September 7, 1939, 3.
71 Wilson, *Century of Canadian Grain*, 661.
72 Canada, *House of Commons Debates*, July 25, 1940 (bill introduced by J.A. MacKinnon), 1906. See also Wilson, *Century of Canadian Grain*, 667.
73 See the many comments on the concerns of Western producers in the debate on the Throne Speech: Canada, *House of Commons Debates*, January 29, 1942 (Castleden), 168; February 3, 1942 (Perley), 266; February 16, 1942 (Graham), 602.
74 Canada, *House of Commons Debates*, January 29, 1942, 167–70.
75 Canada, *House of Commons Debates*, January 30, 1942, 181.
76 Canada, *House of Commons Debates*, introduced by Gardiner March 9, 1942, 1127, and passed on March 24, 1942, 1187. See also Wilson, *Century of Canadian Grain*, 685–7.
77 Canada, *House of Commons Debates*, April 9, 1943, 2016. See also MacGibbon, *Canadian Grain Trade*, 55.
78 Canada, *House of Commons Debates*, March 12, 1942 (Perley), 1631; March 29, 1943 (Wright), 1633; March 29, 1943 (Castleden), 1638; March 29, 1943 (Diefenbaker), 1646.
79 Canada. *House of Commons Debates*, March 30, 1943, 1672.
80 See Fowke, *National Policy and the Wheat Economy*, 275; MacGibbon, *Canadian Grain Trade*, 101, 142. Wilson, *Century of Canadian Grain*, chap. 32, notes that the change was made during a period of potentially significant price increases resulting in inflation. In addition, there were Canadian wartime commitments to Britain. See also Irwin, "Farmers and 'Orderly Marketing,'" 99–100.
81 MacGibbon, *Canadian Grain Trade*, 64.
82 See, for example, Mr. Gardiner's March 9, 1942, amendments to the *Prairie Farm Assistance Act* and Mr. MacKinnon's amendments to the *Canadian Wheat Board Act* on March 6, 1942.

83 See Albert Rose, "Leonard Marsh," *Canadian Encyclopedia*, last modified December 16, 2013, https://www.thecanadianencyclopedia.ca/en/article/leonard-marsh; "Leonard Marsh," Canadian Museum of History, *Making Medicare: The History of Health Care in Canada, 1914–2007*, last modified April 21, 2010, https://www.historymuseum.ca/cmc/exhibitions/hist/medicare/medic-3k09e.html.
84 Robert W. Dimand, "Beveridge on Unemployment and Cycles Before 'The General Theory,'" *History of Economic Ideas* 7, no. 3 (2000): 33–51, and Thomas F. Cooley and Lee E. Ohanian, "Postwar British Economic Growth and the Legacy of Keynes," *Journal of Political Economy* 105, no. 3 (June 1997): 439–72.
85 Reginald Whitaker, "Political Thought and Political Action in Mackenzie King," *Journal of Canadian Studies/Revue d'études canadiennes* 13, no. 4 (Winter 1978–9): 57.
86 Donald Creighton, *Dominion of the North* (Toronto: Macmillan Company of Canada, 1969), 502–3.
87 Donald Creighton, *The Forked Road: Canada, 1937–1957* (Toronto: McClelland and Stewart, 1976), 37.
88 Creighton, 44.
89 Creighton, 54. A more favourable analysis (along with the text of the agreement) can be found in J.L. Granatstein and R.D. Duff, "The Hyde Park Declaration 1941: Origins and Significance," *Canadian Historical Review* 55, no. 1 (March 1974): 59–80.
90 Creighton, *Forked Road*, 43.
91 Creighton, 64.
92 Norrie and Owram, *History of the Canadian Economy*, 522–3.
93 George Grant, *Lament for a Nation* (Ottawa: Carlton Library Series, 1965), 47.
94 Grant, 86.
95 Canada, *House of Commons Debates*, July 24, 1944 (Gardiner notice of motion), 5313; July 29, 1944 (second reading), 5573; July 31, 1944 (third reading and passage of bill), 5654. For an assessment, see J.F. Booth, "The Canadian Agricultural Price Support Program," *Canadian Journal of Economics and Political Science/Revue canadienne d'Economique et de Science politique* 17, no. 3 (August 1951): 334–43; J.C. Gilson, "A Canadian View of Conflicts and Consistencies in the Agricultural Policies of Canada and the United States," *American Journal of Agricultural Economics* 55, no. 5 (December 1973): 785–90. For a detailed list of the commodities impacted, see A.H. Turner, "Canada's Experience in Agricultural Support Measures," *Journal of Farm Economics* 41, no. 5 (December 1959): 1250–65.
96 Canada, ParlInfo, *Speeches from the Throne*, 21st Parliament, October 9, 1951, 3–5.
97 Canada, *House of Commons Debates*, November 6, 1951 (Gardiner), 739.
98 Canada, *House of Commons Debates*, November 13, 1951 (bill introduced), 973; November 13, 1951 (Charlton supports), 973; November 13, 1951 (Fair representing Social Credit Party does likewise), 977; November 13, 1951 (Argue), 981.

99 Douglas Hedley, "The Evolution of Agricultural Support Policy," CAES Fellows Paper 2015-1 (2015), https://caes-scae.ca/wp-content/uploads/2018/11/2015-Hedley-Evolution-Ag-Policy-Fellows-Paper-R1.pdf.
100 Canada, *House of Commons Debates*, September 20, 1945 (Fair), 333, and April 30, 1946, 1065.
101 Canada, *House of Commons Debates*, February 10, 1947 (first reading), 231; extensive debate held February 18, 20, and 24–8, 1947; passed March 13, 1947.
102 Canada, *House of Commons Debates*, February 27, 1948, 1677.
103 Canada, *House of Commons Debates*, February 1, 1957 (Howe), 889, (Diefenbaker), 892.
104 Canada, *House of Commons Debates*, October 31, 1957, 595. The debate continued in January 1958. See January 14, 1958, 3330, and January 25, 2957.
105 Canada, *House of Commons Debates*, January 14, 1958 (Lewry), and January 25, 1958 (third reading and passage of bill), 3839.
106 Ralph Olson, "The International Wheat Agreement," *Southwestern Social Science Quarterly* 32, no. 1 (June 1951): 40. See also Frank H. Golay, "The International Wheat Agreement of 1949," *Quarterly Journal of Economics* 64, no. 3 (August 1950): 442–63.
107 Colleen M. O'Connor, "Going against the Grain: The Regulation of the International Wheat Trade from 1933 to the 1980 Soviet Grain Embargo," *Boston College International & Comparative Law Review* 5, no. 1 (1982): 238–43; Theodore Cohn, "The 1978–9 Negotiations for an International Wheat Agreement: An Opportunity Lost?," *International Journal* 35, no. 1 (Winter 1979–80): 132–49; David L. Macfarlane, "The International Wheat Agreement of 1956: A Canadian View," *International Affairs* 32, no. 4 (Oct. 1956) 427–35; Helen C. Farnsworth, "International Wheat Agreements and Problems, 1949–56," *Quarterly Journal of Economics* 70, no. 2 (May 1956): 217–48.
108 William Morriss, *Chosen Instrument II* (Winnipeg: Canadian Wheat Board, 2000), 7–9.
109 Canada, *House of Commons Debates*, February 9, 1956, 31, also 1027–38.
110 Canada, *House of Commons Debates*, January 27, 1956 (Howe), 601, (Argue), 611–12. See also February 24, 1956 (Diefenbaker on final reading), 1541; and February 28, 1956, 1617–18. The bill passed February 28, 1956. On CWB legislation, see February 28, 1956 (Howe).
111 Canada, *House of Commons Debates*, January 12, 1956 (Howe), 31, and February 9, 1956 (McCullough), 1027.
112 Denis Smith, "Walter Lockhart Gordon," *Canadian Encyclopedia*, last modified December 16, 2013, https://www.thecanadianencyclopedia.ca/en/article/walter-lockhart-gordon.
113 Canada, *Royal Commission on Canada's Economic Prospects: Final Report* (Ottawa: Royal Commission on Canada's Economic Prospects, 1958), 283, https://publications.gc.ca/collections/collection_2016/bcp-pco/Z1-1955-2-2-eng.pdf.

114 Canada, 390–1.
115 Creighton, *Forked Road*, 270.
116 Creighton, *Canada's First Century*, 300.
117 Canada, *House of Commons Debates*, resolution introduced on June 25, 1959, 4710; June 29, 1959 (second reading), 4736; June 29, 1959 (Harkness), 5254.
118 Canada, *House of Commons Debates*, June 29, 1959, 5255. See also A.H. Turner, "Federal Farm Credit Assistance," *Canadian Journal of Agricultural Economics* 8, no. 1 (March 1953): 72–81.
119 Canada, *House of Commons Debates*, August 30, 1958, 4346. Diefenbaker lays out the elements at 4346–7.
120 Canada, *House of Commons Debates*, January 25, 1961, 1403.
121 Canada, *House of Commons Debates*, May 1, 1961 (Jorgenson), 4183; May 31, 1961; May 2, 1961 (Rogers), 4263.
122 James N. McCrorie, ARDA: *An Experiment in Development Planning* (Ottawa: Canadian Council on Rural Development, 1969), 37–9.
123 John G. Diefenbaker, *One Canada: Memoirs of the Right Honourable John G. Diefenbaker, vol. 2, The Tumultuous Years 1962 to 1967* (Toronto: Macmillan of Canada, 1977), 279.
124 Canada, *House of Commons Debates*, October 24, 1957, 351.
125 Canada, *House of Commons Debates*, October 24, 1957, 458.
126 Canada, *House of Commons Debates*, October 28, 1959 (bill introduced); October 30, 1957 (second reading); October 31, 1957 (passage).
127 Western Producer, *Prairie Farm Guide* (Saskatoon: Western Producer, 1977), 27.
128 Canada, *House of Commons Debates*, October 31, 1957 (Harkness). The exceptions of "wheat, oats and barley grown in the wheat board area" is noted in the debate of December 11, 1957.
129 Canada, *House of Commons Debates*, January 24, 1958 (Argue), 3614–15.
130 Canada, *House of Commons Debates*, March 9, 1959 (Hees), 1725. Debated March 24, 1959, 2207; March 25, 1959, 2228; April 7, 1959, 2322; May 18, 1959, 3747; and passed on May 18, 1959, 3766.
131 Canada, *Royal Commission on Transportation, vol. 1* (Ottawa: Queen's Printer, March 1961), appendix A, http://epe.lac-bac.gc.ca/100/200/301/pco-bcp/commissions-ef/macpherson1961-eng/macpherson1961vol1-eng/macpherson1961vol1-eng.pdf.
132 Canada, 1:1.
133 Canada, 1:39–40.
134 Canada, *Royal Commission on Transportation, vol. 2* (Ottawa: Queen's Printer, December 1961), 188, https://publications.gc.ca/collections/collection_2014/bcp-pco/Z1-1959-3-2-2-eng.pdf.
135 Commissioner A.R. Gobiel presented a dissenting view. See Canada, *Royal Commission on Transportation*, 1:77.

136 Morriss, *Chosen Instrument II*, 7–9.
137 Donaghy and Stevenson, "The Limits of Alliance: Cold War Solidarity and Canadian Wheat Exports to China, 1950–1963," *Agricultural History* 83, no. 1 (Winter 2009): 32.
138 John G. Diefenbaker, *One Canada: Memoirs of the Right Honourable John G. Diefenbaker*, vol. 1, *Years of Achievement 1956 to 1962* (Toronto: Macmillan of Canada, 1977), 178–83; Morriss, *Chosen Instrument II*, 14–20.
139 Morriss, *Chosen Instrument II*, 59–62, 73.
140 Creighton, *Canada's First Century*, 309 and chap. 13; Grant, *Lament for a Nation*, 13–36.
141 Mitch Potter, "JFK's War with Diefenbaker," *Toronto Star*, November 18, 2013, https://www.thestar.com/news/world/2013/11/18/jfks_war_with_diefenbaker.html.
142 Diefenbaker, *One Canada*, 2:107.
143 Diefenbaker, 240–1.
144 Canada, *House of Commons Debates*, May 25, 1967, 574–5.
145 Canada, *House of Commons Debates*, May 25, 1967 (Jorgenson), 578, (Knowles), 581.
146 Canada, *House of Commons Debates*, May 11, 1964 (Hayes), 3106; June 2, 1964, 3862.
147 Canada, *House of Commons Debates*, June 12, 1964, 4267.
148 Canada, *House of Commons Debates*, August 29, 1966 (back-to-work legislation tabled by prime minister), 7766; September 1, 1966 (Minister Pickersgill introduces amendments to *Railroad Act*), 7888.
149 John Munro, "New Directions in Canadian Transportation Policy," *Transportation Journal* 8, no. 2 (Winter 1968): 38.
150 Canada, *House of Commons Debates*, September 6, 1966 (e.g., Horner), 8065.
151 E.J. Chambers, M. James Dunn, David W. Gillen, and D. Gordon Tyndall, "Bill C-20: An Evaluation from the Perspective of Current Transportation Policy and Regulatory Performance," *Canadian Public Policy/Analyse de Politiques* 6, no. 1 (Winter 1980): 55.
152 Canada, *House of Commons Debates*, September 1, 1966 (Pickersgill), 7997. In debate, Horner repeated Pickersgill's commitment to the Crow Rate. See *House of Commons Debates*, September 6, 1955, 8063.
153 Canada, *House of Commons Debates*, May 27, 1966 (announcement of commission and terms of reference, Green), 5599 and 5601. See also Clarence L. Barber, *Report of the Royal Commission on Farm Machinery* (Ottawa: Information Canada, 1971), iii and iv.
154 Barber, *Report of the Royal Commission on Farm Machinery*, 13–21.
155 Barber, 254–5.
156 Barber, 290.
157 Barber, 231.
158 Barber, 493–4.

159 Canada, *House of Commons Debates*, June 8, 1971 (Murta's question to minister of agriculture), 6470, and September 27, 1971 (Thompson), 8184.
160 Canada, *House of Commons Debates*, October 5, 1971 (Yewchuk), 8468; October 22, 1971 (Nystrom), 8930; and October 22, 1971 (Trudeau's reply), 8930.
161 Canada, *House of Commons Debates*, December 14, 1971 (Thomson), 10478.
162 Barber, "Farm Machinery Industry," 822.
163 Terrence S. Veeman and Michele M. Veeman, "The Changing Organization, Structure, and Control of Canadian Agriculture," *American Journal of Agricultural Economics* 60, no. 5 (December 1978): 764.
164 Canada, *House of Commons Debates*, July 13, 1955 (e.g., Bryson), 6044–6.
165 Enno Kruse, "Royal Commissions as Instruments of Policy-Making in Saskatchewan: The Royal Commission on Agriculture and Rural Life A Case Study" (master's thesis, University of Saskatchewan, 1989), 19.
166 Patrick Kyba, *Alvin: A Biography of the Honourable Alvin Hamilton, P.C.* (Regina: Canadian Plains Research Centre, 1989), 155–6.
167 "Table M1-11: Farm Population, Census Data, Canada and by Province, 1931 to 1971," Statistics Canada, last modified July 2, 2014, https://www150.statcan.gc.ca/n1/pub/11-516-x/sectionm/4057754-eng.htm#1.
168 Canada, *House of Commons Debates*, Harkness provided this information in answer to a question on March 5, 1959, 1628. See also Karen Briere, "Now: Tens of Thousands of Farmers Participate in Protests; Then: Ottawa Delegation to Be 1000 Strong," *Western Producer*, December 23, 2013, https://www.producer.com/news/ottawa-delegation-to-be-1000-strong.
169 Kybak, *Alvin*, 155–7.
170 Canada, *Report of Royal Commission on Price Spreads of Food Products*, vol. 1 (Ottawa: Queen's Printer, September 1959), vii, http://epe.lac-bac.gc.ca/100/200/301/pco-bcp/commissions-ef/stewart1960-eng/stewart1960-v1-eng.pdf.
171 Canada, *Report of Royal Commission on Price Spreads of Food Products*, vol. 1 (Ottawa: Queen's Printer, March 1960), 99, https://publications.gc.ca/collections/collection_2016/bcp-pco/Z1-1957-4-3-1-eng.pdf.
172 Canada, *Report of Royal Commission on Price Spreads of Food Products*, 1:vii, 60.
173 Statistics Canada, 2016 Census of Population, Statistics Canada Catalogue no. 98-400-X2016019.
174 See "Farming," Hutterian Brethren, accessed January 15, 2022, http://www.hutterites.org/day-to-day/livelihood/farming/; Douglas Sanders, "The Hutterites: A Case Study in Minority Rights," *Canadian Bar Review*, no. 42 (1964): 225–42; Barb Glen, "Yes, Hutterites Do Pay Taxes," *Western Producer*, June 14, 2018, https://www.producer.com/2018/06/yes-hutterites-do-pay-taxes/.
175 Gerald Pilger, "The Best Family Farms," *Country Guide*, November 22, 2011, https://www.country-guide.ca/features/the-best-family-farms/.
176 Michael Raine, "Tisdale, Sask., Farm Sells For $26.5 million," *Western Producer*,

September 27, 2016, https://www.producer.com/2016/09/tisdale-sask-farm-sells-for-26-5-million/.

177   There is a website dedicated to the Matador Co-op maintained by Gary and Norma McClelland. Gary's parents were original members of the co-op. See "About Us," Matador Co-op Farm, last updated december 17, 2022, http://www.matadorco-opfarm.ca/about-us.html. See also Waiser, *Saskatchewan*, 346–7.

178   George Melnyk, "Matador Farming Pool and the Cooperative Farming Movement," in *Encyclopedia of Saskatchewan* (Regina: Canadian Plain Research Centre, 2005), 580.

179   See "Trudeau Turns Wrath on Insulting Signs," *Regina Leader-Post*, July 17, 1969, available at https://library.usask.ca/sni/stories/con18a.html.

180   "Farmers Force Legislature Shutdown," *Prairie Fire*, April 7–14, 1970.

4. PHASE 3—UNLEASHING THE MARKET

1   The notion of Keynesian chickens is borrowed from a remarkable essay by Paul Sweezy and Harry Magdoff, "Keynesian Chickens Come Home to Roost," *Monthly Review* 25, no. 11 (April 1974): 1–12.

2   The summary of developments in this paragraph was informed by a number of sources, including Leonard W. Martin, "Stagflation: A Condition Created by Accelerated Demand-Pull Inflation," *American Journal of Economics and Sociology* 44, no. 4 (October 1985): 497–502; Mark A. Lutz, "Stagflation as an Institutional Problem," *Journal of Economic Issues* 15, no. 3 (September 1981): 745–68; Howard Sherman, "Monopoly Power and Stagflation," *Journal of Economic Issues* 11, no. 2 (June 1977): 269–84; and Joan Robinson, "Solving the Stagflation Puzzle," *Challenge* 22, no. 5, (November–December 1979): 40–6.

3   For a basic exposition of monetarist ideas, see F.H. Hahn, "Monetarism and Economic Theory," *Economica*, no. 47 (February 1980): 1–17, and William Frazer, "Milton Friedman and Thatcher's Monetarist Experience," *Journal of Economic Issues* 16, no. 2 (1982): 525–33. See also the following works by Milton Friedman: *A Theory of the Consumption Function* (Princeton, NJ: Princeton University Press, 1957); *Capitalism and Freedom* (Chicago: University of Chicago Press, 1962); and (co-authored with Rose Friedman), *Free to Choose* (New York: Harcourt Brace Jovanovich, 1980).

4   Tejaswini Ganti, "Neoliberalism," *Annual Review of Anthropology*, no. 43 (2014): 91; Margaret Thatcher, "Interview for *Woman's Own* ('No Such Thing as Society')," Margaret Thatcher Foundation, accessed March 7, 2023, https://www.margaretthatcher.org/document/106689.

5   Elizabeth Martinez and Arnoldo Garcia, "What is Neoliberalism? A Brief Definition for Activists," CorpWatch: Holding Corporations Accountable, January 1, 1997, https://corpwatch.org/article/what-neoliberalism.

6   Thatcher, "Interview for *Woman's Own*."
7   Thomas L. Hungerford, "Corporate Tax Rates and Economic Growth Since 1947," Economic Policy Institute, June 4, 2013, https://www.epi.org/publication/ib364-corporate-tax-rates-and-economic-growth/.
8   David Harvey, *The Enigma of Capital and the Crisis of Capitalism* (New York: Oxford University Press, 2010), 10. Harvey repeats this argument in *A Brief History of Neoliberalism* (Oxford: Oxford University Press, 2005), 15–16.
9   Thomas DeGrace, "The Dot Com Bubble Burst that Caused the 2000 Stock Market Crash," StockPicksSystem.com, April 11, 2011, http://www.stockpickssystem.com/2000-stock-market-crash/.
10 Canada, ParlInfo, *Speeches from the Throne*, 28th Parliament, September 12, 1968, 14.
11 Canada, *House of Commons Debates*, October 22, 1968 (Benson), 1681.
12 Canada, *House of Commons Debates*, June 3, 1969 (Benson), 9413–17.
13 Canada, ParlInfo, *Speeches from the Throne*, 27th Parliament, May 8, 1967, 8–9.
14 Canada, *Canadian Agriculture in the Seventies: Report of the Federal Task Force on Agriculture* (Ottawa: Agriculture and Agri-Food Canada, December 1969), 457, http://epe.lac-bac.gc.ca/100/200/301/pco-bcp/commissions-ef/campbell1969-eng/campbell1969-eng.htm. Hereafter cited as Task Force Report.
15 Canada, *House of Commons Debates*, May 10, 1967 (Diefenbaker), 41.
16 Canada, *House of Commons Debates*, March 4, 1968 (Green), 7203.
17 Canada, *House of Commons Debates*, February 2, 1969 (report received), May 19, 1970 (report tabled), 7057.
18 Canada, *Task Force Report*, 10.
19 Canada, 10.
20 Canada, 21.
21 Canada, 263.
22 Canada, 263.
23 Canada, *House of Commons Debates*, May 21, 1970 (Olson), 7161.
24 Canada, *House of Commons Debates*, September 13, 1973 9benjamin), 6549, and September 13, 1970 (Horner), 6550.
25 Grace Skogstad, *Internationalization and Canadian Agriculture: Policy and Governing Paradigms* (Toronto: University of Toronto Press, 2008), 52.
26 Jack Carr, *Wage and Price Controls: Panacea for Inflation or Prescription for Disaster* (Vancouver: Fraser Institute, 1976), 3.
27 First there was a Special Committee on Trends in Food Prices. See Canada, *House of Commons Debates*, April 10, 1973 (MacInnis), 3143, and the committee's recommendations at 3144. Mr. Gray announced the establishment of the Food Prices Review Board by Order-in-Council on May 7, 1973, 3562.
28 James Laxer, Herbert Laxer, and Robert Laxer, *The Liberal Idea of Canada: Pierre Trudeau and the Question of Canada's Survival* (Toronto: J. Lorimer, 1977), 70–1.

29 Canada, *House of Commons Debates*, October 14, 1975 (introduced by Macdonald and debated remainder of the day), 8191–8216; October 17, 1975, 8306–26.
30 Ian Urquhart, "Balking at Trudeau's Medicine," *Maclean's*, November 3, 1975, 18.
31 Canada, *House of Commons Debates*, Broadbent moved to reject the program on November 14, 1975, 9073; for Stanfield's critique, see November 14, 1975, 9077. The debate carried on occupying the House most of the fall of 1975. See December 1, 1975 (Nystrom); third reading started on December 1, 1975, with passage on December 3, 1975, 9690.
32 Denis Smith, "Walter Lockhart Gordon," *Canadian Encyclopedia*, last modified December 16, 2013, https://www.thecanadianencyclopedia.ca/en/article/walter-lockhart-gordon.
33 The fate of the task force's report seemed uncertain because at the time it was likely not to be made public. Canada, *House of Commons Debates*, November 15, 1967, 4309, but Mr. Sharp presented it to cabinet January 22, 1968, then finally it was tabled. Canada, *House of Commons Debates*, February 15, 1968, 6749. The report's official title was *Foreign Ownership and the Structure of Canadian Industry: Report of the Task Force on the Structure of Canadian Industry*. See also Mel Watkins, "Task Force on Foreign Ownership and the Structure of Canadian Investment," *Canadian Encyclopedia*, last modified December 16, 2013, https://www.thecanadianencyclopedia.ca/en/article/task-force-on-foreign-ownership-and-the-structure-of-canadian-investment; Harry G. Johnson, "Towards a New National Policy," *International Journal* 23, no. 4 (Autumn 1968): 615–22.
34 Canada, ParlInfo, *Speeches from the Throne*, 28th Parliament, October 8, 1970, 4.
35 Canada, *House of Commons Debates*, February 27, 1970 (Lang's announcement of program), 4159.
36 "'Operation LIFT' to Lower Wheat Surplus," *Manitoba Co-operator*, March 21, 2018, https://www.manitobacooperator.ca/country-crossroads/our-history/our-history-1970-operation-lift-to-lower-wheat-surplus/. There was a long and raucous debate in the House on March 2 that lasted until after 1:00 a.m.
37 Canada, *House of Commons Debates*, October 13, 1970 (Burton), 73–5; October 15, 1970 (Nystrom), 176; October 20, 1970 (Mazankowski), 407–8.
38 Canada, *House of Commons Debates*, November 9, 1970 (Olson), 991; February 10, 1971 (Lang), 3238.
39 Canada, *House of Commons Debates*, January 10, 1973 (Diefenbaker), 149; February 22, 1973 (Horner), 1552. Horner later estimated the cost in lost sales of wheat not produced at $600 million: February 1973, 1288.
40 Canada, *House of Commons Debates*, October 26, 1970 (MacEachen), 541; November 2, 1970 (Olson on second reading), 812.
41 Grace Skogstad, "The Farm Products Marketing Agencies Act: A Case Study of Agricultural Policy," *Canadian Public Policy/Analyse de Politiques* 6, no. 1 (Winter 1980): 91.

42 Canada, *House of Commons Debates*, November 2, 1970 (Olson), 812.
43 Canada, *House of Commons Debates*, April 27, 1971 (Horner), 5294-5; November 2, 1970 (Gleave), 817.
44 See Canada, House of Commons Committees, 28th Parliament, Standing Committee of Agriculture, 1970, vols. 1-3. at https://parl.canadiana.ca/browse/eng/c/committees/28-2. For a full account of this legislation see Skogstad, "Farm Products Marketing Agencies Act."
45 Canada, *House of Commons Debates*, December 30, 1971, 10954.
46 Jodey Nurse and Bruce Muirhead, "A Crisis in National Unity? The Chicken and Egg War, 1970-1971," *Journal of Canadian Studies* 56, no. 1 (Winter 2022): 124-45.
47 Nurse and Muirhead, 142.
48 Skogstad, "Farm Products Marketing Agencies Act," 99.
49 Canada, *House of Commons Debates*, April 23, 1971 (Land), 5175; May 4, 1971 (second reading), 5490.
50 Canada, *House of Commons Debates*, May 4, 1971, 5500-2.
51 Canada, *House of Commons Debates*, May 6, 1971 (Horner), 5568; May 4, 1971 (Burton), 5503.
52 Ian MacLachlan, "The Historical Development of Cattle Production in Canada" (unpublished manuscript; originally written 1996; last edited 2006), OPUS: Open Ulethbridge Scholarship, accessed January 21, 2020, https://opus.uleth.ca/bitstream/handle/10133/303/Historical_cattle_Canada.pdf;jsessionid=1503DC39113E5A9C79EDCBB99C9B9F34?sequence=3. See especially p. 20.
53 Canada, *House of Commons Debates*, June 13, 1973 (Fortin), 4719; June 19, 1973, 4888; June 21, 1973 (lambert), 4990-2; June 21, 1973 (Whicher), 5006-7; June 21, 1973 (Gleave), 4989; June 26, 1973, 5055.
54 William Morriss, *Chosen Instrument II* (Winnipeg: Canadian Wheat Board, 2000), 118-21.
55 Canada, *House of Commons Debates*, July 13, 1973 (Caouette), 5581; July 16, 1973 (Gleave), 5651.
56 Canada, *House of Commons Debates*, July 16, 1973 (Lang), 5657.
57 See, for example, Canada, *House of Commons Debates*, July 27, 1973 (Nystrom), 6054; August 30, 1973 (Korchinski), 6070; August 31, 1973 (Gleave), 6095.
58 Morriss, *Chosen Instrument II*, 121.
59 Canada, *House of Commons Debates*, December 12, 1974 (Horner), 2199.
60 Canada, *House of Commons Debates*, April 26, 1976 (Lang), 12865; April 26, 1976 (Hamilton), 12882; on the advisory committee, June 22, 1976.
61 Hamilton was complementary in his support. See Canada, *House of Commons Debates*, June 13, 1977, 6008. For Nystrom's concerns, see June 13, 1977, 6610-12.
62 Lorne Weston, "The FLQ: The Life and Times of a Terrorist Organization" (master's thesis, McGill University, 1989); Marc Laurendeau, "Front De Libération Du Québec," *Canadian Encyclopedia*, last modified September 19,

2016, https://www.thecanadianencyclopedia.ca/en/article/front-de-liberation-du-quebec.

63 Canada, ParlInfo, *Speeches from the Throne*, 30th Parliament, September 30, 1974, 8.

64 Canada, *House of Commons Debates*, March 12, 1975 (Macdonald), 4036; March 12, 1975 (Gillies for the Progressive Conservatives), 4039.

65 Canada, *House of Commons Debates*, March 12, 1975 (Douglas), 4042. When Mr. Bawden claimed that the prime minister had bowed to the demands of the NDP in creating this company, the NDP member from Winnipeg North Central, Knowles, replied, "Hear, hear." See July 10, 1975, 7470.

66 Canada, *House of Commons Debates*, November 5, 1976 (introduced by Lambert), 807; November 6, 1976 (Saltsman), 808.

67 See, for example, Canada, *House of Commons Debates*, November 16, 1976 (Railton), 1026; November 8, 1976 (Clarke), 845; November 8, 1976 (Knowles), 849; October 18, 1976 (Benjamin), 182; November 10, 1976 (Nystrom), 964.

68 Canada, *House of Commons Debates*, February 10, 1975 (Sharp), 3049.

69 Canada, *House of Commons Debates*, March 5, 1975 (Whelan), 381.

70 Canada, *House of Commons Debates*, July 10, 1975 (third reading and passage), 7423; the bill passed the same day. For an analysis, see John Spriggs, "Economic Analysis of the Western Grain Stabilization Program," *Canadian Journal of Agricultural Economics*, no. 33 (1985): 209–30, and John Spriggs and G.C. Van Kooten, "Rationale for Government Intervention in Canadian Agriculture: A Review of Stabilization Programs," *Canadian Journal of Agricultural Economics*, no. 36 (1988): 1–21.

71 Canada, *House of Commons Debates*, November 1, 1976 (introduced by Faulkner), 634; November 5, 1976 (second reading), 803–4.

72 Canada, *Commission on the Costs of Transporting Grail by Rail*, vol. 1 (Ottawa: Minister Supply and Services, 1976), 1, http://epe.lac-bac.gc.ca/100/200/301/pco-bcp/commissions-ef/snavely1976-eng/snavely1976-v2-eng.pdf.

73 Canada, 1:2.

74 Canada, *Commission on the Costs of Transporting Grain by Rail*, vol. 2 (Ottawa: Minister Supply and Services, 1977), 145–6, http://epe.lac-bac.gc.ca/100/200/301/pco-bcp/commissions-ef/snavely1976-eng/snavely1976-v2-eng.pdf1.

75 Canada, 2:155–6.

76 Canada, 2:183.

77 Canada, *House of Commons Debates*, February 28, 1978 (Goodale), 3311–12.

78 Canada, *House of Commons Debates*, December 4, 1974 (introduced by Lang), 1925; February 27, 1975 (Mr. Whelan notes the $250 million allocated), 3657.

79 Canada, *House of Commons Debates*, April 20, 1975 (Benjamin), 5351–3; May 1, 1975 (second reading), 5375; May 6, 1975 (bill sent to committee), 5484; January 28, 1975 (bill passed), 10405.

80 Canada, *Review of Western Grain Stabilization Program, 1976–1978* (Ottawa: Information Services Canada, 1976), https://archive.org/stream/reviewofwesterngoocana/reviewofwesterngoocana_djvu.txt.
81 D. Lynn Cameron and John Spriggs, "International Effects of Canada's Western Grain Program," *Western Journal of Agricultural Economics* 16, no. 2 (December 1991): 435.
82 Canada, *House of Commons Debates*, May 1, 1933 (Manion), 4432. The second and third readings took place on May 3, 1933. The bill passed without any debate.
83 Canada, *Grain and Rail Transportation in Western Canada: Report of the Grain Handling and Transportation Commission, vol. 1* (Ottawa: Grain Handling and Transportation Commission, 1977), 5. See also Greg Mason, "The Grain Handling and Transportation Commission," *Canadian Public Policy/Analyse de Politiques* 4, no. 2 (Spring 1978): 236.
84 Canada, *Grain and Rail Transportation in Western Canada*, 1:5.
85 Canada, 1:chap. 1.
86 Canada, 1:520–1.
87 Canada, 1:521–2.
88 Canada, 1:336.
89 Canada, 1:538.
90 Canada, *House of Commons Debates*, May 16, 1977 (report tabled by Minister Lang), 5665; May 17, 1977 (Mr. Hnatyshyn moved to commend Hall), 5705, (also moved by Hamilton, Trudeau, and Lang), 5706.
91 Canada, *House of Commons Debates*, May 17, 1977, 5706. See Mr. Hnatyshyn and Mr. Lang's exchange on the Crow Rate, May 18, 1977, and Mr. Lang on no rail decisions, May 19, 1977.
92 Canada, *House of Commons Debates*, May 18, 1977 (Williams), 5758, with Lang's immediate answer.
93 Canada, *House of Commons Debates*, May 24, 1977, 5877.
94 See the testy exchange between Mr. Diefenbaker and Mr. Lang, Canada, *House of Commons Debates*, May 26, 1977, 5968.
95 Canada, ParlInfo, *Speeches from the Throne*, 30th Parliament, October 11, 1978, 5.
96 Canada, *House of Commons Debates*, November 20, 1978 (Clark), 1290.
97 Canada, ParlInfo, *Speeches from the Throne*, 31st Parliament, October 9, 1979, 32.
98 Canada, *House of Commons Debates*, October 26, 1979, 650, and on the consultation remark, October 30, 1979, 743.
99 Canada, *House of Commons Debates*, November 14, 1979 (Lumley and Stevens), 1296. On the value of the rates see November 14, 1979 (Howie), 1296.
100 Canada, *House of Commons Debates*, November 15, 1979 (Broadbent), 1347.
101 Canada, *House of Commons Debates*, November 16, 1979 (Clark), 1395.
102 Canada, Archived Budget Documents, Budget Speech, December 11, 1979, 2. Note: the Government of Canada website Archived Budget Documents contains

links to all budgets from 1968 to 2015 (see https://www.budget.canada.ca/pdfarch/index-eng.html). All subsequent references refer to the links on this site.
103   Canada, ParlInfo, *Speeches from the Throne*, 32nd Parliament, April 14, 1980, 10.
104   Canada, Archived Budget Documents, Budget Speech, October 28, 1980, 3.
105   Canada, Archived Budget Documents, Budget Speech, November 12, 1981, 1.
106   Canada, 5.
107   Canada, ParlInfo, *Speeches from the Throne*, 32nd Parliament, April 14, 1980, 9.
108   Canada, Archived Budget Documents, Budget Speech, October 28, 1980, 6.
109   François Bregha, "National Energy Program," *Canadian Encyclopedia*, last modified April 29, 2016, https://www.thecanadianencyclopedia.ca/en/article/national-energy-program.
110   "Alberta and the National Energy Program," CBC News, accessed March 7, 2023, https://www.cbc.ca/alberta/features/tories40/nep.html.
111   Tammy Nemeth, "Pat Carney and the Dismantling of the National Energy Program" (master's thesis, University of Alberta, 1997), https://era.library.ualberta.ca/items/b447ba08-b092-4600-af10-0d4f6d91d034/view/34ac8632-ef37-4ea3-9885-312709080b74/MQ22547.pdf. At the time the media carried story after story decrying the impact of the NEP, including many tales of investment loss because of it. The Independent Petroleum Association of Canada took out full-page ads demanding the NEP be scrapped. See, for example, *Financial Post*, April 18, 1981, 11.
112   Canada, Archived Budget Documents, Budget Speech, November 12, 1981, 5.
113   Canada, Archived Budget Documents, Budget Speech, June 28, 1982, 13.
114   Canada, Archived Budget Documents, Budget Speech, April 19, 1983, 9–10.
115   Canada, *House of Commons Debates*, December 8, 1981, Whelan introduces bill (13834); Whelan moves second reading and refers to committee (14286); Wise for the Progressive Conservatives immediately expresses caution and concern (14288); Althouse indicates the NDP's support in principle (14292). Among the more fervid claims were those of Mr. Doug Neil, with his talk of Liberal fascism on January 29, 1982, 14471. See also the claims of Don Mazankowski on February 5, 1982, that the private sector was being replaced (14713–14), and those of Thacker on July 8, 1982, comparing Canada to Russia, then a communist state (19145).
116   Canada, Archived Budget Documents, Budget Speech, February 14, 1984, 1.
117   Canada, *House of Commons Debates*, February 8, 1982 (Broadbent, and Trudeau's response), 14746.
118   Canada, *House of Commons Debates*, February 9, 1982 (Mazankowski and Nystrom), 14814.
119   Canada, *House of Commons Debates*, February 8, 1982 (Whelan), 14747–8.
120   Canada, *House of Commons Debates*, July 16, 1982 (Althouse), 19406.
121   Canada, *House of Commons Debates*, August 4, 1982 (Pépin), 20015, (Mazankowski and Benjamin) 20016.

122 For an analysis, see Bruce Gordon Pollard, *The Year in Review, 1983: Intergovernmental Relations in Canada* (Kingston: Queen's University Institute of Intergovernmental Relations, 1983), 107–9. Also see K.K. Klein, S.N. Kulshreshtha, B. Stennes, G. Fox, W.A. Kerr, and J. Corman, "Transportation Issues in Canadian Agriculture II: Analysis of the Western Grain Transportation and Feed Freight Assistance Acts," *Canadian Journal of Regional Science/Revue canadienne des sciences régionales* 17, no. 1 (Spring 1994): 45–70.
123 Canada, *House of Commons Debates*, January 27, 1983 (Benjamin and Pépin's response), 22283.
124 Canada, *House of Commons Debates*, February 1, 1983 (Hnatyshyn), 22348.
125 Canada, *House of Commons Debates*, February 1, 1983 (Trudeau), 22386.
126 Canada, *House of Commons Debates*, May 10, 1983 (introduced), 15315. Second reading took place May 12, 1983, 15315, and the debated occupied much of remainder of the month.
127 Canada, *House of Commons Debates*, May 12, 1983 (Pépin), 25377–8.
128 Darcie Doan, Brian Paddock, and Jan Dyer, "Grain Transportation Policy and Transformation in Western Canadian Agriculture," Agriculture and Agri-food Canada, 2006, https://pdfs.semanticscholar.org/b7c0/b228313a692fa439c0723a93ec88c418229a.pdf.
129 Canada, *House of Commons Debates*, May 12, 1983 (Nystrom), 25424, and May 16, 1983, 25513.
130 Canada, *House of Commons Debates*, May 16, 1983 (Hnatyshyn), 2556.
131 See various speakers in Canada, *House of Commons Debates*, May 16, 1983: Murta (15504), Schellenberger (25508), and Malone (25509).
132 Canada, *House of Commons Debates*, May 16, 1983 (Whelan), 25500.
133 Canada, *House of Commons Debates*, November 15, 1983 (Hovdebo), 28884.
134 Canada, *House of Commons Debates*, October 19, 1983, 28129.
135 Canada, *House of Commons Debates*, October 26, 1983 (Mazankowski), 28352.
136 Doan, Paddock, and Dyer, "Reform of Grain Transportation Policy and Transformation," 163–4.
137 Manuel Álvarez-Rivera, "Election Resources on the Internet: Federal Elections in Canada—Elections to the House of Commons," ManuelAlvarez.net, last modified October 7, 2021, http://www.electionresources.org/ca/.
138 Canada, ParlInfo, *Speeches from the Throne*, 33rd Parliament, November 5, 1984, 25.
139 Canada, ParlInfo, *Speeches from the Throne*, 33rd Parliament, November 5, 1984, 28.
140 Canada, Archived Budget Documents, Budget Speech, May 23, 1985, 25.
141 Canada, *House of Commons Debates*, November 22, 1984, 474.
142 Canada, *House of Commons Debates*, June 25, 1985 (Wise), 6166.
143 Canada, *House of Commons Debates*, February 13, 1985 (Mayer), 2312, and February 15, 1985 (passage of bill), 2401.

144 Canada, *House of Commons Debates*, April 26, 1985 (Mazankowski), 4148, and June 27, 1985 (passage of bill), 6322.
145 Canada, ParlInfo, *Speeches from the Throne*, 33rd Parliament, October 1, 1986, 8.
146 Canada, *House of Commons Debates*, October 3, 1986 (Mulroney), 49. Also see the remarks by Mr. Althouse, October 3, 1986, 68.
147 Canada, *House of Commons Debates*, December 15, 1986 (Wise), 2088.
148 Canada, *House of Commons Debates*, October 3, 1986 (introduced by Wise), 38. For rationale, see Wise's comments on October 20, 1986, 509.
149 Canada, *House of Commons Debates*, October 20, 1986 (Althouse), 528.
150 Canada, *House of Commons Debates*, October 3, 1986 (Mulroney), 49, where the prime minister confirmed meetings with the provinces on the question. The matter was repeatedly raised in question period over the course of the entire session. There was never a specific bill to implement the program since the money was allocated under the budget. See Wise's comments on December 18, 1986, 2242.
151 Canada, *House of Commons Debates*, October 21, 1986 (Mayer), 586; October 28, 1986 (second reading), 795; and March 5, 1987 (passage of the bill), 3861.
152 Canada, *House of Commons Debates*, November 20, 1987 (Oliver), 11316; December 9, 1987 (second reading), 11631; and July 15, 1988 (for the bill's passage), 17597.
153 Canada, *House of Commons Debates*, June 6, 1988 (introduced by Lewis), 16140, and July 26, 1988 (bill passes), 17944.
154 Canada, *House of Commons Debates*, February 12, 1988 (Mayer), 12930, and July 26, 1988 (bill passes), 17948.
155 Canada, *House of Commons Debates*, September 27, 1989, introduced (Lewis), 3978, second reading, October 3, 1989 (Mazankowski), 4259–61. Co-introduced October 25, 1989, 5096.
156 Government of Canada, ParlInfo, *Speeches from the Throne*, 33rd Parliament, October 1, 1986, 8.
157 Canada, *House of Commons Debates*, November 4, 1986 (Crosbie), 1035. Also see December 19, 1986, 2318.
158 Canada, *House of Commons Debates*, January 28, 1987 (Kilgour), 2798. The factious bet offer from Benjamin is January 28, 1987, 2798.
159 Canada, *House of Commons Debates*, June 15, 1987 (Hnatyshn), 7071.
160 Canada Transportation Act, S.C. 1996, c. 10, https://laws-lois.justice.gc.ca/eng/Acts/C-10.4/index.html.
161 Canada, Archived Budget Documents, Budget Speech, February 26, 1986. Among the Crown corporations to be sold were De Havilland, Northern Transportation, CBC, and Canagrex.
162 Rose, "Exposing Big Government." See also Canada, *House of Commons Debates*, March 11, 1986.

163 Barry Wilson, "What Can Ottawa Gain By Helping Farmers Now?," *Western Producer*, October 22, 1998, https://www.producer.com/1998/10/what-can-ottawa-gain-by-helping-farmers-now/.

164 Canada, *House of Commons Debates*, December 16, 1987 (Gottselig), 11844. The $750 million was cited by Althouse, March 10, 1988, 13607. See also July 26, 1988, 17944. It appears that the funds were spent by 1988, as per Winegard June 27, 1988, 16818.

165 Canada, Archived Budget Documents, Budget Speech, February 18, 1987, 7.

166 Canada, Archived Budget Documents, Budget Speech, February 10, 1988, 10. For an alternate analysis of the role of European Union subsidies in creating an environment in Europe in which family farming is better able to thrive and a critical assessment of the subsidy blaming policies of Canadian governments, see Darrin Qualman, "The Farm Crisis and Corporate Power," Canadian Centre for Policy Alternatives, April 25, 2001, https://www.policyalternatives.ca/publications/reports/farm-crisis-and-corporate-power.

167 Government of Canada, ParlInfo, *Speeches from the Throne*, 34th Parliament, December 12, 1988.

168 Government of Canada, ParlInfo, *Speeches from the Throne*, 34rd Parliament, April 3, 1989, 6.

169 Canada, Archived Budget Documents, Budget Speech, April 27, 1989, 2, 5, and 16.

170 Canadian Agri-Food Policy Institute, *Overview of Federal-Provincial-Territorial Relations and Canadian Agriculture* (Ottawa: CAPI, December 2021), https://capi-icpa.ca/wp-content/uploads/2021/12/EN_CAPI-AG_FPT-What-We-Heard_Dec-16-2021-1.pdf.

171 Canadian Agri-Food Policy Institute, *Understanding Our Past and Present: Designing Our Future: Federal Provincial Territorial Policy Making in Canadian Agriculture* (Ottawa: CAPI, July 2021), https://capi-icpa.ca/wp-content/uploads/2021/07/FPT_Ag_Framework_Douglas_Hedley_Perspective_Report_EN.pdf.

172 Douglas Hedley, "The Evolution of Agricultural Support Policy," CASE Fellows Paper 2015-1 (2015), 30, https://caes-scae.ca/wp-content/uploads/2018/11/2015-Hedley-Evolution-Ag-Policy-Fellows-Paper-RI.pdf.

173 Agriculture Canada, *Growing Together: A Vision for Canada's Agri-Food Industry* (Ottawa: Supply and Services Canada, 1989), https://archive.org/details/growingtogethervoocana/page/n1/mode/2up.

174 Agriculture Canada, 35.

175 Agriculture Canada, 40.

176 Canada, Archived Budget Documents, Budget Speech, February 20, 1990, 1–2, 5–6.

177 Canada, Archived Budget Documents, Budget Speech, February 26, 1991, 8, 64, 100.

178 Canada, Archived Budget Documents, Budget Speech, February 25, 1992, 2, 10, 17.

179 Canada, Archived Budget Documents, Budget Speech, March 26, 1993, 1, 58.

180 See Mylène Levac and Philip Wooldridge, "The Fiscal Impact of Privatization in Canada," *Bank of Canada Review*, August 14, 1997, https://www.bankofcanada.ca/1997/08/summer-1997/.

181 Anthony E. Boardman and Aidan R. Vining, "A Review and Assessment of Privatization in Canada," University of Calgary, School of Public Policy, SPP *Research Papers* 5, no. 4 (January 2012): 4, https://www.policyschool.ca/wp-content/uploads/2016/03/boardman-vining-privatization.pdf.

182 Kevin Wipf, "From Farm Crisis to Food Crisis: Neoliberal Reform in Canadian Agriculture and the Future of Agri-Food Policy" (PhD diss., University of Alberta, 2013), 135.

183 Canada, ParlInfo, *Speeches from the Throne*, 34th Parliament, December 12, 1988, contains a one-page Speech from the Throne with free trade the only proposed item.

184 William Miner, "The Rise and Fall of the Canadian Wheat Board," CASE Fellows Paper 2015-2 (2015), 19–20, https://caes-scae.ca/wp-content/uploads/2018/11/2015-Miner-Evolution-Ag-Policy-Fellows-Paper-R1.pdf; Canada, *House of Commons Debates*, September 24, 1991 (Laporte), 2603; Grace Skogstad, "The Dynamics of Institutional Transformation: The Case of the Canadian Wheat Board," *Canadian Journal of Political Science* 38, no. 3 (September 2005): 538.

185 Skogstad, "Dynamics of Institutional Transformation," 538.

186 Canada, *House of Commons Debates*, March 4, 1991 (Blais), 17907; March 7, 1991 (Mazankowski), 18143; March 7, 1991 (Althouse), 18158.

187 Canada, *House of Commons Debates*, March 4, 1991 (Mazankowski), 17907, and March 7, 1991, 18143.

188 Canada, *House of Commons Debates*, March 21, 1991, 18148; November 8, 1991 (Althouse), 4826. A variety of technical issues resulted in various amendments, but the bill passed on March 25, 1991.

189 For some excellent analysis of GRIP and NISA, see Grace Skogstad, "Agriculture and Food Policy," *Canadian Encyclopedia*, last modified July 31, 2014, https://www.thecanadianencyclopedia.ca/en/article/agriculture-and-food-policy; Alen Asselstine, "Canada's Net Income Stabilization Account (NISA)," paper presented at the 43rd Conference of the Australian Agricultural and Resource Economics Society, Christchurch, New Zealand, January 20–2, 1999, DOI: 10.22004/ag.econ.123759.

190 Wipf, *From Farm Crisis to Food Crisis*, 138. On the rallies, see 137–9.

191 Canada, *House of Commons Debates*, January 18, 1994.

192 Canada, Archived Budget Documents, Budget Plan, February 22,1994, 1.

193 Canada, Archived Budget Documents, Budget Speech, February 27, 1995, 2.

194 Canada, 4.

195 Canada, 11.

196 Peter C. Newman, "The Crash Landing of the Crow," *Maclean's*, April 17, 1995, 53.

197 Steve Pratte, "Western Canadian Grain Transportation and the Maximum Revenue Entitlement: Process, Design Considerations and Final Implementation," Canadian Canola Growers Association, accessed March 12, 2023, https://ctrf.ca/wp-content/uploads/2017/05/CTRF2017PratteAgriculturalTransportationMRE-.pdf.
198 Pratte, 3.
199 Canada, ParlInfo, *Speeches from the Throne*, 37th Parliament, June 14, 2000.
200 Canada, *House of Commons Debates*, September 19, 1994 (introduced by Goodale), 6822. See also Hermanson's comments, September 23, 1994, 6098.
201 Canada, *House of Commons Debates*, May 18, 1995 (introduced by Gagliano), 12761; June 8, 1995 (second reading), 13452–5; June 22, 1995 (third reading and passage), 14489.
202 Canada, *House of Commons Debates*, May 15, 1995 (bill introduced by Young), 12573; June 20, 1995 (bill passed with Reform Party support in principle), 14209.
203 Canada, *House of Commons Debates*, September 23, 1994 (Goodale explains name change), 6076. See also Mr. Hermanson's comments at 6098.
204 Canada, *House of Commons Debates*, June 17, 1996 (Anderson), 3945.
205 Canada, *House of Commons Debates*, June 17, 1996 (Hermanson), 3948.
206 Canada, *House of Commons Debates*, April 17, 1997 (Pickard), 9872.
207 William W. Wilson and Bruce L. Dahl, "Reciprocal Access in U.S./Canadian Grain Trade: Background Issues for the U.S. Grain Trade," AE 98001, prepared for USDA/FAS (January 1998), https://www.researchgate.net/publication/23514623_reciprocal_access_in_uscanadian_grain_trade_background_issues_for_the_us_grain_trade.
208 André Magnan, *When Wheat Was King: The Rise and Fall of the Canada–UK Grain Trade* (Vancouver: UBC Press, 2016), 114; Skogstad, "Dynamics of Institutional Transformation," 538.
209 Adrian Ewins, "Grain Marketing Panel Prepares to Hit the Road," CBC News, December 14, 1995, https://www.producer.com/1995/12/grain-marketing-panel-prepares-to-hit-the-road/.
210 Grace Skogstad, "The Liberal Party, Insensitivity, and Western Agriculture," in *Continuity and Change in Canadian Politics: Essay in Honour of David E. Smith*, ed. Hans Michelmann and Cristine Clercy (Toronto: University of Toronto Press, 2006), 236–7.
211 Skogstad, 238.
212 Skogstad, 238.
213 The story even made the venerable *New York Times*. See Anthony Depalma, "On Canada's Prairie, a Farmers' Rebellion Flares," *New York Times*, January 3, 1997. See also Alexander J. Black, "Winnowing the Chaff: Canadian Grain Trade and International Law," *American University International Law Review* 12, no. 1 (1999): 16.
214 Michael Raine, "Farmers for Justice Hold Protest Rally," *Western Producer*, August 14, 1997, https://www.producer.com/1997/08/farmers-for-justice-hold-protest-rally/.

215 See "13 Alberta Farmers Jailed for Violating Custom Rules by Hauling Grain to U.S.," Agrivill.com, November 3, 2002, https://www.agriville.com/threads/2077-13-alberta-farmers-jailed-news-stories.
216 Canada, *House of Commons Debates*, December 3, 1996 (Goodale), 7000.
217 Canada, *House of Commons Debates*, December 3, 1996 (Goodale), 7000.
218 For the text of Bill C-4, see Parliament of Canada, LEGISinfo, "Bill C-4" (1997), https://www.parl.ca/DocumentViewer/en/36-1/bill/C-4/royal-assent/page-ToC.
219 Canada, *House of Commons Debates*, February 18, 1997 (Hermanson), 8238.
220 Canada, *House of Commons Debates*, April 24, 1997, (Benoit), 10153; April 25, 1997 (Hermanson), 10149.
221 Canada, *House of Commons Debates*, April 26, 2001 (Vanclief), 1554.
222 Canada, *House of Commons Debates*, April 30, 2001 (Hilstrom), 1200.
223 See the excellent account of various events in "Federal Sponsorship Scandal," CBC News, October 26, 2006, https://www.cbc.ca/news2/background/groupaction/.
224 Jordan Michael Smith, "Reinventing Canada: Stephen Harper's Conservative Revolution," *World Affairs* 174, no. 6 (March–April 2012): 27.
225 Canada, ParlInfo, *Speeches from the Throne*, 39th Parliament, April 4, 2006.
226 Canada, ParlInfo, *Speeches from the Throne*, 39th Parliament, September 16, 2007.
227 Schmitz, "Canadian Agricultural Programs," 378.
228 Canada, ParlInfo, *Speeches from the Throne*, 40th Parliament, November 19, 2008, https://lop.parl.ca/sites/ParlInfo/default/en_CA/Parliament/procedure/throneSpeech/speech401.
229 Canada, ParlInfo, *Speeches from the Throne*, 40th Parliament, January 26, 2009, https://lop.parl.ca/sites/ParlInfo/default/en_CA/Parliament/procedure/throneSpeech/speech402.
230 Canada, ParlInfo, *Speeches from the Throne*, 41st Parliament, June 3, 2011, https://lop.parl.ca/sites/ParlInfo/default/en_ca/Parliament/procedure/throneSpeech/speech411.
231 Canada, ParlInfo, *Speeches from the Throne*, 41st Parliament, June 3, 2011, https://lop.parl.ca/sites/ParlInfo/default/en_ca/Parliament/procedure/throneSpeech/speech411.
232 Canada, *House of Commons Debates*, June 5, 2006 (Strahl), 1235.
233 Canada, *House of Commons Debates*, February 25, 2008: see comments from Laüzon (2201) and Easter (2220).
234 Canada, *House of Commons Debates*, May 22, 2009 (Lemieux), 1210.
235 Canada, *House of Commons Debates*, May 11, 2009 (Easter), 1215.
236 Canada, *House of Commons Debates*, May 11, 2009, 1230.
237 For an early account of the grain industry, see Dan Morgan, *Merchants of Grain: The Power and Profits of the Five Giant Companies at the Center of the World's Food Supply* (London: Penguin, 1980).
238 Canada, *House of Commons Debates*, May 20, 1971 (Korchinski), 6001. See also comments from Horner on the same date (5999).

239 Canada, *House of Commons Debates*, July 11, 1973 (Diefenbaker), 5514.
240 Canada, *House of Commons Debates*, March 3, 2008 (comments from Ritz and Easter), 1515.
241 "Canadian Wheat Board," in *Canadian Annual Review of Politics and Public Affairs 2008*, ed. David Mutimer (Toronto: University of Toronto Press, 2015), 45.
242 Canada, *House of Commons Debates*, October 18, 2011 (Ritz), 1005.
243 Canada, *House of Commons Debates*, October 19, 2011 (Harper), 1425.
244 Magnan, *When Wheat Was King*, 140–2.
245 Paul Waldie, "Prairie Farmers Vote to Keep the Canadian Wheat Board," *Globe and Mail*, September 12, 2011, https://www.theglobeandmail.com/report-on-business/prairie-farmers-vote-to-keep-canadian-wheat-board/article556370/.
246 Magnan, *When Wheat Was King*, 145.
247 Canada, *House of Commons Debates*, October 19, 2011 (Van Loan), 1010.
248 Canada, *House of Commons Debates*, November 23, 2011 (Van Loan), 1540.
249 Canada, *House of Commons Debates*, November 23, 2011 (Van Loan), 1540.
250 Canada, *House of Commons Debates*, November 28, 2011, 3673.
251 Magnan, *When Wheat Was King*, 146.
252 Janice McGregor, "'Oppressive' No More: Harper's 'Reorganized' Wheat Board," CBC News, October 17, 2011, https://www.cbc.ca/news/politics/analysis-oppressive-no-more-harper-s-reorganized-wheat-board-1.1023216.
253 "Wheat Board Vote a 'Non-binding Survey,' Says Ritz," CBC News, September 12, 2011, https://www.cbc.ca/news/canada/saskatchewan/wheat-board-vote-a-non-binding-survey-says-ritz-1.984620.
254 Gordon Pitts, "Canada's Prairie Agricultural Economy Prepares for a Seismic Shift," *Globe and Mail*, September 10, 2011, https://www.theglobeandmail.com/report-on-business/canadas-prairie-agricultural-economy-prepares-for-a-seismic-shift/article594032/.
255 Nick Pearce, "Farmers in 'Dire Straits' over Unfulfilled Grain Contracts," *Saskatoon StarPhoenix*, September 19, 2021, https://thestarphoenix.com/news/local-news/farmers-in-dire-straits-over-unfulfilled-grain-contracts.
256 "About G3 FEP," G3 Canada, accessed March 12, 2023, https://www.g3.ca/en/farmers-equity-plan. See also Kevin Hursh, "What's the Real Story at G3 Canada?," *Western Producer*, April 12, 2018, https://www.producer.com/2018/04/whats-the-real-story-at-g3-canada/, and Alan Dawson, "Newly Created Buyer G3 to Take Majority Ownership of Government-Owned CWB," *Manitoba Co-operator*, April 23, 2015, https://www.manitobacooperator.ca/news-opinion/news/national/newly-created-buyer-g3-to-take-majority-ownership-of-government-owned-cwb/.
257 Laura Payton, "Harper Pardons Farmers Arrested under Old Wheat Board Law," CBC News, August 1, 2012, https://www.cbc.ca/news/politics/harper-pardons-farmers-arrested-under-old-wheat-board-law-1.1146436; Jennifer Graham, "Harper Pardons Farmers Convicted Years Ago of Selling Grain in the U.S.," *Globe*

and Mail, August 1, 2012, https://www.theglobeandmail.com/news/politics/harper-pardons-farmers-convicted-years-ago-of-selling-grain-in-the-us/article4456953/.

258 Canada, Agriculture and Agri-Food Canada, *2013–14 Report on Plans and Priorities* (Ottawa: Agriculture and Agri-Food Canada, 2013), https://publications.gc.ca/collections/collection_2013/aac-aafc/A1-9-2013-eng.pdf. For the details on the plans, see "AgriStability: Growing Forward 2—Program Guidelines (Consolidated Version)," Agriculture and Agri-Food Canada, February 6, 2014, https://agriculture.canada.ca/en/programs/agristability/resources/growing-forward-2-program-guidelines-consolidated.

259 Canada, *House of Commons Debates*, March 3, 2014. The entire complex bill is available at Parliament of Canada, LEGISinfo, "Bill C-18" (2015), https://www.parl.ca/DocumentViewer/en/41-2/bill/C-18/royal-assent.

260 Barry Wilson, "Ritz Reshapes the AG Sector," *Western Producer*, January 3, 2016, https://www.producer.com/2014/01/ritz-reshapes-ag-sector/.

5. A TENUOUS LOCATION IN THE FOOD CHAIN

1 Bill Curry and Barrie McKenna, "Stimulus Gamble: How Ottawa Saved the Economy—and Wasted Billions," *Globe and Mail*, February 8, 2014, https://www.theglobeandmail.com/report-on-business/stimulus-gamble-how-ottawa-saved-the-economy-and-wasted-billions/article16760149/.

2 Robert Rich, "The Great Recession: December 2007–June 2009," Federal Reserve History, November 22, 2013, https://www.federalreservehistory.org/essays/great-recession-of-200709.

3 John F. Conway and Robert R. Stirling, "Fractions among Prairie Farmers," in *The Political Economy of Agriculture in Western Canada*, ed. G.S. Basaran and D. Hay (Toronto: SRU and Garamond Press, 1988), 73–86.

4 Al Mussell, "Stratification in Canadian Agriculture: Surveying the Implications," Agri-Food Economic Systems, Policy Concepts Paper (November 2021), 18–19, http://www.agrifoodecon.ca/uploads/userfiles/files/stratification%20in%20canadian%20agriculture%20november%202021.pdf.

5 As per "Table 32-10-0065-01: Farm Families and Average Total Income by Typology Group, Unincorporated Sector, Canada," Statistics Canada, January 15, 2016, https://www150.statcan.gc.ca/t1/tbl1/en/tv.action?pid=3210006501. It is doubtful that those belonging to category 1, low-income farms, were in fact operating farms. No data is available, but very likely this group were low-income people living on farms and in rural areas.

6 "Saskatchewan Remains the Breadbasket of Canada," Statistics Canada, May 10, 2017, https://www150.statcan.gc.ca/n1/pub/95-640-x/2016001/article/14807-eng.htm.

7 "Table 32-10-0158-01: Farms Classified by Operating Arrangement, Census of Agriculture Historical Data," Statistics Canada, May 11, 2022, https://www150.

statcan.gc.ca/t1/tbl1/en/tv.action?pid=3210015801.
8 "Table 32-10-0439-01: Paid Labour, Census of Agriculture, 2011 and 2016, Inactive," Statistics Canada, May 10, 2017, https://www150.statcan.gc.ca/t1/tbl1/en/tv.action?pid=3210043901.
9 "Saskatchewan Potash," Saskatchewan Mining Association, accessed January 16, 2023, http://saskmining.ca/ckfinder/userfiles/files/SMA-potash-fact-sheet-2019-V4revised.pdf.
10 Emily Eaton and Valerie Zinc, *Fault Lines Life and Landscapes in Saskatchewan's Oil Economy* (Winnipeg: University of Manitoba Press, 2016), 51, 61, 71, 95.
11 "Table 32-10-0052-01: Net Farm Income (x 1,000)," Statistics Canada, November 28, 2022, https://www150.statcan.gc.ca/t1/tbl1/en/tv.action?pid=3210005201.
12 "Table 32-10-0051-01: Farm Debt Outstanding, Classified by Lender (x 1,000)," Statistics Canada, November 28, 2022, https://www150.statcan.gc.ca/t1/tbl1/en/tv.action?pid=3210005101.
13 Monette Farms website: https://www.monettefarms.ca/.
14 Meredith MacLeod, "Farmers Warning of Supply Issues Due to Delay in Arrival of Migrant Workers," CTV News, April 10, 2020, https://www.ctvnews.ca/health/coronavirus/farmers-warning-of-supply-issues-due-to-delay-in-arrival-of-migrant-workers-1.4892015.
15 See the Delage Farms website at https://www.delagefarms.ca/.
16 "In the Beginning," Kambeitz Farms, accessed January 19, 2023, https://kambeitzfarms.com/in-the-beginning/.
17 See "About Us," Carefoot Farms, accessed January 19, 2023, http://www.carefootfarms.ca/about_us.html.
18 See, for example, Robert Arnason, "40,000-Acre Farm Goes Organic," *Western Producer*, March 22, 2018, https://www.producer.com/2018/03/40000-acre-farm-goes-organic/; Katelyn Wilson, "Sask. Farmer Converts 40,000 Acres into Canada's Largest Organic Farm," *Global News*, September 13, 2018, https://globalnews.ca/news/4447635/sask-farmer-converts-40000-acres-into-canadas-largest-organic-farm/; Gord Gilmour, "Too Big to Be True? Can Really Large Organic Farms Stay True to the Spirit of the Sector?," *Manitoba Co-operator*, February 26, 2019, https://www.manitobacooperator.ca/crops/too-big-to-be-true/.
19 André Magnan and Annette Aurélie Desmarais, "Who Is Buying the Farm? Farmland Investment Patterns in Saskatchewan, 2003–14," Canadian Centre for Policy Alternatives, March 2017, 6–7, https://policyalternatives.ca/sites/default/files/uploads/publications/Saskatchewan%20Office/2017/03/Who_is_Buying_the_Farm_SK_2003-14.pdf.
20 "The Andjelic Story," Andjelic Land, accessed March 7, 2023, https://andjelic.ca/about. See also Jason Kirby, "Farmland Inc.," *Globe and Mail*, September 10, 2022, https://www.theglobeandmail.com/business/article-farmland-ownership-canada-andjelic/.

21 Al Mussell and Douglas Hedley, "Size Economies and Stratification in Primary Agriculture: Understanding the Implications," Agri-Food Economic Systems, September 2021, http://www.agrifoodecon.ca/uploads/userfiles/files/stratification%20in%20primary%20agriculture%20sep-21.pdf.
22 Alfons Weersink, "The Growing Heterogeneity in the Farm Sector and Its Implications," *Canadian Journal of Agricultural Economics* 66, no. 1 (2018): 28.
23 Weersink, 39.
24 United States Securities and Exchange Commission, "Form 10-K Deere & Co Annual Report," Commission File no. 1-1421, 5, https://www.sec.gov/Archives/edgar/data/27673/000155837020014439/jdcc-20201101x10k.htm.
25 United States Securities and Exchange Commission.
26 "Selected Farm Machinery Manufacturers Worldwide in FY 2021, Based on Revenue," Statista, accessed January 19, 2023, https://www.statista.com/statistics/461428/revenue-of-major-farm-machinery-manufacturers-worldwide/.
27 United States Securities and Exchange Commission, Form 20-F, "CNH Industrial N.V.," Commission File No. 001-36085, 19–20, https://www.sec.gov/Archives/edgar/data/1567094/000162828022004478/cnhi-20211231.htm.
28 United States Securities and Exchange Commission, Form 10-K 1, "AGCO Corporation," Commission File No. 1-12930, 1, https://www.sec.gov/Archives/edgar/data/880266/000088026616000044/a2015agco10-k.htm.
29 United States Securities and Exchange Commission, Form 20-F, "CNH Industrial N.V.," Commission File No. 001-36085, 19–20, https://www.sec.gov/Archives/edgar/data/880266/000088026616000044/a2015agco10-k.htm.
30 United States Securities and Exchange Commission, Form 20-F, "Kabushiki Kaisha Kubota," Commission File No. 1-07294, 9, https://www.sec.gov/Archives/edgar/data/109821/000119312513273651/d450658d20f.htm.
31 Jennifer Reibel, "Manufacturer Consolidation Reshaping the Farm Equipment Marketplace," *Manufacturer News*, August 29, 2018, https://www.farm-equipment.com/articles/15962-manufacturer-consolidation-reshaping-the-farm-equipment-marketplace.
32 Susan Reidy, "AGI Posts Record Quarterly, Half-Year Trade Sales," World-Grain.com, September 8, 2019, https://www.world-grain.com/articles/12450-agi-posts-record-quarterly-half-year-trade-sales. Anyone watching recent Tim Hortons Briers will be familiar with AGI. See also "Our History," AGI, accessed January 20, 2023, https://www.aggrowth.com/en-us/about-us/agi-history, and Karen Briere, "Ag Growth CEO Helped Expand Implement Maker," *Western Producer*, October 28, 2010, https://www.producer.com/2010/10/ag-growth-ceo-helped-expand-implement-maker/.
33 See Douglas Faller, "Degradation of Farm Work and Resistance to Deskilling in the Canadian Prairies: The Case of Farm Machinery" (master's thesis, University of Regina, 1998).

34　Michael Gertler, JoAnn Jaffe, and Mary A. Beckie, "Duelling Discourses of Sustainability: Neo-conventional and Organic Farming on the Canadian Prairies," in *Contested Sustainability Discourses in the Agrifood System*, ed. Douglas H. Constance, Jason Konefal, and Maki Hatanaka (New York: Routledge, 2018), 163–87.

35　See Brandt's website at https://www.brandt.ca/ for more information on the company's operations.

36　Olivia Paschal, "The Unexpected Side Effects of Trump's Trade War," *The Atlantic*, March 19, 2019, https://www.theatlantic.com/politics/archive/2019/03/tariffs-drive-farm-income-down-and-equipment-prices/583684/.

37　Jennifer Blair, "Pricey Farm Machinery and Soft Commodity Prices Don't Add Up," *Alberta Farmer Express*, March 3, 2020, https://www.albertafarmexpress.ca/2020/03/03/pricey-farm-machinery-and-soft-commodity-prices-dont-add-up/.

38　See Clarence L. Barber, *Report of the Royal Commission on Farm Machinery* (Ottawa: Information Canada, 1971), 63–4.

39　For example, Wakaw was officially incorporated in 1911 and had forty businesses by 1914, including three machinery dealers: Massey-Harris, Oliver and Cockshutt, and International Harvester. See Jean Brunanski and Ed Brunanski, *Wakaw: 80 Years of History, 1898–1978* (Wakaw, SK: Wakaw Recorder, 1978). To pick another random example based on an accessible source, Aberdeen had three farm machinery dealers one year after incorporation, including John Deere, Massey-Harris, and one not specified. See Town of Aberdeen, *Aberdeen, 1907–1981* (Edmonton: Friesen Printers, 1982).

40　See "Saskatchewan Farm Equipment Dealers," Farms.com, accessed January 21, 2023, https://www.farms.com/farm-equipment-dealers-canada/saskatchewan-farm-equipment-dealers.aspx.

41　"Pattison Merges Deere Dealership Chains," AGCanada, January 10, 2017, https://www.agcanada.com/daily/pattison-merges-deere-dealership-chains.

42　Pattison Agriculture is but one part of a much larger holding company, the Jim Pattison Group, which originated in a General Motors dealership in the 1960s. Having undergone significant expansion, the company now operates various divisions, including an extensive network of food retail stores, a fishing company, the world's largest integrated forest products company, a chain of wine stores, the Guinness World Records operation, a major outdoor advertising business, several marketing and distribution enterprises, nearly seventy radio and online news and entertainment outlets, a coal port, a large leasing firm, as well as various automotive and truck retail outlets. See "About Us," Jim Pattison Group, accessed January 22, 2023, https://www.jimpattison.com/about/our-story/.

43　"Table 6: Pesticide Use on Canadian Crop Farms—Provinces and Region," Statistics Canada, last modified November 27, 2015, https://www150.statcan.gc.ca/n1/pub/21-023-x/2013001/t006-eng.htm.

44 "Table 32-10-0209-01: Type of Pesticides Used on Farms," Statistics Canada, December 3, 2019, https://www150.statcan.gc.ca/t1/tbl1/en/tv.action?pid=3210020901.
45 For the range of products see "ADAMA," Syngenta Group, accessed March 8, 2023, https://www.syngentagroup.com/en/about/adama, and for profits, see "Syngenta Group Reports 2021 Performance, Growing 23%, with $28.2 Billion Sales," Syngenta Group, March 31, 2022, https://www.syngentagroup.com/en/media/syngenta-news/year/2022/syngenta-group-reports-2021-performance-growing-23-282-billion-sales. See also Sudeep Chakravarty, "World's Top 10 Agrochemical Companies: Industry Forecast and Trends," *Market Research Reports*, September 25, 2019, https://www.marketresearchreports.com/blog/2019/09/25/worlds-top-10-agrochemical-companies-industry-forecast-and-trends.
46 "Profile and Organization," Bayer Global, accessed January 22, 2023, https://www.bayer.com/en/profile-and-organization.aspx.
47 Caroline Winter and Tim Loh, "With Each Roundup Verdict, Bayer's Monsanto Purchase Looks Worse," *Bloomberg Business*, September 24, 2019, https://www.bloomberg.com/news/features/2019-09-19/bayer-s-monsanto-purchase-looks-worse-with-each-roundup-verdict, and "Bayer Wins U.S. Nod for Monsanto Deal to Create Agriculture Giant," *Western Producer*, June 7, 2018, https://www.producer.com/2018/06/bayer-wins-u-s-nod-for-monsanto-deal-to-create-agriculture-giant-2/.
48 See "Seed & Crop Protection Products," Bayer Crop Science Canada, accessed March 8, 2023, https://www.cropscience.bayer.ca/en/Products.
49 "Business Segments: Agricultural Solutions," BASF, accessed January 22, 2023, https://www.basf.com/global/en/who-we-are/organization/business-segments.html; "Innovation for Successful Agriculture," BASF, accessed January 22, 2023, https://www.agricentre.basf.co.uk/en/.
50 Alexander H. Tullo, "DowDuPont Completed Final Split to Form DuPont and Corteva," *Chemical and Engineering News*, June 7, 2019, https://cen.acs.org/business/mergers-acquisitions/DowDuPont-completes-final-split-form/97/i23; Christopher M. Matthews, "A Different Dow Emerges Following Merger with DuPont," *Wall Street Journal*, April 1, 2019, https://www.wsj.com/articles/a-different-dow-emerges-following-merger-with-dupont-11554150629.
51 "2021 Fact Sheet," Corteva Agriscience, accessed March 9, 2023, https://investors.corteva.com/static-files/a46f4e73-0261-4949-acff-71791cb188a0.
52 United States Securities and Exchange Commission, 40-F Annual Report, "Nutrien Ltd., Annual Information Form, Year Ended December 31, 2021," Exhibit 99.1, 9, https://last10k.com/sec-filings/ntr.
53 Canadian Press, "Nutrien Shares Begin Trading on TSX and NYSE after Agrium, Potash Corp. Merger," *Calgary Herald*, January 2, 2018, https://calgaryherald.com/commodities/mining/nutrien-shares-begin-trading-on-tsx-and-nyse-after-agrium-potash-corp-merger/wcm/2f6884c3-5cb3-45a5-992c-b22c8a4a0990,

and "Fact Sheet," Nutrien, accessed march 9, 2023, https://nutrien-prod-asset. s3.us-east-2.amazonaws.com/s3fs-public/uploads/2020-07/Nutrien%20Fact%20 Sheet_2020.pdf.

54 United Grain Growers, *Grain Growers Record, 1906 to 1943* (Winnipeg: Public Press, 1944), https://openlibrary.org/books/OL6487727M/The_grain_growers_ record_1906_to_1943, 24.

55 Brett Fairburn, "United Grain Growers (Agricore United)," in *Encyclopedia of Saskatchewan* (Regina: Canadian Plains Research Centre, 2005), 969.

56 David Parkinson, "Agricore and UGG Agree to Merge," *Globe and Mail*, July 31, 2001, https://www.theglobeandmail.com/report-on-business/agricore-and-ugg-agree-to-merge/article1032609/.

57 Brett Fairburn, "Saskatchewan Wheat Pool," in *Encyclopedia of the Great Plains*, ed. David J. Wishart (Lincoln: University of Nebraska, 2011), http:// plainshumanities.unl.edu/encyclopedia/doc/egp.ag.057.

58 Laureen Gatin, "Restructuring the Saskatchewan Wheat Pool" (master's thesis, University of Regina, 1999), 42–3.

59 "Wheat Pool to Become Viterra?," CBC News, August 29, 2007, https://www.cbc. ca/news/canada/saskatchewan/sask-wheat-pool-to-become-viterra-1.653478.

60 *Western Producer*, January 18, 1996.

61 *Western Producer*, February 1, 1996.

62 Ben Dummett, "Glencore to Buy Viterra for $6.2 Billion," *Wall Street Journal*, March 20, 2012, https://www.wsj.com/articles/SB10001424052702304636404577293350190169954.

63 "Glencore Completes Acquisition of Viterra and Announces Key Management Appointments," Cision, December 17, 2012, https://www.newswire.ca/news-releases/glencore-completes-acquisition-of-viterra-and-announces-key-management-appointments-511391011.html.

64 "Notices of Rail Line Discontinuance," Canadian Transportation Agency, last modified September 21, 2015, https://otc-cta.gc.ca/eng/notices-rail-line-discontinuance.

65 "Archer-Daniels-Midland Company (ADM)," Market Screener, accessed January 22, 2023, https://www.marketscreener.com/archer-daniels-midland-co-11533/financials/.

66 Bunge, *2018 Annual Report: Embracing Change, Building on Our Mission* (White Plains, NY: Bunge, 2019), 3, https://www.bunge.com/2018ar.pdf.

67 Cargill, *Extraordinary Times: Cargill 2021 Annual Report* (Minneapolis: Cargill, 2021), https://www.cargill.com/doc/1432194192294/2021-cargill-annual-report.pdf.

68 Statista, "Glencore—Statistics and Facts," Statista, March 23, 2022, https://www. statista.com/topics/2081/glencorexstrata/; "Louis Dreyfus Company Reports Solid 2018 Financial Results," Louis Dreyfus Company, March 25, 2019, https://www.ldc. com/press-releases/louis-dreyfus-company-reports-solid-2018-financial-results/.

69 Jennifer Clapp, "ABCD and Beyond: From Grain Merchants to Agricultural Value Chain Managers," *Canadian Food Studies* 2, no. 2 (September 2015): 126.
70 Clapp, 126.
71 "About Us," Richardson International, accessed January 22, 2023, https://www.richardson.ca/about-us/.
72 "About," Paterson Grain, accessed January 22, 2023, https://www.patersongrain.com/about/.
73 "About Us," Parrish & Heimbecker, accessed January 22, 2023, https://parrishandheimbecker.com/about-us/. Sales figures are from "2018 Top 100 Food and Beverage Companies," Food Engineering, accessed January 22, 2023, https://www.foodengineeringmag.com/2018-top-100-food-beverage-companies.
74 "About," Oxfam, Behind the Brands, accessed January 23, 2023, https://www.behindthebrands.org/about/. For a comprehensive analysis of recent developments in the food industry, see Anthony Winson, *The Industrial Diet: The Degradation of Food and the Struggle for Healthy Eating* (New York: New York University Press, 2014).
75 "History," Nestlé, accessed January 23, 2023, https://www.corporate.nestle.ca/en/aboutus/history. For a dizzying array of Nestlé brands, see "Everything Owned by Nestlé," Wyoming Trust & LLC Attorney, accessed January 23, 2023, https://wyomingllcattorney.com/Blog/Everything-Owned-by-Nestle.
76 See "General Mills, Inc.," *Encyclopedia Britannica*, accessed January 23, 2023, https://www.britannica.com/topic/General-Mills-Inc.
77 Tom Risen, "Warren Buffett to Merge Kraft, Heinz," *US News and World Report*, March 25, 2015, https://www.usnews.com/news/articles/2015/03/25/warren-buffett-to-merge-kraft-heinz.
78 Jacob Davidson, "One Image That Shows Just How Insane the Kraft Heinz Empire Will Be," *Money*, March 25, 2015, https://money.com/kraft-heinz-merger-brands/.
79 "Who We Are," Kellogg's, accessed January 23, 2023, https://www.kelloggs.com/en_US/who-we-are.html.
80 Nathan Reiff, "Top 8 Companies Owned by Kellogg's," Investopedia, last modified December 14, 2022, https://www.investopedia.com/articles/company-insights/081716/top-8-companies-owned-kelloggs-k.asp.
81 Joe Cornell, "Kellogg Company Announces Plan to Separate into Three Independent Publicly Traded Companies," *Forbes*, June 24, 2022, https://www.forbes.com/sites/joecornell/2022/06/24/kellogg-company-announces-plan-to-separate-into-three-independent-publicly-traded-companies/?sh=7a22f61111f5.
82 United States Securities and Exchange Commission, Form 10-K, "PepsiCo, Inc.," Commission File No. 1-1183, 3, 9, 27, https://pepsico.gcs-web.com/static-files/60b79d40-4d73-46c8-8e7f-ebb9dab597c6.
83 United States Securities and Exchange Commission, Form 10-K, "Coca-Cola Company," Commission File No. 001-022172, 3, https://www.sec.gov/Archives/

edgar/data/21344/000002134416000050/a2015123110-k.htm#s07dc370cb59e5a36e7 30cef8ce6cfa7a.

84 R.B. Fleming, "The Golden Age of the General Store: Life Before Malls," *The Beaver*, December 4, 2018, https://www.canadashistory.ca/explore/business-industry/the-golden-age-of-the-general-store.
85 "About the Company," IGA, accessed January 23, 2023, https://www.igastoresbc.com/about-us/overview/.
86 "The Oshawa Group Limited: History," Funding Universe, accessed January 23, 2023, http://www.fundinguniverse.com/company-histories/the-oshawa-group-limited-history/.
87 Jack Trevena, *Prairie Co-operation: A Diary* (Saskatoon: Co-operative College of Canada, 1976), 78.
88 John Archer, "The Saskatchewan Purchasing Company," *Saskatchewan History* 5, no. 2 (Spring 1952): 55–65.
89 "About FCL," Federated Co-operatives Limited, accessed January 23, 2023, https://www.fcl.crs/about-us.
90 See "Safeway Inc.," *Encyclopaedia Britannica*, accessed January 23, 2023, https://www.britannica.com/topic/Safeway-Inc.
91 "Celebrating Over 85 Years at Safeway," Safeway, accessed January 23, 2023, https://www.safeway.ca/about-us/history/.
92 "Canada's Food and Pharmacy Leader," Loblaw Companies Limited, accessed January 23, 2023, https://www.loblaw.ca/en/about-us/history.html. See also "Canada's Leading Pharmacy Retailer," Shoppers Drug Mart, accessed January 23, 2023, https://corporate.shoppersdrugmart.ca/en-ca/about-us/our-history.
93 "The Weston Family Empire Expands Again," CBC News, July 16, 2013, https://www.cbc.ca/news/canada/the-weston-family-empire-expands-again-1.1313575; "About George Weston Limited," Weston, accessed January 24, 2023, https://www.weston.ca/en/our-company.aspx.
94 Sasha Yusufali and Derrick Clements, "George Weston Limited," *Canadian Encyclopedia*, last modified March 21, 2019, https://www.thecanadianencyclopedia.ca/en/article/george-weston-limited.
95 Robert Heilbroner, *Twenty First Century Capitalism* (Concord, ON: Anansi, 1992), 74.
96 Grace Skogstad, "Interest Groups, Representation and Conflict Management in the Standing Committees of the House of Commons," *Canadian Journal of Political Science* 18, no. 4 (December 1985): 739–72.
97 "Walter Charles (Wally) Nelson," Saskatchewan Agricultural Hall of Fame, accessed January 24, 2023, https://www.sahf.ca/copy-of-a-3.
98 See the Western Canadian Wheat Growers website at https://wheatgrowers.ca/.
99 "Who We Are," Western Canadian Wheat Growers Association, accessed January 24, 2023, https://wheatgrowers.ca/about-us/advocating-for-you/.

100 See Western Canadian Wheat Growers Association, "Premier Scott Moe Thanks the Wheat Growers," YouTube, May 26, 2919, https://www.youtube.com/watch?v=73t0qgUIJ60&t=2s&ab_channel=WesternCanadianWheatGrowersAssociation.
101 James N. McCrorie, *In Union Is Strength* (Saskatoon: Centre for Community Studies, 1964).
102 The information that follows is drawn from the NFU website. See "About the National Farmers Union," National Farmers Union, accessed January 24, 2023, https://www.nfu.ca/about.
103 See "Statement of Purpose—1969," National Farmers Union, accessed January 29, 2023, https://www.nfu.ca/about.
104 "About Us," Agricultural Producers Association of Saskatchewan, accessed January 24, 2023, https://apas.ca/about-us.
105 For a now dated but comprehensive list of farm organizations, see Gary Carlson, *Farm Voices: A Brief History and Reference Guide of Prairie Farm Organizations and Their Leaders, 1870 to 1980* (Regina: Saskatchewan Federation of Agriculture, 1981).
106 Grace Skogstad, *The Politics of Agricultural Policy-Making in Canada* (Toronto: University of Toronto Press, 1987), 58.
107 *Organized Farmer*, June 10, 1967, quoted in Carrol Jaques, *Unifarm: A Story of Conflict and Change* (Calgary: University of Calgary Press, 2001), 44.

6. MEANWHILE, BACK ON THE FARM

1 See "Canadian Agricultural Partnership: A Cornerstone for the Continued Growth of a Key Economic Sector," Agriculture and Agri-Food, news release, April 3, 2018, https://www.canada.ca/en/agriculture-agri-food/news/2018/04/canadian-agricultural-partnership-a-cornerstone-for-the-continued-growth-of-a-key-economic-sector.html.
2 "Canadian Agricultural Partnership," Agriculture and Agri-Food, last modified August 29, 2022, https://www.agr.gc.ca/eng/about-our-department/key-departmental-initiatives/canadian-agricultural-partnership/?id=1461767369849.
3 "The Canadian Agricultural Partnership," Canadian Federation of Agriculture, accessed January 24, 2023, https://www.cfa-fca.ca/issues/the-next-agriculture-policy-framework/.
4 Stephen Metcalf, "Neoliberalism: The Idea that Swallowed the World," *The Guardian*, August 18, 2017, https://www.theguardian.com/news/2017/aug/18/neoliberalism-the-idea-that-changed-the-world.
5 Linda Lobao and Katherine Meyer, "The Great Agricultural Transition: Crisis, Change, and Social Consequences of Twentieth Century US Farming," *Annual Review of Sociology*, no. 27 (2001): 103.
6 Lobao and Meyer, 119.

7   Caroline Tauxe, "Family Cohesion vs. Capitalist Hegemony: Cultural Accommodation on the North Dakota Farm," *Dialectical Anthropology* 17, no. 3 (1992): 291–317.
8   Curtis E. Beus and Riley E. Dunlap, "Conventional versus Alternative Agriculture: The Paradigmatic Roots of the Debate," *Rural Sociology* 55, no. 4 (1990): 594.
9   Beus and Dunlap, 594.
10 Marta Chiappe and Cornelia Butler Flora, "Gendered Elements of the Alternate Agricultural Paradigm," *Rural Sociology* 63, no. 3 (1998): 376.
11 Shannon Bell, Alicia Hullinger, and Lilian Brislen, "Manipulate Masculinities: Agribusiness, Deskilling, and the Rise of the Businessman-Farmer in the United States," *Rural Sociology* 80, no. 3 (2015): 285–313.
12 Kathryn Dudley, "The Entrepreneurial Self," in *Fighting for the Farm: Rural America Transformed*, ed. Jane Adams (Philadelphia: University of Pennsylvania Press, 2003), 182–3.
13 Michael Gertler, JoAnn Jaffe, and Mary A. Beckie, "Duelling Discourses of Sustainability: Neo-conventional and Organic Farming on the Canadian Prairies," in *Contested Sustainability Discourses in the Agrifood System*, ed. Douglas H. Constance, Jason Konefal, and Maki Hatanaka (New York: Routledge, 2018), 162–86.
14 Quoted in Colton Wiens, "Former Premier Warns Agricultural Industry," CTV News, November 20, 2018, https://regina.ctvnews.ca/former-premier-warns-agricultural-industry-1.4185399. See also Karen Briere, "Bad Labels Can Stick, Former Premier Warns Agriculture," *Western Producer*, December 6, 2018, https://www.producer.com/2018/12/bad-labels-can-stick-former-premier-warns-agriculture/.
15 Wall has served on the board of NexGen Energy Ltd. (which is exploring uranium opportunities in Saskatchewan), as a special business adviser to Avenue Living Asset Management, and as special adviser for the business law firm Osler, Hoskin, and Harcourt. See the following for information on some of Mr. Wall's corporate activities after leaving office: "NexGen Announces Appointment of Brad Wall, the Former Premier of Saskatchewan, to Its Board of Directors," Cision, March 21, 2019, https://www.newswire.ca/news-releases/nexgen-announces-appointment-of-brad-wall-the-former-premier-of-saskatchewan-to-its-board-of-directors-829945845.html; also "Why Osler," Osler, Hoskin, and Harcourt LLP, accessed January 24, 2023, https://www.osler.com/en/why-osler.
16 Alan Drengson, "Two Philosophies of Agriculture: From Industrial Paradigms to Natural Patterns," *The Trumpeter* 2, no. 2 (Spring 1980), 1, http://trumpeter.athabascau.ca/index.php/trumpet/article/view/534/904.
17 Amanda Petrusich, "Going Home with Wendell Berry," *New Yorker*, July 14, 2019, https://www.newyorker.com/culture/the-new-yorker-interview/going-home-with-wendell-berry.

18 Emily Eaton, *Growing Resistance: Canadian Farmers and the Politics of Genetically Modified Wheat* (Winnipeg: University of Manitoba Press, 2013), 147.
19 Jack Stabler, M. Rose Olfert, and Murray E. Fulton, *The Changing Role of Rural Communities in an Urbanizing World: Saskatchewan 1961–1990* (Regina: Canadian Plains Research Centre, 1992); Jack Stabler and M. Rose Olfert, *The Changing Role of Rural Communities in an Urbanizing World: Saskatchewan—an Update to 1995* (Regina: Canadian Plains Research Centre, 2002).
20 Stabler and Olfret's classification system for urban communities is based on "functional categories"—namely, the range of services provided and the activities undertaken. They rank centres into one of six categories, ranging from primary wholesale-retail as the most comprehensive centres, with secondary wholesale-retail occupying a second tier and complete shopping centre third. The fourth, fifth, and final classifications are as follows: partial shopping centres, full convenience centres, and minimum convenience centres. They first traced the trajectory of 598 Saskatchewan centres between 1961 and 1995, finding little change in the top two classifications. Saskatoon and Regina remained alone in the top tier and the number of secondary wholesale-retail remained at 8 (Estevan, Lloydminster, Moose Jaw, Prince Albert, Swift Current, Weyburn, Melfort, and Yorkton). The remaining classifications changed significantly between 1961 and 1995, with the number of complete shopping centres dropping from 29 to just 7, while partial shopping centres fell from 99 to 22, and full convenience centres declined from 189 to 59. The only increase was among minimum convenience centres, defined as the "smallest, and functionally simplest trade centres, offering a small set of services such as a gasoline station or a restaurant." Concurrent with the decline of larger towns and villages, minimum convenience centres increased from 271 to 500. In a subsequent update for 2001, they reported that, while the top classifications remained virtually unchanged, the partial shopping centres fell from 22 to 6, while the lower tier of full convenience centres increased from 59 to 72, and there were 2 more minimum convenience centres, bringing the total to 502.
21 For a variety of related sources, see "Demography, Census Reports and Statistics," Government of Saskatchewan, accessed March 9, 2023, https://www.saskatchewan.ca/government/government-data/bureau-of-statistics/population-and-census, and especially the "Population by Community" link.
22 See "Organized Hamlets Changed to Hamlet Status," Saskatchewan Ministry of Municipal Affairs, https://web.archive.org/web/20080325234149/http://www.municipal.gov.sk.ca/div/munadvisory/munchanges/orghamlet2hamlet.html, and "Restructured Villages," Saskatchewan Ministry of Municipal Affairs, https://web.archive.org/web/20080325234155/http://www.municipal.gov.sk.ca/div/munadvisory/munchanges/restructvillages.html (both accessed January 24, 2023). A village must have a population of 300 or more, 150 dwellings and business premises, and a taxable assessment of $30 million or more. Organized hamlet

designation requires a population of 100 or more, 150 dwellings and business premises, and a taxable assessment of $35 million or more.

23 Alan Davidson, *Social Determinants of Health* (Don Mills, ON: Oxford University Press, 2014); Dennis Raphael, *About Canada: Health and Illness* (Halifax: Fernwood Publishing, 2010).

24 Lise Hartling and William Pickett, "The Canadian Agricultural Injury Surveillance Program: A New Injury Control Initiative," *Chronic Diseases in Canada* 19, no. 3 (1998): 108.

25 Canadian Agricultural Injury Reporting, *Agricultural Fatalities in Canada, 1990–2008* (Edmonton: Canadian Agricultural Injury Reporting, 2011), 5, 17–18, https://www.casa-acsa.ca/wp-content/uploads/2013-00_Agricultural_Fatalities_Canada_1990-2008_Full_EN.pdf.

26 Louise Hagel, Niels Koehncke, and Joshua Neudorf, *Fatal Farm Injuries in Saskatchewan, 1990 to 2013* (Saskatoon: Canadian Centre for Health and Safety in Agriculture, University of Saskatchewan, n.d.), 10, https://www.casa-acsa.ca/wp-content/uploads/FatalFarmInjuriesSK1990_2013.pdf.

27 See "What Is the Network?," Agricultural Health and Safety Network, University of Saskatchewan, accessed January 24, 2023, https://cchsa-ccssma.usask.ca/aghealth/about-us/what-is-the-network.php.

28 Chandima Karunanayake, Donna C. Rennie, Louise Hagel, Joshua Lawson, Bonnie Janzen, William Pickett, James A. Dosman, and Punam Pahwa, "Access to Specialist Care in Rural Saskatchewan: The Saskatchewan Rural Health Study," *Healthcare* 3, no. 1 (2014): 84–99; Roland Dyck, Chandima Karunanayake, Punam Pahwa, Louise Hagel, Josh Lawson, Donna Rennie, and James Dosman, "Prevalence, Risk Factors and Co-morbidities of Diabetes among Adults in Rural Saskatchewan: The Influence of Farm Residence and Agriculture-Based Exposures," *BMC Public Health*, no. 13 (2013), https://bmcpublichealth.biomedcentral.com/articles/10.1186/1471-2458-13-7; Meenu Sharma, Joshua A. Lawson, Rani Kanthan, Chandima Karunanayake, Louise Hagel, Donna Rennie, James A. Dosman, and Punam Pahwa, "Factors Associated with the Prevalence of Prostate Cancer in Rural Saskatchewan: The Saskatchewan Rural Health Study," *Journal of Rural Health* 32, no. 2 (Spring 2016): 125–35.

29 Stefani Langenegger, "More Suicide Support, Mental Health Services Called for in Agriculture," CBC News, June 28, 2017, https://www.cbc.ca/news/canada/saskatchewan/agricultural-producers-association-of-saskatchewan-concerns-1.4181668.

30 Samara McPhedran, "Farmer Suicide Isn't Just a Mental Health Issue," *The Conversation*, September 24, 2012, http://theconversation.com/farmer-suicide-isnt-just-a-mental-health-issue-9381. See also Gunisha Kaur, "The Country Where 30 Farmers Die Each Day," CNN, March 17, 2022, https://www.cnn.com/2022/03/17/opinions/india-farmer-suicide-agriculture-reform-kaur/index.html.

31 Michael Rosmann, "Farmer Suicide Continues to Be Unresolved Problem," Farm and Ranch Guide, July 21, 2017, https://www.agupdate.com/farmandranchguide/opinion/columnists/farm_and_ranch_life/farmer-suicide-continues-to-be-unresolved-problem/article_843c55dc-ca22-11e7-a811-33c48d52e1dd.html.
32 Kelly Provost, "Sask. Farm Stress Line Calls Up 74% Over Same Time Last Year," CBC News, November 4, 2019, https://www.cbc.ca/news/canada/saskatoon/farm-stress-line-calls-increase-1.5347024.
33 Canada, House of Commons Standing Committee on Agriculture and Agri-Food, October 2, 2018 (M. Reynolds), https://www.ourcommons.ca/DocumentViewer/en/42-1/AGRI/meeting-108/evidence.
34 Canada, House of Commons Standing Committee on Agriculture and Agri-Food, *Mental Health: A Priority for Our Farmers* (Ottawa: House of Commons, 2019), 5, https://www.ourcommons.ca/Content/Committee/421/AGRI/Reports/RP10508975/agrirp16/agrirp16-e.pdf.
35 C.B. Macpherson, *Democracy in Alberta: Social Credit and the Party System* (Toronto: University of Toronto Press, 1953), 226.
36 Macpherson, 224–6, 227.
37 See, for example, Otis Dudley Duncan and Beverly Davis, "An Alternative to Ecological Correlation," American Sociological Review 18, no. 6 (1953): 665–6, and W.S. Robinson, "Ecological Correlations and the Behavior of Individuals," *American Sociological Review* 15, no. 3 (1950): 351–7.
38 W.L. Morton, *The Progressive Party in Canada* (Toronto: University of Toronto Press, 1950). Data from Andrew Heard, "Canadian Election Results by Party 1867 to 2021," Elections, Simon Fraser University, accessed March 9, 2023, https://www.sfu.ca/~aheard/elections/1867-present.html.
39 For some thoughtful analysis of these developments, see Dale Eisler, *From Left to Right: Saskatchewan's Political and Economic Transformation* (Regina: University of Regina Press, 2022). Also see David McGrane, "Which Third Way? A Comparison of the Romanow and Calvert NDP Governments from 1991 to 2007," in *Saskatchewan Politics: Crowding the Centre*, ed. Howard Leeson (Regina: Canadian Plains Research Centre, 2008), 143–63, and Leeson, "The 2007 Saskatchewan Election: Watershed or Way Stations?," 119–40, in the same volume.
40 Pankaj Mishra, *Age of Anger: A History of the Present* (London: Allen Lane, 2018), 14.
41 Jeremy Simes, "The Rise on the Right: Inside Saskatchewan's Shifting Political Landscape," *Regina Leader-Post*, June 3, 2022, https://leaderpost.com/news/local-news/sask-politics/the-rise-on-the-right-inside-saskatchewans-shifting-political-landscape; Phil Tank, "Unified Grassroots Sounds Less about Unity the Closer You Listen," *Saskatoon StarPhoenix*, January 6, 2022, https://thestarphoenix.com/opinion/columnists/tank-unified-grassroots-sounds-less-about-unity-the-closer-you-listen.

42 Nik Nanos, "Data Dive with Nik Nanos: Canadians Are Losing Faith in the Country's Most Vital Institutions," *Globe and Mail*, February 11, 2022, https://www.theglobeandmail.com/opinion/article-data-dive-with-nik-nanos-canadians-are-losing-faith-in-the-countrys/.

43 See Tauxe, "Family Cohesion vs. Capitalist Hegemony," and Parvin Ghorayshi, "The Identification of Capitalist Farms," *Sociologica Ruralis* 26, no. 2 (1986): 146–59.

44 Kelly Bronson, Irena Knezevic, and Chantal Clement, "The Canadian Family Farm, in Literature and in Practice," *Journal of Rural Studies*, no. 66 (2019): 105.

45 Bronson, Knezevic, and Clement, 109.

46 Bronson, Knezevic, and Clement, 109.

47 André Magnan, Melissa Davidson, and Annette Aurélie Desmarais, "'They Call It Progress, but We Don't See It as Progress': Farm Consolidation and Land Concentration in Saskatchewan, Canada," *Agriculture and Human Values*, no. 40 (2023): 277.

48 Magnan, Davidson, and Desmarais, 277.

49 See "Treaty Map," Office of the Treaty Commissioner, accessed January 24, 2023, http://www.otc.ca/pages/treaty_map.html.

50 See Truth and Reconciliation Commission of Canada, *Truth and Reconciliation Commission of Canada: Calls to Action* (Winnipeg: Truth and Reconciliation Commission of Canada, 2012), 4–5, https://crc-canada.org/wp-content/uploads/2016/03/trc-calls-to-action-english.pdf.

51 See "Treaty Land Entitlement," Government of Saskatchewan, accessed January 24, 2023, https://www.saskatchewan.ca/government/partnerships-for-success/profiles/treaty-land-entitlement.

52 "Saskatchewan's One Millionth Acre," Crown-Indigenous Relations and Northern Affairs Canada, last modified April 10, 2015, https://www.rcaanc-cirnac.gc.ca/eng/1428677852854/1539954110358.

53 Nicolas Gauthier and Julia White, "Aboriginal Peoples and Agriculture in 2016: A Portrait," Statistics Canada, January 17, 2019, https://www150.statcan.gc.ca/n1/pub/96-325-x/2019001/article/00001-eng.htm.

54 Melissa M. Arcand, Lori Bradford, Dale F. Worme, Graham E.H. Strickert, Ken Bear, Anthony Blair, Dreaver Johnston, Sheldon M. Wuttunee, Alfred Gamble, and Debra Shewfelt, "Sowing a Way Towards Revitalizing Indigenous Agriculture: Creating Meaning from a Forum Discussion in Saskatchewan, Canada," *FACETS* 5, no. 1 (2020): 619–41, https://www.facetsjournal.com/doi/10.1139/facets-2020-0004. See also the web page devoted to the forum: "Forum on Indigenous Agriculture in Saskatchewan: Sowing a Way Towards Revitalizing Indigenous Agriculture," University of Saskatchewan, accessed January 19, 2023, https://research-groups.usask.ca/indigenousag/#Welcome.

55 Arcand et al., 619.

56 Arcand et al., 626–35.
57 Katelyn Duncan, "Canada's First Nations People Were Country's First Farmers," *Western Producer*, June 17, 2021, https://www.producer.com/crops/canadas-first-nations-people-were-countrys-first-farmers/.
58 Jeremy Simes, "Racism: Not Someone Else's Problem," *Western Producer*, June 25, 2020, https://www.producer.com/news/racism-not-someone-elses-problem/; Pamela Cowan, "Saskatchewan: Land of Living Skies and a Racial Divide," *Regina Leader-Post*, August 4, 2017, https://leaderpost.com/news/local-news/saskatchewan-land-of-living-skies-and-a-racial-divide; Nicole Di Donato, "'It's Blatant Racism': Renewed Calls for Education, Reconciliation after Racist Sign Posted on Sask. First Nation," CTV News, July 15, 2021, https://saskatoon.ctvnews.ca/it-s-blatant-racism-renewed-calls-for-education-reconciliation-after-racist-sign-posted-on-sask-first-nation-1.5509708; Bryan Eneas, "Sask. Premier Acknowledges Systemic Racism Exists, Asks People to Treat Others with Respect," CBC News, June 17, 2020, https://www.cbc.ca/news/canada/saskatchewan/sk-premier-systemic-racism-exists-treat-others-respsect-1.5616645.
59 Brenda Macdougall, "After Boushie: It's Time For Honest Talk about Racism in Saskatchewan," *Globe and Mail*, August 24, 2016, https://www.theglobeandmail.com/opinion/after-boushie-its-time-for-honest-talk-about-racism-in-saskatchewan/article31537479/.
60 Dayne Patterson, "Network of Sask. Farmers, Ranchers Open Land to Indigenous People to Practise Treaty Rights," CBC News, July 16, 2021, https://www.cbc.ca/news/canada/saskatchewan/indigenous-treaty-land-network-rural-farm-1.6104966. See also the Treaty Land Sharing Network website at https://treatylandsharingnetwork.ca/access-land/.
61 "Indigenous, Environmental, and Agricultural Organizations across Saskatchewan Call on the Province to Halt the Liquidation of Crown Land," National Farmers Union, March 21, 2017, https://www.nfu.ca/indigenous-environmental-and-agricultural-organizations-across-saskatchewan-call-on-the-province-to-halt-the-liquidation-of-crown-land/.
62 "New Trespass Legislation Coming into Force on January 1, 2022," Government of Saskatchewan, December 16, 2021, https://www.saskatchewan.ca/government/news-and-media/2021/december/16/new-trespass-legislation-coming-into-force-on-january-1-2022. Concern has been raised that this law further abrogates treaty rights. See Laura Sciarpelletti, "New Sask. Trespassing Legislation Infringes on Treaty Rights, Says Treaty Land Sharing Network," CBC News, January 22, 2022, https://www.cbc.ca/news/canada/saskatchewan/treaty-land-sharing-network-opposition-trespassing-legislation-1.6323227.

EPILOGUE: UNANSWERED QUESTIONS

1. For a discussion of these issues with reference to Saskatchewan, see Annette Desmarais, Darrin Qualman, André Magnan, and Nettie Wiebe, "Investor Ownership or Social Investment? Changing Farmland Ownership in Saskatchewan and Canada," *Agriculture and Human Values*, no. 34 (2017): 149–66.
2. Jen Skerritt, "Tyson Foods Helped Create the Meat Crisis It Now Warns Against," BNN *Bloomberg*, April 29, 2020, https://www.bnnbloomberg.ca/tyson-foods-helped-create-the-meat-crisis-it-now-warns-against-1.1428579.
3. K. Murray Knuttila, "The Impact of the Western Canadian Agrarian Movement on Federal Government Policy, 1900–1930: An Assessment and Analysis" (PhD diss., University of Toronto, 1982). Also see Knuttila, "Matters of the State Still Matter," in *Power and Resistance: Critical Thinking about Canadian Social Issues*, ed. Les Samuelson, Jessica Anthony, and Wayne Anthony, 6th ed. (Halifax: Fernwood Publishing, 2017), 22–50.
4. Melanie Sommerville and André Magnan, "'Pinstripes on the Prairies': Examining the Financialization of Farming Systems in the Canadian Prairie Provinces," *Journal of Peasant Studies* 42, no. 1 (2015): 119–44, and André Magnan and Sean Sunley, "Farmland Investment and Financialization in Saskatchewan, 2003–2014: An Empirical Analysis of Farmland Transactions," *Journal of Rural Studies*, no. 49 (2017): 92–103.
5. See Tim Clune and Heather Downey, "Very Good Farmers, Not Particularly Good Businesspeople: A Rural Financial Councillor Perspective on Rural Business Failure," *Journal of Rural Studies*, no. 95 (2022): 256–67, and Lee Hart, "No Clear-Cut Fix in Right to Repair Debate," *Grainews*, September 22, 2022, https://www.grainews.ca/machinery/no-clear-cut-fix-in-right-to-repair-debate.
6. Mark Halsall, "The Most Common Grain Marketing Mistakes," *Grainews*, September 27, 2021, https://www.grainews.ca/features/the-most-common-grain-marketing-mistakes; Rebecca Hannam, "Four Things to Know about Grain Contracts," *Manitoba Co-operator*, August 24, 2022, https://www.manitobacooperator.ca/markets/four-things-to-know-about-grain-contracts; James Snell, "Grain Contracts a Dilemma for Farmers This Year," *Alberta Farmer*, June 27, 2022, https://www.albertafarmexpress.ca/news/grain-contracts-a-dilemma-for-farmers-this-year.

INDEX

A

ABB Grain (Australia), 218
An Act to Amend Certain Acts Relating to Agriculture and Agri-Food (Agricultural Growth Act), 191
An Act to Authorize a Subsidy for a Railway through the Crow's Nest Pass, 39
Advance Payments for Crops Act, 163, 167, 177
AGCO Corporation (US), 211
The Age of Anger, 243
Ag Growth International (AGI), 212
agrarian commodity producers, independent
  change in class position, xxiv, 194, 199–200, 207, 229, 244–45
  class status of, xiii, xxv, xxviii, 49, 199, 240, 244
  declining numbers of, 242
  engaging in non-farm paid labour, 205
  establishment of, 46
  growing importance of wage labour to, 50, 204, 245
  importance of farm equity to, 122
  losses and stress suffered by, 239
  operating with considerable uncertainty, 196
  as petite bourgeoisie, xxviii, 61, 66, 199, 240
  reliance on commodity sale income, xxix, 42, 64, 205
  specialization by, 197–98, 200–201, 226
  See also cost-price squeeze, on grain producers; farmers
agrarianism, xxiii–xxiv, 44, 61–62, 64, 227, 233
agrarian movement/protest, 44, 48, 67
agribusiness, 132, 138, 216, 233
Agricore United, 217–18
Agricultural Health and Safety Network, 238
Agricultural Marketing Programs Act, 177, 184, 191
Agricultural Prices Support Act, 96
Agricultural Producers Association of Saskatchewan (APAS), 189, 228, 239
Agricultural Products Act, 98
Agricultural Products Board, 98, 169
Agricultural Products Board Act, 177
Agricultural Products Cooperative Marketing Act, 88, 177
Agricultural Products Marketing Board, 97
Agricultural Stabilization Act, 107, 147, 171
Agricultural Stabilization Board, 144
agriculture. *See* farming/farm sector
Agriculture and Agri-Food Administrative Monetary Penalties Act, 177, 191

Agriculture and Rural Development Act, 105
agri-food industry, 168, 176, 253
Agrium, 215
Aid for the Advancement of Agricultural Instruction in the Provinces Act, 38
Air Canada, 144, 170
Alberta
    agrarian consciousness among farmers, 200, 240
    agricultural treaty land in, 247
    anti-NEP campaign in, 154
    civil disobedience by farmers in, 179
    creation of, 34
    fall in per capita income during Depression, 76
    farm machinery dealerships in, 213
    in favour of elimination CWB, 187
    immigration to, 57
    investment in railroads, 36
    oil industry in, 154
    origin of Reform party, 172
    part of Rupert's Land, 2, 13
    population growth in, 35
    rehabilitation of drought areas in, 80, 84
Alberta Barley Commission, 179
Alberta Farmers' Co-operative Elevator Company, 216
Alberta Wheat Pool, 217
Allen, Richard, 64–65
Allen, Sir Hugh, 12
Allied Purchasing Agency, 47
Allis Chalmers, 54
Althouse, Vic, 162
Altria Group, 222
Amendments Respecting Rate per Bushel, Emergency Payments, Extension and Application to Rye, Flaxseed and Rapeseed, 140
Amendment to Fertilizer Act, 56

Anderson, Alan, 57
Anderson, Gary, 212
Andjelic Land, 208
Andres, Robert, 145
Anglo-American Convention of 1818, 3
Anti-Inflation Act, 135
Archer, John, 224
Archer-Daniels-Midland (ADM), 220
Argue, Hazen, 101
Australian Wheat Board, 218
Auto Pact, 186

B
Bank of Canada, 79, 170
Bank of Montreal, 61
Bank of Toronto, 61
Baran, Paul, xvii, xxx
Barber, Dr. Clarence/Barber Report, 113–14
barley
    cultivation of, 30, 138, 145, 180
    sales on open market, 184, 186, 188
    sales under jurisdiction of CWB, 99, 107, 109, 140, 170, 178–79
    as specialized commodity, 197
BASF, 215, 227
Bayer Group, 215, 227
Beaudoin, Gérald A., 7
Beckie, Mary Ann, 235
Bednasek, Drew, 31
beef industry
    beef as specialized commodity, 197
    beef production, 201, 254
    cash advances for producers, 184
    growth in Ontario and Quebec, 141
Benjamin, Leslie, 134, 151
Bennett, R.B.
    belief in efficacy of tariffs, 76
    establishing CBC to counter US culture, 79
    increasing government spending, 72

INDEX • 321

leader of Progressive Conservative
Party, 66, 76
legacy of, 83
providing farm relief/loans, 77–78
wheat marketing crisis, 80–83, 94, 241
Berkshire Hathaway, 222
Berry, Wendell, 235
Beveridge Report (UK), 93
Bill C-18 (protecting plant breeders' rights), 191
Bill C-19 (enabling government restraint), 145
Bill C-34 (amending *Canada Transportation Act*), 142, 176
Bill C-73 (creating *Anti-Inflation Act*), 135
Bill C-239 (enabling interest charge on advances to farmers), 140
Blais, Pierre, 170
Blake, Edward, 18–20
Board of Grain Commissioners, 87
Board of Grain Supervisors, 47
Board of Railway Commissioners, 37, 40, 148
Borden, Robert, 46, 64, 66, 77
Bourgault Industries Ltd., 213
Boushie, Colten, 250
Brandt Group of Companies, 213
Bretton Woods Agreement, 95
brewing and distilling industry, 4
British North America (BNA), 1–2, 5, 17, 36
British North America Act, 5–6, 22
Broadbent, Ed, 152
Brown, Lorne, 83
Bryson, Scott, 115
buffalo, loss of, 15, 18, 29
Buffalo Party, 243
Buffett, Warren, 222
Bunge Limited, 190, 220–21
Burton, John, 137
Business Council of Manitoba, 188

C
Call to Action #45 (TRC), 247
Calvert, Lorne, 243
Campbell, Kim, 172
Canada
agricultural policy of, xvii–xviii, xxi, xxix, 49, 98, 104, 139, 168, 190
clearing Prairies for agrarian settlement, 28
close identification with North American economy, 103
dependence on US, 67–68
emergence of urban-industrial society in, 67
foreign (US) ownership of economy, 101, 136
government deficits, 125, 144, 152–53, 160–61, 166–67, 173
interventionist policy of, 92–93, 136
nationalism and control of own economy, 136, 153
temporary foreign workers program, 184
Western agriculture as lesser priority, 154
See also economy, Canadian
Canada, government spending
investment to create Petro-Canada, 144
as preventing global collapse, xix
reduction in, xx, 151–52, 167, 175
restraint in, 131, 145, 150, 152, 193
as stimulating economic growth, 72, 92–93
transfers to provinces, 130, 167
Canada Development Corporation, 136, 170
Canada Grain Act, 49, 87, 163
Canadair, 170
Canada Pension Plan, 110
Canada Student Loans Plan, 97

Canada Transportation Act, 175–76
Canada–United States Free Trade
　Agreement, 170, 177
Canada–United States Joint
　Commission on Grains, 178
Canadian Agricultural Economics
　Society, 209
Canadian Agricultural Income
　Stabilization Program, 183
Canadian Agricultural Partnership, 231,
　255
Canadian Agricultural Policy, xvi
Canadian Alliance, 182, 242
Canadian Bank of Commerce, 61
Canadian Broadcasting Corporation
　(CBC), 97, 129, 144, 165, 238–39
Canadian Centre for Health and Safety
　in Agriculture, 238
Canadian Chamber of Commerce, 136
Canadian Charter of Rights and
　Freedoms, 179
Canadian Council of Agriculture, 48, 99
Canadian Dairy Commission, 145
Canadian Environmental Advisory
　Council, 169
Canadian Farmers for Justice, 179
Canadian Farm Loan Act, 78, 103–4
Canadian Farm Loan Board, 53
Canadian Federation of Agriculture, 141,
　178, 228, 232
Canadian Grain Bill, 82
Canadian Grain Commission, 163, 180
Canadian Institute for International
　Peace and Security, 169
Canadian Labour Congress, 136
Canadian Manufacturers' Association, 21
Canadian National Railroad (CN), 37, 176
Canadian Northern Railway, 35–37
Canadian Pacific Railway (CPR)
　creation/construction of, 12, 15, 35,
　　107, 255

financing of, 19, 36, 108
freight rates of, 39
and grain handling and
　transportation, 41
growth of, 158
not allotting railcars to farmers, 43
scandal of, 12, 15–16, 19
selling lands to support immigration,
　32–33
urging removal of rate cap, 175
See also rail transportation system
Canadian Reform Alliance (Canadian
　Alliance), 173
Canadian Transportation Agency, 219
Canadian Transport Commission, 112,
　164
Canadian Western Agribition, 235
Canadian Wheat Board (CWB)
　as agent for international sales, 109,
　　141–42, 149, 156, 189
　demand for retention of, 98
　effectiveness of, 163
　future of, 86, 170
　jurisdictional areas of, 107, 145, 170,
　　178–79, 186
　made a permanent agency, 111
　main role to set minimum prices,
　　87, 92
　management of, 179–81
　monopoly power of, 99, 140, 142, 179,
　　189
　offering crop insurance, 74
　paying advance price to farmers, 48,
　　91, 101, 106
　selling wheat in competition to US,
　　100
　as single-desk seller of wheat, 118, 242
　termination of, xxiv, 185, 187–88,
　　190–91, 194, 255
　as unresponsive to needs of
　　producers, 177

value to grain farmers, 88, 216, 226
weakening authority of, 143, 176
Canadian Wheat Board Act, 86, 90, 99, 111, 170, 177
  amendments to, 142, 162, 176, 179, 186, 188
Canagrex, 155, 162
capital
  accumulation guaranteed by Keynesian policies, 93, 95
  as beneficiary of National Policy, 58
  concentration and centralization of, xxiv, 24, 53, 114, 118, 129, 155
  investment in farmland for gain, 253
  joint-stock companies, xviii, 25, 217
  multinational sources of, 110, 128
  needed for purchasing acreage and equipment, 53, 66, 160, 197, 199, 234, 245
  supplemented by farm credit, 104
  value of farm land and machinery, 123, 203–4, 209
capitalism
  advanced, xxvi, xxviii
  changing nature, stages of, xviii, 75, 129, 229
  competitive, 55
  corporate, xviii–xx, 55, 71
  global, xviii, xx, xxiii, xxiv, 126, 196, 229
  in the industrial economy, xviii, 3, 24, 28
  in Keynesian ideology, xix, xxi
  in market-based societies, xxv, 28, 127
  and neoliberalism, 125–27, 196
  profit making as goal of, 96
  promoting growth and development, 68, 75
  and transformation of class structures, 244
  use of periodization to analyze transitions in, xviii, xxi, 66

Carefoot Farms, 208
Careless, J.M.S., 23
Cargill, Incorporated, 188, 220–21, 254
Cartier, George-Étienne, 5
Case IH, 227
Castleden, George, 90
Central Selling Agency, for wheat pools, 81
cereal grains
  grading of new varieties of, 49
  producers of, xxix, 115, 168, 196–97, 200, 220, 226
  prominent Prairie crop, xvii, xxii, xxix, 37, 67, 95, 111, 141
  reduction in number of farms, 194
  See also wheat production and marketing
Cervus Equipment, 213
Charlottetown Conference, 5
chemicals, agricultural, 42, 67, 73, 115, 196, 210, 214–15, 221, 254
Chrétien, Jean, 172, 181
Churchill, Gordon, 106
CLAAS Group (Germany), 212
Clark, Joe, 151–52, 173
class. *See* social class/class structure
CN Commercialization Act, 176
CNH Industrial, 211
Coca-Cola Company, 223
Cold War, 73, 102, 125
colonialism, xxx, 3, 5, 10, 17, 31, 96
Cominco Fertilizer Partnership, 215
Commission of Inquiry into the Sponsorship Program and Advertising Activities, 182
Committee on Railways and Canals, 43
Community Pasture Program (CPP), 83–84
competition/competitiveness
  among agricultural producers, 191, 216, 220, 225, 227, 235, 257

competition/competitiveness *(continued)*
  among rail lines, 112–13, 164–65, 175
  call for co-operation instead of, 63, 120, 127, 243
  difficult for small family farmers, 133
  in export/international markets, 39, 43, 55, 100, 183, 228
  in industrial capitalism, xviii, 24, 66
  in prices, 114, 213
  with private sector enterprises, 181
  tariff protection from, 15
Confederation
  and expansion of agricultural frontier, 22, 86
  and formation of Canada, 7, 11, 15, 34, 75
  as framework to address problems, xxii, 6
  Indigenous Peoples as full partners in, 248
  laissez-faire ideologies at time of, 27
  and National Policy, 17, 25, 40, 58, 229
  as start of industrialization policy, xiii, xxi, 72
  transportation system built after, 35
  See also National Policy
Connell, Charles, 9
Conserva Pak Seeding Systems, 213
Conservative Party (1867–1942)
  advocating policy of protective tariffs, 17, 23, 46, 77
  embracing National Policy, 66
  facing wheat marketing crisis, 80
  increasing government spending, 72
  perceived regard for farmers, 64, 78
Conservative Party of Canada
  abandoning Keynesian economics, 195
  adherence to neoliberalism, 192
  birth of, 173, 182, 243
  enabling commercial, incorporated agricultural enterprises, 194

promoting fiscal restraint, 183
  supporting freedom of farmers to market their grain, 186–88
  supporting retention of tariffs, 241
Constitution Act, 74
continentalism, xx, 193, 210
Conway, John, 198, 201
Cooperating Friends of the Pool, 218
Co-operative Commonwealth Federation (CCF), 64–65, 97–98, 241–42
co-operatives
  as alternative farm arrangement, 67, 121
  for creameries, 47
  as farmer owned, 47, 88, 121, 177, 216, 218, 255
  for grain handling and storage, 64, 80, 120, 210, 218
  intergenerational transfer of farm assets as problematic, 122
  land grants to establish, 122
  purchasing and retail sales activities of, 224
Corn Laws, 5
Corteva, Inc., 215, 227
cost-price squeeze, on grain producers
  due to instability in markets, 99, 115, 118–19, 242
  exacerbated by mechanization of production, 113
  increased by inflation, 133, 136
  leading to protests against government, 120, 122
  not reduced by *Agricultural Stabilization Act*, 107
Cowessess First Nation, as agricultural producers, 249–50
Creighton, Donald, 16, 19, 94–96, 102, 110–11, 136
crop insurance, 74, 104–5, 171, 183, 228

Crop Insurance Act/Crop Insurance
    Program, 171
crops, 38, 40, 86, 174
    See also barley; cereal grains; wheat
        production and marketing
Crosbie, John, 152, 164
Crow Benefit, 157–59, 175, 193
Crown corporations
    Canagrex established, 155
    dissolution or sale of, 151, 162, 165, 167
    seeking private sector financing, 145
    as undesired government presence in
        the economy, 151
    used during WWII military effort, 95
Crown lands, 74–75, 251
Crow Rate
    abandonment of, 151–52, 157, 174–76,
        255
    causing restrictions on producers, 242
    designed to lower shipping costs,
        39–40, 144, 149
    future of, 147, 150–51, 156, 226
    as not remunerative for the railways,
        112, 146, 157, 192
    replaced by Crow Benefit, 158, 175, 193
Crow's Nest Pass Agreement, xxiv, 39,
    108, 149, 158

D

dairy industry, 141
Danysk, Cecilia, 50, 206
Daschuk, James, xxii, 3, 18, 29
De Havilland Aircraft of Canada
    Limited, 170
Delage Farms, 207
Delorme, Chief Cadmus, 249
deregulation, of markets, xix, 217, 230, 242
    economic effects of, 128–29, 131
    negative impacts of, xxii, xxiv, 164
    as neoliberal approach, xx, 127, 169,
        193, 195

as part of an economic renewal
    strategy, 161, 166
seen to create employment, 160
See also markets
Desmarais, Annette Aurélie, 208, 253
Deutz-Allis, 211
Devine, Grant, 162
Diefenbaker, John
    agricultural policy of, 104–7, 111, 131,
        144, 150, 161–62, 186
    follower of Keynesian economics, 241
    relationship with US, 109–10
    support for farmers, 90, 103, 137, 144,
        242
    support for wheat board, 99
Dieter, Chief Francis, 31
Doctrine of Discovery, repudiation of,
    247
Dole Food Company, 223
*Dominion Lands Act (An Act Respecting
    the Public Lands of the Dominion)*,
    10, 17, 32, 58, 247, 255
Donnelly, Thomas, 53
Douglas, James, 43
Douglas, T.C., 91, 143
DowDuPont, 215
Drengson, Alan, 235
Drew, George, 97
drought
    of 1930s, xxiii
    impact on grain production, 30, 76,
        83, 87, 256
    rehabilitation of lands affected by,
        80, 84
    support for farmers during, 106, 189
Duplessis, Maurice, 143
DuPont Corteva Agriscience, 215

E

Easter, Wayne, 185–86
Eaton, Emily, 206, 236

Economic Council of Canada, 169
economy, Canadian
  carbon tax, 227
  changing environment in, 177, 194, 200
  collapse of 1929, xix, 68–69, 71, 195
  crisis of 2008–09, xix, xxi, 183, 192, 195, 230
  development of, 6–7, 13, 27, 75, 77
  dominated by US, 110, 136
  effects of unemployment on, xix, 71–72, 77, 126, 160, 195–96
  goods and services tax, 167
  impacted by global economic system, xvii–xx, 25, 65, 68, 135, 167, 229
  independence of, 62
  inflation, 91, 126, 130, 133, 135–36, 144
  stimulus package to protect farming, 183–84, 195
  wage and price controls, 135
egg and poultry production, 139, 141, 203, 229
entrepreneurship
  among grain companies, 41, 43, 225
  contributing to agricultural success, 197, 212, 234, 242, 246
  and individualism, 194, 243
  in world view, xxiv
environment, natural
  and climate change, 253
  impacting agricultural producers, 37, 253–54
  protection of, 84, 168–69, 233–34
  sustainability of, 228, 245
  toxicants in, 238
  water conservation, 83
Estey, Justice Willard, 175
Euler, W.D., 86
Evans, John, 54
Experimental Farms, 38

F
Fair, Robert, 98
Fairbairn, Brett, 41, 47, 217
Family Farm Foundation, 178
family farms
  as backbone of economy/democracy, xxii, 62, 105, 133
  belonging to agrarian-based class, 240
  business structure/typology of, 198–200, 204, 216, 254
  capitalization of, 116, 155, 198, 244
  debt carried by, 206
  definition of, 245–46
  developing into high-input agriculture, 66
  effect of agricultural policies on, xviii, xxi, xxix
  environmental sustainability, 245
  established on Prairies through government policies, xiii
  expanding population of, 67
  family-based labour on, 50, 197, 245
  health and wellness of, 228
  ideologies and mythologies of, 233
  impact of neoliberalism on, xxiv, 129
  income streams on, 198–99
  intergenerational transfers of assets, 185
  at middle of input-output nexus, 196
  as oil producing, xxii
  reduction in number, increase in size, xxiii, 111, 134, 194, 201, 225, 232–33
  restructuring and future of, xxiii, 245, 257
  wage labourers hired on, 50, 205
  See also cost-price squeeze, on grain producers; farmers
farm credit, 53, 78, 103–4, 111, 161, 193
Farm Credit Corporation (FCC) (now Farm Credit Canada)
  borrowing costs of, 153–54

funds granted to for lending, 111, 155, 165
funds owed by lendees, 206
providing credit to farmers, 156, 161, 193, 255
services provided by, 181
Farm Credit Corporation Act, 181
Farm Debt Mediation Act, 191
Farm Debt Review Act, 177
Farmer Automatic, 211
farmers
    advance payment (loan) to, 101, 106, 119, 140, 193
    civil disobedience by, 179
    class structure differentiation among, 198
    entrepreneurial self-concept of, 234
    experiencing inner satisfaction as creative producers, xxvii
    freedom of choice in grain sales, 184
    grievances of, 44, 54–55
    health and wellness of, 131, 228, 238–39
    homogeneity and growing heterogeneity of, 56, 65, 209, 226
    indebtedness/growing poverty of, xxiii, 79, 105, 111, 154–56, 163, 166, 185, 195–96
    new class of commercial, entrepreneurial producers, 194
    off-farm income of, 198–99, 244
    prevalence of suicide among, 238, 240
    pushing for their own grain-handling system, 64
    regarding the health and wellness of, 228
    relief program and supports for, 74, 77, 147, 162, 164, 167, 170–71, 181–83
    self-sufficiency of, 132

Farmers' Creditors Arrangement Act, 78, 80
Farmers Equity Trust, 190
Farmers for Justice, 187
Farmers' Platform, 45, 63, 241
Farmers Union of Canada (Saskatchewan Section), 227
Farm Improvement Loan Act, 160–61, 185
farm income
    affected by drought, 76
    classifying enterprises by, 200, 206, 217
    as decreasing, 175
    government role in supporting, 98–100, 106, 159
    largely dependent on international commodity prices, 206
    percentage used to pay for crop insurance, 86
    of Saskatchewan farmers, 79, 117
    stabilization of, 106–7, 144, 182, 193
    as sustainable, 185
Farm Income Protection Act, 170, 172
farming/farm sector
    alternative modes of, 121, 234
    capitalization of, 198, 206, 256
    as central to societal development, 253
    changing scene of, 209, 225, 246
    commercial, 40
    comprehensive assessment of, 131
    corporate model of, 204, 233, 254
    as dangerous occupation, 238
    demonstration farms, 80
    differentiation or stratification in, 209
    diversification of, 137, 140
    dominated by wheat, cereal grain, livestock production, 141
    effects of neoliberalism on, 232
    farm size and number, 114, 134, 201
    high-input/low-input, 66, 208, 210, 214, 233–35, 238, 253–54

farming/farm sector *(continued)*
   lack of effective international rules
      for, 166
   loans and subsidies for, 107, 133, 135,
      161, 185
   as market-oriented, 52, 177
   mechanization of, xxiii, 75, 103, 114,
      226
   multinational enterprises in, 210, 220,
      226–27
   overproduction and lagging sales in,
      100, 109, 120, 192–93
   restructuring of, 132–34, 175, 237
   role in national economy, xvii, xxi,
      168, 193
   stabilization of, 107, 228
   tripartite funding for, 171
   wage labourers in, 198–99, 245
farming practices
   conventional, 234–35
   Hutterite form of agriculture, 121–22
   mixed, xvii, xxii, 194
   neo-conventional, 235
   no-till/zero-till (ZT) systems, 212
   organic, 235
   strip, 80
   as sustainable, 234–35
   See also industrialization
farm machinery
   high costs of owning and
      maintaining, 54, 113, 120, 203
   instrumental in agricultural
      expansion, 38
   needed by family farms, 196
   producers and providers of, 210
   reducing costs of production, 53
   transitions and innovations in, 52–53,
      212–13, 256
   See also tractors, farm
farm machinery industry
   affected by drop in farm incomes, 159

Barber Report recommendations
   on, 113
capital concentration and
   centralization in, 53, 118
competition in and restructuring of,
   113–14
economies of scale encouraging
   multinationals, 115
high financial returns for companies,
   54
Farm Products Marketing Act, 160
Farm Products Marketing Agencies, 145
Farm Products Marketing Agencies Act, 139
Faulkner, James, 145
Federated Co-operatives Limited, 224
Feeds Act, 191
Fendt (Germany), 211
fertilizers
   costs of, 55–56
   economies of scale encouraging
      multinationals, 115, 212, 220
   as facilitating agricultural expansion, 38
   farmer purchases of, 42, 67, 196
   long-term implications of use, 254
   as part of high-input farming, 210,
      214, 234
Fertilizers Act, 191
financial sector
   banking industry, 61, 129, 185, 195
   collapse of system during 1930s, xix, 79
   credit unions, 47, 206
   crisis of 2008–09, 195, 230
   dominance of US in, 95
   financial services operations, xviii,
      211, 220, 256
Finkle, Alvin, 82
First Nations in Canada
   as agricultural producers, 248–49
   effects on of loss of buffalo, 15
   land surrendered to Crown for
      immigrant influx, 28, 31

sharing of land through treaties, 28–29
See also Indigenous Peoples
Fleming, R.B., 224
FlexiCoil, 213
food chain, agricultural
    components in, 4, 120, 196, 222, 256–57
    farmers' position in, 229
    as global, xvi, xxiv, 233, 253
Food Prices Review Board, 135
Forbes magazine, 225
Fordism, 73, 126
Foreign Investment Review Agency, 136
Forum on Indigenous Agriculture, 249
Foster, George, 23, 48
Fowke, Vernon, xvi–xvii, xxi, xxv, 6, 17, 23, 86, 118
FRAME (AGI), 212
free trade
    basis for New National Policy, 46
    benefitting farm machinery industry, 113, 212
    in British economy, 3, 5
    effects on agricultural producers, 170, 177, 191
    free trade agreements, 15, 21, 46, 128, 166, 191
    Liberal Party position on, 15, 18–19, 21
    and neoliberalism, 128
    Progressive Conservative position on, 155, 170
    See also Canada–United States Free Trade Agreement
freight rates. *See* rail transportation system
Friedman, Milton, 126
Friggstad Farm Equipment, 213
Frito-Lay North America, 223
Front de libération du Québec, 143
fungicides, 214–15, 238

G
G3 Canada Limited, 190
Garcia, Arnoldo, 127
Gardiner, James G., 83, 87, 91
Gatin, Laureen, 217
gender order
    in agricultural production, xxix–xxx, 65, 254
    farmers' attitudes on, 228, 234
    imbalance during Western settlement, 52
    lives of farm women, 50–52
General Agreement on Tariffs and Trade (GATT), 170, 177
General Mills, 222
George Weston Ltd., 225
Gertler, Michael, 212, 235
Gilson, Dr. Clay, 156–57
Gleave, A.P., 138
Glencore International, 218, 220
global capitalism. *See* capitalism, global
globalization, xx–xxii, 167, 193
Globe and Mail, 188
Goodale, Ralph, 147, 172, 176–80, 188
Gordon, Walter, royal commission chair, 101–2, 136
Gottselig, Bill, 165
Government Expenditure Restraint Act, 144
Graham, William Morris, 31
grain elevators
    companies, 41, 47, 88, 237
    decline in number of, 219
    farmer-owned, co-operative, 46
    government ownership of, 45
grain farms/grain production
    advance payments for, 163, 177, 193
    complexity of, 256
    declining number of, 244
    feed grains, 141–42, 186
    impact of drought on, 87

grain farms/grain production *(continued)*
    reducing income instability in, 147
    subsidies eliminated for, 174
Grain Futures Act, 87
Grain Growers' Grain Company, 47, 62, 216
Grain Growers' Guide, 45, 62, 64, 66
grain handling and transportation
    affected by rail line abandonments, 164
    costs of, 149
    equipment for, 212
    grain delivery points, 41–42, 47, 190
    grain delivery quota system, 90
    ownership of facilities for, 41, 46, 185, 187–88, 227
    regulation of, 46
    royal commission on, 49, 146–47
    structure and organization of, 149, 152, 157, 174–75, 217
    See also grain elevators; rail transportation system
grain marketing/grain trade
    effects of free trade on, 177
    facilitated by expanded/restructured rail lines, 41, 146
    freedom of choice in, 183
    as fundamental economic issue, 242
    gain from purchase and resale of grain, 42
    government encouragement of, 49
    importance of futures markets, 189
    international grain market, 80
    marketing pools for, 48, 87–88, 98, 107, 111, 142–43, 190, 226
    multinational trade agreements, 108, 118, 152
    prices for, 166
    as private, 41, 61, 64, 67, 81, 210, 216, 220, 255
    regulation of, 106, 226
    return of tariffs governing, 241

select committee to study, 86–87
See also markets; wheat production and marketing
Grand Trunk Pacific Railway, 36–37
Grand Trunk Railway, 36–37, 42
Grant, George, 95–96, 110, 136
Great Depression
    causing hardships on farmers, 118, 241
    economic crisis of, xiii, xix–xx, xxiii, 60, 68, 74, 76, 97, 126, 128, 185
    emergence of CCF, 64
    existence of farm machinery industry during, 54–55, 59
    fertilizer expenditures during, 56
    growth of farms at the beginning of, 35
    growth of railways by start of, 37
    integrated manufacturing in aftermath of, 219
    Keynesian economics as working, 72, 92
    marking end of phase 1 of agricultural phases, xxi–xxii, 94
    marking the end of the National Policy, 23, 25, 66, 229, 231
    necessitating tariff reductions, 46
    need for revenue from natural resources, 75
    PFRA established to aid farmers, 83
Green, Joe, 229
Green Party, 191
Grey, Deborah, 172
grocery distribution, 222, 224
Gross Revenue Insurance Plan (GRIP), 171
Growing Forward, 183, 231
Growing Forward 2, 190–91, 231
Growing Resistance, 236
Growing Together: A Vision for Canada's Agri-Food Industry, 168, 231

H

Hall, Justice Emmett, 148–50, 157
   royal commissions chair, 148, 150, 161, 186, 219
Hamilton, Alvin, 104–5, 143, 150
Hansard, 107, 156
Hansen, Phillip, xxvii
Harkness, D.S., 99, 103
Harper, Stephen, 173, 182, 184, 186–87, 190, 192
Harris, Alanson, 54
Harrison, Robert, 9
Harvey, David, 73, 128
Hayek, Friedrich August von, 126
Hays, Harry, 111
health care, national public system, 148
Health of Animals Act, 191
Hedley, Douglas, 98, 208
Hees, George, 107
Heide, Travis, organic farm, 208
Heilbroner, Robert, 55, 68, 225
Heimbecker, Norman, 41
Heinz Foods, 222
herbicides, 210, 214–15, 234, 254
Hermanson, Elwin, 176–77, 180–81, 186
Herriot, Trevor, 85
Hesston Corporation, 211
Hilstrom, Howard, 181
Hnatyshyn, Ray, 158
Hofstadter, Richard, 63
homesteading
   agrarian ideology for, 62
   allowance for off-homestead income, 32
   expanding into the open ranges of ranchers, 141
   harsh conditions endured, 30, 52
   lands designated for, 22
   large numbers taken up prior to WWI, 56, 208
   laws regulating, 32, 257
   requirements for, 11

Horner, Jack, 134, 138, 140, 142
Howe, C.D., 95, 99, 101, 112
Hudson's Bay Company (HBC)
   capital activities of, 128
   control of Rupert's Land, 7, 10
   land grant to, 2, 22, 32
   paternalistic treatment of Indigenous people, 9
   quasi-state status of, 3
   selling of lands to support immigration, 33
Hyde Park Declaration, 94

I

immigration
   African American immigrants to Prairies, 57
   campaigns to encourage, 62
   chain migration, 57
   contribution to economy, 9, 24
   creating need for railways, 12
   facilitating Western expansion, 8, 31, 35
   federal and provincial jurisdictions on, 22–23
   as government priority, 33
   by pioneer families, 56
   policies for, xxii
   See also National Policy; settlers, white European; Western settlement
Immigration Act, 22
Imperial Oil, 109
Independent Grocers Alliance (IGA), 224
Indian Act, 30
Indigenous Peoples
   as agricultural producers, 30, 248–49, 251
   dominion relations with, 13
   forced assimilation of, 18
   fur trapping by, 1

Indigenous Peoples *(continued)*
    impact of Western settlement on, 254, 257
    integrating laws and legal traditions into agreements, 248
    land rights/land claims, 31, 247–48, 251
    movement restricted by pass system, 30
    prevented from taking up farming, 247
    relationship with land, 13–14, 28
    removed from traditional lands, xiii, xxii, xxx, 9, 17, 29, 31, 40, 56, 85
    subjected to racism, 250
    traditional ceremonies, knowledge, practices, 249–51
    truth and reconciliation with, xxv
    See also First Nations in Canada
individualism, xv, 127, 194, 233, 243
    See also neoconservative ideology
industrialization
    of Canadian heartland, 17
    demanding new form of economic organization, xviii
    development strategy for, xi, xiii, xxii, 6, 16
    emergence of, 4
    enabled by National Policy, xxi, 16, 24, 40
    enabling advanced farming practices, 53, 254
    facilitated by strong national government, 6, 25, 27, 72
    fate of agriculture in, xvi
    promotion of, 40
    See also farm machinery
insecticides, 215, 238
International Centre for Ocean Development, 169
International Harvester (IH), 53–54
International Wheat Agreement, 82, 100, 109

Intersystems Holding, 211
irrigation, 80, 83–84, 211

J
Jaffe, JoAnn, 235
James Richardson & Sons, 41
JayDee AgTech, 214
JBS Foods, 254
Jefferson, Thomas, 62
J.I. Case Company, 54
John Deere, 54, 210, 214, 227
John Deere Capital Corporation, 211
Joly, Henry, 9

K
Kambeitz Farms, 208
Kellogg Company, 222–23
Kennedy, John F., 109–10
Keurig Dr Pepper Inc., 223
Keynes, John Maynard, 72, 126
Keynesianism
    of the 1930s, 196
    active role of Canadian state, 72, 83
    adopted by governing Liberals, 101
    effectiveness of, 92–93
    enabling government intervention in the market, 112, 195
    followed by the CCF, 97, 241
    neoliberal attacks on, xxiv, 145
    opposed by Friedman free-marketers, 126
    stabilizing economic order and institutions, 96, 128, 130
    supporting family farming and Western agriculture, xxi, 74, 98
    transition to neoliberalism in 1970s, xix, 193
Keystone Agricultural Producers, 178
Klein, Ralph, 179
Knuttila, Charles, xvi
Korchinski, Stanley, 140

Kraft Foods Inc., 222
Krasowski, Sheldon, 28–29
Kroger, Arthur, 175
Kubota Corporation (Japan), 211

L
laissez-faire ideology, 27, 93, 127, 132
Lake of the Woods Milling Company, 43
Lang, Otto, 137–38, 140, 142–43, 147, 150, 186
Laurier, Sir Wilfrid
  advocating government ownership of grain terminals, 45
  appeal to manufacturers to supply the West, 21
  banning Black people from entering Canada, 57
  creation of Saskatchewan and Alberta, 34
  embracing National Policy objectives, 20
  endorsing need for transportation system, 112
  making immigration as high priority, 22, 33
  promoting Canadian development, 59
  resolving conflict between farmers and CPR, 43
Law Reform Commission, 169
Leger-Anderson, Ann, 51
Legumex Walker Inc., 221
Lemieux, Pierre, 185
Lewis, Doug, 163
Lewry, Louis, 99
Liberal Party
  addressing free-trade grain marketing, 15, 18, 177
  adopting National Policy, 19
  advocating government restraint, 130, 144, 152, 172
  assistance to farmers during 1930's drought, 83
  bringing in wage and price controls, 136
  calling for regulation of fertilizer industry, 56
  change in support for the Crow Rate, 156, 158–59
  dealing with farming-related issues, 43
  dealing with grain transportation issues, 111
  dealing with overproduction and sagging prices, 109
  dealing with Quebec nationalism, 152, 181
  energy policy of, 153
  espousing protectionism, 21, 23, 46, 66
  establishing farm machinery testing institute, 114
  establishing national marketing agencies for farm products, 138
  facing right-wing alternative party, 173
  following Keynesian approach to economics, 72, 97, 101
  opposed to deregulation in agriculture, 164
  presence in Saskatchewan, 241–43
  privatization of CN Railroad, 176
  promoting immigration, 33
  promoting north-south alignment on trade and commerce, 94, 103
  sponsorship scandal of, 182
  supporting cash advances to farmers, 184
  supporting farmers to produce their own seed, 191
  supporting wheat marketing board, 48, 82, 91, 99, 142, 186–87
  traditional values and programs of, 64
LIFT (Lower Inventories for Tomorrow) Program, 137–38
Little Black Bear Reserve, residential school, 31

livestock
	animal husbandry, 38, 234
	breeds of, 226
	covered under *Agricultural Marketing Programs Act*, 184
	equipment for handling, 212
	production of, xxix, 40, 141, 198, 209, 229
	as specialized commodity, 197
	value of, 201, 203
	watering dams for, 84
Loblaw Companies Ltd., 225
Louis-Dreyfus Group (France), 220–21
Lukiwski, Tom, 188

M

MacAulay, Lawrence, 231
Macdonald, Donald, 135
Macdonald, Sir John A., 5, 10, 12, 16–19, 38, 77, 94, 112
Macdougall, Brenda, 250
MacKay, Peter, 173
Mackenzie, Alexander, 9, 12–13, 15, 18, 20
Mackenzie King, William Lyon
	as embracing National Policy, 66
	favouring Keynesian approach to economics, 72, 93
	opposing a private central bank, 79
	relations with the US, 94–95
	supporting a Canadian grain/wheat board, 82, 86, 92, 111
	supporting family farms, 78
	supporting old-age pensions, 241
	supporting soil reclamation projects, 80
Mackintosh, W.A., 36
MacKirdy, K.A., 17
Maclean's magazine, 33, 51, 175
Macpherson, C.B., xxvii–xxviii, 240, 255
MacPherson, M.A., royal commission chair, 107, 111–12

Magnan, André, 187, 208
Manitoba
	agricultural lands in treaty areas, 14, 247
	attempt to extend western boundary of, 34
	cereal and plant-oil producers in, 200
	creation as a province, 11, 15
	egg and poultry farming in, 139
	fall in per capita income during Depression, 76
	farm income crisis in, 172
	farm machinery dealerships in, 214
	grain delivery points on rail line, 42
	needing railroad to counter isolation, 13, 35
	as part of Rupert's Land, 2
	rehabilitation of drought areas, 80, 84
Manitoba College of Agriculture, 65
Manitoba Grain Act, 44–46, 255
Manitoba Grain Growers Association, 45
Manitoba Pool Elevators, 217
Manning, Ernest, 172
Manning, Preston, 171
manufacturing industry, 4, 68
Maple Farm Equipment, 214
Marchildon, Gregory, 75–76
Marketing Act (1934), 78
Marketing Freedom for Grain Farmers Act, 187, 194
markets
	bread-price-fixing scheme, 225
	and competition, 257
	as free/deregulated, xix, 126–28, 155, 160, 167, 189, 227, 229
	international markets, xix, 129
	mechanism for controlling production and distribution of goods, xxvi
	national scheme for farm products, 138–39

as necessary contrivance for
    economic decisions, 256
and net transfer of power, xxvii–
    xxviii, 255–56
See also competition/competitiveness;
    deregulation, of markets;
    free trade
Marquis Wheat, 38
Marsh, Leonard, 93
Marshall Plan reconstruction, 95
Martin, Paul, 144, 173–75, 181
Martinez, Elizabeth, 127
Martin-McGuire, Peggy, 30
Massey, Daniel, 54
Massey Ferguson, 211
Massey-Harris Co., 54–55
Matador Co-op Farm, 122
Mayer, Charles, 162, 170, 186
Mazankowski, Don, 151, 161, 163, 168–69
McCrorie, James, 24
McDougall, William, 9
McGabe Grain, 216
McKnight, Bill, 172
Meech Lake Accord, 167
Meighen, Arthur, 48, 66
Mental Health: A Priority for Our Farmers, 240
Metcalf, Stephen, 232
Métis Nation, 11, 22, 85
Midland and Pacific Grain Corporation Ltd., 216
Miller, Jim, 18
Miller, Marc, apology for victimization, 31
milling industry, 4
Mills, C. Wright, xvi
Minneapolis Moline tractors, 54
Mishra, Pankaj, 243
Mitchell, Broadus, 68
Moe, Scott, 227, 235–36, 250
Monette Farms, 207

Monod, David, 53
Monsanto Company, 215, 236
Morrison, John, 55, 213
Motherwell, W.R., 49
Muirhead, Bruce, 139
Mulroney, Brian, 154, 160, 162, 166, 169–70, 172
Mussell, Al, 199, 201, 208

N
National Citizens Coalition, 182
National Energy Program (NEP), 153
National Farmers Union (NFU), 142, 178, 187, 218, 228, 251
National Farm Products Marketing Council, 138
National Housing Act, 97
National Policy
    core elements of, xxii, 18–19, 23, 35, 39, 44–46, 54, 94, 118, 193
    definitions of, 16–18
    as economic development framework, xxi, 15–17, 25, 40
    embraced by all political parties, 66
    enabling industrialization, 24, 28
    family farmers as class central to, xxiii, 210, 244
    foundation for agricultural policies/practices, xi, 229, 231
    importance of immigration to, 62
    legacy of, 58, 67–68, 75, 78
    replaced by continentalism, xx
    role of the West in, 20, 24–25, 58, 61
    winding down of, 59, 77
National Progressive Party, 47
National Transcontinental Railway, 36
National Transportation Act, 112, 148, 164, 219
National Transportation Agency, 164
Nature Saskatchewan, 251
Nelson, Walter "Wally," 226–27

neoconservative ideology, 50–51, 127–28, 131
See also individualism
neoliberalism
  approach not protecting farmers but freeing them, xiii, 191
  attacking Keynesian welfare state, xiii, xxiv, 145
  definition of, 131, 232
  as dominating economic and political policy, xxi, 195–96, 230
  ideology/key elements of, xx, 127–28, 165, 167, 169, 173, 176, 190, 192–93
Nestlé company, 222
Net Income Stabilization Account (NISA), 171
New Democratic Party (NDP)
  endorsing creation of Canagrex, 155, 162
  endorsing creation of Petro-Canada, 144
  opposing deregulation in agriculture, 164
  opposing wage and price controls, 136
  promoting farmers' interests in production and pricing, 138, 140, 143, 152
  Reform Party viewed as alternative to, 172–73
  strong Western base of, 135, 243
  succeeding the CCF, 134, 242
  supporting Canadian Wheat Board, 176, 178, 187
  supporting Crow Rate, 156, 158–59
  supporting right of farmers to produce their own seed, 191
New Holland equipment, 227
Newman, Peter C., 175
New National Policy, 46
Nixon, Richard M., 126

N.M. Paterson and Sons, 41
Nordion International, 170
Norrie, Kenneth, 4, 15, 67–68
North America Beverages, 223
Northern Pacific Railway, 36
North West Company, 2
Northwest Elevator Association, 43
North West Grain Dealers Association, 43–44
North-West Mounted Police (NWMP), 17
North-West Territories, 13, 17
North-West Territories Act, 13
No Surrender: The Land Remains Indigenous, 29
Nurse, Jodey, 139
Nutrien, 215, 227
Nystrom, Lorne, 136, 143

O

October Crisis of 1970, 143
Office of the Treaty Commissioner (Sask), 247, 251
Ogdensburg Agreement, 94
Ogilvie, William, 41
oil and energy sector
  farm dependence on fossil fuels, 67
  government policy for, 153
  international oil cartels, 193
  oil and gas extraction, 206
  oil prices, 144, 166, 206
  oil production, xxii, 154, 196
  petroleum energy, 125
oilseed production
  affected by move to free markets, 229
  commodity specialization in, 200–201
  on family farms, xv, xxiv
  funds allotted for producers, 162
  policy areas affecting, xxix, 168
  in private grain trade, 220
  rapeseed (canola), 138, 140, 143, 163, 186
  size and number of farms, 244

Olfert, Rose, 236
Oliver, Frank, 45
Oliver Farm Equipment, 54, 211
Olson, Bud, 131
Ontario
    beef production in, 141
    car manufacturing in, 141
    early governance of, 13
    egg and poultry production in, 139, 141
    fall in per capita income during Depression, 76
    originally part of Rupert's Land, 2
    part of Canada at Confederation, 5
    railroad construction in, 36
    role in National Policy, 20
    wheat and cereal grain production in, 141
An Ordinance Providing for the Organization of Schools in the North-West Territories, 58
Oregon Treaty, 3
Organization of Arab Petroleum Exporting Countries, 126
Oshawa Group, 224
Owram, Douglas, 4, 15, 67–68

P

Palliser Wheat Growers Association, 227
Parker, Thomas, 9
Parrish, William, 41
Parrish & Heimbecker Ltd., 221
Partridge, E.A., 62–63, 66
Paterson Grain (Winnipeg), 221
Patrons of Industry, agrarian organization, 62
Pattison Agriculture, 214
Patton, Harold, 44
Pearson, Lester, 102, 109–10
Peavy Company (US), 41
Peepeekisis Cree Nation, 31

Pépin, Jean-Luc, 156–57
PepsiCo, 223
periodization, analytical tool, xviii, xxi, 66
Permanent Joint Board on Defense, 94
pesticides, 210, 214, 234, 254
Petro-Canada, 143–44, 169–70
Philip Morris International Inc., 222
Phillips, Dave, 84–85
Pickard, Jerry, 179
Pickersgill, James, 111–12
pipelines, 84, 102–3
plant breeders' rights, 191
Plant Protection Act, 191
Polanyi, Karl, 28
Polk, James, 3
pork industry, 141, 184
Potash Corporation of Saskatchewan, 215
potash industry, 206, 215
power, net transfer of. *See* markets
The Practice of Technology, 235
Prairie Farm Assistance Act, 86
Prairie Farm Assistance Administration (PFAA), 86, 255
Prairie Farm Rehabilitation Act (formerly *Rehabilitation of Drought Areas Bill*), 80, 83, 85
Prairie Farm Rehabilitation Administration (PFRA), 80, 83–85, 166, 255
Prairie Grain Advance Payments Act, 106, 140, 162–63, 167, 177
Prairie Rail Authority, 149
Prairie settlement. *See* Western settlement
Precision Planting (Precision Ag Products Inc.), 211
private sector
    advocating abolition of CWB, 188
    capital accumulation in, 93
    as deregulated, 166
    expansion of, 151–52, 156

private sector *(continued)*
  as natural order of things, 127
  partnerships with, 183
  relations with Crown corporations, 145, 181
privatization
  element of neoliberal approach, xix–xx, 127, 131
  government savings as a result of, 170
  initiatives for, 162
  negative effects on family farms, xxii
  as primary route to creating jobs, 160
  of public assets and services, xxiv, 128, 144, 167, 169, 193
  reducing government intrusion into marketplace, 166
Progressive Conservative Party (1942–2003)
  achieving free trade agreement with US, 170
  challenged by Reform Party, 171, 173
  dismantling of the National Energy Program, 154
  espousing free market policies, 155
  espousing reducing deficit and public debt, 160
  expressing support for Canadian Wheat Board, 142, 186
  favouring neoliberal approach to economics, 164, 169
  instituting commission on railroads, 108
  merged with Canadian Alliance into Conservative Party of Canada, 182
  opposed to creation of Petro-Canada, 143
  opposed to more centralized grain handling, 158
  opposed to national marketing agencies, 138
  opposed to wage and price controls, 136
  placing moratorium on branch line abandonment, 161
  preferring to retain Crow Rate, 150, 156
  presence in Saskatchewan, 241–43
  promoting farm income stabilization, 107
  promoting fiscal restraint, 144, 151
  promoting lower taxes and less government, 97
  recommending younger farmers transition to another occupation, 134
  reluctance to accommodate US nuclear warheads in Canada, 110
  supporting Prairie family farmers, 77, 103, 105, 140
Progressive Party (1920–1930), 40, 47–48, 64–65, 241
public spending. *See* Canada, government spending

Q
Quaker Foods North America, 223
Qualman, Darrin, 66, 210
Quebec
  asbestos worker strike, 97
  beef production in, 141
  Bloc Québécois, 172
  egg and poultry producers in, 139, 141
  fall in per capita income during Depression, 76, 78
  governance of, 13
  included in Rupert's Land, 2
  nationalism/sovereignty of, 143, 152, 173, 181, 193
  as part of federated Canada, 5, 96
  protections for francophones, 6
  role in National Policy, 20
  wheat and cereal grain production in, 141–42
Quiet Revolution, 143

R

racism, 57, 250
Railroad Act, 112, 192
rail transportation system
   compensation for, 158
   construction of, 10, 35–36
   deregulation of, 178
   economic function of, 108
   expansion of rail network, 41, 67, 148
   freight rates, 107, 111–12, 146, 149, 156, 158–59, 161, 176
   land grants and subsidies given to, 35, 108, 112
   means of achieving National Policy, 108
   private ownership of, 36
   rail line abandonment, 112, 146–50, 161, 164, 193, 219, 242
   rail line rehabilitation, 167
   restructuring of, 226
   role in agrarian communities, 61
   as transcontinental, 12, 17
   See also Western settlement
Railway Act, 107, 145
Ray, Arthur, 18
Rebellions of 1837 & 1838, 4
Red River Resistance, 32
Reform Association of Canada, 171
Reform Party, 171, 173, 176–77, 180–82, 186, 192, 242–43
Regina Riot, 83
Report of the Royal Commission on Banking and Currency, 79
Report on Social Security for Canada (Marsh Report), 93
residential schools, 31
Respecting Experimental Farm Stations, 38
Revenue Insurance Program, 171
Rhodes, E.N., 79
Richardson International Ltd., 188, 220–21, 227
Richardson Pioneer (Winnipeg), 220–21

Riel, Louis/Riel Rebellion, 11, 32, 85
Ritz, Gerry, 183, 186, 188, 190–91
Romanow, Roy, 175
Roosevelt, Franklin D., 72, 93–95
Rosmann, Dr. Mike, 239
Royal Bank of Canada, 61
Royal Canadian Mounted Policy (RCMP), 250
Royal Commission on Canada's Economic Prospects (Gordon Commission, 1955), 101, 136
Royal Commission on Grain Handling and Transportation (Hall Commission, 1975), 148, 150, 161, 186, 219
Royal Commission on the Grain Trade of Canada (1906), 44
Royal Commission on Health Care in Canada (Hall Commission, 1973), 148
Royal Commission on Health Services (1961), 97
Royal Commission to Inquire into Trading in Grain Futures (Stamp Commission, 1931), 81
Royal Commission on Price Spreads of Food Products (1959), 120
Royal Commission on the Shipment and Transportation of Grain (1899), 43–44
Royal Commission on Transportation (MacPherson Commission, 1959), 107, 111–12
Royal Grain Inquiry commissions (Turgeon Commission, 1923 & 1936), 49, 87
Royal Proclamation of 1763, 28, 247
Rupert's Land, 2–4, 6–7, 9, 32
   transferred to Canada, 10, 13, 17
rural communities, 217, 228, 235, 242
   See also towns and villages

S

Safeway Canada, 224
SALIC (Saudi Agricultural and Livestock Investment Company), 190
Saltsman, Max, 144
Sandwell, R.W., 52
Saskatchewan
  activities of PFRA in, 84
  agricultural lands in treaty areas, 14, 29, 247–48
  agriculture linked to economic patterns occurring in Canada, xvii, xxiv
  aid for farmers during grain trade war, 165
  changing character of cities and towns, 236–37
  control over land and natural resources, 74–75
  co-operative farms in, 121–22
  creation of, 34, 59, 74
  crisis service calls from farmers, 239
  decline in number of grain elevators, 219
  differentiation among agrarian producers, 198, 200, 209
  dire condition of farmers, 78, 90, 105
  effects of branch line abandonment on, 164
  fall in per capita income during Depression, 76, 79
  farmer disagreement on grain marketing, 227–28
  farmers engaged in non-farm work, 205–6
  farm income in, 79, 117, 171
  farming curriculum taught at residential school, 31
  farmland ownership patterns in, 208
  farm machinery dealers in, 213–14
  farm operators engaging in non-farm paid work, 205
  future of agricultural production in, 257
  global manufacturing companies in, 212–14
  growth of large/highly capitalized farms in, 53, 118, 201, 207, 246
  immigration to, 57–58
  Indigenous agriculture in, 248–49, 251
  inland terminal operators in, 221
  investment in railroads, 36, 42
  major Canadian farm organizations in, 229
  number and size of farms/farming enterprises, 119, 201–2, 204, 207–8, 244, 246
  occupational injuries sustained in, 238
  oil industry in, xxii
  part of Rupert's Land, 2, 13
  pioneer women in, 51–52
  population growth in, 35, 50, 58, 60
  potash industry in, 215–16
  racism as an issue, 250
  rehabilitation of drought areas in, 80
  support for political parties in, 47–48, 64, 159, 241–43
  total farm capital in, 203–4
  total farm debt in, 206
  transformation of rural areas, xii, 59
  transition of class of agrarian producers, 200, 232, 235, 240, 242
  value of productive farm assets, 203
  See also rural communities; towns and villages
Saskatchewan Act, 74
Saskatchewan Association of Rural Municipalities, 228
Saskatchewan Farmers Union, 228
Saskatchewan Federation of Labour, 251

Saskatchewan Grain Growers
    Association, 45, 227
Saskatchewan Indian Agriculture
    Program, 249
Saskatchewan Progressive Conservative
    Party, 103
Saskatchewan Register of Heritage
    Property, 58
Saskatchewan Treaty Land Entitlement
    Framework Agreement, 248
Saskatchewan United Party, 243
Saskatchewan Wheat Pool (SWP), xv,
    178, 217–18
Saskcan Pulse Trading, 221
schools. *See* towns and villages
Science Council of Canada, 169
SDF Group, 211
Seed Hawk air drills, 213
SeedMaster seeding tools, 213
seeds
    grass seeds, 80
    high-tech, patented seeds, 67
    machinery for seeding, 207, 211–13
    oilseeds, xxix, 162–63
    produced by farmers, 191
    supplied by seed companies, 196, 212,
        215
    of weeds mixed in the grain, 42
Seeds Act, 191
settlers, white European
    acquiring land taken from
        Indigenous Peoples, xxii, 10, 85,
        247, 257
    co-operative spirit of, 61–62
    cultivating cereal grain as main
        occupation, 216
    fertility rates of, 50
    locating on the Prairies, 21–23, 32, 34,
        40, 56, 58–59, 197
    needing railroad for movement and
        supplies, 12, 35
    replacing Indigenous Peoples, xxx, 28,
        30–31, 40, 247, 250
    See also gender order
Settling Saskatchewan, 57
Shepard, Bruce, 53
Shiloh People, 57
Shoppers Drug Mart Corporation, 225
Siege of Ottawa (1911), 45
Sifton, Clifford, 21, 33–34, 44, 62
Simpson Seeds Inc., 221
Skogstad, Dr. Grace, 139, 229
Smiley, Donald, 16
Smith, Adam, 226
Snavely Commission, 146, 219
Sobeys Inc., 224–25
social class/class structure
    affecting Western independent
        commodity producers, xxv–xxvi
    approach to analysis of, xxv–xxvi
    within dynamic nature of capitalism,
        xvii, 128, 229
    homogeneity in, 197
    and society's notion of freedom, 190
    and transformation of rural Prairie
        communities, xii, 61, 232, 237, 244
Social Credit Party, 65, 98
Social Gospel, 64–65
social programs/social safety net
    attacks on by neoliberalism, 145
    expenditures financed through taxes,
        97, 127
    family allowances, 92, 145
    health care, 73
    old-age pensions/old-age security, 97,
        110, 241
    as providing jobs and government
        debt, 125
    providing security and stability, 130
    and social contract of companies and
        unions, 72
    See also welfare state

soil
  available for farming, 8, 51
  cultivation of, 29, 64
  degraded, poor, 85, 122, 166
  protection for, 56
  reclamation projects, 80
South Saskatchewan River Project, 97
soybean producers, 162
Special Canadian Grains Program, 162
Special Farm Financial Assistance
    Program, 154
Stabler, Jack, 236
Stamp, Josiah, royal commission chair, 81
Stanfield, Robert, 110
Stanley, Gerald, 250
Starbucks Coffee Company, 223
Statute of Westminster, 75
Steedsman, James, 55
Ste. Madeleine, displacement of Métis
    people, 85
Stenson, Art & Rob, 212
Stephen, Sir George, 43
Steward, Charles, 75
Stirling, Bob, 198, 201
St. Laurent, Louis, 97, 101, 111
Strahl, Charles, 184
Suez Canal crisis, 102–3, 110
suicide, of agricultural producers. *See*
    farmers, suicide
Supreme Court of Canada, 40, 139
Syngenta Group, 215

T
tariffs
  main source of government revenue,
    15
  part of industrialization program, xxii
  policy concerning, 18, 23–24, 94
  as protective of markets, 17–18, 45–47,
    94, 226, 241
  reform/reductions in, 45–46, 76–77, 94

Task Force on Agriculture, xxiii, 130–31,
    137, 193
  recommendations of, 132–35
Task Force on Program Review, 165
Task Force on the Structure of Canadian
    Industry, 136
Tauxe, Caroline, 233
Taylor, F.W., 73
Taylor, Jeffery, 65–66
Teleglobe Canada, 170
Telesat Canada, 169–70
Temporary Wheat Reserves Act, 101
Territorial Grain Growers Association, 44
textile industry, 4
Thatcher, Margaret, 127
Thompson, E.P., 244
Thoreau, Henry David, 62
3G Capital, 222
Tilley, Samuel, 12, 18
Tolmie, John, 55
Toronto Stock Exchange, 217
Tough, Frank, 18
towns and villages
  class structure of, 61, 237
  decline in number of, 236–37
  emergence and development of,
    59–60
  general stores in, 224
  local merchants as important
    element, 223, 237
  schools established, 10, 22, 32, 56, 58,
    125, 237
  See also rural communities
tractors, farm
  annual sales of, 53, 66, 213
  companies producing and selling,
    211–12
  increase in number on farms, 118
  used on large agricultural enterprises,
    207
  See also farm machinery

treaties
    agricultural land in treaty territories, 14, 29, 247–48
    between government and Indigenous Peoples, 248
    imply surrender of land or sharing of land, 29
    Indigenous rights guaranteed in, 251
    made to obtain land for European settlers, 28
    See also Indigenous Peoples, land rights/land claims
Treaty 1, 14
Treaty 2, 14, 247
Treaty 4, 14, 29, 247
Treaty 5, 247
Treaty 6, 14, 247
Treaty 7, 247
Treaty 8, 247
Treaty 10, 247
Treaty Land Sharing Network, 251
Treaty of Niagara of 1764, 247
Treaty of Paris (1763), 2
Trespass to Property Amendment Act, 251
Trespass to Property Consequential Amendments Act, 251
Trudeau, Justin, 192
Trudeau, Pierre
    accused of misunderstanding Western farmers, 138
    agenda to stabilize farm incomes, 143
    and the Barber recommendations, 114
    bringing in wage and price controls, 135
    calling for restraint on spending, 130, 156
    tour of the West, 122–23
True North Saskatchewan, 243
Truth and Reconciliation Commission of Canada, 247
Tupper, Charles, 8, 19–20

Turgeon, William F.A., royal commissions chair, 49, 87
Turner, John, 156
Tyson Foods Inc., 254

U
Unemployment Assistance Act, 97
Unified Grassroots, 243
Unilever, 223
Unionist Party, 241
United Farmers of Alberta, 45
United Grain Growers (UGG), 216–17
United Nations Declaration on the Rights of Indigenous Peoples, 248
United States
    dollar as global standard currency, 95, 126
    dominance in world politics, 103
    dominance of global grain market, 108
    domination of/integration with Canadian economy, xx, 95, 109–10, 136
    free trade agreement with Canada, 166
    increasing trade with Canada, 161
    Manifest Destiny doctrine, 5
    restored partnership with Canada, 160
    subsidies given to US farmers, 158, 170
    use of Canadian pipelines by US oil and gas companies, 102–3
    See also Canada–United States Free Trade Agreement
University of Manitoba, 156
University of Saskatchewan, 238
US Federal Trade Commission, 55

V
Valtra Inc., 211
Van Horne, William Cornelius, 43
Van Loan, Peter, 187
Veterans' Land Administration, 169

Via Rail, 165
Viterra, global agri-business, 188, 218, 221, 227

W
Waiser, Bill, 122
Wall, Brad, 235–36, 243
War Measures Act, 39, 47, 91, 98
Watkins, Mel, 136
Weber, Max, xxix
Weersink, Alfons, 209
Weir, Robert, 78
welfare state
    created by activist states, xix
    falling into disfavour with neoliberalism, 145, 193
    producing greater degree of social equality, 73, 125–26
    as sapping individual work ethic, 127
    spending and taxation associated with, 128
    See also social programs/social safety net
Westeel (AGI), 212
Western Barley Growers Association, 179, 187
Western Canadian Wheat Growers Association (WCWGA), 178, 187, 227–28, 235
Western Grain Marketing Panel, 177–78
Western Grain Stabilization Act, 145, 147, 161, 163, 171
Western Grain Stabilization Fund, 163, 165
Western Grain Transition Payment Program, 159
Western Grain Transportation Act, 157, 159, 161, 169, 174–75, 186
Western Grocers, 225
Western settlement
    by agrarian populations, xi, xxii, 28, 38, 40, 61, 75, 95, 118, 240
    aided by optimistic, co-operative spirit of settlers, 50, 62
    aided by railroad construction, 4, 17, 36
    as component of National Policy, 8, 16
    developing national industrial economy, 24
    during early twentieth century, 49
    facilitated by grain handling sites and rail line networks, 219
    halted during Great Depression, xxiii, 94–95
    historical myth of, 250
    impact on Indigenous Peoples and their lands, 18, 31, 85, 254
    land survey system, 10, 32
    occupied by homesteads, 141
    occurring post-Confederation, 11
    See also homesteading; immigration; National Policy
Westfield Industries, 212
Weston, Galen & Garfield, 225
Wheat Cooperative Marketing Act, 88
wheat production and marketing
    collapse in prices, 109
    co-operative marketing of, 87
    genetically modified grain, 254
    and international wheat agreements, 100
    international wheat markets, 137, 178, 187, 242
    removing lands from, 137–38
    storage of wheat, 99, 101
    wheat pools, 47, 80–81, 87, 187
    wheat prices, xvi, 81–82, 91–92, 109
    See also Canadian Wheat Board (CWB); cereal grains; Saskatchewan Wheat Board
Whelan, Ed, 144
Whelan, Eugene, 155, 159

Whitaker, Reginald, 93
White, Sir Thomas, 37
White Farm Equipment, 211
Whitehorse Accord, 168
Wilson, C.F., 88
Wilson, Michael, 160, 165–66, 169
Winnipeg Grain Exchange, 40–41, 47–48, 87, 91–92, 98
Wipf, Kevin, 170
Wise, John, 162
women pioneers. *See* gender order
Woodsworth, J.S., 79
Woolford, Andrew, 17
World War, First
    common economic interests prior to, 226
    costs of farm machinery before, 113
    emergence of new political parties after, 64
    global disruption caused by, 35–36, 40, 47
    high-input farming increasing since the end of, 210
    homogeneity of settlers prior to, 61
    institution of a wheat board after, 81, 185
    large number of Western settlers prior to, 56
    towns and villages prior to, 223
    US as dominant economic power after, 68
World War, Second
    Canada declaring war on Germany, 89
    Canada's status in world after, 110
    changes to grain trade in aftermath, 106, 210, 226
    co-operative farms in Saskatchewan after, 121
    decline in number of cereal grain producers since, 194, 219
    effect on the economy, xiii, xx–xxi, 60, 72–73, 94
    farm machinery sector in post-war period, 53, 55
    halting Prairie expansion, xxiii
    impact on independent Prairie stores and retail services, 224
    Keynesian economics proven to work by end of, 92
    massive government spending during and after, 126

Y

Yalnizyan, Armine, 74

Murray Knuttila is professor emeritus at the University of Regina and Brock University. He resides in Regina and is the author of several books, including *That Man Partridge* and *Paying for Masculinity*.